Carthage, now a spectacular ruin on the north coast of Africa, was the capital of one of the ancient world's most powerful empires. This book describes its history, from foundation by the Phoenicians in the ninth century BC to destruction by the Romans some six centuries later.

The volume opens with a narrative account of the expansion of the Phoenician trade empire from the tenth to the fifth centuries BC. The author then examines the growth of Carthage from a colony of Tyre to the capital of a western empire that stretched across Africa from modern-day Libya to the coast beyond the Pillars of Hercules, and in Europe from Spain through Sardinia to Sicily.

The central part of the book creates a portrait of Carthage at the peak of its power. Professor Lancel describes its society, trade, rituals and religion. He presents a vivid picture of the Carthaginian urban and rural landscape, the latter featuring great estates, sprawling villas and huge parks, constructed and maintained by large numbers of slaves, and protected against slave revolts and piratic invasions by extensive walls and defensive towers. This was a sophisticated, urbane and cultured society.

The two penultimate chapters tell the story of the great conflict with Rome, famously featuring Hannibal's crossing of the Alps, and concluding with the city's destruction in 146 BC. The author ends with an essay on what parts of Punic culture survived the demise of the city.

Accessibly written for a wide readership, the book draws on the latest findings of archaeological research throughout th
research from many d
contemporary writing.
250 maps and photog
chronology, bibliograp
further reading for Eng
been prepared by Henry Hurst of the University of Cambridge.

CARTHAGE

Byrsa I. Mission archéologique française à Carthage.
Rapports préliminaires des fouilles 1974–1976,
sous la direction de Serge Lancel.
(Collection de l'École française de Rome, 41) Rome, 1979.

Byrsa II. Mission archéologique française à Carthage.
Rapports préliminaires sur les fouilles 1977–1978: niveaux
et vestiges puniques,
sous la direction de Serge Lancel.
(Collection de l'École française de Rome, 41) Rome, 1981.

Introduction à la connaissance de Carthage:
la colline de Byrsa à l'époque punique.
Paris: Édition Recherches sur les Civilisations, 1983.

CARTHAGE

A HISTORY

Serge Lancel

Translated by
Antonia Nevill

BLACKWELL
Oxford UK & Cambridge USA

Copyright © Librairie Arthème Fayard, 1992

English translation © Basil Blackwell Ltd, 1995

First published as *Carthage* by Librairie Arthème Fayard, 1992
English edition first published 1995

Blackwell Publishers
108 Cowley Road
Oxford OX4 1JF
UK

238 Main Street
Cambridge, Massachusetts 02142
USA

British Library Cataloguing in Publication Data

A CIP catalogue record for this book is available from the British Library.

Library of Congress Cataloging-in-Publication Data

A CIP catalogue entry has been requested.

ISBN 1 557 86468 3
Typeset in 10½ on 12½ pt Sabon by Pure Tech Corporation Ltd,
Pondicherry, India
Printed in Great Britain by TJ Press Ltd, Padstow, Cornwall

This book is printed on acid-free paper

This book is dedicated to the memory of those volunteer archaeologists – especially Louis Carton, François Icard and Charles Saumagne – who, in the first half of this century, laboured with sincerity, generosity and passion for greater knowledge and protection of Punic Carthage.

Contents

Translator's Preface

It has been both a privilege and a delight to translate Dr Lancel's enthralling work. It is a book which will enable those of us who cannot visit Carthage in person to explore it in these pages in the company of an expert whose passionate enthusiasm for his subject will carry the reader with him across the centuries to that legendary city. I thank him for his unfailing patience in answering my questions. I am greatly indebted also to Mr Henry Hurst of the University of Cambridge for his invaluable expertise and technical guidance.

Antonia Nevill

Foreword

The traveller approaching Carthage by sea during the small hours
will find himself entering a sort of purse net whose edges gradually
draw closer together. On the starboard side, in passing, he will have
caught sight of Plane Island, then the sharp point of Ras-el-Djebel,
the *promontorium Apollinis* of the Ancients, before perceiving
from the muddy waters bordering it the confused estuary of the
Medjerda, the *Bagradas* of old. On the port side, in clear weather,
the Aegimuran Isles Zembra and Zembretta, sentinels at the entry
to the gulf, stand out from the surface of the water. Beyond, the
high and formidable prow of Cap Bon blocks the horizon towards
the east, then slopes down and rises again approaching Tunis with
the double knoll of Bou Kornine, which is to this landscape what
Vesuvius is to the Bay of Naples. Drawing level with it, if our
traveller looks to the right he will now see, very near, the line of hills
forming the site of Carthage: the promontory of Sidi-bou-Saïd,
then the indentations that end at Byrsa. He will recall that long,
long ago in this place a queen from the east concluded a strange
transaction with the natives; that much later a crusader king died
there and, for a time, gave it his name, and that, nearer our own
time, a cardinal primate of Africa built a cathedral, with cupolas
that still rise as a seamark: three unequally significant moments in
an exceptional destiny. History clings to those places it has once
chosen.

Such, if legend is to be believed, was the destination of Phoenician
immigrants, at the end of the ninth century BC. Today the traveller
disembarks at La Goulette, midway along the sandbar separating
the sea from what still remains of the Lake of Tunis. Where did
Elissa's companions beach their first boats? Perhaps, as we shall
see, on the shore of 'Salammbô' – shades of Flaubert! – where the

basins of the present-day lagoons did not yet exist; or in a little bay long since filled in, where now the vestiges of the Antonine Baths may be seen; or perhaps on the red sandy beach of 'Hamilcar's gully', whence thirteen centuries later the young Augustine, as yet dreaming of earthly glory, set sail for Rome.

Overlooking this coast, the village of Sidi-bou-Saïd displays in several tiers the whiteness of its houses, emphasized by the blue of their door-frames and grilles. From there our traveller, surely like Dido's companions in the past, will get a better idea of the actual site, which is even more maritime than the first approach by sea may have led him to suppose. To the south and towards the west – and more so yesterday than today when man, searching for places to build on, banks up and fills in without taking heed of a natural balance – the waters of the Lake of Tunis lap the southern shore of the isthmus linking the peninsula to the mainland. To the north-west the sebkha er-Riana, a briny marsh that is encrusted with salt in the dry season, spreads its dull blue-green shadows and recalls the centuries when the sea largely filled the gulf of Utica. From the top of Sidi-bou-Saïd the site of Carthage appears very much as it used to be, the head of an arrow pointing east, whose shaft would one day be cut by a fortification barring the isthmus, once more turning the peninsula into the island it had been at the dawn of human times.

It is obvious that such a situation enticed the Phoenician sailors accompanying Dido-Elissa. The Carthage they would found there, just beyond the barrier of Cap Bon – a formidable euphemism! – would be the first colonial foundation on African soil of people from the east, Semitic or Greek. On African soil, or rather on the African littoral: *Carthago ad Africam*, as it was said of Alexandria that it was on the fringe of Egypt: *Alexandria ad Aegyptum.*

Marginal but not precarious, Carthage thus lived for a long time turned towards the outside world, the most outstanding example of those maritime cities of which Cicero, in a celebrated text, said 'their inhabitants do not stay bound to their homes, but are always drawn far away by hopes and expectations which continually give wings to their heels.' Later the time would come when the fellow-citizens of Hanno the Navigator became those of Mago the Agronomist and gave the old Punic city a solid foothold in the countryside of its hinterland, to the point where – supreme paradox – a product of that land, the fig brandished by Cato in the Senate in Rome, would give the age-old enemy the signal to go after the spoils. But it has been said that Carthaginian power was first and foremost that of an 'empire of the sea'. The fruits of that constant openness to the outside world were the remarkable flexibility of this state which remained Semitic to its very core – notably as regards religion – yet became also Greek, Iberian, even Italian, and naturally in the long term African; its capacity, in return, to export its products and beliefs throughout the length and breadth of the western Mediterranean; but also, in a less beneficial fashion, its inability – except in the terrible days of its long death-throes – to form in its bosom that cement of patriotism against which Hannibal's attacks in Italy had foundered.

Looking at this gulf where, as night falls, indigo turns to black, the traveller will have realized that a great part of Carthage's history was written in advance into the very landscape.

1

The Founding of Carthage

The founding of Carthage, around the end of the ninth century BC, was for many hundreds of years a determining factor in the political and cultural destiny of the western Mediterranean basin. But that foundation was not an isolated act: it was part of a vast movement which, in successive waves, deposited on those shores explorers and traders coming from the east. The historian encounters many difficulties in obtaining the facts. Making sure of their reality and true character, assessing their relative importance, fixing their chronology: many frequently arduous tasks are based on a critique of a body of literary, archaeological, sometimes even epigraphic data, that by their confusion have contributed not a little to blurring the view of Phoenician expansion in the west.

TEXTUAL TRADITIONS AND THEIR CRITIQUE

The sources of this history have not always been so complex and varied. Around the end of last century, when the textual tradition was the only one that could be taken into consideration, things seemed relatively simple. This tradition attributed the most distant destinations and the most ancient dates to Phoenician expansion. As if to mark out their territory, the oriental navigators would appear first to have gone the greatest distance, establishing beyond the 'Pillars of Hercules' – our Straits of Gibraltar – the bridgeheads for future undertakings. If we are to believe a Latin author, Velleius Paterculus, Gades (Cadiz), on the Atlantic coast of Andalusia, was founded in 1110 BC. On the opposite shore, the founding of Lixus

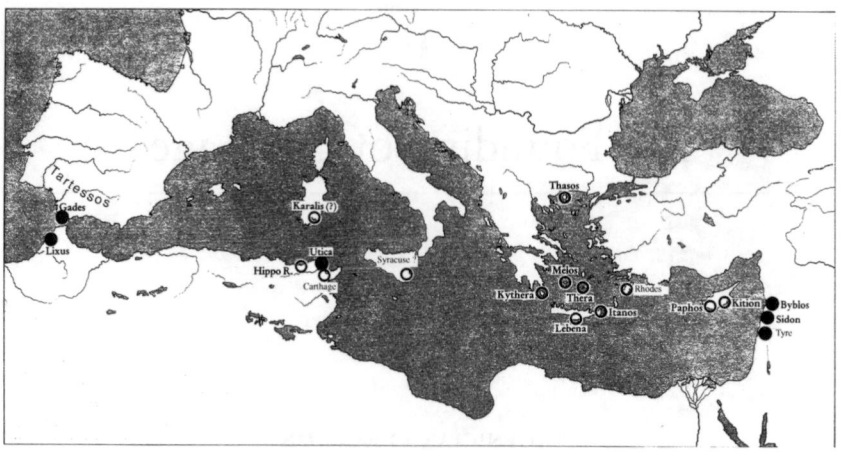

FIGURE 1   *The first Phoenician expansion in the Mediterranean,*
according to literary tradition (after H. G. Niemeyer, Die Phönizier im
Zeitalter Homers, *1984).*
• *The founder cities in Phoenicia and the most ancient foundations in*
the west.
○ *Settlements attested by literary sources.*

(Larache, in Morocco) dates back even further, according to Pliny
the Elder (*NH*, XIX, 63) (figure 1).

Having fixed those two farthest points, the occupation of Utica,
in the north of Tunisia, at the mouth of the Medjerda, and at the
end of a bay then accessible from the open sea, would seem shortly
afterwards to have initiated the Phoenician hold on the northern
shores of the Maghreb. Pliny, in his great work dedicated to the
Emperor Titus in AD 77, remarked that in the Temple of Apollo at
Utica wooden beams of Numidian cedar were still to be seen, in the
state in which they had been placed in position 1178 years earlier,
that is, 1101 BC. That figure matches the one already supplied by
the Pseudo-Aristotle (*Concerning Reported Wonders*, 134), according to whom the founding of Utica predated that of Carthage by
287 years, if the latter is assumed to be 814 BC. It will be seen later
that, with these two tallying indications, we are in the chronological system of Timaeus of Taormina. Other settlements spaced out
along the African shores would seem to have completed this arrangement. According to Phoenician sources, echoed by the Latin
historian Sallust (*Jugurtha*, XIX, 1), this appears to have been the
case, for a Hippo on that same north coast of the Maghreb, about
whose identity one may hesitate between Hippo Regius (Annaba,

formerly Bône, in Algeria) and Hippo Dhiarrytus (today Bizerta in Tunisia); along the east coast of present-day Tunisia, Hadrumetum (Sousse), then much farther south, Leptis Magna, in Libya, would at that time have formed invaluable relay-points or stepping-stones on the return journey to the east. The same Tyrian annals, reported by Menander of Ephesus, a historian of the Hellenistic era, placed in the first half of the ninth century BC the founding in 'Libya' (in its widest ancient geographical sense), by King Ithobaal of Tyre, of a town named Auza, the whereabouts of which are unclear and for which Algiers or even Oran has been suggested, as there is such a problem over identification with the city of Auzia (Sour-el-Ghozlane, formerly Aumale), attested in Roman times on the high plateaux of the Algiers region. For Carthage, according to textual tradition alone, there is in theory an uncertain choice between a very ancient date, going back to the end of the thirteenth century BC, and another, later by three centuries: it will be seen further on that there is general acceptance, not without some difficulty, of the date of 814 BC, give or take a few years.

The first inclination of specialists and the learned public was to accept these chronological markers, in spite of their surprising antiquity. Without a doubt, that scholarly confidence (especially of the German, F. Movers, who in the middle of the nineteenth century published a three-volume survey of the Phoenicians which was for a long time accepted as authoritative), can be regarded as one of the expressions of an orientalism much in vogue at the time, and more particularly marked in literature, as far as Carthage was concerned, by the publication of Flaubert's *Salammbô* in 1862. People were then happy to credit the Phoenicians with every great initiative. To the virtue of having 'invented' the alphabet was added that of having outshone the Greeks in the knowledge and use of maritime routes. Homer himself, according to Victor Bérard, discovered in some oriental manual of *Nautical Instruction* the essence of the geographical framework of the *Odyssey*, as well as the outlines of the legend of Ulysses in some Phoenician 'periplus' (Bérard, 1930, p. 146). In due course – for a much later period – we shall encounter these textual questions in connection with the *Periplus of Hanno*.

ARCHAEOLOGICAL DATA

The first reactions from this excessive confidence in the primacy of eastern initiative were linked with the upsurge in archaeology at the end of last century. First of all, the excavations in the Greek or rather Aegean world, at Knossos and Mycenae, positively demonstrated the originality and importance of proto-Greek civilizations, and so provided support for believers in the 'Greek miracle' against the allure of the 'eastern mirage'. 'Phoenicomania' was tenacious, however, since in 1894 W. Helbig was still explaining that Mycenaean civilization was due to the Phoenicians. Archaeology played its full role later, but this time negatively, in the western basin of the Mediterranean, since in none of the sites mentioned above (notably Lixus, Utica and Carthage) were archaeologists able to verify the remote dates of literary tradition. These negative findings were swift to arouse the excesses of what may be called 'hypercriticism' in the other direction. Thus, according to some, the great development of Phoenician colonization waited until the seventh century BC, appreciably after the first phases of Greek colonization in Sicily and southern Italy: a dating that would in fact have seriously compromised its possibility, the more so because what is known of the difficulties suffered at the hands of the Assyrians in Phoenicia itself (in Cyprus, Sidon and above all in Tyre) at the beginning of the seventh century virtually ruled out the launching of any great undertaking towards the west in that era.

In the last two or three decades, and particularly in recent years, the progress of archaeological research has both greatly increased the quantity and complexity of the data and cleared a path to more carefully considered solutions, equally removed from the excesses of 'Phoenicomania' and from the misapplications of the later dating. The realities of Phoenician expansion are clearer; they were achieved during slow and gradual processes and are not compatible with the precise accounts of the legendary foundations. From simple acceptance of the mythical account – a study of which maintains all its interest in a structural perspective – we have progressed to the painstaking elaboration of a history based chiefly on data incorporated within outlines of probability: the probability of the conditions of navigation in ancient times, the actual possibilities of trading in the defined geographical areas. Luckily, literary texts once more intervene to provide a content and substance to these outlines. For example, the lines from the *Odyssey* (XV, 414 ff.) in which the swineherd Eumaeus, in a story of his own childhood that he tells to Ulysses, mentions 'those men from Phoenicia, those rapacious sailors who, in their black vessel, have a thousand gewgaws (*athyrmata*)'. And the Homeric poem gives us a glimpse of those sailors, who come ashore for just as long as it takes to revictual the ship and seduce the girls, and cast off again after a bit of furtive trading. It has recently been stressed (Gras, 1989, pp. 106–7) that this vision of the Phoenician trader is dated and that the image is fully valid only for that period (between the tenth and seventh centuries BC) when the bulk of maritime traffic from one part to another of the Mediterranean eluded political control, in particular of the Phoenician sovereigns, to fall into the hands of a class of pirate merchants. A little later, Herodotus (I, 1) still conveys what had meanwhile become a cliché, in an account describing the Greek port of Argos:

> Having arrived in the land, the Phoenicians sought to sell their wares; five or six days after their arrival, when they had sold nearly all their cargo, a large group of women came down to the shore, and among them was Io, daughter of King Inachos. While they were bargaining for what they wanted, near to the stern of the boat, the Phoenicians fell upon them: the majority fled, but Io and a few others were captured and the Phoenicians threw them into their boat, which set sail in the direction of Egypt.

Herodotus speaks of 'goods', without being more specific. As for the word used in the Homeric text, it suggests luxury goods or those of a trifling nature, leaving one perplexed: *athyrmata*, 'trinkets', or what our consumer society might call 'gadgets'. Around the end of the sixth century, a passage in the *Periplus* of the Pseudo-Scylax would be more precise about what the Phoenician traders were then offering the 'Ethiopians': perfumed oil, gems from Egypt, wild boar and Attic pottery. But what did they have at the beginning of the first millennium? However, the objects behind the words are not without importance because, in the eyes of the archaeologist, it is the discovery of currency, or rather objects of trade on the Phoenician side, that establishes the reality of such trade and allows a chronological approach to it. Let it be added that not all objects are easy to identify in their various dimensions and that the use of certain discoveries sometimes remains problematical.

Let us take the now classic example of the bronze statuette fished out of the sea, about thirty years ago, off the shore of Selinunte, on the southern coast of Sicily (figure 2). The non-specialist will doubtless be surprised to learn how vast a literature – scores of articles in learned journals, hundreds of pages – was aroused by this figurine, which was admittedly venerable and enjoyed greater prestige for having been saved from the sea. At first it was seen as the god

FIGURE 2   *The statuette from Selinunte (Palermo Museum).*

Melqart – the Greek Herakles, the Latin Hercules. In fact this
figurine belongs in the series of representations of what Middle East
archaeologists call a 'smiting god': the god striding towards the
enemy and preparing to smite him with a weapon brandished in his
raised right hand. If it is permissible to recognize it as a divinity
of the Syrio-Phoenician world – a Baal or Reshef, rather than a
Melqart – is it equally permissible to turn it into a testimony of
Phoenician expansion in the west, as was proposed some twenty
years ago? The best item for comparison is a statuette found at
Ugarit (Ras Shamra in Syria), preserved in the Louvre Museum, and
dated between the fourteenth and thirteenth centuries BC. If that is
also a plausible approximate date for the Selinunte statuette, unless
one supposes somewhat gratuitously that the object travelled two
or three centuries after it was made, its transport cannot be attributed to Phoenician navigation. On the other hand, it is tempting
to attribute it to Mycenean expansion, which is known from pottery evidence to have reached southern Italy (Apulia and Calabria),
south-eastern Sicily and the Aeolian Isles before the end of

Mycaenean IIIB, that is, before the destruction of the Mycenean palaces around 1200 BC. However, following intensive analyses carried out for the last fifteen or so years on the bronzes found in Sicily and Sardinia, and comparisons that have been made between figurines of similar 'smiting gods' in Cyprus (notably at Kition) and Syrio-Palestinian models from the Bronze Age, the export of these bronzes, including the Melqart or Reshef of Selinunte, now tends to be placed at the height of Cypriot influence, at the beginning of the first millennium (Bisi, 1980, pp. 5–15).

It may be added that, as regards Phoenicia itself, strong historical data further diminish the belief in the earliest dating of western foundations and support evidence for placing the great colonial undertakings between the tenth and eighth centuries BC. After the golden age of the middle of the second millennium and then the rule of the great empires – the Hittites for the north, pharaonic Egypt for the south – followed by the intrusion of the Peoples of the Sea, the start of the first millennium was an era of veritable rebirth for the maritime cities of Phoenicia. Lacking political unity, at that time they achieved a certain cultural unity. Then too, decisive technical advances seemed to take place in shipbuilding which would provide the best opportunities for long-distance navigation, for example, the use of bitumen to render keels watertight, and constructing hulls with ribs that would give vessels the necessary robustness to tackle the open sea with ease.

FROM CYPRUS TO THE PILLARS OF HERCULES

It is not surprising that the Phoenician presence beyond the coasts of present-day Lebanon is first clearly attested in the eastern basin of the Mediterranean (figure 3): to begin with, on the eastern coast of Cyprus, which for the Phoenician sailors was the first shore facing them, at Kition (Larnaka); on the island of Rhodes, at Ialyssos; in Crete, where two ports on the south coast bear the significant name of Phoinix. In the advance towards the west, Sicily was in a key position. The discussion of the Selinunte bronze has just given a glimpse of the problems. It may be added that in the south-east corner of the island (where the site of Thapsos, north of Syracuse, bears a Semitic name) the fairly clear imprint of a Phoenician influence, recognizable as much in the 'Siculean' vases as in the finds of fibulae, razors and axes, stands out from the distinctive local cultural background of the so-called Cassibile civilization.

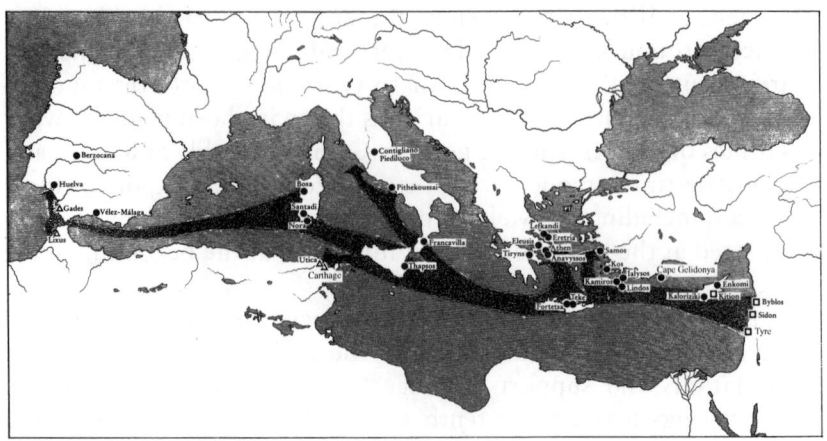

FIGURE 3   *The first Phoenician colonization, according to H. G. Niemeyer.*
▫ *The founder cities in Phoenicia and Cyprus.*
▲ *Very early Phoenician settlements in the west, according to literary tradition.*
• *Important archaeological sites of the archaic period.*

These traces are dated, rather vaguely, to the eleventh or tenth century, and one may justly hesitate to relate them to a passage from the Greek historian Thucydides (VI, 2, 6) which states that the Phoenicians had installed themselves around the whole of the island, and fell back to the western part on the arrival of the Greeks. The reason given by the historian for the area of retreat chosen, the geographical proximity of Carthage, renders his testimony chronologically suspect. Still farther west, on the south coast of Sardinia, an important chronological marker is provided by the inscribed stone of Nora (figure 4), which remains the most ancient text in the Phoenician language in the western basin, with a dating placed in the second half of the ninth century BC (Amadasi-Guzzo, 1990, pp. 72–3). It would seem to be a trace of a Phoenician proto-history, linked with the local culture of the *nuraghe*.

From Nora, on the southern tip of Sardinia, it was still a long sea journey to the Pillars of Hercules, on either side of the Straits of Gibraltar. As has been said, there are no grounds for supporting the traditions giving very early dates for these foundations in the extreme west. At Lixus, in particular, on the Atlantic coast of Morocco, not one piece of the excavated material brought to light seems earlier than the seventh century (Ponsich, 1982, p. 826). In contrast, on the other side, in Andalusia, where archaeological research

FIGURE 4 *The stele of Nora (Istituto per la civiltà fenicia e punica, Rome).*

has been very active for about twenty years, the gap between factual data and textual indications is tending to narrow.

TARTESSUS AND THE PHOENICIANS IN SPAIN

It is in fact probably this region of southern Spain that is referred to in the biblical passages which make the tenth century a literally golden age for the Phoenician city of Tyre. There are passages in the first book of Kings and the second book of Chronicles which assign two principal destinations to the combined fleets of King Hiram and his ally King Solomon of Israel: Ophir, where they seek gold, and Tarsis (or rather Tarshish) whence, every three years, they brought back not only gold and silver, but ivory, monkeys and peacocks (or, according to another reading, which may be preferable: elephant ivory, daggers and axes). There is general agreement in situating Ophir – a region rather than a precise place – on the coast of Arabia or India. As for the word Tarsis, it is ambiguous: when the Old Testament (I Kings, 10:23; Isaiah, 23:1; 60:9) speaks of the 'Tarsis fleet' or 'Tarsis vessels', one may think of a category of ship, a certain type of vessel, probably long-distance, so designated by virtue of a customary destination or perhaps of a particular kind of freight; but other texts, and sometimes the same ones (I Kings, 10:23; II Chronicles, 9:21) indicate very clearly that Tarsis is also a country or a region, certainly a long way away, as it takes three years to return bearing precious goods, but also, according to the words of the prophet Ezekiel (27:12) at the beginning of the sixth century BC, a source of equally valuable mineral riches, such as tin, iron and lead.

Such metalliferous deposits in fact created the wealth of an Andalusian Eldorado which, following Herodotus, Greek and subsequently Latin authors named Tartessus. In those texts the toponym frequently applies to a city – as in Herodotus, who made it a harbour town, a maritime trading-place – over which, when they mention it, authors are divided between Gades (Cadiz) and Carteia. For others Tartessus was a region, a kingdom, on either side of a river, in which may be recognized the lower valley of the present-day Guadalquivir, bordered on the north by the large mining massif of the Rio Tinto, still being worked. The problem is to know whether one can be sure of the identity of Tarsis and Tartessus: it seems at least that if there were perhaps several places known as Tarsis – including Tarsus in Cilicia – one of those Semitic localities was none other than the Tartessus of the classical authors. For one of the latest scholars to have made a careful study, especially from a philological standpoint, Tarshish/Tartessus would appear to be no more than the variable expression of a root having a consonantal variation *trs/trt* in the indigenous language of the southern Iberians (Koch, 1984, pp. 139–40). That identification at least seems certain at the time of the second treaty concluded between Rome and Carthage – which has been dated to the middle of the fourth century BC – where in Polybius' text, which informs us of it, there is a Punic town in Spain whose name, Mastia Tarseion, suggests that at that date the inhabitants of Tarsis were identical with those of the Tartessus region. And a Greek lexicon of Late Roman Empire date has preserved the equation, 'Tarsis, Baetica', explaining the ancient Old Testament place-name by reference to the name which Andalusia then bore in the nomenclature of the Empire's provinces.

Beside this textual record, the archaeology of southern Spain has lined up some impressive findings over the last twenty or so years. Two publications in particular are milestones in this research. In 1968, at Jerez de la Frontera, Spanish archaeologists devoted a great international congress to 'Tartessus and its problems' (*Tartessos y sus problemas*, Barcelona, 1969). Fifteen years later, the team from the German Archaeological Institute of Madrid, who had combined their efforts with those of their Spanish colleagues, gave an account in Cologne of the extent of the progress achieved on the

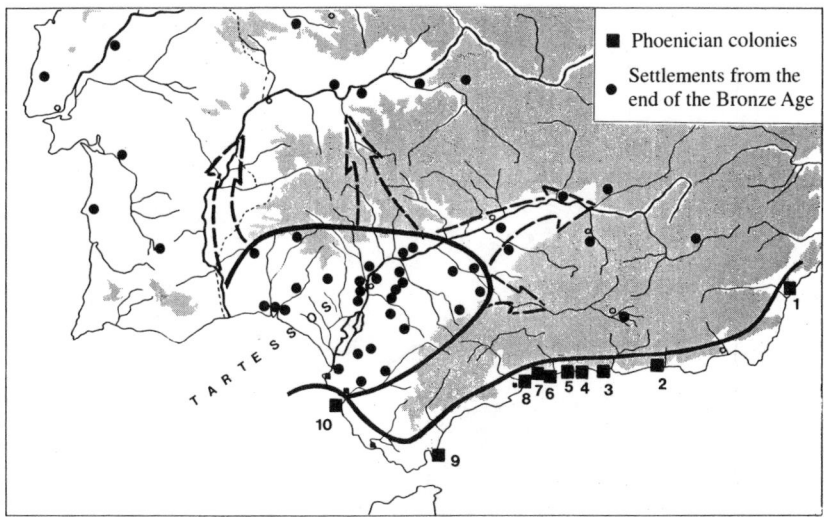

FIGURE 5 *Phoenician colonies of the Costa del Sol as far as Cadiz and the sites of the end of the Bronze Age in the Tartessus region (the lower valley of the Guadalquivir) (after M. E. Aubert-Semmler in* Phönizier im Westen). *The arrows show the 'orientalizing' expansion of the sixth century. 1 Villaricos; 2 Adra; 3 Almuñecar; 4 Chorreras; 5 Toscanos; 6 Mezquitilla; 7 Malaga; 8 Guadalhorce; 9 Gibraltar; 10 Cadiz.*

'Phoenicians in the west' (*Phönizier im Westen*, Mainz, 1982). And that assessment has already been overtaken by the latest results of very active research on the coastal sites of southern Spain (figure 5).

The essential point here is that what emerges above all from these works, apart from new discoveries, is a better characterization of the known sites and more detailed analyses of their facies. Thus, in the Guadalquivir valley, archaeological surveys had long ago discovered traces of an ancient rural settlement, apparently prosperous if one is to judge, for example, by the quality of the ivories unearthed from the tombs of Carmona, north of Seville, or by that of the hoard of gold jewellery from nearby El Carambolo. Like that of Aliseda, in the mid-valley of the Tagus, this jewellery – datable to the seventh and sixth centuries – certainly did not go back to the first times of Phoenician expansion, but revealed clear Phoenician influences within the sphere of local production. One can now get a better picture of how those 'Tartessian' sites, whose earliest development goes back to the Bronze Age and whose wealth in ancient times was based on the mineral exploitation of the Sierra

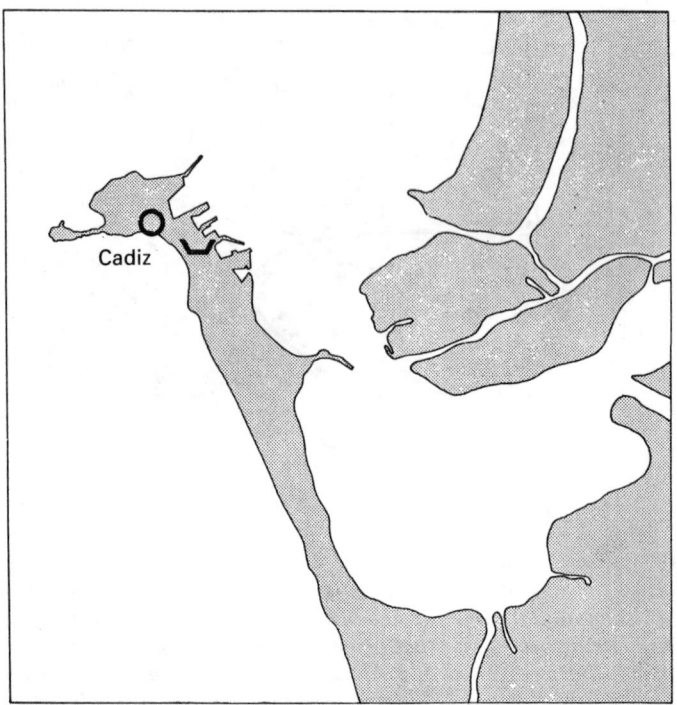

FIGURE 6 *The site of Cadiz (Gades) (after A. Garcia y Bellido).*

Morena, were enriched culturally and strengthened economically by the Phoenician coastal settlements (Aubet-Semmler, 1982, pp. 311–20).

Gades (Cadiz) springs first to mind, with the help of literary tradition, and also because the site – which itself evokes that of Tyre, with its isle parallel to the shore from which it is separated by a narrow channel (figure 6) – is a Phoenician landscape *par excellence*. Mistrusting the mainland, the Phoenician gets as close as he can without actually settling on it: 'the Phoenicians always install themselves between land and sea' (Gras et al., 1989, pp. 53–61). Unfortunately, setting aside some problematic discoveries – such as the figurine of what seems likely to be a Ptah (figure 7) – the archaeological record goes back no further than the sixth century on this site, which has been constantly occupied since remotest antiquity and has suffered a great deal of disturbance. The possibility remains, however, that more precise excavations may allow us to go back much earlier, and such hope has been greatly encouraged since the settlement of Doña Blanca, at the mouth of the

FIGURE 7   *The Ptah from Cadiz (National Archaeological Museum, Madrid).*

Guadalete and opposite the Phoenician islet of Cadiz, yielded oriental material of the eighth century (Ruiz Mata, 1985, pp. 241–63).

On the other hand, some striking discoveries have recently been made on the Mediterranean coast of Andalusia, which the navigators from the east had to touch before passing the Straits. First of all, going from east to west, near Almuñecar, on what would have been the site of Sexi, where Strabo (III, 5, 5) indicates that the Tyrians, invited by an oracle to found a settlement at the Pillars of Hercules, stopped and made a sacrifice to Melqart. There a cremation cemetery contains tombs dating from the end of the eighth century, but with an Egyptian aspect strongly indicated by alabaster jars bearing pharaonic cartouches belonging to the ninth century, while one of them shows, alongside pseudo-hieroglyphic inscriptions, a text in Phoenician (Pellicer Catalan, 1962).

Thirty kilometres away to the west, at Toscanos, near Torre del Mar, some structures in monumental masonry date back to the middle of the eighth century. It has been possible to identify them

FIGURE 8   *Trayamar: burial chamber 1 (H. G. Niemeyer and H. Schubart).*

as shops, in the form of oblong rooms where amphorae and other storage vessels were piled up; recent digging has established that a modestly built-up area of shore served as a port there. In the same sector, the cemeteries of the Rio Guadalhorce and Rio Algarrobo, at Trayamar, have produced tombs constructed of monumental masonry, whose finds place them in the second half of the seventh century (figure 8). But two adjacent sites, Chorreras and Morro de Mezquitilla, include a domestic settlement, with houses having walls of dried clay bricks, whose first stage dates to the eighth century. In the province of Cadiz, a small site at Cerro del Prado, at the mouth of the Rio Guadarranque, may date from the end of the seventh century (Schubart, 1982, pp. 207–31). So, if one allows that the first archaeological evidence for a site may show a certain delay – possibly of several decades – in relation to its first human settlement, it will be recognized that all the south-eastern coast of the Iberian peninsula, the last stretch before passing the Pillars of Hercules, was densely colonized by the easterners from the eighth century and doubtless even a little before that. For the most westerly of these *comptoirs* (as the commercial role of the Andalusian sites is evident) the last foothills of the Baetican Cordillera were no longer a barrier on the route to the land of Tartessus and its mineral riches.

BEYOND THE PILLARS OF HERCULES: FROM LIXUS TO UTICA

On the other side of the Straits, on African soil, the realities on the ground appear very different, as if the texts that place Gades and Lixus on either side like the two pillars of a very ancient Phoenician colonization had created a forced and artifical symmetry (figure 9).

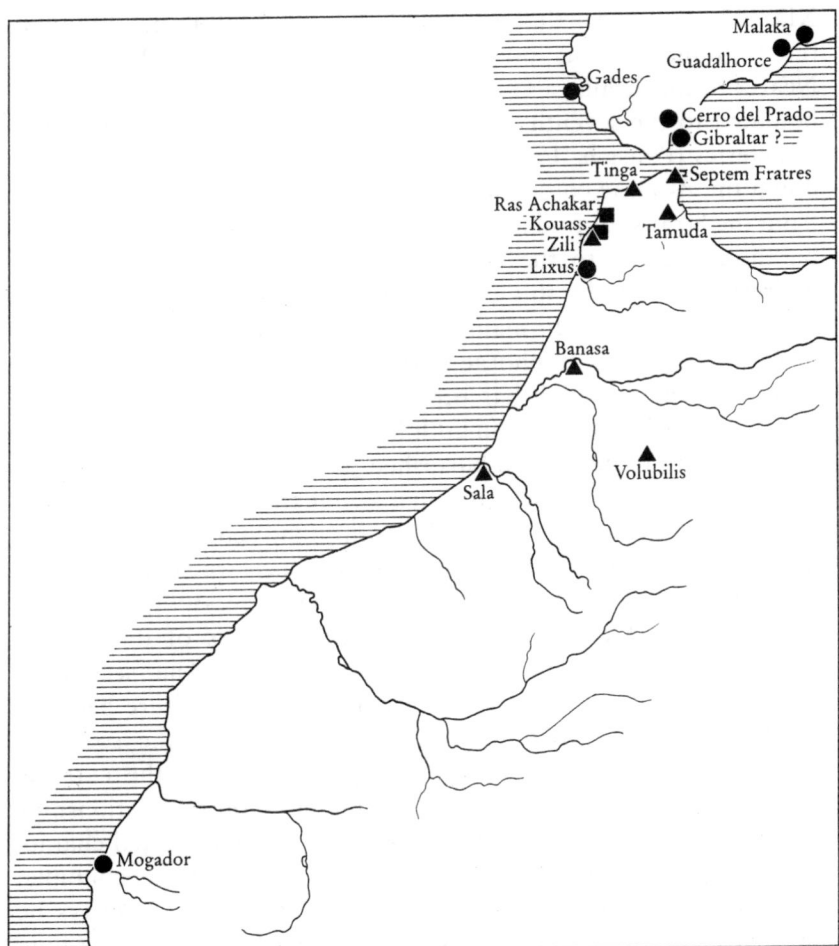

FIGURE 9 *The Phoenicians on both sides of the Straits of Gibraltar and on the Atlantic coast of Morocco (after M. Ponsich).*
- *First Phoenician settlements.*
- ▲ *Cities with Punic mints.*
- ■ *Punic archaeological sites.*

Nevertheless Lixus, like Gades, is in its own way a perfect example of a Phoenician site: it lies on an estuary, which facilitates the anchorage of boats, with the additional attraction, as it happens, of a hill circled by a meander of the Wadi Loukkos, forming a real landmark for oriental sailors and an acropolis cum belvedere for the occupants of the site. But, at the present stage of research, the oldest levels of a vast complex of superimposed temples – whose first stage could be the temple of Melqart, according to Pliny (*NH*, XIX, 63) even older than that of Gades – go back no further than the beginning of the seventh century (Ponsich, 1982, p. 438). Nearer to the Straits, a Phoenician presence in Tingis (Tangier) can be dated to the seventh century, at the earliest, by finds from the cemeteries (Ponsich, 1967). And one must go much farther south, down the Atlantic coast as far as Mogador, almost 700 kilometres from the Straits, to find another landfall, dating from the same era, on the sea route to the Great South (Jodin, 1966). The special interest presented by this distant site – itself typically Phoenician, on an island close to the mainland – is that it has revealed fragments of Attic and Ionian amphorae of the middle of the seventh century, no equivalent of which has been found at Carthage or the other Punic sites in Tunisia. And in both Mogador and Lixus, excavations have brought to light a red burnished pottery of Phoenician origin, which ceases to be present in Carthage at the beginning or, at the latest, in the middle of the seventh century. Two conclusions may be drawn from these findings. The first, to which we shall return, is that Carthage seems to have kept apart from the east-west sea route which carried Phoenician navigators and traders of the earliest times towards the most westerly settlements. The second is that from that period there was a community of culture between the strongly entrenched Phoenician civilization in the south of Spain and the much more scattered settlements in the extreme African west. This early symbiosis and later favoured relationships on the north-south axis would remain one of the principal characteristics of the region. It must be borne in mind that in economic, cultural and even broadly geopolitical terms it would always be distinct from the rest of the Maghreb, whose destiny we must now examine.

The hypothesis has been advanced that at this period (ninth(?) to eighth century) ships from Phoenicia heading to the far west by a more northerly route, using the Balearic Islands as a stepping-stone, would return to the east, laden with minerals from Tarsis-Tartessus,

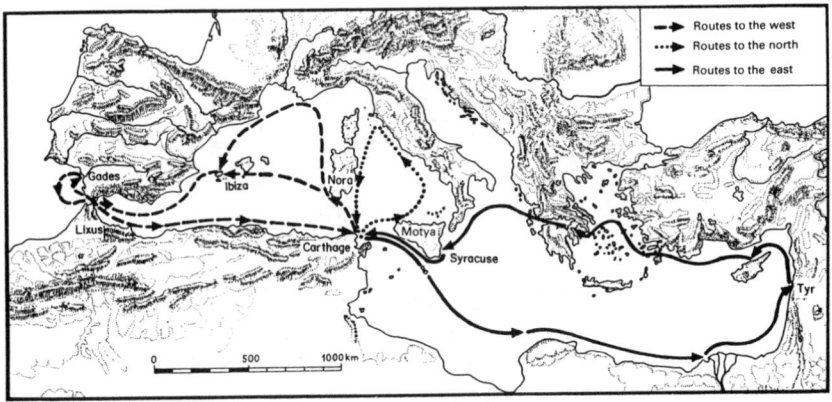

FIGURE 10 *Phoenician routes in the Mediterranean (after C. Picard in* Phönizier im Westen).

by sailing along the African coast and putting in at Carthage, where they would unload only a small part of their cargo (C. Picard, 1982, p. 170). The interest of this hypothesis lies in recognizing the very small number – if not the total absence – of archaeological traces at Carthage of trade between the African city and the land of Tartessus in early times. But – and herein lies the difficulty – those ships, which obviously could not make that long sea journey along the north coasts of the Maghreb in one stretch, have left not one single trace – at least, as far as we know at present – of their passage along hundreds of kilometres of shores. It will be seen that on these coasts the ports of call so far picked out are not Phoenician but 'Punic', and appreciably later (seventh to sixth century).

UTICA

In the earliest times, before they came to Carthage, their only landfall attested by tradition – if one excepts the hypothetical Hippo – was Utica (figure 11). The ancient city has suffered the common fate of many estuarine sites – in France one has only to think of Aigues-Mortes or Brouage – of being gradually embedded in the alluvial deposits of a river that has distanced them from the sea: the little promontory on which the Phoenician settlement was founded, at the mouth of the Medjerda, now looks out on a marshy plain into which the contours of the ancient site have partly merged

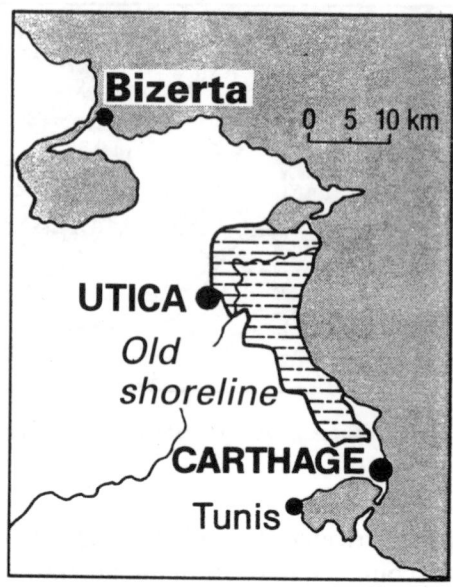

FIGURE 11   *The sites of Utica and Carthage.*

FIGURE 12   *Aerial view of the 'shore cemetery' at Utica (P. Cintas).*

(figure 12). From the fanciful and romantic reconstructions of the engineer Daux under Napoleon III right up to the persistent efforts of Pierre Cintas in the middle of this century, the site has greatly disappointed those who had let themselves be beguiled by the mirage of its origins. Only cemeteries have been excavated among the pre-Roman levels. Certainly these are spectacular and have yielded far from negligible material, but their oldest tombs appear no earlier than the eighth century, despite the efforts exerted by their finder to add to their age (Cintas, 1970, pp. 294–308), so we are left a long way from the venerable date of 1101 BC which Pliny the Elder ascribed to the construction of Apollo's temple. Much remains to be done at Utica, and there is always a hope that we shall see the archaeologists reduce the considerable gap that separates them from the early dates of tradition, but conditions are difficult. Utica is a site that has for the most part been spoilt, abandoned for too long to the initiative of landowners, and where often chaotic excavations have further aggravated the upheavals due to natural causes. Fortunately, it is not the same for Carthage, where textual and archaeological evidence is far more substantial, even though correlation between the two, as regards the earliest city, is still problematical.

FIGURE 13 *The 'shore cemetery' at Utica (P. Cintas).*

THE FOUNDING OF CARTHAGE

Carthage has not escaped the efforts of classical traditions to endow western Phoenician cities with the most ancient origins. Historically, it is a quite understandable phenomenon, as those traditions were developed at dates – starting from the fourth century BC – when Carthaginian power in the western Mediterranean had become a major fact: it needed origins in keeping with that power. This explains why the African city features in the computations and calculations that also concerned its great rival, Rome, and which have the destruction of Troy as their chronological starting-point.

'EARLY' AND 'LATE' TRADITIONS

Thus a fragmentary text of a Greek historian of the first half of the fourth century, Philistos of Syracuse, states that 'Carthage was founded *at that time* by the Tyrians, Azoros and Karkhedon' (Jacoby, *Fragmenta historiae graecae*, II, B, No. 556, fragm. 47). The 'time' in question is indicated in his *Chronicle* by Saint Jerome who, eight centuries later, resumed this tradition by quoting Philistos and pinpointing the date of Carthage's founding in 'the year of Abraham 802' or 1215 BC. This date is thirty-three years before the fall of Troy according to the chronicle of Eusebius, and thirty years before according to Apollodorus. So Philistos fixed the founding of Carthage a generation before the fall of Troy and thus placed himself in the tradition of the Greek tragedians – for example, Euripides, *The Trojans* – who were already evoking Carthage in connection with events prior to the Trojan War. Another fourth-century Greek historian subscribes to this tradition, in apparently independent fashion – Eudoxus of Cnidus, according to whom 'it was shortly before the Trojan War that the Tyrians colonized Carthage under the leadership of Azoros and Karkhedon, from whom the town received its name.' The tradition fixed in this way in the classical Greek era was favoured, as it is to be found again in an author of the second century AD who remains one of our most important sources on the history of Carthage, Appian, who writes (*Libyca*, 1): 'The Phoenicians founded Carthage in Libya fifty years before the fall of Troy; the founders were Zoros and Karkhedon.' Apart from the date, the common factor in the different versions of

FIGURE 14 *Excavation in the cemetery at Utica. The photograph shows the major difference in depth in relation to the Roman level (P. Cintas).*

this tradition is the role played by the two founder-heroes, Azoros or Zoros, surely a derivation of the name Tyre (= Sor or Sur, 'rock' in Phoenician) and Karkhedon, whose eponymous nature is obvious, as his name is nothing more than the Greek transcription of the Semitic name, Qart Hadasht, of the 'New Town' founded in Cyprus before one was founded at Carthage. How were the supporters of this tradition, following Philistos and Eudoxus – and before them Euripides – led to put back the founding of Carthage to a time earlier than the fall of Troy? The following ingenious explanation has been advanced: reading the *Odyssey* would have given rise to the belief that the Mediterranean west had been known to the Greeks at the time of the Trojan War. As it was known, furthermore, that Carthage was already in existence when the Greeks came to found their colonies in the western Mediterranean (notably in Sicily: at Syracuse, at Megara Hyblaea), the conclusion was drawn that the Phoenician city belonged to an era earlier than the fall of Troy.

In comparison with this early tradition, the sources that date the foundation of the Tyrian colony to the end of the ninth century BC and mention the circumstances of the foundation are impressive for their number, agreement and coherence. Above all, unlike those we have just seen, they are based on a structure of official historical records. The Phoenician metropolis, Tyre, kept chronicles that included in particular royal lists, with lengths of reigns and mention of the most noteworthy events (Teixidor, 1989, pp. 47–8). The originals of those annals, and even their local transcriptions, are lost, but Greek historiography made partial use of them. This was notably the case of a Sicilian Greek, Timaeus of Taormina, at the beginning of the third century, who was in contact with Punic people who had settled on the island and had the opportunity to be well informed about what the Carthaginians themselves knew of their past. According to Timaeus, Carthage had been founded thirty-eight years before the first Olympiad, that is, in 814/813 BC. To within a year, that is the date mentioned later by Cicero in his *De Republica* (II, 23, 42) and the same indications are also to be found in Velleius Paterculus and Saint Jerome's *Chronicle*. It may be that these authors were deriving their information from Timaeus, but different sources cannot be ruled out. At all events, the soundness of the tradition that sets the foundation of the city in 814 BC is again confirmed by the testimony of another Greek historian, in the first half of the second century BC, about whom we are certain that he made use of and translated Phoenician written sources: Menander of Ephesus. His notes were collected, at the end of the first century AD, by Flavius Josephus, a Hellenized Jew in the entourage of the Emperor Titus. He states that the foundation of Carthage took place in the seventh year of the reign of King Pygmalion in Tyre.

Transferred to a definite chronology by reference to Tyrian annals, this corresponds to the year 819 BC, or again, using other calculations, to the year 814 with Timaeus and 824 with Justin (XVIII, 4–5). These variations of a few years can be explained by the inexactness of conversions starting from different eras and are in themselves negligible; the least ancient variant, giving the date 814, is the one generally accepted.

THE FOUNDATION MYTH

The sources also agree on the circumstances of the foundation. It was reported more or less identically by Timaeus and Menander, immortalized by Virgil, and described more explicitly in the second century AD in the digest of Justin, already mentioned. The common element in these different versions is the drama that began at Tyre when King Pygmalion, through greed, killed the husband of his sister Elissa. The latter fled, together with a certain number of loyal followers, among whom were important personages from the city. She landed in Cyprus and, after a few journeys, which, says Timaeus, earned her the name of Dido (*Deido*) among the natives, she arrived in Libya. In detail, this plot has a number of variants, particularly as regards the names of its protagonists, which may be explained by the difficulty of transcribing Semitic names into the classical languages. As regards the name of the heroine, Elishat, transcribed as Elissa by the Greeks, is attested on many occasions by Punic ex-votos at Carthage. However, the name Dido has prevailed for the woman who founded Carthage, perhaps because it featured in the Latin sources of Naevius, Ennius and Virgil especially. Dido is a surname for Elissa. The woman who was called Elissa in Tyre became Dido in Africa: the 'wanderer', as she was known, according to Timaeus; the 'virile woman' (*virago*), according to the grammarian Servius, Virgil's commentator; the 'husband-murderer', according to Eustathius, a Byzantine commentator on Homer. Modern scholars have been no more successful in their efforts to link this name with a stem that is meaningful in Semitic or even in Greek. The reader of Virgil, the listener to Purcell's opera, the music buff who actually enjoys Berlioz and his *Trojans*, will surely not mind that the name which bears such an aura should be given an additional touch of mystery in its philological obscurity.

In the epic of Elissa-Dido there are two especially outstanding features worthy of comment. After she had founded Carthage, the king of the Libyans, Hiarbas, wanted to marry her. Rather than be unfaithful to her first husband, who had been killed by Pygmalion in Tyre, she pretended to carry out an expiatory ceremony and climbed on to the pyre she had just lit. We know what passionate and romantic use was later made of this standard version, common to Timaeus and Justin, by Virgil, who erected the funeral pyre of betrayed passion on Carthage's shore within view of the vessels carrying Aeneas on his divine mission. Behind this myth of Elissa-Dido perishing amid the flames, we can see the outlines of the religious practice of self-sacrifice which a Phoenician king or queen was obliged to carry out in a grave crisis – in the present case, in order to perpetuate the foundation in the face of threat from the natives. The sacrifice of children by fire in the *tophet* (sacred area) was perhaps only a ritual derivation of that exceptional practice. It will be noted that, according to Justin (VI, 6), Elissa-Dido had the pyre built at the edge of the town; and it will be seen that the sacrificial area of the *tophet* was situated at the southern fringe of Punic Carthage. The myth preserved its full vigour up to the end of Carthage. In the spring of 146, when the soldiers of Scipio Aemilianus took the town by storm, the wife of the defeated general, Hasdrubal, cast herself and her children into the flames from the last bastion of the city's resistance, the temple of Aesculapius (Eschmoun) on the summit of the hill of Byrsa (Appian, *Libyca*, 131). Myth and history came together full circle, with a similar emblematic female figure in both instances.

The second salient feature of the foundation myth is in fact an explanatory, aetiological image of the name Byrsa for the Punic citadel. Virgil knew of it and, supposing his public also to be familiar with Dido-Elissa's ruse, made only an oblique allusion: the Tyrians, he said (*Aeneid*, I, 367–8), 'bought as much land as they could encircle with the skin of a bull, for which reason it was called Byrsa'. Justin's account shows with greater detail how the trick worked, as it relied on the use of a word with a double meaning. Elissa bought as much ground as the hide of an ox could 'cover' (*tegere* or *tenere*), then had the skin cut into very fine strips so as to encircle, in a manner obviously unforeseen by the other party to the bargain, an area estimated by Servius, Virgil's commentator, at 22 *stadia*, or about 4 kilometres in circumference. It is certain that this story was told in Greek at the time of Timaeus or perhaps even earlier, and it must be supposed therefore that *bursa*, ox-hide in Greek (*bourse* in French), formed a pun in Greek with a still unknown Semitic root, which was used by Elissa's companions to designate their first settlement. Before considering what must be understood in topographic terms by Byrsa, it may be noted that even before the Romans made a proverb of *fides Punica* – 'Punic perfidy' – the Greeks had emphasized the *sophisma* (in Latin *calliditas*) of the Phoenician queen, in contrast with the naïve ingenuousness of the Libyans (Scheid and Svenbro, 1985, pp. 328–42). The art of turning negotiations to its own advantage and misrepresenting an agreement by twisting the terms, which was Carthage's strength and was experienced by the Greeks in Sicily before the Romans encountered it, was thus already symbolized by Dido's ruse.

THE REALITIES ON THE GROUND

Certainly, it is every archaeologist's dream to match the realities of a site with textual data. At Carthage archaeologists have had many dreams, with varying success. Their first efforts were directed entirely towards a search for origins. In 1858 Flaubert spent the spring in Carthage in order to immerse himself in the place where the characters of *Salammbô* would evolve. The following year an archaeologist, Beulé, better known as the 'discoverer' of the Propylaea of the Acropolis in Athens, occupied the plateau of Byrsa, then known as the hill of Saint–Louis, and discovered the famous enclosure of Carthage. At the conclusion of work carried out with great integrity, the report of which contains observations that are still useful, he unearthed a segment of the mighty retaining wall with which the Romans, in the era of the Emperor Augustus, had 'corseted' the hill, which they had previously decapitated and transformed into a plateau.

THE ARCHAIC CEMETERIES

The first Carthage remained to be discovered (figure 15). It was the focus of an archaeology chiefly concerned with funerary remains that was very active from the last decades of the nineteenth century. It was carried out by the Tunisian Department of Antiquities, especially its second director, P. Gauckler, one of the best excavators of his time, in keen rivalry with a White Father, A.-L. Delattre. To them we are indebted for the majority of the discoveries made, rather hastily, in order to supply objects to the museums that were

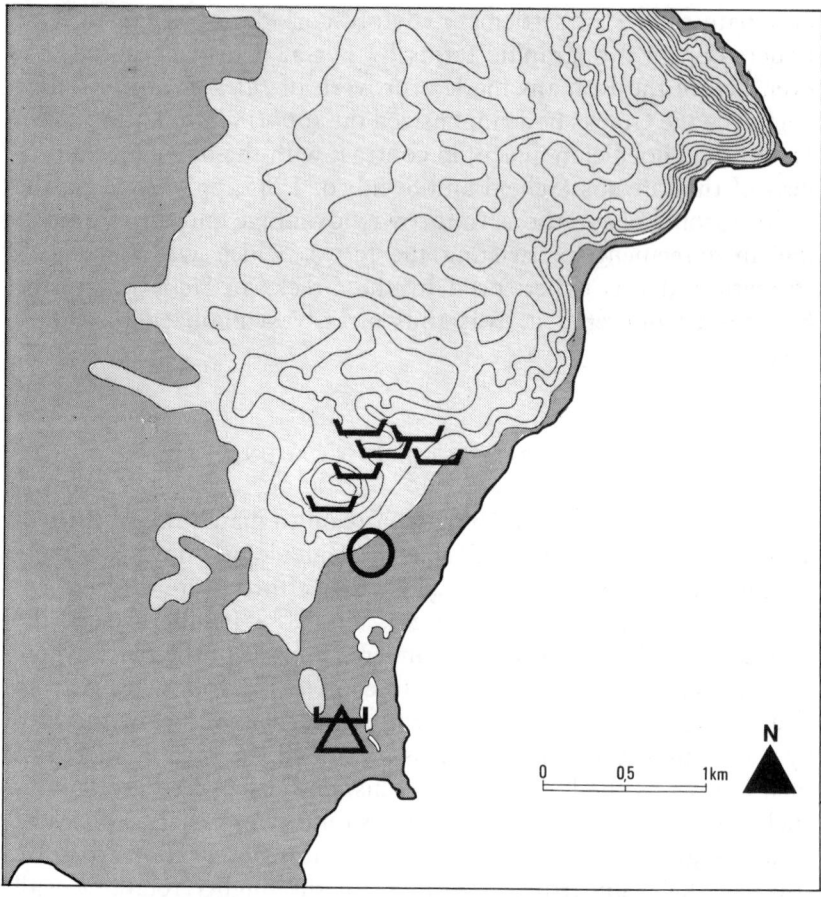

FIGURE 15 *Schematic plan of ancient Carthage: in the north, the cemeteries; in the centre, the urban settlement; to the south, the tophet (after H. G. Niemeyer,* Die Phönizier im Zeitalter Homers, *1984).*

being opened here and there, but first of all in Carthage. At the very beginning of the twentieth century, the layout of the earliest cemeteries of the Punic city was known in broad outline; this topography was later supplemented only in detail (Bénichou-Safar, 1982, pp. 13–60). The tombs of the archaic period formed an arc following the contours of the high ground from the hill of Saint-Louis (today Byrsa) as far as the area called Dermech, slightly behind the present remains of the Antonine Baths: the contemporary settlement was most likely to be found between that arc and the shoreline.

Here the difficult problem of dating the material retrieved from these tombs must be considered. As will be seen, grave goods constitute, if not the only, at least one of the best sources of our knowledge of Punic arts and crafts, particularly in the earliest times. They varied – amulets, pendants, jewels, masks and razors – but most common were terracotta vessels. This last category of material provides the best criteria for dating, particularly pottery imported from the Greek world, among which certain series can be dated to within a quarter of a century or so. While proto-Attic pottery is a rarity – unlike the extreme west in the south of Spain and Morocco, as has been seen – material originating from Corinth is especially plentiful in the archaic tombs of Carthage (Boucher, 1953, pp. 11–29). But few objects of that provenance – proto-Corinthian pot-bellied aryballoi – date from earlier than the beginning of the seventh century. Therefore only a few tombs on the eastern slopes of the so-called 'Hill of Juno' or the lower slopes of Dermech can be dated to the end of the eighth century, while tombs belonging to the seventh century abound in these areas and on the southern flank of the hill of Byrsa (Bénichou-Safar, 1982, pp. 321–5; Lancel, 1982, pp. 357–9). Certainly, it is possible that the most ancient tombs in Carthage, contemporary with or slightly later than its foundation (the beginning of the eighth century), may not yet have been located. They might lie in the internal fringe of these burial zones, nearest to the settlement to which they related (Cintas, 1970, pp. 441–2). We shall see that the recent location of several parts of that archaic settlement now enables us to try to pinpoint these relationships. But at present almost a century separates the traditional date of 814 from the burials dated *convincingly* as the most ancient.

THE TOPHET

Let me emphasize this last qualification, for the possibility also exists that tombs of the earliest period may not have been recognized from the material they contain, or that we have not wanted to recognize them as such. This raises the problem of dating pottery in the Phoenician tradition, which naturally forms the main part of these grave goods. The question was again posed, with a mass of extra evidence, as a result of the excavation of the tophet, particularly when it was explored under the supervision of P. Cintas between 1944 and 1947. We shall return later, at greater length, to this sacrificial area (see p. 227). For the moment, suffice it to say that the archaeological evidence it reveals consists of an accumulation, over the centuries, of votive deposits comprising a stele or cippus surmounting one or two cinerary urns. This accumulation has produced more or less overlapping layers, in the deepest of which lie the most ancient deposits, touching the natural subsoil. At this level, and on part of the site which was possibly, with a different coastal configuration, the shore of the lagoon where the first

FIGURE 16 *Greek pottery from the deposit in the 'Cintas chapel'. 1 and 2 cotyles; 3 bottle; 4 askos; 5 to 7 oenochoi (P. Cintas).*

Phoenicians landed, Cintas brought to light what seemed to him to be a kind of sanctuary established, if not at the very origin, at least in the first years of the foundation of the site (Cintas, 1948). A natural crevice in the rock had been turned into a little vault, which contained two distinct types of objects: right at the bottom, Greek vessels: two little skyphoi, three small oenochoi, a bottle (figure 16); above, resting on a layer of sedimentation, a later deposit comprised a Phoenician amphora and a lamp with two spouts. The Greek vessels of the lowest layer were proto-Corinthian or related, of the same date as the pot-bellied aryballos, that is, contemporary with the vessels which date the most ancient burials, as we have seen. Of course, the absolute chronology of this pottery is not fixed beyond doubt: at the time of Cintas's discovery, there was a tendency to lower the dating of this whole series for which F. Johansen, in his *Vases sicyoniens*, had formerly proposed a broad margin, between 800 and 725 BC. As for the finely-made askos in the shape of a bird, which was associated with the collection of proto-Corinthian vessels though it is of a type developed in the ninth century, it is likely to be an island copy, possibly Euboean, and its date evidently must not be separated from that of the associated vessels (Gras, 1989, p. 214).

Cintas therefore had to transfer his hopes of establishing a very early date for the beginnings of the tophet to another find, made at the same time, not in the vault, but in a 'foundation deposit' situated at the base of a low wall adjoining the 'chapel'. This deposit contained a lamp with a single spout – presumed to be of an early date since all bowl-lamps that can be dated to the seventh century have two spouts – and an amphora with twisted handles which he hoped to identify as 'sub-Mycenaean' and date to the end of the tenth century (figure 17). But a specialist, at the very time of the discovery (Demargne, 1951, p. 50), linked this vessel with the series of late geometric or subgeometric vases of the Greek islands – Thera, Delos – that similarly bear a decoration of chequered triangles alternating with concentric circles on the shoulder and, on the neck, bands of zigzags between triglyphs. And even the most generous chronology does not allow us to place this amphora any earlier than 750 BC. That disappointment subsequently led the finder of this 'sanctuary' to minimize the importance of his discovery and make little of his 'chapel' (Cintas, 1970, pp. 315–24; it may be added that the present trend is to consider this well-known find a votive deposit of a particular type: Gras, 1989, p. 218), and to stress the importance of non-Greek pottery in establishing the site's chronology.

FIGURE 17   *The late geometric amphora from the 'foundation deposit'*
(P. Cintas).

The latter approach seems legitimate. First, because there appears
to be no reason why a class of pottery that has been well studied on
eastern sites since the end of the Bronze Age should be ruled out as
dating evidence; second, because at Carthage this approach was
based on an extremely interesting observation. It will be seen
further on that the excavators of the tophet allowed a distinction
between two major strata in its earliest levels: 'Tanit I' and 'Tanit
II'. It would appear that, with a few rare exceptions – where they
are associated with proto-Corinthian pottery of the second half of
the eighth century – most of the pottery of Tanit I is absent from the
grave deposits, even in the earliest part of Carthage's cemeteries.
This is particularly true of 'thistle-head' vessels, but also of several
forms of amphorae with either vertical or horizontal handles, partly
coated in wide bands around the belly or lower part with bright red
slip, and most frequently decorated on the shoulder with strigils,

FIGURE 18 *Archaic amphorae from the tophet (Tanit I) of Phoenician tradition (excavations and photographs by P. Cintas).*

zigzags or horizontal or vertical strokes that stand out from a light surface (figure 18). It can thus be assumed that tombs furnished with these early objects have yet to be discovered in the cemeteries.

One last question remains: can one really break free from the chronological framework of Greek pottery for dating the earliest evidence of the Punic metropolis? Generally speaking, one would shy away from doing so, as from taking a leap in the dark. All Cintas's comparative studies, for example (1970, pp. 330–70) have shown that the pottery of Tanit I must be related to the series whose shape and decoration it parallels, found in Cyprus and the Near East, and so must fit into Near Eastern chronologies with dates ranging from 850 to 700 for the majority of these articles: a very broad margin, as may be seen – too broad to provide discriminatory criteria in the present case. But there is still a strong presumption that certain archaic amphorae of the tophet may date back to the beginning of the eighth century.

THE PRESENT STATE OF ARCHAEOLOGICAL DATING

So, in this debate, Greek pottery is going to have the last word! The hypothesis of an early dating is still made, with the backing of a recent re-examination of the cotyles (or scyphoi) from the vault of 'Cintas's chapel'. These two small bowls with horizontal handles of the 'Aetos 666 types' – in reference to an example discovered in excavations of Aetos on the island of Ithaca – appear in fact to be datable to the second quarter or middle of the eighth century (D'Agostino, 1977, pp. 48–9). And a cup with chevrons from the cemetery of the so-called hill of Juno also seems to belong to the end of the first half of the eighth century (figure 19), these three pieces of pottery coming perhaps, not from Greece itself, but from workshops on Ischia, off the coast of Naples. We may add the expert observations – for the moment the penultimate, if not the final

FIGURE 19 *Cup with chevrons from the hill of Juno cemetery (Musée national de Carthage).*

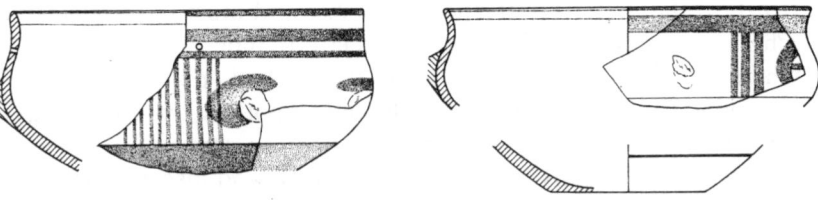

FIGURE 20 *Fragments of two Euboean cups (middle of the eighth century BC) from the archaic settlement of Carthage (after M. Vegas, 1989, p. 217).*

FIGURE 21 *An amphora from the tophet of Carthage (Lapeyre excavations) (drawing and photograph by P. Cintas).*

word on the matter! – of one of the best and most knowledgeable scholars of both Greek and Phoenician archaic material. A little while ago the late lamented A.-M. Bisi (1983, pp. 693–715) re-examined the whole question of the oldest pottery from Carthage's tophet, and notably that from the 'foundation deposit'. In the light of recent excavations at Pithecusae in Italy, and also in the Greek island of Euboea (Evvoia), it seems that products of Euboean or Euboeo-Cycladic influence were associated with objects typical of the early proto-Corinthian era, which may be dated to the second quarter or middle of the eighth century.

Very recently, deep excavations in the archaic period settlement, at the very heart of earliest Carthage, have brought to light large fragments of cups of the later Geometric period originating from Euboea (Evvoia) and datable to the second or, at the latest, third quarter of the eighth century (Vegas, 1989, pp. 213–14) (figure 20). It is difficult to say precisely whether they came directly from Euboea or by way of central Italy. In certain cases even, it is not impossible that vessels of typically Phoenician shape but with ob-viously Greek ornamentation were made in Carthage, with help from either the Corinthian or Euboean workshops. This might be the case of an exceptional item from the excavations carried out at the tophet of Salammbô by Père Lapeyre in 1934: an urn with red burnish, except for a band on a level with the handles, where birds (in Euboean style) are depicted alternating with stylized 'diabolos' characteristic of the workshops of Corinth (figure 21). Without making an archaeological fantasy, it can be suggested that this urn may have contained the cremated remains of a child of mixed parentage, the decorator of the vase possibly being the child's father (Gras, 1989, pp. 219–20). To return to our subject, we may con-clude that a whole mass of recent archaeological indications tends to narrow the gap that still persists between the earliest remains and the textual traditions that place the founding of Carthage at the end of the ninth century.

2

The Establishment of the City

Compared with other more or less contemporary Phoenician settlements in the west, particularly those on the Andalusian coasts which are now the best known archaeologically, Carthage is the only one that meets the criteria of a town. And it is surely not by chance that Carthage is the only instance where we have a Semitic legend about its founding comparable with the legends of the foundation of the Greek colonies. As we have seen, that legend established between Carthage and the mother-city, Tyre, a relationship of *apoikia*, to use the Greek term, in the unusual and romanticized form of a split provoked by the murder by Pygmalion of the husband of his sister, Elissa-Dido. Some citizens, *politai* according to Timaeus, *senatores* (leading figures) according to Justin (IV, 15) accompanied Elissa in her flight, part therefore of the Tyrian aristocracy, which would provide the town that was to be founded with a complete social stratification. Similarly, the eighty *virgines* rescued by Elissa from their sacred prostitution in the service of Venus, when landfall was made in Cyprus (Justin, V, 4–5) were to ensure the peopling of the new city. This, of course, parallels the rape of the Sabine women, which similarly contributed to the demographic development of Rome, and from this repetition one may suspect the existence of a structural outline peculiar to these stories; but, in this instance, the ancient links between Tyre and Cyprus confer on this deportation of young women the character of a veritable *deductio*, or a politically organized transfer of population.

FROM THE TYRIAN COLONY TO THE AFRICAN METROPOLIS

As in Rome the influx of foreigners attracted by the hope of refuge, so in Carthage the contribution of Africans lured by the possibilities of trade would do the rest: 'Out of this crowd of men,' says Justin (V, 11), 'a sort of state was formed.' Nothing seemed to be lacking from the success of this foundation, and envoys from Utica came to give it their blessing: 'The deputies from Utica,' says Justin (V, 12), 'seeing them as kinsfolk, also brought them gifts and urged them to found a town on the spot where destiny had given them a settlement.' The approach is ambiguous: the exhortation to found a city suggests patronage, which is given the lie by the offer of presents, as that rather implies allegiance. That is the initial ambiguity of the relationship between Utica, whose traditions proclaim its precedence without fixing its status as a settlement, and a later foundation, Carthage, clearly marked out by other traditions to become the metropolis of the Phoenicians of the west.

When she left Tyre, Elissa-Dido had brought with her not only a delegation of the town's nobility. She had also brought away what Justin (IV, 15) calls the *sacra Herculis*, the liturgical articles of the cult of Hercules, the name taken by the Phoenician god Melqart in the *interpretatio Romana*. Faithful to his story line, Justin presents this as an act of fidelity to the memory of Acherbas, Elissa's husband, who had been a priest of Hercules-Melqart in Tyre. But it is known that Melqart (the 'king of the city' in Phoenician) was the tutelary divinity of Tyre. At the time of an initial phase of colonization in the far west, his cult had already spread, as we have seen, to Gades (Cadiz) and Lixus (Larache), on either side of the appropriately named Pillars of Hercules. Bringing away the *sacra Herculis* ensured a religious consecration for the founding of the colony, just as the presence of citizens and notables in Elissa's entourage had given it a political basis.

We shall see that Melqart did not preserve his rank of leading divinity in Carthage, since his cult was eclipsed by those of the two supreme deities, the couple Tanit and Baal Hammon; but the link between the 'new town' and the mother-city would be marked for several centuries by the embassy which, every year, left Carthage to celebrate a sacrifice in the temple of Melqart in Tyre (Quintus Curtius, IV, 2, 10). According to Diodorus of Sicily (XX, 14), the offering brought by the Carthaginians on those occasions originally took the form of a tithe in the strict sense of the word, one-tenth of the African city's revenue. Subsequently their prosperity made the Carthaginians somewhat forgetful of their duties of allegiance but, Diodorus adds, the dangers they encountered at the end of the fourth century at the time of Agathocles' expedition recalled them smartly to a respect for those duties and they then sent sumptuous offerings to Melqart of Tyre. Meanwhile, victories achieved by Carthage had occasioned extraordinary gifts to the mother-city: in the sixth century, part of the booty seized by Malchus in Sicily was taken to the Tyrian Hercules by that general's son, on the orders of the Carthaginian senate (Justin, XVIII, 7, 7): at the end of the fifth century a bronze statue of the god Apollo, coming from Gela in Sicily, was sent to Tyre to be placed in the sanctuary of Hercules. A few years before the fall of Carthage, Polybius (XXXI, 12) was still mentioning the ships that would carry the offerings destined for the gods of Tyre, and we shall see that in 195 when Hannibal, fleeing his homeland secretly, was recognized at Cercina (Kerkenna, off the coast of Sfax) by Phoenician merchants, he could claim that he was being sent to Tyre by the senate in Carthage. So strong did the ties remain across the centuries between the old Phoenician city and the 'new town' – ties that are not similarly attested for any other Phoenician town in the west – that there is no doubt that we must accept, beyond the romanticized stories of the foundation legends, the evidence of numerous texts (Diodorus, XVII, 40; Strabo, XVII, 3, 15: Livy, XXXIII, 49) that Carthage was at the outset a colony officially organized by Tyre.

From the start Carthage thus assumed a special destiny: neither a bridgehead towards the extreme west or at the tip of the Maghreb, like the first foundations (Gades, Lixus, Utica), nor a *comptoir* or trading-post set up with an eye to mercantile strategy, like the settlements on the southern coast of Spain, which were perhaps established in the eighth and seventh centuries in order to consolidate earlier trading relations with Phoenicia, then threatened by Greek colonizing enterprises in the western Mediterranean. Carthage was installed alongside Utica, but with a time-lag that in itself suggests a different historic purpose, in a strong geopolitical position in the midpoint of Mediterranean Africa, a 'target territory' for the artisanal and commercial civilization of the Phoenicians. And archaeology bears abundant witness that the skills they brought with them would be implanted without much competition in the palaeo-Berber setting of protohistoric times.

From the account of the founding we must, however, remember those features which show that the Phoenician vessel approaching Carthage was not going to put in to a land totally lacking in political organization. Apart from its aetiological function, the story of the ox-skin cut into fine strips implies the payment of a tribute that had to be made to a recognized authority. This is confirmed and made more specific later in the account when, according to both Timaeus of Taormina and Justin (VI, 1), Elissa-Dido was sought in marriage by the king of the Libyans, or to be more exact, someone whom Justin calls Hiarbas and claims is the king of the Maxitani. In these Maxitani is recognizable the name, only slightly altered, of the inhabitants of territory near to Carthage, the *pagus Muxi*, a former Punic territorial district in Romanized form (Desanges, 1967, pp. 304–8). It may be seen that, despite the variations it acquired with the passage of time, the legendary account still describes a political coexistence, at the origins of Carthage, between the founders of the colony, who had come from the east, and a Libyan sovereignty (Camps, 1979, p. 44). Of course, the legend adds that Elissa sacrificed herself on the pyre to escape the entreaties of the king of the Maxitani, which shows that there were limits to that coexistence. But it is important to note that the Phoenician immigrants did not introduce their artisanal and commercial *savoir-faire* into an ethnic and political vacuum. What we term Punic civilization – religious and funerary practices, ways of life, arts and crafts – was born of a meeting on African soil between a Libyco-Berber substratum which was still at a proto-historic stage and a Semitic culture proven by history. It could be said that it was the product of a successful graft.

EARLIEST CARTHAGE

None the less, whatever Virgil may say, Carthage was a creation *ex nihilo*, as archaeology has shown, on the peninsula where it took root, at that time still very nearly the island it had been in the dawn of human times, before the alluvial deposits of the Medjerda created the sandbar which was to link it to the mainland.

Virgil described the material birth of Carthage in his own way, that of a poet, abbreviating and compressing into the vision of an immense building site all the elements making up a town that was both real and idealized throughout its lifetime:

> Aeneas admired this building site, a while ago merely simple shacks; he marvelled at the gates, the hustle and bustle and the paving of the streets. The Tyrians work with enthusiasm; some extend the walls, build the citadel . . . Here, some are digging out harbours, there, others are making deep foundations for theatres . . . Oh, happy are they whose walls already stand, said Aeneas, and raising his eyes he contemplated the rooftops that crowned the city (*Aeneid* I, 421–7).

This town that he watches rising is both the Rome he himself dreams of founding and the Carthage that Augustus finally decided to rebuild, shortly before the beginning of the Christian era, on the site of the city destroyed in 146 BC, at least partly on its ruins. Thus the harbours were superimposed on the ancient 'cothons'.

No one will be surprised to find that, in comparison with the rich images in this text of the raising of the first Carthage, archaeology can offer only a pretty meagre picture (figure 22). Archaeologists are well aware that on any site the vestiges of a first settlement will be to a large extent damaged, if not totally destroyed by re-use, and buried under the deepest backfills and superimposed material, so that they very often leave only the barest perceptible traces.

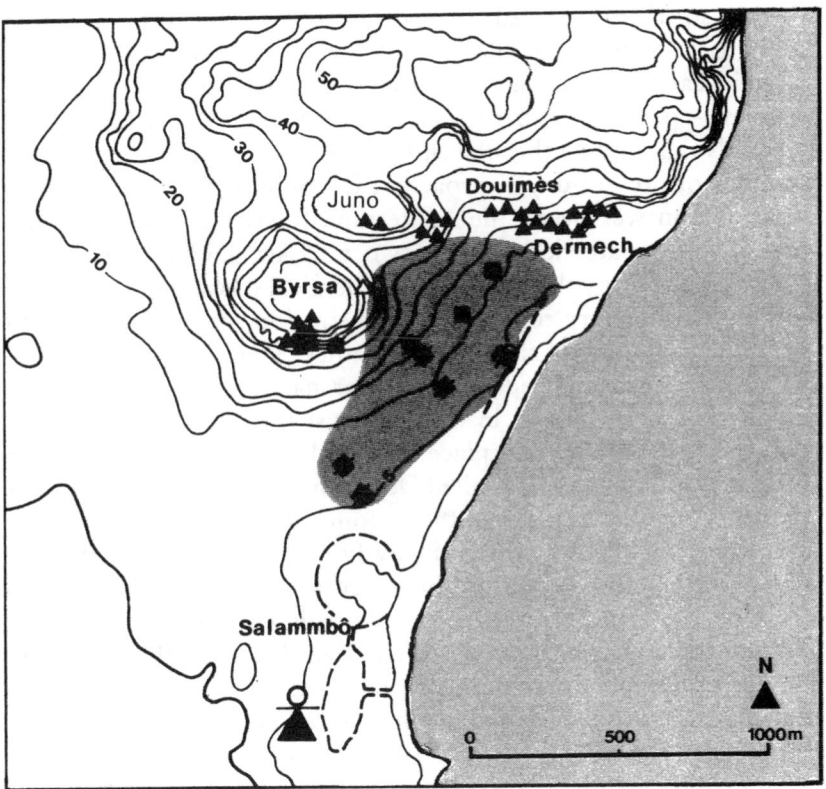

FIGURE 22 *Archaic Carthage. The zone in dark grey represents the hypothetical extent of the city, surrounded by the cemeteries of Byrsa, Juno, Douimès and Dermech. In the Salammbô area, the ports to the east of the tophet were not yet in existence (after a survey by the German archaeological mission, F. Rakob, 1987).*

One can imagine what will be left of a site that witnessed fifteen centuries of rearrangements, destructions and rebuildings up until the almost definitive end of its life in 698, in a town whose remains were subsequently, over the years, dismembered to be carted away by the builders of Tunis and Kairouan, and even by those of Pisa and Genoa in Italy. In the pages that follow there will be further occasion to repeat that in Carthage the most frequent archaeological situation, far from presenting the elevations of structures and walls, is to show 'negatives', not only of those walls but even of their foundations, picked away stone by stone through the ages, right up to the present, to the point where, in the campaign of international excavations recently sponsored by UNESCO, the excavators' vocabulary was enriched by a new term to describe the finding so often recorded in reports: 'robber trench' or 'fosse de spoliation' or 'fosse de pillage'.

I said earlier that when – in the second half of the nineteenth century – people began to search the ground of Carthage, with methods that had neither the skill, the sensitivity nor the scientific scruples of present-day approaches, the only things that began to yield an answer were the subterranean settings of the dead, preserved from attack by their very depth. Although recent excavations (1976–85) by the French archaeological mission have brought to light the funerary role of the southern slope of the hill of Byrsa from the beginning of the seventh century (Lancel, 1982, pp. 263–364), and thus completed the map of archaic cemeteries, that topography had been known in outline for several decades. We know that the first burials took place in part directly north of the small littoral plain, in the areas called Dermech (today in the upper parts of the archaeological park of the Antonine Baths) and Douimès (on the other side of the TGM railway line), and in part on the low exposed slopes on the east of the hill of Juno. As we saw earlier, in these two sectors certain grave goods are dated by Greek pottery of the end of the eighth century, and we have also noted the possibility that certain tombs containing only material of Phoenician tradition may be earlier. To the south of the hill of Juno, dates almost as early – first half of the seventh century – are registered by numerous grave goods from the hill of Byrsa. Directly south of the site, on the western edge of what would later be the commercial harbour, the sacrificial area of the tophet – discovered in 1922 – completes the panorama of the burial sites (Bénichou-Safar, 1982, pp. 13–60).

Until very recently, only these data were available to help reconstruct the location of the first city, with the aid of analogy. It is known that in the civilizations of the classical world cemeteries were pushed out to the periphery of the settlement, outside the walls if it had defences. It is not certain that the separation of the living and the dead – a religious ruling that was infringed, for example, in sixth-century Athens – was strictly observed in Semitic circles. Simple practical reasons, however, allow us to suggest that the settlement relating to these burial zones lay within the fairly large area which they bordered, at the southern edge of which the tophet would also be located: that would be the place at the farthest end of the town, according to Justin (VI, 6), where Elissa-Dido had her pyre built, in a ritual act of foundation.

THE EARLIEST SETTLEMENT: RECENT RESEARCH

That hypothesis remained to be confirmed by discovering traces of the archaic settlement within the limits thus defined. In 1978–9, in the excavations of the German archaeological mission, bordering on the seafront and facing the former Bey's palace, a first observation was noted of archaic pottery with pieces attributable to the end of the eighth century, in layers underlying a Punic occupation area of the end of the fifth century. This meant that, a few dozen metres back from the present shoreline, an archaic occupation area (of which two fragments of seventh-century walls survived) which had been levelled subsequently, had served as a base for later constructions. To the right of this area, but more inland, at the foot of the south-east side of the hill of Byrsa, and on the line of what subsequently became the Roman *decumanus maximus*, an excavation made in 1983 (Rakob, 1984, pp. 3–4) unearthed structures *in situ*, albeit modest: the sill of a wall, in unbaked bricks, together with a beaten clay floor and pottery datable to the end of the eighth century (point 5 on figure 23).

   In recent years a whole series of observations, made in careful stratigraphic excavations at various points in the northern part of the coastal plain, between the shore and the lower slopes of the Juno and Byrsa hills, have allowed us to realize the extent of the archaic town, if not always convincingly before the end of the eighth century, at least between the beginning of the seventh century and the sixth (figure 23). It may be noted as a point of minor history, which thus links up with the main story, that quite a number of these observations were made by a team of British archaeologists who recorded archaeological layers exposed in

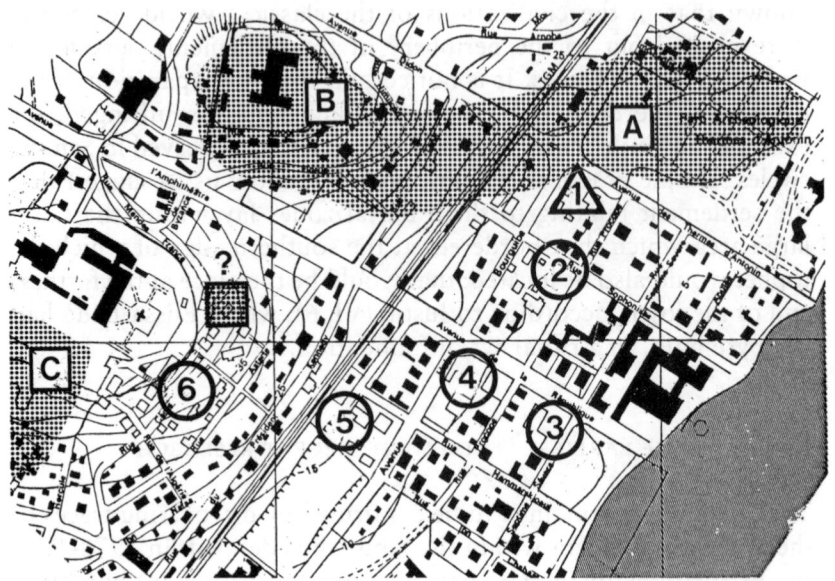

FIGURE 23   *The north part of the urban area of Punic Carthage. The stippled areas show the zones of the cemeteries: A Dermech-Douimès; B hill of Juno; C south and south-west slopes of Byrsa; on the east slope, the stippled square with a question mark shows the hypothetical 'Saumagne tombs'. At the corner of Avenue Habib Bourguiba and Avenue des Thermes d'Antonin, the triangle marked 1 shows the site of an archaic tomb excavated by P. Cintas (Manuel d'Archéologie punique, vol. I, 1970, p. 441). Figures 2 to 6 in circles show recently excavated sites in the archaic settlement. (A diagram by S. Lancel on the basis of plan 0934 of the District of Tunis.)*

trenches dug in spring 1986 for the installation of a sewerage system in the streets of the present settlement. Until then, while Roman Carthage had used sewers laid out along all its principal roadways, its modern successor had lived in Punic style, pouring its liquid waste into the same type of soakaway that the French archaeological mission found (as we shall see) in the area on the south slope of Byrsa in Hellenistic times.

The northern limit – perhaps in the form of a defensive system, which has been sought in vain – has not been discovered between the nearest known tombs and the archaic settlement. In the absence of structural evidence for habitation, strata under the present Rue Sophonisbe, between the Roman *decumani* II and III (Ellis, 1987, p. 12) (point 2 on figure 23), dated by finds of the sixth century, may nevertheless constitute evidence that the settlement extended this far. An additional marker is similarly provided, more to the south, by strata of the beginning of the seventh century without structures *in situ*, at the corner of the Avenue Bourguiba and the Avenue de la République (Chelbi, 1983, p. 80) (point 4 on figure 23). However, the best evidence for the archaic settlement is in the central part of the coastal plain. In addition to the 1983 investigation under the levels of the Roman *decumanus maximus*, two other probes carried out on the same line, one at the crossing of *cardo* X, the other at the crossing of *cardo* XIII (point 5 on figure 23), revealed fragments of walls and floors datable to the end of the eighth and beginning of the seventh century (Rakob, 1989, pp. 34–7). Closer to the modern sea front, between Roman *cardines* XIII and XIV, along the Rue Septime Sévère, an excavation in 1987–8 revealed a sequence of eleven floor levels, of which the earliest are datable to the eighth century and bear obvious traces of industrial activity, consisting of metalwork (iron slag, tuyères to activate a furnace) and dyeing (deposits of crushed murex) (point 3 on figure 23). It seems likely that a peripheral crafts area was located there, on the edge of a shoreline that was then several dozen metres farther back than its present position, between the edge of the sea and the main nucleus of the settlement. Fragments of Euboean cups were found there, bearing witness to imports from the Aegean Sea to Carthage in the middle of the eighth century, and at present they are the earliest evidence discovered in a dwelling area at Carthage (Vegas, 1989, pp. 213–16; above, figure 20).

To the south of the line formed by the Roman *decumanus maximus* and between that line and the tophet, traces of occupation in the archaic period are still meagre. Their clearest indication is the existence, at a distance of 35 metres north of the Roman *decumanus* IV, of another artisanal quarter, characterized by potters' kilns datable between the second half of the seventh century and the sixth – a kind of industrial suburb, in earliest times, between the settlement and the tophet (Rakob, 1990, pp. 39–41). As far as these very careful investigations allow the sequence to be charted, it would seem that the first urban nucleus, perceptible in the second half of the seventh century – so fitting the earliest dates of the cemeteries and the tophet – was formed in the northern sector of the coastal plain, to the right of the hills of Juno and Byrsa, then spread eastward toward the sea, and principally southward, in the direction of the tophet, from which it was originally a kilometre distant. That advance towards the south was at first represented by early craft installations and cannot have involved the whole of that southern zone. The stratigraphy of excavations in this area has in fact showed that the lower part of the small coastal plain was unusable before being filled in. On this side of the 5-metre contour above sea level, there was at that time the shore of a lagoon which remained outside Carthage's first urban layout (Lancel, 1990, pp. 12–13). As for the port installations, of which the present-day lagoons convey a more or less accurate impression, they did not exist then, at least in that form. We shall see that the first ports of the city that was to be a principally maritime power for centuries to come remain a mystery.

The most recent archaeological investigations also leave the problem of the archaic city's acropolis without a solution. Virgil's text relating to Dido's ruse of cutting into fine strips the ox-hide intended to mark out her territory – 'for this reason known as Byrsa' – was added to in the form of a gloss by his commentator of the fourth century AD, the grammarian Servius: 'Carthage,' he says, 'was at first called Byrsa' (*Ad Aeneidem*, IV, 670). What are we to think? First, it will be noticed that the ox-hide legend 'at least shows that the Greek or Hellenized Carthaginian who put it into circulation considered the region of Carthage called *Byrsa* to be the spot chosen for a first settlement by the founders of the colony' (Gsell, *HAAN*, vol. II, 1921, p. 8). That consideration alone may incline us to admit that the name Byrsa may have been the principal name of the city and may, from the outset, have been applied to what remained its central core, according to all later texts. One of those texts which describes the urban situation in the Hellenistic era says, 'in the middle of the town stood the acropolis, known as Byrsa' (Strabo, XVII, 3, 14). It is extremely probable that the citadel did not change its position during Punic times, and was already, in the archaic era, situated where it is clearly located by texts other than Strabo relating to the capture of the town in 146 BC (Lancel, 1988, pp. 61–89).

We have just seen that, starting from the middle of the seventh century, according to present knowledge, the first city developed nearest to the archaic cemeteries, and especially between the sea and the hill known as 'Byrsa Hill', a recent name for what was formerly called Saint-Louis, modern place-naming thus clearly taking sides in the debate. There are therefore serious grounds for thinking that the summit, at least, of this hill (for the entire south flank was occupied by a cemetery in archaic times) bore the upper town corresponding with the partly known settlement on the littoral plain. Alas! It was one of the discoveries – in this instance, unfortunately negative – in the latest work of the French archaeological mission that the hilltop in the Augustan era – at the end of the first century BC – had been cut away and transformed into a plateau by the engineers preparing the ground for the new Roman colony (Lancel, 1983, pp. 5–9). That eradication, which was not without political motives, removed all trace of what in all probability was the religious heart of the Punic metropolis, right from its origins.

To emphasize the limits of the latest investigations – and let us add our ignorance of the existence and location, in that period, of a defensive wall – is not to minimize their importance for our knowledge of the archaic town. First of all, our knowledge of its extent: the seventh-century settlement already occupied a sizeable part of the littoral plain – hundreds of metres in both directions – not to mention the possible occupation of the heights of Byrsa. A suburban fringe of workshops (metalworkers, fullers, dyers, potters) ensured the production necessary for daily living, and already perhaps, as regards pottery for example, for export as well. The building alignments discovered show that at least in the central part of the littoral plain (other orientations still seem questionable), in the seventh century, the settlement was not established in haphazard fashion, but followed a generalized layout roughly parallel to the shoreline: in this part of the site, all later rearrangements kept to it and the Roman surveyors later made use of it generally in the layout of the Augustan colony.

Nevertheless, considerable grey areas still remain. The little that these excavations tell us about the character of this settlement shows it to have been modest in the earliest period, with its fragments of mud-brick walls and beaten clay floors. The plans of the houses, and consequently their arrangement and the inhabitants' way of life, are unknown to us. I have already remarked on our lack of information about the ports, the citadel and the town's defences. Nor is anything known about public monuments or civic and religious life, apart from the tophet and the cemeteries.

INFORMATION FROM FUNERARY ARCHAEOLOGY

It is necessary, therefore, to go back to these funerary contexts in order to fill out what is known of archaic Carthage, and first of all to its cemeteries. Perhaps nowhere better than in the Punic city has this archaeology of the enclosed and sealed environment, the frozen world of the dead, better compensated for the lack of documentary evidence and the limitations of information gleaned from the world of the living.

FIGURE 24 *The opening of a Punic tomb in Carthage during the* belle époque *(after P. Gauckler, 1915, vol. I, p. 1, pl. VIII).*

At the beginning of the century our predecessors made use in their operations of that marvellous instrument of 'excavation' (and destruction!) known as a 'Decauville': a narrow-gauge railway on which ran little wagons that were filled with excavated spoil. On a site like Carthage, where the cemeteries are on the hillside, the railway was placed at the foot of or midway up the slopes and, as Père Delattre remarked at some point in an innocent and picturesque fashion, speaking of the deep tombs, 'one could get at them on the level.' Thanks to such vertical exposures, the visitor can still see, on the south flank of the hill of Byrsa as at Dermech, in the park of the Antonine Baths, carefully built subterranean chamber tombs of eastern style, at the bottom of pits several metres deep. Slightly before and after 1900, about a hundred of these monuments were the focus of excavations which were sometimes pretexts for fashionable gatherings (figure 24).

TYPOLOGY OF THE TOMBS

The architectural arrangement of these tombs is almost always the same, with a few variations. The burial chamber, a large cubic stone

FIGURE 25   *The discovery of Punic tombs at Dermech at the beginning of the century (P. Gauckler).*

receptacle, either contains niches and cells formed in the walls or houses stone sarcophagi; there are most often two, and in fact, apart from some exceptional reburials, excavations have generally shown a double occupation of these tombs. This implies that, except when the two intended occupants died at the same time, to inter the second occupant it would have been necessary to clear the pit of the sand with which it would have been filled after the first inhumation had been sealed with the heavy closing slab. The slabs forming a pitched roof over the ceiling of the burial chamber, which were concealed at the front by a facing wall built in horizontal courses, had the principal function of acting as a relieving arch, easing the load of earth and sand on the tomb's ceiling (figures 25 and 26). This arrangement explains why the burial chambers were for the most part discovered intact and filled with little or no soil. In these conditions it is also understandable that excavations should sometimes have revealed, still in place, part of the fine-grained brilliant white stucco which coated the internal walls of the best-finished tombs; these were so well constructed, with their blocks carefully dressed and assembled with dry joints, that they could well have done without that extra touch (Bénichou-Safar,

FIGURE 26   *Punic tombs on the south slope of Byrsa, discovered by Père Delattre and displayed in 1980 by the French archaeological mission (S. Lancel).*

1982, pp. 160–1). In the richest tombs the stone ceiling, formed by the perfectly squared underside of the covering slabs, was lined on the inside with wooden panelling of various kinds of trees, among which thuya, sandalwood, cedar and cypress are recognizable. These were in part available in the forests near the Khroumiri, north-west of present-day Tunisia. There is nothing left of these wooden ceilings, of which only a few fragments survived at the time of the excavations at the beginning of the century, but horizontal grooves still visible in certain tombs, arranged just below the stone ceiling, bear witness to the skill of the carpenters of the seventh century BC (Bénichou-Safar, 1982, p. 162). As for the grave goods, they were placed in niches hollowed out of the walls and around the body (figure 27), or over the lid of the stone sarcophagus, if that was the method of burial adopted.

These built tombs were much in the minority, since among all the archaic cemeteries they number less than about a hundred, out of almost a thousand explored burials. The cost of such monuments in materials and labour is enough on its own to explain their comparative rarity. They were probably intended as the 'eternal abode' of rich notables, although the quality of the grave goods found in

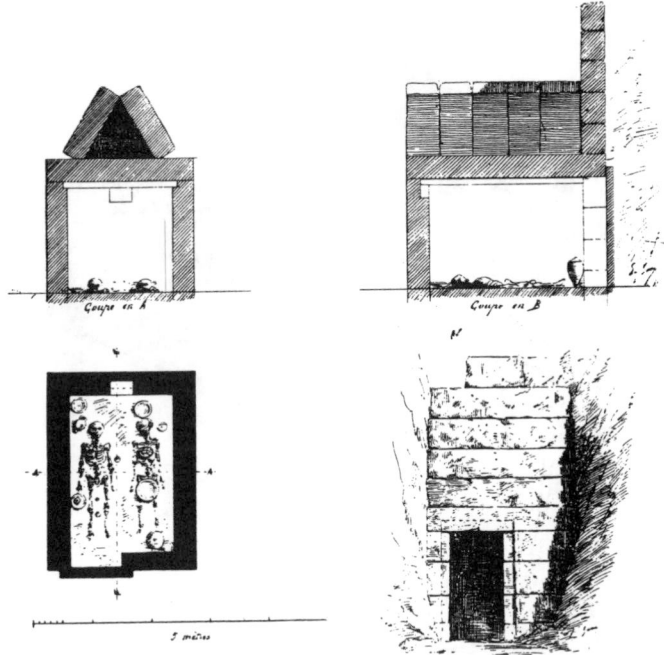

FIGURE 27 *A tomb at Dermech excavated by P. Gauckler in 1889, in which the burial chamber had a cedar-wood ceiling (drawing by Sadoux).*

FIGURE 28 *Cist burials from the south slope of Byrsa (S. Lancel).*

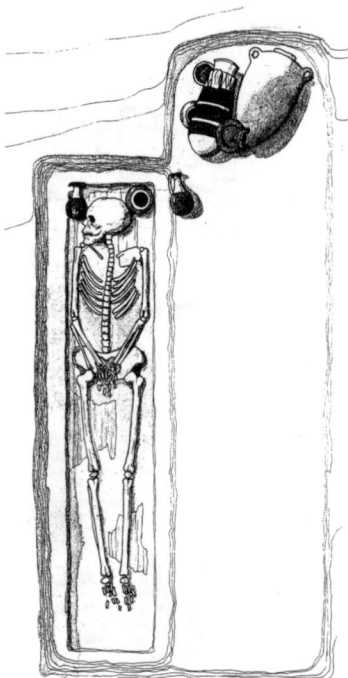
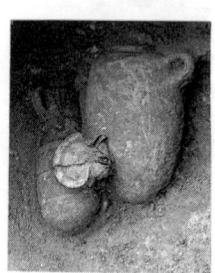

FIGURE 29   *A pit burial from the cemetery on the south slope of Byrsa;
the remains of a coffin or a simple wooden stretcher can be seen under
the skeleton. Most of the grave goods are situated outside the tomb
(drawing by P. de Carbonnières, photograph by S. Lancel).*

them, as far as they can be identified after the event, does not fully
bear out this impression of wealth.

Less monumental and less elaborate is a second type of burial,
made in the shape of a cist (figure 28) in which large slabs were
assembled in such a way as to form a complete box, whose floor,
walls and lid were of a size to fit a single body (Bénichou-Safar,
1982, pp. 102–5). In the best made of these cists the interior
surfaces received a coating of stucco, and it is not uncommon to
detect the remains of a timber coffin (figure 29). The grave goods
were placed either on the floor of the cist, alongside the body, or in
a niche either inside or outside the tomb.

These cists may be considered as an improvement on the form of
burial which, together with cremations *a pozzo*, seems to be the
most ancient on the site of Carthage. They were simple pits dug in
the natural soil – sometimes a calcareous sandstone, but more often

FIGURE 30 *A pit burial on the south slope of Byrsa, lined with slabs.*
The grave goods are outside it (S. Lancel).

heavy clay streaked with whitish marl and plentiful sandy veins.
The depth of the pit – which was the size of a body – from the level
of the natural soil is varied, but may be between four and five
metres. Once the desired depth was attained, the body was placed
on the ground, which had been carefully tamped down, in a coffin
or at least on a wooden support, traces of which often appear on
the base of the excavated grave (see, for Byrsa, Lancel, 1982,
pp. 263 ff.). The grave goods were laid out alongside the body,
without any fixed rules for their position, and two or three crudely
hewn limestone slabs covered this fairly modest burial-place. An
elaboration consisted of lining the walls of the pit with a few
upright slabs, but not the base, unlike the cists (figure 30).

FUNERAL RITES

Lastly, the excavations have revealed the coexistence in the archaic
era of the rite of cremation – very much in the minority, but well

FIGURE 31 *From the cemetery on the south slope of Byrsa, a 'Canaanite' amphora containing cremated remains (S. Lancel).*

attested – with that of inhumation, notably in the areas of the cemetery of Douimès and the hills of Juno and Byrsa. Whereas in the later period when this ritual, as we shall see, was much more frequent, the burnt remains were for the most part placed in an ossuary, the ashes of archaic cremations were either put into an amphora which was itself sometimes placed in a cavity formed with slabs (figure 31: tomb A.143 of Byrsa: Lancel, 1982, pp. 340–8), or else, more generally, laid on the base of a tomb that looked like a round and fairly shallow well (tombs *a pozzo*). No trace of fire has ever been noticed *in situ*, which means that the body was not cremated on the spot.

The dates attributable to these cremation burials are often very early. Palaeographic analysis of an inscription on an amphora from the hill of Juno, containing the cremated remains of someone bearing the theophoric name GRB'L, would indicate a date somewhere at the beginning of the seventh century (Bénichou- Safar, 1982, pp. 328–9). Such a dating has been confirmed on a number of occasions by analysis of the pottery accompanying the cremated remains, among which the frequent presence has been noticed of articles in ivory (rare in inhumations) which have every appearance of having been burnt at the same time as the body (Delattre, 1921,

p. 96; Lancel, 1982, pp. 345–7). Features common to these archaic cremation burials have been observed: they are grouped together where they occur (cemeteries of Juno and of Byrsa), in small areas where this rite seems homogeneous (Lancel, 1981, p. 160); the elongated ovoid amphora of 'Canaanite' tradition is common among associated finds (cf. figure 31); their grave goods include, frequently enough to be significant, manufactured ivory articles which, as we shall see later, are among the most representative objects of a Phoenician heritage. Is this enough for an interpretation of this cremation rite which then contrasted so strongly with the majority practice of inhumation? The first excavators, such as A. Merlin (1918, pp. 310–11) saw in the rite of cremation the mark of an indigenous, non-'Phoenicized' part of the population, but in a population already widely mixed at the beginning of the seventh century, I would see cremation reflecting a particular loyalty to a practice well attested in Phoenicia itself and in the archaic cenetery of Motya, in Sicily (Gsell, *HAAN*, vol. IV, 1924, pp. 442–3; Tusa, 1972, pp. 7–81; 1978, pp. 7–98). We shall see later that the probable origin of the 'Canaanite' amphorae supports this interpretation.

On the other hand, certain ritual practices observable in the inhumation graves reflect the Libyan contribution which probably formed an important and surely even a majority component of Carthage's population at the beginning of the seventh century, some three or four generations after the city's foundation, assuming the traditional date. For example, the application to the corpse's face of a thick layer of bright red make-up, made of cinnabar, which subsequently formed a deposit on the bones after the flesh had decomposed (Lancel, 1979, pp. 256–8). Sometimes this sulphide of mercury was simply put in a little dish beside the body, but its symbolic value and power, in the colour red – the colour of blood – remained the same. That practice was not Phoenician but indigenous, and much more in evidence in the provincial 'Libyphoenician' world (Cap Bon, the Sahel and, farther, at Tipasa in Algeria) than at Carthage itself. On the other hand, the placing of the corpse in a flexed lateral position (on its side with the legs drawn up), characteristic of burials in Libyco-Berber contexts (cf. below, p. 297) was entirely unknown in Carthage, in any period. Even if they had not been previously placed in a coffin or on a wooden support, the skeletons appear to have been stretched out full-length on their backs.

Some observations of these rituals, made during the course of excavations, are as useful as a written account of the burial ceremony. Thus I noted the coincidence of two phenomena, in the exploration of graves on the southern side of Byrsa: the sand mixed with crumbled clay with which the grave pits were filled after the burial invariably included fine particles of charcoal, so that the presence of these particles, found in clearance of the surface soil, would be a sure indication of the existence of a grave; moreover, this sand in-fill always – or almost always – included numerous fragments of plates and dishes, the latter with a wide red-glazed border typical of archaic Punic pottery (Lancel, 1982, p. 362). The only plausible explanation is that the placing of the body in the trench was accompanied by a funerary feasting ritual, to which both the charcoal and the receptacles that were deliberately smashed and thrown into the tomb at the same time as the sand bear witness. Various other observations also suggest that the ritual slaughter of an animal probably occurred on the occasion of funerals (Bénichou-Safar, 1982, p. 281). This poses a question that is equally valid for non-Punic contexts: what was the meaning of those feasts and the purpose of those sacrifices? Were they intended for the dead, or for deities with whom those closest to the departed interceded on his behalf? Only one text offers an answer to such a question: an inscription from the Punic cemetery of Cagliari in Sardinia shows that the foodstuffs mentioned were offered by the dead man and his wife to a divinity, HWT; on the threshold of the next world, the dead would thus address the chthonian deities.

It may therefore be suggested that part of the solid and liquid foods placed in Carthaginian tombs were an offering from the dead to the gods, the other part being intended for their own nourishment *post mortem*. Did the placing of these foodstuffs, discovered in the form of residues or sediments at the bottom of the receptacles that had contained them, or as the remains of fish, birds and small mammals (Bénichou-Safar, 1982, p. 264), correspond with a real belief in the 'bodily' survival of the dead? This act, at Carthage as elsewhere, was part of a symbolism which without doubt figures among the oldest human traditions and goes back to time immemorial. Confirmation of its symbolic nature is provided by the common observation that the containers of these food offerings were sometimes placed outside the sarcophagus or cist containing the body (cf. figure 30): physically out of reach of the dead person, but symbolically within his grasp!

GRAVE GOODS

The consistency of the offerings should be reflected in the composition of the groups of receptacles intended to contain them. In fact, although one may find variations in the finds from the most ancient tombs, a basic set of grave goods – one might almost say a canon – can be seen to have established itself from the first half or at the latest the middle of the seventh century (Lancel, 1982, p. 364). These 'standard pottery groups', to quote P. Gauckler, always comprise two kinds of pouring vessels: on one hand an 'oenochoe' (the Greek word implies that the content was wine, which is probable but not always certain in the earliest times) with a three-lobed mouth, the earliest examples of which (up to the middle of the seventh century) invariably present the same characteristics – a double cylindrical handle, and a little bulge on the body on a level with the lower attachment of the handle (figure 32). This very functional form, which seems to have been copied from that of bronze vases, closely imitates Palestinian examples of the end of the Bronze Age, but is also paralleled in other Mediterranean contexts.

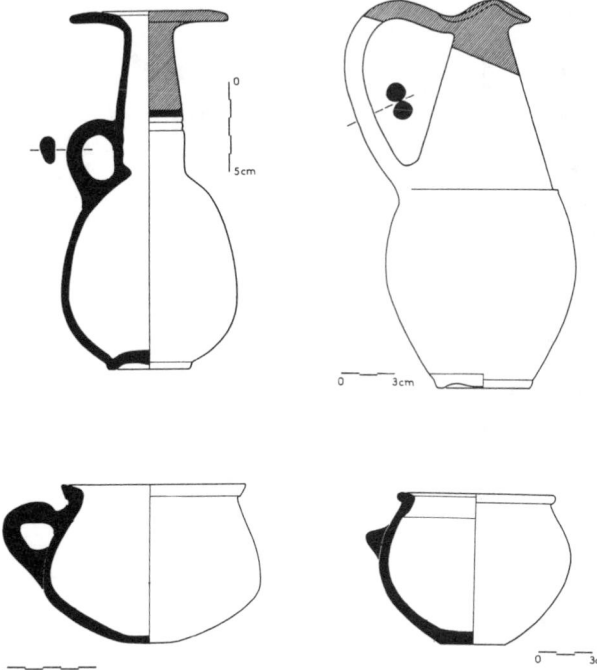

FIGURE 32 *The four basic grave-good vessels from archaic tombs of Carthage (P. de Carbonnières).*

The second vessel has a shape typical of the Syrio-Palestinian repertoire, with no occurrence outside the Semitic world, and its mouth with a broad, flattened rim has caused English-speaking writers to christen it the 'mushroom vase' and French archaeologists to refer to it as the 'oenochoe à bobèche' (candle-ring oenochoe). This name is arguable since, as in the previous case, it presupposes the function of this little jug, which had a small capacity and a peculiarly shaped mouth that would render it totally unsuitable for pouring liquids. Rather than seeing it as a wine container, we should recognize it as a vessel intended to contain perfumed oils, which would not be poured, properly speaking, but tipped out of the flask for application. Solid foodstuffs were placed in two – there is very rarely only one – small, globe-shaped, pots with a single handle or thumb-grip, and very frequently, when excavated, their bases show signs of carbonization, indicating that they had been placed on a fire shortly before the closing of the tomb (figure 32).

In addition to these four basic funerary articles there was commonly a large amphora without a foot, doubtless the water supply

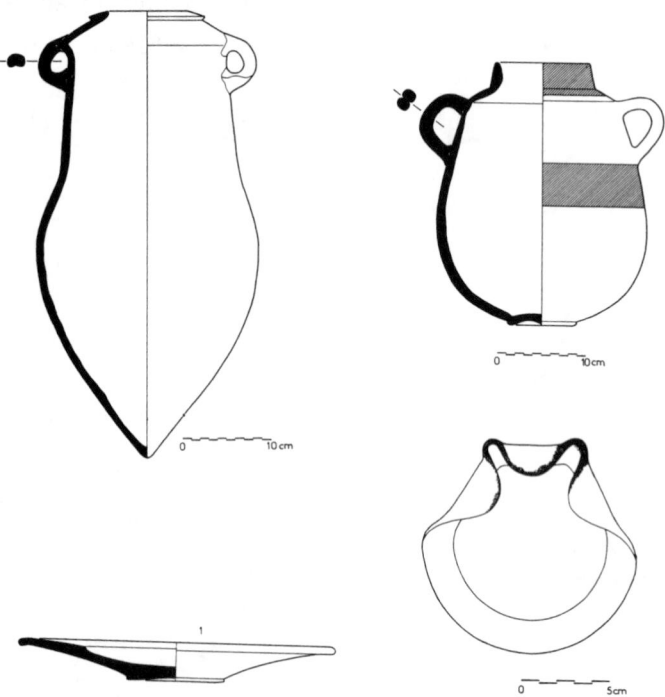

FIGURE 33 *The large amphora without a foot, the small amphora, the lamp and its patera (P. de Carbonnières).*

for the deceased (even if its initial use had been for wine), often a smaller amphora with a foot or base, a plate and also often one of the bowl-shaped oil lamps, on which the pinching of the rim in two places close together creates two lips or spouts. Usually, if not always, these lips are found blackened with soot, which suggests that the lamp had been placed in the tomb alight, just before it was filled (figure 33).

Among these standard grave goods, the most characteristic of the Syrio-Palestinian pottery tradition, apart from the 'mushroom vase' already referred to, are the two-lipped lamp and the broad-rimmed patera which was sometimes used for its stand. In the earliest tombs (end of the eighth century, beginning of the seventh), these articles were coated with thick, shiny red slip (figure 34). That red slip appears only partially on the same objects in tombs of the middle of the seventh century and afterwards disappears. In the view of the most knowledgeable expert on Punic pottery, there was no doubt that these vessels coated with red slip had been imported from Phoenicia, the first potters working in Carthage having lacked the ability or knowledge to carry out this technique for finishing the vessels (Cintas, 1970, pp. 376–80). In fact, though this method of red gloss is basically oriental, its translation on western sites was not uniform. Many variations exist in the details and methods of application, and these may also be noted in the archaic material at

FIGURE 34 *The articles from tomb A.136 on the south slope of Byrsa. Note, in the centre, the proto-Corinthian cotyle, and the bright red slip on the mouths of the two pouring vessels (S. Lancel).*

Carthage. It has been found that this red gloss went out of fashion before the end of the seventh century, though no one as yet has been able to explain why.

As for the amphorae of the archaic tombs, they are recognizable as descendants of two 'Canaanite' series, with shapes typical of the Syrio-Palestinian products of the end of the Bronze Age (Lancel, 1980, pp. 1–7): both the large amphora with the carinated shoulders (Cintas 282/283 shape) and a large, ovoid receptacle with a narrow mouth, equipped with two little handles like ears (this is the amphora of the type Cintas 268) that is also to be found at Motya, Gela and Milazzo in Sicily, and on archaic Italian sites (Ischia, Castel di Decima, Capua, Viterbo and Vulci) from the second half of the eighth century (cf. figure 31). The Phoenician origin of this type is not in doubt, but it is far from certain that the examples found in the west over such a vast area were manufactured in a Semitic country. There is rather a tendency towards the hypothesis (Gras, 1985, pp. 291–320) that these receptacles were made on the western sites in imitation of 'Canaanite' prototypes imported from the east at the beginning of the first millennium BC. Carthage, like Motya in Sicily or some Etruscan sites, may have been one of the centres of manufacture of these amphorae. However, there is a difficulty: the amphorae are meant for wine. Now, as far as we know, it is doubtful whether Carthage had been able to develop enough wine production before the middle of the seventh century to justify the large-scale manufacture of such containers. The fact that they have been found in greater numbers at Motya, in Sicily, where the development of wine-growing in the archaic era seems more probable, favours the hypothesis of a Sicilian (or Campanian) origin for these amphorae of typically Phoenician shape. It will be remembered that at Carthage they are characteristic of a cremation context, a ritual that was in a very small minority in the African city, and would have affected only a limited category of people who had special links with Phoenician circles in central Italy and Sicily. Attention must, however, be drawn to a recent suggestion (Guerrero, 1989, pp. 147–64) that these amphorae, in particular the streamlined shape Cintas 282/283, would indicate imports of wines from the east, to Carthage as to other western sites.

The archaeologist excavating one of these archaic tombs in Carthage knows that there is every possibility of finding a complete collection of these vessels: the 'funerary service', which of course borrowed its components from the tableware and cooking pots of the living. It will have been noticed that this collection does not

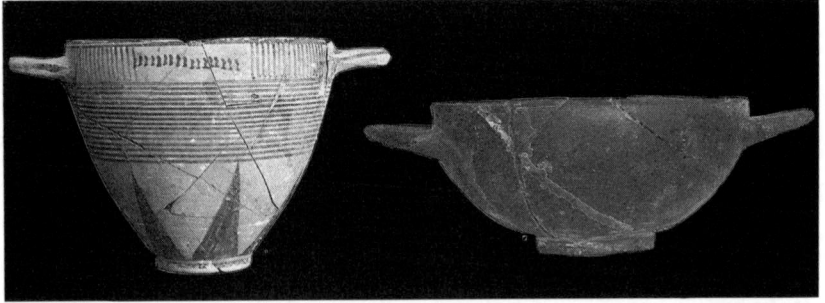

FIGURE 35 *Left, a subgeometric proto- Corinthian cotyle (second half of the seventh century) and right, an Etruscan cup in* bucchero nero *(end of the seventh century) from the archaic cemetery on the hill of Byrsa (S. Lancel).*

include drinking vessels, goblets or cups: very occasionally one comes across a bowl of Palestinian type, perhaps the squat proto-type of the specifically Punic 'thistle-head' vase. When these goblets are found, they are additional to and stand out even more from the collection of pottery of Phoenician tradition because they belong to a different order. It is as if the Carthaginians of the end of the eighth century and the seventh were reluctant, even after death, to sip from the thick rim of one of those bowls or stemmed chalices so well attested on the sites of Phoenicia proper. They liked to drink from the slender rims of proto-Corinthian cotyles – marvels indeed of both strength and lightness, given the technical conditions of ancient potting – with their thin, well-fired sides that ring like crystal (figure 35). At all events, it is thanks to these cotyles with two horizontal handles that we are able, as I said earlier, to put a date on these tombs in Carthage, where they are to be found in abundance from the end of the eighth up till the middle of the seventh century. Subsequently, and until the beginning of the sixth century, they were superseded for the same functions by cups of *bucchero nero sottile*, with sides no less slender and resonant, in particular by a form of rimless cylix which, in our Byrsa tombs, appeared once as if it was in use with an oenochoe with a three-lobed spout, made of the same material (Lancel, 1985, p. 732). These are thin-sided *bucchero* forms that are to be found hardly anywhere but Carthage, except of course in mainland Italy (Thuillier, 1985, p. 159). These types of vessels are particularly frequent at Caere, in southern Etruria: I shall have occasion, later on, to refer to Carthage's relations with the Cerveteri region at the beginning of the sixth century, in connection with the gold sheets of Pyrgi, the port of Caere. But, with these vessels in *bucchero sottile* from the Byrsa tombs, which can be dated to the third quarter or the end of the seventh century, we may have an additional indication, for a slightly earlier period, of relations between the Punic city and the Etruscan world.

It is certainly important to note that these 'drinking vessels', whose use is connected with the consumption of wine in 'banquets' or meals taken communally, were first Greek and then Etruscan and that both kinds were rivalled by local imitations from the sixth century. The presence of these vessels in the 'funerary service' is without doubt explained not only by their technical quality and the seductive slenderness of their sides and rims, but also by the attraction the Carthaginians, who were constantly in contact with the Greeks in Sicily, must have felt for that Greek ritual of drinking wine in communal meals – 'syssitia'. The adoption in Carthage of this religious and social practice may well be regarded as one of the first signs of the western acculturation of these Orientals.

MASKS AND TERRACOTTAS

From the large amphora derived from the 'Canaanite jars' to the most slender of the small Greek bowls with handles, we are still

FIGURE 36 *A grimacing mask from a Dermech tomb (seventh to sixth century) (Musée national du Bardo, Tunis).*

FIGURE 37 *A negroid mask from Dermech (seventh to sixth century)* *(Musée national du Bardo, Tunis).*

concerned with the material survival of the deceased, or rather the continuation of that material life symbolized by these articles. But pottery has other applications. Tombs of that period also yield other terracotta objects whose significance is not always obvious. This is notably true of masks, the most ancient of which were unearthed by P. Gauckler in the Dermech tombs that go back to the end of the eighth century or the beginning of the seventh (figures 36–9). Later, while these masks were evolving towards a greater stylization and at the same time becoming Hellenized, alongside them there appeared masculine and feminine 'protomes', whose eyes and mouths, unlike the masks, are not perforated. We are talking here of real masks or perhaps reproductions, for although the eyes and mouths are pierced, their dimensions (less than about twenty centimetres) would never have allowed them to be worn on real faces. The oldest masks, which are extremely expressive, are of two types: 'negroid', its mouth twisted in a rictus, and a 'grimacing' or grotesque type, whose face is very wrinkled and lined. There is general agreement that placing these demoniacal masks in the tomb was a response to the need for the protection of the dead man, as the mask would exercise an apotropaic effect against evil powers. However, as every object placed in a tomb, with rare exceptions, had a previous use other than funerary, the question remains as to

FIGURE 38   *The 'Saumagne mask' from the south slope of Byrsa (end of the sixth century) (Musée national de Carthage).*

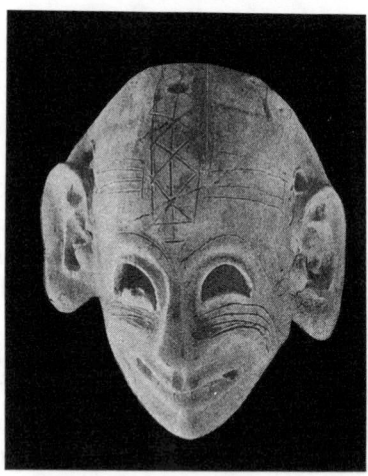

FIGURE 39   *A grimacing mask with a headband (end of the seventh century) (Musée national du Bardo, Tunis).*

what the primary purpose of these masks was. Perhaps they were used in ritual costumes, made out of wood and cloth, in a fashion more suitable for that purpose. Despite their weight, life-size masks in terracotta could be used for that function, which would have been the case for the famous masks of the sanctuary of Artemis Orthia at Sparta, perhaps also for the great Cypriot and eastern examples (notably those of Gezer in Palestine). Interpretations differ with the place of discovery: the masks brought to light in the tophet of Motya may have been used to cover the faces of sacrificial victims (Ciasca, 1988, p. 354). One thing seems almost certain: in the western Semitic world these masks, in their archaic form, are a legacy of Phoenicia proper, but that legacy went by way of Carthage. They are virtually absent from Phoenician sites in southern Spain, but as in Carthage, they were abundant from the end of the seventh century in Sicily (at Motya), in Sardinia (at Tharros chiefly) and Ibiza, that is, in Carthage's direct zone of influence, from the end of the seventh century.

We remain in the realms of ritual and the sacred with the terracotta figurines of very primitive appearance unearthed at Carthage in the two funerary deposits (rarely in the tombs, mainly in the tophet). These are articles that were turned on a wheel – which explains their bell-like or campaniform shape – to which the craftsman has added in barbotine (as wet clay) the defining elements of the body: arms, sometimes the head and, in the case of a male, stylized sexual organs. The female sex is summarily depicted by an incised triangle above which, sometimes, the navel protrudes (figure 40). Red-coloured bands embellish the body, on which they cross over or suggest a robe, probably the remains of a priestly robe attested on Cypriot figurines (Bisi, 1979, pp. 24–6). The head, made separately, was very frequently socketed on to the body, which is why a number of these heads have been found, in particular in the tophet of Carthage, detached from the body (figure 40). The masculine heads are always rendered according to the same brutally expressive design which is also found in Ibiza and Sardinia in the sixth century: protruding ears, a strong hooked nose, its line extending that of the cranium, plunging to meet the chin, with its jutting profile further accentuated by a short beard; between the two, a thick-lipped mouth. Such figurines are attested in Cyprus at the end of the Bronze Age, but they are most widespread in the world of the western Phoenicians, especially in the strictly Punic area, starting with the types in the Carthage tophet dated to the end of the eighth century. It is thought that these terracotta dolls may have played a role in rites of sorcery or possession. From the contexts in which they are found in Carthage, one is inclined to ascribe more of a votive use to them. However, various observations, chiefly relating to the position of these figurines' arms, which are often raised in an attitude of prayer, have suggested that they may be not so much ex-votos as praying figurines, placed in the

FIGURE 40   *Campaniform figurines from the tophet of Carthage (P. Cintas).*

sacrificial areas to secure the family's fertility (Ferron and Aubet, 1974).

The funerary levels have yielded other, more elaborate, terracotta figurines, made in a mould and afterwards retouched and hand-painted by the craftsman. Some of them are very close to their eastern origins, for example, two little statuettes from the same tomb in Dermech, which can be dated from its finds to the middle of the seventh century (figure 41). It is apparent that these images are two variations of the same representation, which is well attested in the east – one has her hands crossed over her belly and holds a large fan in the shape of a palm leaf, covering her bosom, while the posture of the other emphasizes her pregnancy. But whereas in Phoenicia (in Akhziv, Tyre, Sarepta) these 'pregnant women' or 'pregnant goddesses' are shown standing, with long robes falling to their feet hiding their condition, here they are shown seated. The coloured decoration on the robes combines vertical black bands with traces of blue and red (the latter being particularly used on the

FIGURE 41 *Two seated figurines from a Dermech tomb (mid-seventh century) (Musée national du Bardo, Tunis).*

ears, which are largely uncovered and carved in the round). The arrangement of the hair in two equal tresses falling over the shoulders on either side of the face is typical of an eastern tradition well represented in Syria-Palestine, which goes back ultimately to an Egyptian design.

An Egyptianizing style is in any case a feature of many of these statuettes from the tombs of the seventh century, and even of the sixth, which often have the stiffness of a mummy, whether they are represented with their arms alongside their body or, like that shown in figure 42a, dated to the sixth century, from a Douimès tomb excavated by Père Delattre, with the left arm across the breast. Its eyes are huge ovals, outlined by make-up applied equally lavishly on the cheeks and lips; the bands painted on the body suggest clothing, while two motifs, inspired by the *oudja* eye, on the shoulders, endow the figure with their protective power.

FIGURE 42   *An Egyptianizing figurine from a Douimès tomb (a) (Musée national de Carthage) and one in a Greek style (beginning of the fifth century) from Dar-el-Morali (b) (Musée national du Bardo, Tunis).*

A little later, but from the end of the seventh century, one sees the appearance in the tombs of Carthage of figurines fashioned in bas-relief, following eastern tradition – the lower part of the body remaining as if in a sheath that conceals its shape – but presenting a certain number of features that reveal Ionian influence. That influence is particularly noticeable in one of the best preserved examples of the 'goddess with the drum', from the cemetery of Dar-el-Morali, where the two traditions may be seen to coexist (figure 42b). What remains of the rigid hieratic style is offset by the living quality of the bare feet emerging from beneath her dress, by her smiling eyes and mouth, while the borrowing from Asian Greece is shown by the treatment of the hair, so different from the eastern fashion: in front of the *stephane* or diadem, the front of the hairstyle is continuous waves from which descend three plaits on each side, falling over the shoulders to a level with the breasts. On the other hand, the rosettes decorating the embroidered vertical band on her garment and the braids adorned with tongues at bust level mark a return to the standard repertoire of eastern ornament. In this figurine of mixed influences we may recognize Astarte, whose drum – here clasped to her breast with both hands – was an attribute in the east from the very earliest times. It is probable (Ferron, 1969, p. 32) that these figurines were introduced into burials as protective talismans.

SCARABS AND AMULETS

When he reaches the final phase of an excavation, sifting the sand and clay that have infiltrated into badly covered graves, the archaeologist eventually gains access to the world where magic is ever present. The humble people of the 'Punic amulets', bearing no inscriptions, are so numerous, so rich in their diversity that the most knowledgeable scholar of Carthaginian archaeology in the middle of this century was able to devote his first work to them (Cintas, 1946). Certain Dermech tombs excavated by P. Gauckler turned up a veritable profusion of these little talismans, in the form of pendants which would have been attached next to one another on necklaces; sometimes there were as many as several dozen in one tomb. It has been observed that these amulets are especially plentiful in what must be rich tombs, judging by their material, which can be explained by the price that could be fetched for these little articles, very probably imported from Egypt. Those from tombs dated in the seventh and sixth centuries, at least, are genuinely Egyptian, as evidenced by their material – a porous and friable siliceous clay coated with enamel which is usually blue – their technique, style and, still more, the themes represented. Among the amulets without a hieroglyphic legend, by far the most frequent is the *oudja* eye, followed by the *uraeus* and the god Ptah-Patech. Several copies of these three favourite amulets are often found within the same tomb. Then come the *Bes* and the Anubis figures, all amulets equally popular in Egypt in the same era (figure 43). It has been noticed – and used as a reason for asserting their Egyptian provenance – that certain amulets peculiar to the XXVIth dynasty (the white crown, the writing tablet, Khnoum or Amon, the aegis of Sekmet) are to be found in plenty at Carthage in tombs dated between the middle of the seventh and the sixth century, contemporary with that dynasty (Vercoutter, 1945, p. 282). At the very beginning of their history, the Carthaginians were steeped in that Egyptian magic which would continue to dominate them for centuries to come.

The scarab is prominent among these talismans that the deceased carried with him into the tomb, there to extend the protection they were deemed to have afforded him during his lifetime. Already several decades ago it was possible to catalogue almost a thousand

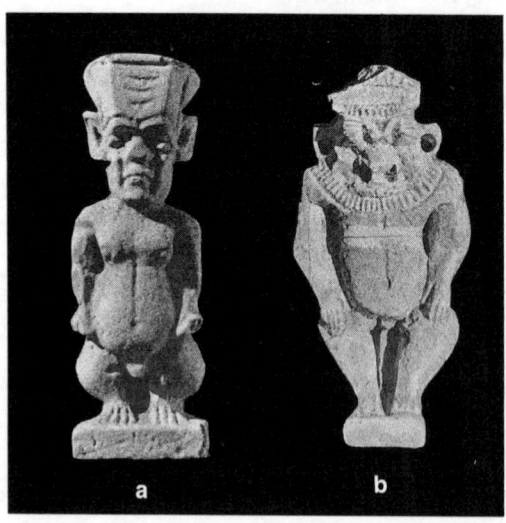

FIGURE 43　*Egyptian-style amulets in glazed earthenware: Ptah-Patech on the left (Musée national de Carthage) and Bes on the right (Musée national du Bardo, Tunis).*

of these scarabs and scaraboeoids, many of which had been able to
escape the attention of the first excavators of Carthage's cemeteries.
Nearly every seventh-century tomb yields some to the sieves (Lancel,
1982, pp. 269, 276, 320). Until the sixth century, they are of frit or
faience like the amulets, and their material, technique and the
inscriptions they bear give them a similarity to the scarabs found in
Egypt on sites of the XXVIth dynasty (Vercoutter, 1945, p. 338).
The names of the pharaohs of that era often appear on the scarabs
excavated from Carthaginian tombs; more than thirty have been
counted which bear the fairly well transcribed names of the first
Saitic pharaohs. The talisman's magic effectiveness rested largely on
that reference to the king and his power. Thus the forename of
Psammetichus I can be read on the lower part of the complex
composition on the flat surface of a white paste scarab from
Dermech (figure 44a). In the upper portion lies a sphinx, surmounted by an ankh and with a ewer in front of it; in the lower
portion a crouching god faces the goddess Bastet. The Saitic epoch,
with strong leanings towards the archaic, had tried hard to revive
the golden age of Egyptian civilization, and it will be no surprise to
find the name of Mykerinos, the builder of one of the three great
pyramids at Gizeh, on a blue-green paste scarab from the Douimès
cemetery, the lower portion showing the pharaoh's cartouche
preceded by royal symbols (figure 44b): the falcon holding the
flagellum and the *uraeus* (Leclant, 1968, p. 95). Sometimes the
magic works on its own, without the help of a pharaoh but with
that of a divinity, as witnessed by a scarab in white paste from
Dermech, its flat surface showing the plume of Maat (goddess of
Justice) and an *uraeus*, each preceded by the hieroglyphic sign *nfr*
(figure 44c). On several scarabs found in archaic tombs at Carthage

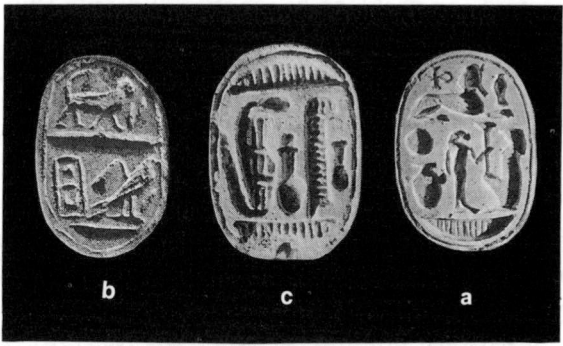

FIGURE 44 *Scarabs from the Dermech cemetery (seventh century):*
(a) and (c) Musée national du Bardo; (b) Musée national de Carthage).

only the crown of Lower Egypt appears, and with reference to these one may wonder if they go back to the period of the divisions of Egypt just prior to the XXVIth dynasty, when the north was independent of the south (Vercoutter, 1945, p. 338, note 1).

The jewels of that era, whose gold may happen to glint in the fingers of the excavator of burials, rarely escape in their conception from the preoccupation with magical protection. This is particularly true of the little cases for carrying amulets (Quillard, 1971, pp. 5–32). They are to be found at Carthage in enamelled paste, and then their Egyptian origin seems indisputable, but they are also found fashioned in gold, like the case with the ram's head (figure 45a), where local manufacture seems probable (Leclant, 1980, pp. 102–3). These cases contained strips of cloth or ribbons, bearing Egyptian-style motifs or scenes, which have disappeared if they were of perishable material (papyrus or fabric). But their reality is attested by three thin plates of gold that can be dated to the end of the seventh and the beginning of the sixth century and reproduce the same themes with variations (the decans and a whole cohort of Egyptian divinities). This repetition of the motifs suggests that an Egyptian model was reproduced at Carthage, and similar strips have been discovered in Sardinia. At all events, the majority of Carthaginian jewellery of the archaic era is to be classified, like these cases, as talismans, and many pieces bear Egyptian-style motifs, whether they are earrings in the form of a cross with its top forming a loop to go through the ear (figure 45c), which are very frequently found, or necklace pendants (Quillard, 1979), such as the circular one from a Douimès tomb, its upper portion showing a winged solar disc surmounting another disc inserted into a crescent, while on the lower portion two *uraei* flank a *sacrum* covered with granulation (figure 45e). Also from the Douimès sector and dating from the end of the seventh century comes a pendant in the form of an arched niche in which, enthroned on an altar with an Egyptian throat, the two *uraei* rear up, this time facing to the front, flanking a bottle-shaped idol with a granulated surface (figure 45f). A pendant frequently reproduced is one on which the solar disc is shown set into a downward-pointing crescent (figure 45d). A separate classification is required for a medallion that has no analogue in Egypt, whereas it may be compared to a pendant found at Byblos

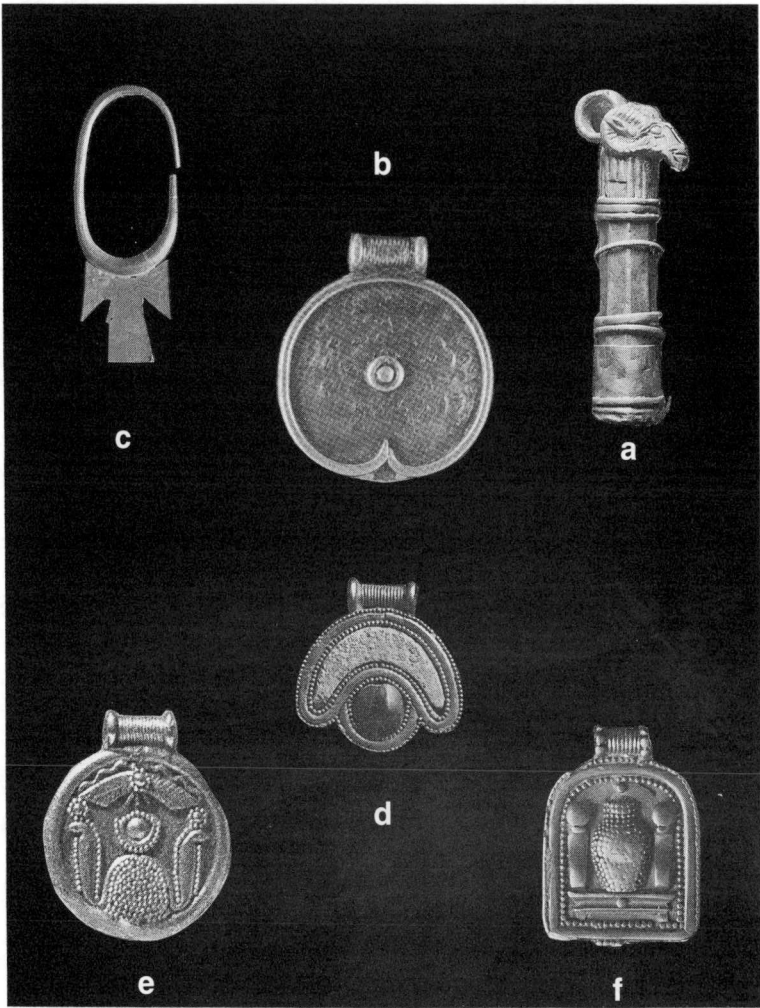

FIGURE 45 *Gold jewellery from the cemeteries of Dermech and Douimès (seventh to sixth century) (Musée national de Carthage and Musée national du Bardo, Tunis).*

by P. Montet. On this medallion, which also comes from the Douimès cemetery and can be dated to the seventh century, may be seen, around a central boss and on a field surrounded by an outer ring whose two points meet and turn inwards, engraved in microscopic characters (the object is no more than 18 mm long) a text of six little lines that is the most ancient Punic inscription discovered at Carthage (figure 45b): it reveals to us the name of the person who owned the medallion, Yadamalek (Ferron, 1958).

IVORIES

Last, with a little luck, the excavator of Carthage's archaic tombs may light upon products of the valuable lineage of the most characteristically Phoenician craft, in carved ivory. Here again the influence of Egyptian iconography is revealed, clearly present in two mirror handles, one of which comes from the Douimès cemetery and is datable to the first half of the seventh century (figure 46a). It represents a woman wearing a *klaft* which leaves her two prominent ears uncovered; her long garment is loosely belted over her hips; her hands, drawn up to her bosom, press her breasts which they support with the four fingers opened into an arc, the thumb extended almost vertically. It is matched by a very similar figurine (figure 46b) brought to light in a tomb of the same era (seventh century) on the hill of Juno, equally Egyptian-style, wearing the

FIGURE 46 *Ivory mirror handles from the Douimès (Musée national de Carthage) and Juno cemeteries (seventh century) (Musée national du Bardo, Tunis).*

same wig and also pressing her breasts. The two statuettes differ only in minor details: the braid at the hem of the dress and what appears to be a tiara do not figure on the Douimès mirror handle. This motif of a woman holding her breasts goes back to an old Mesopotamian and Syrian tradition (though originally the body was nude), and the face with the large almond-shaped eyes framed by a wig belongs to the 'women at the window' of the ivories of Nimrud, in the eighth century. Bearing in mind the difference in quality of these two figurines from comparable pieces from Phoenicia proper, one might assume that they are works executed in Carthage itself in the manner of Syrio-Palestinian models, without excluding the possibility of imports from centres on the Phoenician coast (Byblos, Sidon, Tyre).

A completely different problem is posed by another category of carved ivories, the combs which make their appearance at Carthage during the course of the seventh century. Such is the case of the fine example from the tomb in the Juno cemetery, where in 1918 A. Merlin discovered the mirror handle we have just seen (figure 46b): its decoration – a sphinx and a duck (?) among lotus flowers – is inspired by the Egyptian style, but it is incised instead of being carved in the bas-relief of oriental tradition. Other similar objects, sometimes preserved only in a fragmentary state, have been dug up at Carthage in contexts datable to between the start of the seventh century and the end of the sixth. Here the points of reference are not oriental but belong to the Phoenician world of the extreme west: the carved combs most similar to those of Carthage, with which they are contemporary, come from the 'land of Tartessus' in Andalusia (figures 47 a and c). Unless one allows that the two series of articles came from independent and parallel local producers – which is not strictly impossible – the question then arises as to which workshops produced those pieces which seem not to have an eastern origin. From the technical quality of the Carthaginian specimens, an argument has been made for placing at Carthage workshops which, perhaps about the middle of the eighth century, manufactured these carved ivories whose ornamentation – at least in the earliest – shows great fidelity to Syrio-Palestinian schemes of decoration (Bisi, 1968). On the other hand, judging from the equal quality and above all the far greater quantity of carved ivories brought to light in 'eastern-leaning' sites in southern Spain (chiefly in the Carmona area: at la Cruz del Negro, El Acebuchal, El Bencarron), it has been argued that the Andalusian workshops played the leading role (Aubet, 1980, pp. 47–51). As often happens,

FIGURE 47 *Ivory combs from Carthage: (a) and (c) from Carmona, in Andalusia (seventh to sixth century) and (b) from the hill of Juno (seventh century) (Gallimard, 'Univers des Formes').*

each argument probably contains its grain of truth. More precise chronological analyses suggest that the older group of southern

Spanish ivories could be the work of Carthaginian (rather than oriental) craftsmen who had emigrated to Spain and were active at the beginning of the seventh century. Subsequently, workshops established in the 'land of Tartessus' would develop a very flourishing autonomous production and perhaps export to Carthage from the middle of the sixth century.

This reluctance to credit archaic Carthage with its own independent craftsmen in the field of ivory derives generally from the relative sparseness of the finds of this nature that have been made until recently in the African city. The latest excavations in the cemetery of the south slope of Byrsa have turned up new elements of a kind to place Carthaginian production more fairly in that very specific Phoenician craft tradition. The amphora of a cremation tomb excavated in 1980 contained, among other material dated to the middle of the seventh century by a subgeometric proto-Corinthian cotyle, a little ivory plaque worked in relief, which the cremation fire had caused to split into two (figure 48a). Its motif is frankly Egyptianizing: two figures standing face to face, one male the other female, in a gesture of worship of the winged sun above them. The 'Cushitic' features are very noticeable in the way the two people are portrayed (hair, garments) – to such a degree that the hypothesis that this article comes from the Nile valley must not be excluded – which ties in with the date when this plaque was placed in the tomb (Lancel, 1981, pp. 162–4). Some distance away, in the same part of this cemetery, another cremation tomb of identical

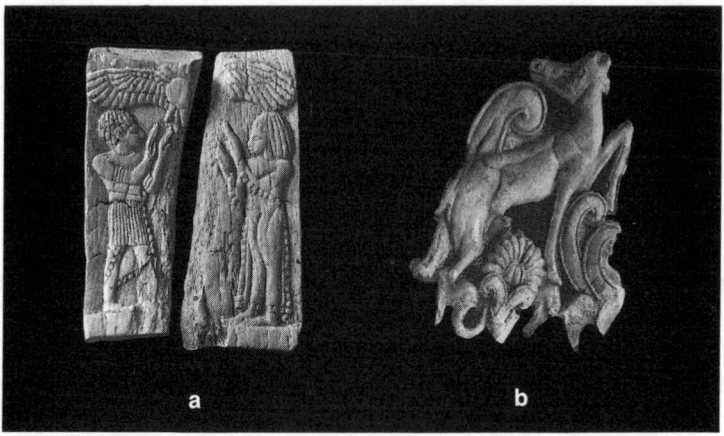

FIGURE 48 *Ivories from the Byrsa cemetery: (a) in an Egyptianizing style and (b) in a Syro-Palestinian tradition (S. Lancel).*

dating had two years earlier produced a whole group of ivory objects, and in particular several pieces including little plaques with openwork carving, copying the same motif that probably formed part of a decorative frieze made of symmetrically placed metopes. The basic motif (figure 48b) is a deer-like animal facing to the right, its head turned back and its left foreleg raised, amid decorative volutes and palm leaves. The most successful realization of this motif, in its various versions, of the deer turning its head to graze the foliage, is achieved by the openwork ivories of Nimrud. A stylistic impoverishment is noticeable in the rendering of the surrounding vegetation, which has become stilted and conventional, but, as regards their theme, these openwork ivories of Carthage appear to be in direct descent from the Nimrud pieces dated to the end of the eighth century. In their technique, despite the differences in size and execution – clearly superior in the Cypriot examples – these ivories from Byrsa may be compared to those of the royal cemetery of Salamis in Cyprus, dated to around 700 BC (Karageorghis, 1973). Half a century, therefore, separates the type specimens of Nimrud and Cyprus from the openwork ivories of Byrsa. This find, without precedent at Carthage, shows that in the middle of the seventh century ivory was being carved in the African city with great fidelity to Syrio-Palestinian models. Pieces of raw ivory – in the form of slices obtained by sawing the end of a tusk into sections – found in the same tomb seem to provide proof that we are not dealing here with imported objects, but production by local craftsmen. This burial (let us emphasize, for cremated remains) would not belong to a lover of ivories, but a craftsman who had taken with him to the next world both the products of his craft and some samples of the raw materials he used (Lancel, 1983a, pp. 691–2).

CARTHAGE AT THE END OF THE SEVENTH CENTURY

It will easily be understood that this rapid glimpse of the contributions provided for over a century by excavating Carthage's cemeteries by no means exhausts their value as a source of information. Rather paradoxically, this funerary documentation infuses life into the still nascent city, whose large extent has been revealed by the latest work on the ground without, however, telling us much about how that space was distributed. To be persuaded, it is enough to reread that page that P. Gauckler (1915, p. 398) was inspired to write by the excavation of what he called the 'tomb of the priestess':

the skeleton of a woman, perhaps a priestess, is stretched out, the skull turned to the east towards the door: she still holds a large bronze mirror in her left hand, and in her right, heavy cymbals of the same metal. The left wrist disappears beneath a bracelet of pearls, scarabs and various figurines; her right arm is encircled by several silver and ivory armbands. The fingers are laden with silver rings and a gold band, with four baboons engraved on the setting; on her left ear, a gold pendant with a tau-shaped cross; round her neck a great necklace of solid gold made up of forty pieces of various shapes, symmetrically placed on either side of a central brooch figuring a crescent of turquoise lying on a disc of jacinth. Another necklace of silver completes the adornment. A Corinthian aryballos and figured alabaster, a large enamel flask covered with gold leaf, a statuette in multi-coloured faience, completely Egyptian in style, painted ostrich-egg discs, pottery and a lamp complete the grave goods.

In its evocative power this description, which would have overjoyed Flaubert when he was feverishly assembling the documentation for his *Salammbô*, wins hands down against any romantic fiction. Thanks to this burial archaeology we know more about archaic Carthage than about any other contemporary city in the western Mediterranean.

Let us halt here for a brief overview, at this image of the Punic city around the end of the seventh century or in the very first years of the sixth. Its horizons are broad: even if it is clear that it looks primarily towards the orient, it already had close contacts with the Greek cultural world, perhaps chiefly through the intermediary of Sicily, and it is probably already in some relationship with the southern Etruscan area and the coasts of Latium. Its connections with southern Spain work in both directions. Its relations with its nearest surroundings are less in evidence. These days, the archaeology of the archaic Mediterranean world is increasingly concerned with trying to define the idea of territory – *chora* in Greek terms – and to put cities back into their settings. It is always difficult even to sketch out a territory for the earliest Carthage, to obtain an idea of its links with its closest, and in theory its elder neighbour, Utica. Archaic Carthage was still for some time to come a head without a body. Its power and wealth came from the wider world.

3

The Beginnings of Empire

At the end of the seventh century the western basin of the Mediterranean was a much frequented stretch of sea, for mastery of which
the Greeks challenged the Phoenico-Punic people, chiefly from the
time of the first settlements of Chalcidian colonization in the island
of Ischia, then at Cumae in Campania, shortly before the middle of
the eighth century. As the Phoenicians had done before, taking
themselves straight away to the farthest reaches of the western
world, the Euboean founders, venturing beyond the plains of Sicily
and southern Italy and along the Tyrrhenian coasts, had as their
aim the conquest of markets and the creation of a trade route
(Heurgon, 1969, p. 151). They were attracted by the mineral
wealth of the Isle of Elba and Etruria, as the easterners had been
earlier by the riches of the Rio Tinto. Once the bridgehead was
established in central Italy, the next step was always to occupy the
intermediate positions firmly, and first of all the Straits of Messina.
That had been achieved at the beginning of the second half of the
eighth century by the founding of Zancle and Rhegium (Reggio
Calabria) on either side of the Straits (Vallet, 1958, p. 56). Archaeological evidence gives an idea of the efficiency of this bottleneck.
Corinthian pottery spread massively in the seventh century at
Taranto and in Sicily (and it is probably via this route that it arrived
at Carthage), but the colonial trade of Corinth stopped short at the
Straits. Only a few rare luxury examples of this pottery got as far
as Etruria, whereas the Chalcidians allowed a veritable flood of
beautiful Attic pottery to pass through the Straits, to be found later
in Etruscan tombs (Vallet, 1958, p. 164). If we are to believe

Thucydides (VI, 13, 1), in the space of a few years the Euboeans had expanded at Naxos, Leontinoi and Catania, on the east coast of Sicily, while a little farther to the south Megara founded Megara Hyblaea and Corinth the town of Syracuse. The south coast did not escape this expansion for long. Gela was founded by the Rhodians at the beginning of the seventh century, and the last Doric colony, Agrigentum, appeared at the beginning of the sixth. Meanwhile, cramped in its little coastal plain, Megara Hyblaea had spread westward in the middle of the seventh century, to Selinunte, on the borders of the world that had remained Phoenico-Punic. And from the last years of the eighth century, at Croton, Sybaris and Taranto, southern Italy had become Magna Graecia.

Greek colonization was not content with having a solid hold on this strategic position in central Italy, with control over the east-west passage and access to the Tyrrhenian Sea. In the second half of the seventh century colonists from Thera in the Cyclades founded Cyrene and thus limited possible expansion towards the east by the Phoenico-Punic people established in the Maghreb and Libya. On that southern shore of the Mediterranean one sees the consequences in linguistic divisions produced by Greek settlement in Cyrenaica over many centuries.

On the northern shores, around 600 BC, sailors from Phocaea in Asia Minor founded the town of Massalia, Marseilles, which took control of the great trading route of the Rhône valley and would for centuries be Carthage's constant rival in the region. Lastly, to the west, the Phoenician private hunting ground in Spain was not spared from encroachment. The Palaeopolis of Ampurias, a Phocaean foundation in Catalonia, goes back no further than the beginning of the sixth century, but on the Andalusian coast Mainake (Malaga) may well be earlier. And Herodotus (IV, 152) recounts how, about 640, the Samian Colaios, travelling to Egypt, was forced off his route by storms as far as the Pillars of Hercules, where he made fat profits by selling his wares to the people of Tartessus. He may well have shown the way to Phocaeans who, towards the end of the seventh century or the beginning of the sixth, followed him and were so well received by the sovereign of the kingdom of Tartessus, Arganthonius, that he is supposed to have invited them to quit Ionia and come to settle in his land, according to Herodotus (I, 163).

In the seventh century BC it was probably even harder for a Greek sailor to differentiate clearly between Carthaginian merchants and their oriental colleagues than it was for the former to make a

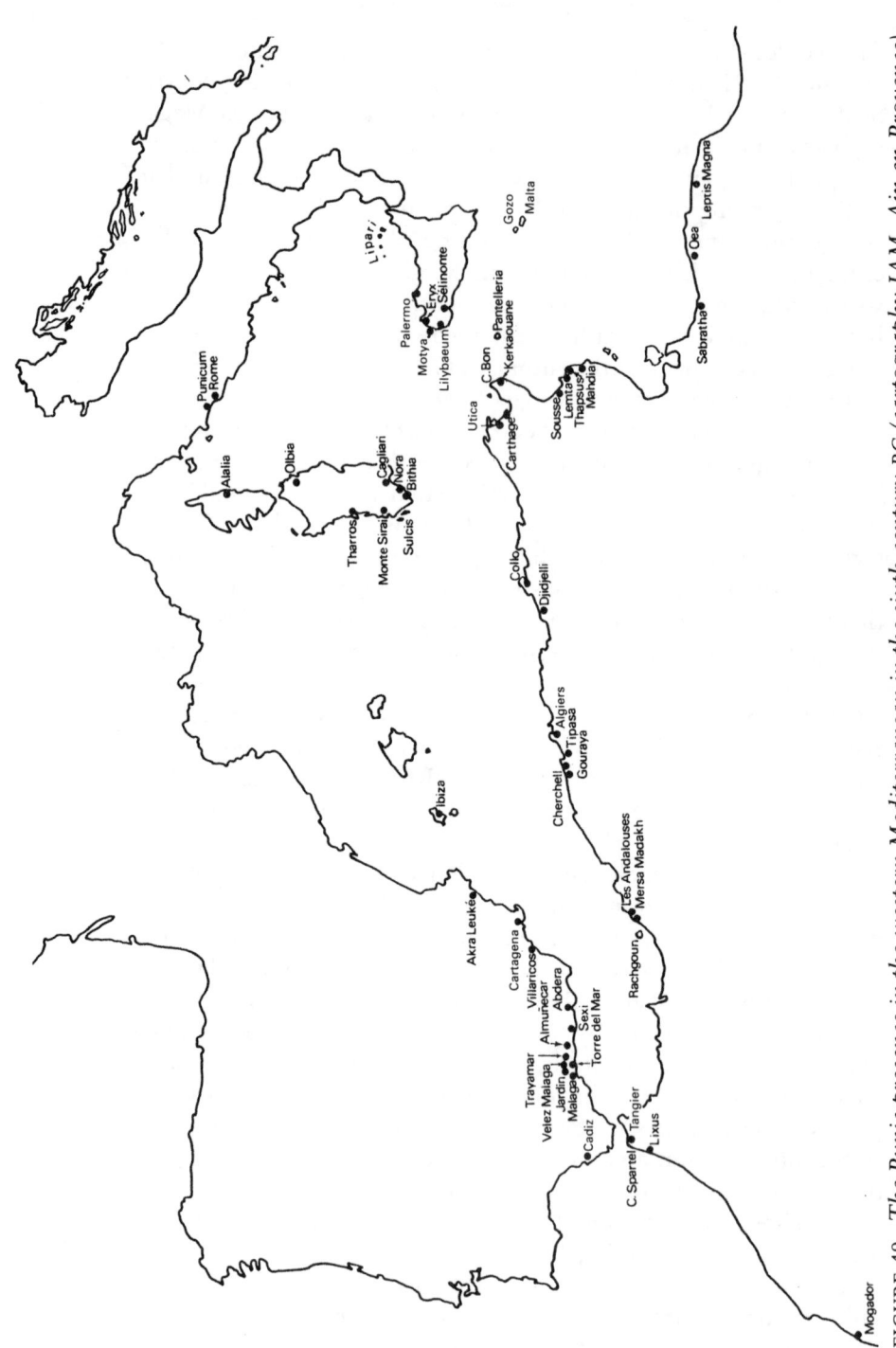

FIGURE 49 *The Punic presence in the western Mediterranean in the sixth century BC (cartography IAM, Aix-en-Provence).*

distinction between Greeks from Greece proper and colonials from the Hellenized territories of the western Mediterranean. Similarly, it is not easy for today's historians always to attribute with certainty, in this appropriation of western space, the share that belongs exclusively to the Punic people (figure 49). That title applies here to the sailors, traders and entrepreneurs of all kinds and of Semitic culture, who operated from Carthage, if not in its name. It may be understood that such an identification is not obvious. It rests chiefly on the analysis of archaeological materials, especially pottery, and on the determination in recognized features of what appears exclusive to Carthage. Furthermore, even though the mother-city, Tyre, suffered many troubles at the hands of the Assyrians during the first half of the seventh century (and until the beginning of the sixth century, in the reign of Nebuchadnezzar), nothing allows us to affirm that the African 'new town', Carthage, could carry on enterprises politically independent of the Phoenician city's control, at least till the middle of the sixth century. Even enfeebled, Tyre would remain the metropolis, still active on the high seas for a long time to come. Around 600 BC, it was to Phoenician sailors that the pharaoh Nechao entrusted the mission of accomplishing a voyage round Africa (Desanges, 1978, pp. 7–16). And the ties between the colony and its mother-city, as we have seen, always remained very strong. They were essentially on a religious plane, but in Antiquity, and especially in Semitic circles, that plane was fundamental. It would take the military conquests of the Carthaginians in Sicily and Sardinia, in the second half of the sixth century, then the victory over the Phocaeans in Corsica, at Alalia (Aleria), for Carthage to form itself *de facto* into an autonomous power. And perhaps one would have to wait until the thalassocracy which it was became an African landed state, starting from the fifth century, in order truly to see it as a sovereign power.

PUNIC ESTABLISHMENTS IN THE WESTERN MEDITERRANEAN

The questions relating to Semitic settlements in the western Mediterranean from the seventh century reflect this ambiguity. Were they originally Phoenician or Punic and, if they were first of all Phoenician, when may they be regarded as part of the 'empire' of Carthage? Let us take the case of Ibiza, in the Balearic Islands.

According to Diodorus of Sicily (V, 16), the Carthaginians established a colony at Ebesos (the Phoenician *Eibshim*), on the island of

Pithyuse, 160 years after the foundation of their own city; if we agree on the date of 814 for that founding, this places us in 654. Recent developments in archaeological research on Ibiza force a reconsideration of that statement, which was still generally accepted not long ago. The inclination now is to identify as Phoenician, by dating it to the middle of the seventh century, a first modest settlement comprising simply the installations necessary to support commercial navigation from the Andalusian coasts towards the north and east: a few houses, warehouses for goods. Only the cemetery of this period is well known, in particular the cremations exhumed at the foot of Puig des Molins hill, which contain fewer grave goods (but with imported pottery, chiefly Etruscan) placed in urns, little cavities or pits. It was therefore a 'Phoenician' establishment, but without intervention from Tyre and a creation of the Phoenicians of the west (Gomez Bellard, 1990, p. 178). There remain some specialists, however, who think that Carthage in the middle of the seventh century was perfectly capable of carrying the colonization of Ibiza to a successful conclusion, and that the archaeological documentation in our possession does not yet allow us formally to reject the testimony of Diodorus (Rouillard, 1989, p. 227). From the beginning of the sixth century, Carthage's influence grew on Ibiza in parallel with the crisis of the Phoenician settlements in the south of Spain, precipitated by the siege and fall of Tyre in 573. That direct Carthaginian influence is well marked by changes in the features of the Puig des Molins cemetery, as much in the typology of the burials (appearance of hypogea, subterranean tombs) as in that of the grave goods (Gomez Bellard, 1990, p. 183). In the tophet of Illa Plana, apparently founded around the end of the sixth century, there was then an abundance of campaniform statuettes with marked sexual characteristics, typical of the Punic area. Unknown on Phoenician sites of southern Spain, they were present at Carthage, as we saw, in a very early period, but also, as we shall see, in Sardinia and Sicily. In the fifth century the island of Ibiza, whose city seems already to have attained its full development, evidently came within Carthage's sphere of influence, just like the whole of the Balearic archipelago, which went on to provide Carthage's armies with the celebrated corps of 'slingers' (the *funditores*) in the fourth century. However, the type of political relationship that linked the archipelago with Carthage eludes us. Hypothetically, one might imagine a military governorship and a garrison.

If the Balearics naturally looked towards Spain and had perhaps received their first Semitic culture from the Phoenician south of the peninsula, Malta, at the other end of the western Mediterranean, in that central position which, with Sicily, made it a barrier, was far more orientated towards the east than the west, towards the Nile delta rather than Carthage (Ciasca, 1988, p. 208). The archaeological features of the island, even in the later Punic era, would always be markedly different from those presented by neighbouring regions (western Sicily, northern Tunisia). However, from a date which cannot be fixed precisely (sixth century?), the Carthaginian hold over Malta is not in doubt. It would cease only in 218, when the Romans seized the island, after taking its military governor and Punic garrison prisoner. In the same sector, Gozo and Lampedusa were occupied by Carthage at least from the middle of the sixth century, as is indicated by the *Periplus* of the Pseudo-Scylax. On Pantelleria remains of fortifications on the acropolis show that the island was a Carthaginian staging post, of which the port at the very least was under Punic control.

SARDINIA AND THE ETRUSCAN WORLD

To the north, the key factor in Carthaginian domination of the western basin of the Mediterranean was Sardinia. There again, certainly the footsteps of the Phoenicians, as Péguy might have said, 'had worked for them'. In particular, at the time of the second phase of Phoenician settlement, from the end of the ninth century, there was a veritable process of colonization starting from the city states of Phoenicia proper. It is thought that Sulcis and Tharros, on the west coast, were founded at the end of the eighth century. And the magnificent seventh- and sixth-century gold and silver jewellery of Tharros (figure 50), superior to that of Carthage in the same era, speaks volumes for the richness of this Phoenician colony which was then independent of the Punic capital (Pisano, 1988, pp. 370–82). Bithia, in the south, as well as Cagliari, were founded later (the end of the seventh century).

This Sardinia of ancient Semitic culture – but solely on its coastal fringes – enters the history of Carthage in the middle of the sixth century. In fact, it is around this era that a defeat is said to have been suffered on the island by the first Carthaginian 'king', called Malchus (Justin, XVIII, 7), who was doubtless grappling with the natives whose pressure on the coastal settlements had to be weakened. Shortly afterwards, towards the end of the sixth century, the Carthaginians again took military action on the island, with the

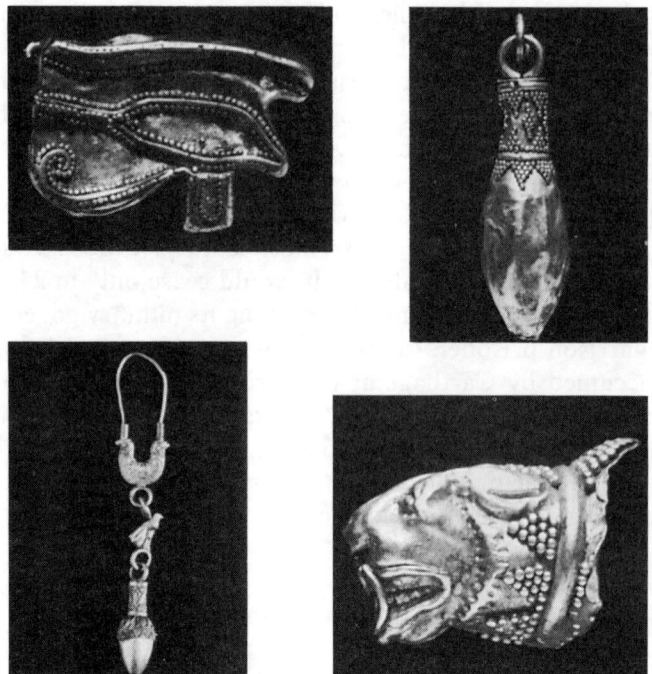

FIGURE 50   *Pieces of gold jewellery from Tharros (seventh to sixth century* BC*) (Archaeological Museum of Cagliari).*

campaigns of the two sons of Mago, Hasdrubal and Hamilcar (Justin, XIX, 1, 6). Already, in 535, the victory of the Carthaginians, allied with the Etruscans against the Phocaeans at Alalia in Corsica, had ensured Sardinia's security against possible Greek operations – of the Phocaeans themselves and their colony Massalia (Marseilles) – by creating a sort of glacis. Lost for the Greeks, Corsica had been left by Carthage at the disposal of its Etruscan allies. Then, when the latter had been destroyed and supplanted by Rome, a kind of *modus vivendi* between Romans and Carthaginians turned the island into a form of neutral territory, which seems nevertheless to have remained more under Carthage's sphere of influence until the time of the first Punic War (the middle of the third century).

For a long time it was thought that the Punic people 'certainly had commercial relations with the Etruscans that necessitated the security of the Tyrrhenian Sea' (Gsell, *HAAN*, vol. I, 1921, p. 245). The nature of those relations and that alliance is now better under-

FIGURE 51 *Bilingual gold sheets from Pyrgi: on the left the Punic text, on the right the Etruscan (Etruscan Museum of the Villa Giulia, Rome).*

stood, since the major discovery in 1963 of Punic-Etruscan bilingual inscriptions, on gold sheets, in Pyrgi, one of the ports of Caere (present-day Cerveteri) (figure 51). These texts are dated around 500 BC, when the Etruscan sovereign of Caere, Thefarius Velinas, expressed his gratitude in an ex-voto to the Punic goddess Astarte (Heurgon, 1965, pp. 89–104). There was in fact a real alliance between Carthage and the principality of southern Etruria, where the name *Punicum*, Caere's second port, gives assurance of the reality of the commercial (and perhaps also demographic) presence of Carthaginians. And recent excavations in the archaic cemetery of the south slope of Byrsa have noticeably increased the number of proofs of imports to Carthage coming from the south of Etruria at a slightly earlier date (Thuillier, 1985, pp. 155–63). Another witness to the trade carried on until at least the beginning of the fifth century between the Etruscan world and Carthage, is a little ivory plaquette from the so-called Sainte-Monique cemetery at Carthage, on which may be read a brief Etruscan text apparently written at Vulci, and which may be translated as follows: 'I am Punic from Carthage,' perhaps a sort of visiting card brought back from Etruria by a Carthaginian merchant (Gras, 1989, p. 227).

THE FIRST TREATY BETWEEN CARTHAGE AND ROME

It seems permissible to place in this light the first treaty between Rome and Carthage, which brings us back, as we shall see, to Sardinia, for the date Polybius assigns to this treaty – within a few years of the Pyrgi tablets – is generally accepted today: 509 BC, or the year of the institution of the republic in Rome. It is worth quoting in its entirety the text handed down by Polybius (III, 1, 22) in Greek, on the basis of a version in archaic Latin of which he underlines the difficulties in interpretation:

> The Romans and their allies will refrain from sailing beyond the Beautiful Promontory, unless storms or an enemy force compel them to do so; if a ship is driven, despite itself, beyond this headland, the crew are forbidden to buy or sell anything, except what may be necessary to render the said ship seaworthy again or to offer a sacrifice. The ship must leave again within five days. For those coming to trade, no transaction may be concluded without the presence of a herald or clerk. Regarding settlement of the purchases made in the presence of these officials, the state will be answerable to the vendor – this applies to sales effected in Sardinia and Africa. Any Roman going to Sicily, in the zone under Carthaginian authority, will enjoy the same rights as others.

As the reader may imagine, the corpus of commentaries relating to this text is one of the fattest. Argument still continues on the single point of what is meant by the 'Beautiful Promontory'. This point is indeed important. In the little commentary which follows the text of the treaty, Polybius begins by making it clear that the 'Beautiful Promontory is the headland jutting out in front of Carthage itself, in a northerly direction'. Following Meltzer and

Gsell, the majority of modern commentators have identified the 'Beautiful Promontory' with Cape Farina, now Ras el-Mekki, which extends its point eastwards and which in fact must be doubled round by ships coming from the north and north-west and entering the gulf of Carthage. This is wrong, for the promontory extending northwards and barring the horizon seen from Carthage is in fact Cap Bon, whose modern name implies a good omen, reflecting the Greek name *Kalon Akroterion* – where *Kalon* means 'favourable' rather than 'beautiful' – and this is an ironic euphemism, for navigation is perilous in the vicinity of Cap Bon, in particular around Ras ed-Drek (Desanges, 1990, p. 30). This explains why Polybius thought it well to add that, if the Carthaginians reckoned that the Romans should be stopped from sailing beyond this cape to the south, it was in order to prevent them from visiting and trading with the rich cities of the Tunisian Sahel – the Byzacena of antiquity – and the *Emporia* of the Syrtis Minor. We shall see later (below, p. 265) that the Carthaginians, perhaps as early as this very time, strove hard to keep Cap Bon bristling with lookouts and guard posts.

Another sentence of Polybius' commentary takes up the essence of the treaty's significance (III, 23): 'This treaty,' he says, 'shows that the Carthaginians looked on Sardinia and Africa as their own domain, but that it was not the same as regards Sicily, where the part of the island subject to Carthage was explicitly distinguished.' In fact, in the treaty of 509, Sardinia appeared to be well under Carthaginian control and Carthage was designated as the sole guarantor for commercial transactions on the island. Around the end of the sixth century, Carthaginian occupation spread towards the interior from the coastal centres and set up a network of strongholds protected by a *limes*, pieces of which are dated between the fifth and third centuries. New establishments were founded in the north of the island, such as Antas, from the end of the sixth century, where the cult of the god Sid would survive in the charming prostyle temple of the Latin *Sardus Pater*. That movement deliberately broke with the 'reluctant colonization' of the Phoenician phase and was accompanied by interpenetration with local populations, as well as by cereal-growing on the great plains and control over access routes to the mining sites of the hinterland. It is agreed that in the fourth century Carthage extended its sway over the whole of the island, and a clause in the second treaty concluded with Rome, dated 348, forcefully affirms the reality of that control: 'The Romans,' says the text, 'may not under any circumstance trade or found towns in Sardinia or Africa' (Polybius, III, 24). And it may be considered as a sign of this integration that Punic Sardinia was included within the Mediterranean monetary system at the beginning of the fourth century.

PHOENICIAN AND PUNIC SICILY

Though Sardinia was completely Punic territory throughout nearly four centuries (from the sixth century to 238 BC), the situation was entirely different in Sicily, the combat zone for relentless battles between Greeks and Carthaginians from the fifth century until the middle of the third, when Rome entered the game and imposed its domination on the island at the outcome of the first Punic War, in 241 BC. There is a celebrated passage in Thucydides (VI, 2, 6) where, in a striking summary, he gives a compressed account of several centuries of pre-Punic Sicilian history:

> The Phoenicians dwelt here and there all over Sicily, after occupying the headlands overlooking the sea and the islets near to the coast . . . Then, when the Greeks came from overseas in large numbers, they left the greater part of the land and were concentrated at Motya, Soluntum and Palermo, where they lived close to the Elymi, reassured by alliance with the Elymi themselves and by the fact that this point of Sicily was very near to Carthage.

At the western extremity of Sicily, like a ship at anchor in its lagoon separated from the open sea by a narrow peninsula, the small isle of Motya is a Phoenician site *par excellence*. As at Syracuse, the oldest proto-Corinthian vases from the archaic cemetery, situated on the north shore of the island, can be dated to 730/720 BC, but the Phoenician foundation probably slightly predated that time. The most ancient parts of the city wall, reinforced by towers, which went right round the island and were washed by the sea, are said to date back as far as the end of the seventh century (Bondi, 1988, p. 266). These defence works thus seem earlier than the Carthaginian occupation of western Sicily, which may be placed in the course of the sixth century. We have seen that at the date of the first treaty with Rome, in 509, mention was expressly made of the part of the island subject to Carthage. To this period we can date a reorganization of the tophet at Motya with artificial terracing and an expansion of the zone reserved for interments

(Gras, 1989, p. 229). A large number of the hundreds of stelae discovered, especially during recent excavations, belong to the same period. Let it be said in passing, two characteristics emerge from even a rapid examination of these little monuments: first, the complete cultural absence, in that period, of the Greek world, which was so close and so powerful; and also the originality, compared with Carthage, of these sculptures, which appear not far removed from their Phoenician origins, yet are rendered in flat relief of a very austere expressiveness (cf. below, figure 202). One would like to be able to state that such independence in the domain of the plastic arts was the reflection of a political liberty with respect to the Punic capital. This is probable. Like Palermo and Soluntum, Motya, protected by Carthage, was not its colony, and there is no evidence that in this era the Carthaginians had founded colonies in the western part of Sicily, which they controlled as far as Selinunte in the south and Himera in the north.

It was precisely at Himera, in 480, that the western Greeks inflicted a sharp check on the Carthaginians, and its synchronism and symmetry with the victory of Salamis against the Persians was celebrated by Herodotus (VII, 166). The synchronism was doubt-less somewhat forced – Aristotle (*Poeticae*, XXIII, 3) says merely 'around the same time' – but what symbolism! At any rate, a combined action of Carthage in Sicily and Xerxes in Greece is not to be ruled out. At that time the Persians were masters of Phoenicia and, according to Diodorus (XI, 1), a treaty on this occasion seems to have linked Carthage and the Great King.

Reduced to their *finistère* of the Sicilian west, the Carthaginians might hope that a decisive victory would give them a complete hold over the island, which was not only rich and fertile, but also in a key position between the two Mediterranean basins. Whoever could hold Sicily would have a lasting grip on the western Mediter-ranean. Two centuries later that was well understood by Rome, which made the island the first province of its empire outside the confines of Italy. For the moment, the Carthaginians could also expect their undivided possession of the island to help them more effectively to contain their enemies from the north, the Phocaeans, already countered at Alalia in 535, but who held the coasts of Gaul and the north-west of Spain, where they restricted Carthage's am-bitions (Morel, 1975, pp. 873–88).

However, the initiative for this major confrontation did not origin-ate from the Carthaginians. It was due to the Doric colonies which, counter to the particularism of the Sicilian cities, tended to create *de facto* two allied states in the face of the Carthaginians. Gelon, the tyrant of Gela on the south-west coast, had already some years before seized power at Syracuse. He made common cause with Theron, tyrant of Agrigentum, who gained possession of Himera, where an ally of the Carthaginians reigned. In place of principalities enfeebled by their isolation, a powerful and formidable bloc was thus created.

Carthage entrusted command of the war against the Greeks of Sicily to 'king' Hamilcar, of the Magonid family, who appears to have taken three years to assemble his armada: 200 warships, 3000 troop transporters, an army of 300,000 men, raised from Africa, Spain, Sardinia, Corsica, Liguria and even the coast of Gaul (Diodorus, XI, 1 and 20). These were enormous numbers for Antiquity, and doubtless exaggerated. But at Himera the defeat suffered at the hands of Gelon and Theron in coalition was so total, the disaster, further aggravated by shipwrecks, so great that, according to Diodorus (XI, 24), a single vessel sailed by a few men was the only one able to return to Carthage. As for Hamilcar, according to Herodotus (VII, 167), seeing the rout of his men, he hurled himself into the fire on which he was in the act of making a sacrifice.

It can be said that the common triumph of Theron of Agrigentum and Gelon of Syracuse marked the beginning of a new era in the history of Greek Sicily, which from then on almost merged with that of Syracuse (Heurgon, 1969, p. 158). I shall not to go into the details of that history here, rich as it was in vicissitudes and destruction on both sides. Thus in 409 Hamilcar's grandson, one Hanni-

FIGURE 52 *Punic coins in silver from western Sicily (third century) (Gallimard 'Univers des Formes').*

bal, destroyed Selinunte and regained Himera and, in 405, after the capture of Agrigentum and Gela by Himilco, the tyrant of Syracuse, the famous Dionysius I, acknowledged by treaty Carthage's possession of western Sicily (figure 52). That stabilization was to have a short duration. Motya was taken and destroyed by Dionysius in 397, and the city was not rebuilt on the same site but became Lilybaeum, the present-day Marsala. For another century and a half Carthage battled on in Sicily with varying success, ebbs and flows to which Rome would finally put a stop. Nevertheless, despite that tenacious effort, quite understandable as Sicily was such a vital stake in the game, Carthage had lost no time in learning its lesson from the defeat at Himera and consolidating its positions in Africa itself.

THE DISCOVERY OF AFRICA

Carthage was not the only bridgehead of the Semitic world in North Africa and, as we have seen, even its founding had been preceded, on either side of the Maghreb, by two foundations traditionally regarded as earlier in date – Lixus in the west, on the Atlantic, north of present-day Morocco, and Utica in the east, another estuarine site, at the mouth of the Medjerda. Even farther east and more to the south, Hadrumetum (now Sousse) and Leptis (Lebda, in present-day Libya) had formed indispensable stopping-points for Phoenician trade on the return journey eastwards. Like Carthage itself, the last two cities are given as colonies of Tyre by ancient writers (Pliny and Silius Italicus for Leptis, Solinus for Hadrumetum), while only Sallust (*Jugurtha*, LXXVIII, 1) mentions the Sidonians as the founders of Leptis Magna; but the term here, as in other contexts, does not mean the inhabitants of Sidon, but Phoenicians in general. It is thus possible that the city-state of Tyre was also behind the establishment of Leptis Magna.

However that may be, there are no grounds for asserting that, in the seventh century, these two cities had reached a stage of development comparable with what we know of Carthage. At Hadrumetum (Sousse), certain deposits in the tophet excavated by P. Cintas under the church built at the end of the nineteenth century may go back to the fourth century, less certainly to the seventh (Cintas, 1947, pp. 4–5); as for the Phoenician, then Punic town, and subsequently the town of the Roman era, they disappeared as early as the Muslim Middle Ages under the town that is Sousse today.

On the site of Leptis Magna, at the mouth of the Wadi Lebda, excavations carried out in 1960 and 1961 seem to have provided archaeological proof of a Phoenician foundation, but one that may go back no further than the end of the sixth century (Carter, 1965, pp. 123–32; Di Vita, 1969, p. 197). In the case of both Leptis and Hadrumetum, the material collected does not allow the supposition of the existence of close relations between those centres and Carthage in the earliest times.

Carthage does not appear to have had any trouble with the Greeks who had established themselves in Cyrenaica in the second half of the seventh century. But the Punic metropolis probably did not wait for the venture of the Lacedaemonian Dorieus in order to establish its presence solidly in the region that the Greeks soon after would call the region of the *Emporia*, 'the markets', to designate the trading posts or even the colonies which Carthage soon set up on the coast, between the Tunisian Sahel and the zone between the two Syrtes, that is, the western part of present-day Libya.

Shortly before the end of the sixth century, the son of a Spartan king, Dorieus, who had had to leave the crown to his brother Cleomenes, left to seek his fortune in Africa and, doubtless encouraged by the people of Cyrene, went to found a colony between the two Syrtes, at the mouth of the River Cinyps (the Wadi Caam), a short distance – 18 kilometres – south-east of Leptis. Such proximity makes one think that the Phoenician colony must have been very weak at the time not to have been able to oppose the Greek settlement; perhaps it had even undergone an eclipse. It may be noted that, from the fourth century, geographical documents in Greek give the name Neapolis to the city then existing on the site of Leptis, which suggests the possibility of a new foundation.

Reaction came from Carthage, which took three years to expel Dorieus. It was probably the experience of this encroachment that gave the Punic capital the idea of fixing the bounds of its zone of influence to the east, at the extremity of the Syrtis Major. It is not known when exactly that frontier materialized, but its establishment would have great importance for many centuries to come, since, apart from being the eastern limit of the Roman province of Africa, it would later determine the dividing line between the linguistic domain of Latin to the west and Greek to the east, and later still the boundary between the empires of the west and east. It is known at least that this frontier existed around the middle of the fourth century, at the time of the composition of the *Periplus* of the Pseudo-Scylax, who cited the concrete form of it on the land, the 'altars of Philaenus' or 'of the Philaeni' (*Philainou* or *Philainon Bomoi, Arae Philaenorum*).

THE 'ALTARS OF THE PHILAENI' AND LIBYPHOENICIAN AFRICA

These 'altars of the Philaeni' fuelled one of those aetiological (or explanatory) accounts in which Antiquity excelled and took such delight. The legend is very probably of Greek origin, as it is in Greek that the name of the two Carthaginian heroes has a meaning: *Philainoi*, the 'lovers of praise'. But it is to Latin authors, and in particular Sallust (*Jugurtha*, LXXIX), that we owe its developed form. According to the Roman historian who, in order to write his *Jugurtha*, had amassed a vast amount of documentation on the past of North Africa, Carthage and Cyrene, weary of the war that set them against each other, agreed that on a certain day their champions would depart at the same time from each town and that their meeting-point would be deemed the territorial boundary. The two champions from Carthage, brothers called Philaenus, covered far more ground than those of Cyrene, who accused them of having started ahead of time and proposed a new agreement: either they accepted being buried alive at the spot they had reached, where the boundary would be fixed, or they would let the Cyrenians advance, on the same conditions. To the Philaeni, who had agreed to sacrifice themselves, Carthage consecrated altars.

There is no knowing what really occurred to give substance to this legendary tale whose plot – the meeting-point of champions bringing a frontier dispute to an end – is to be found elsewhere in Antiquity. At the beginning of the first century AD, Strabo (III, 5, 5) saw the altars as columns or boundary markers that had already ceased to exist in his own time. Slightly later, Pliny the Elder (*NH*, V, 28, 2), mentioning these altars as the eastern limit of the shore of the Lotophagi, states that they were made of sand (*ex harena*): this would suggest one of those *lusus naturae* which, sculpted by erosion, abound in old African landscapes. Moreover, no one knows precisely where to locate this frontier, although it maintained a fine fixity over the centuries: at the far end of the Syrtis Major, and certainly a little south-east of Ras el-Alia, perhaps in the locality of Graret Gser-et-Trab (Desanges, 1980, p. 270).

Never did Carthage's influence, either politically or economically, extend eastwards beyond that limit. But to the west, beginning from the sixth century and more certainly from the fifth, the coastal fringes of the Maghreb seem to have been systematically taken over by the Carthaginians, although the chancy nature of archaeological discovery does not always allow us to affirm the simultaneity of that seizure in every place. An example is the island of the Lotophagi, Djerba, where one would expect to find traces of an earlier Carthaginian occupation, whereas there is no vestige that would allow dating further back than the middle of the fourth century, when the island is mentioned in the *Periplus* of the Pseudo-Scylax (110). In the same way it is very likely, as we saw earlier, that Carthage had positions to defend at the time of the first treaty with Rome (509 BC) on the seaboard of Byzacena, the present-day Tunisian Sahel, where what the Greeks called the *Emporia* must in reality have been the trading posts of economically controlled settlements rather than colonies, at least in the early times. But neither at Gightis (Bou Ghrara), coiled at the end of its little gulf facing Djerba, nor at Tacape (Gabes), in the Syrtis Minor, nor higher up on the sites that regularly punctuate the littoral as far as Hadrumetum (Sousse), has archaeology to this day revealed the remains of a Punic site that pre-dates the fourth century. We shall see, however (below, p. 288) that in what may have been a district (*pagus*) of Carthage's African territory there developed an original material culture called 'Libyphoenician', after a word borrowed from Pliny the Elder, a term that has the merit of happily evoking the symbiosis that took place there between the native substratum and the Semitic contribution. Similarly, in what was Carthage's first rural annexation, if not its territory, its *chora* in the political sense of the term, the Cap Bon which was in fact its 'garden' when Agathocles ravaged it at the end of the fourth century, we still lack precise evidence of a Carthaginian settlement in very early times. But when thorough excavations have been carried out, as at Kerkouane at the extremity of the headland, they have been able to isolate evidence of development from at least the fifth century (Morel, 1969, pp. 473–518; Fantar, 1984, pp. 23–4).

THE NORTHERN SEABOARD OF PUNIC AFRICA

To the west of Carthage, going along the north coasts, a separate case must be made for Utica, the ancient Phoenician city, older than Carthage according to a tradition that archaeology, as we have seen, does not confirm. And the sites of northern Tunisia, including

Bizerta (*Hippo Dhiarrytus*), still conceal any traces of ancient Carthaginian possession, although it is very probable.

Somewhat paradoxically, it is on the long Mediterranean front of present-day Algeria that Punic stepping stones of the very oldest epoch have been revealed. I am borrowing the term 'stepping stones' from P. Cintas who, some decades ago, with great strides of his compasses on the map, was the first to pinpoint these trading posts or ports of call every 30 or 40 kilometres along the coast, sometimes at longer intervals when the configuration of the littoral and landing difficulties made it necessary: *mare saevum, importuosum*, Sallust would say, not without cause. These difficulties thus explain the gap that, in the east of Algeria, separates Hippo Regius (Annaba) from Rusicade (Skikda), on either side of the steeply plunging cliffs of the Edough massif; or Chullu (Collo), to the east of the escarpments of Cap Bougaroun (the *promontorium Metagonium* of the Ancients), from the small islet which, several cable-lengths away from Ziama-Mansouria (Choba), offered an ideal port site to Punic ships, and where we have recently discovered indisputable traces of a small settlement of the Punic era. But, travelling west, beginning from the shores of present-day Kabylia, the settlements follow one another with a noticeable regularity.

Nevertheless, there too the sites are far from presenting homogeneous features and, at the current stage of research, it is not possible everywhere to date Punic settlement back to the same period. It must even be added that not all the place-names starting with the Semitic root *rus*- (the Arab *ras*, 'cape', 'head'), spaced out along these shores (Rusazus, Rusuccurru, Rusguniae, etc.), have yielded absolutely certain traces of a presence that their name undeniably suggests. However, at Kerkouane, where patient and methodical excavation has been carried out, that presence is clearly revealed as early as the end of the sixth century.

Tipasa provides a good example, situated about 60 kilometres west of Algiers (Icosium) (figure 53). It again fell to Cintas, in the middle of this century, to discover there the vestiges of a Punic material culture in the form of graves dug out of the sandstone of the littoral cliffs, some distance to the east of the modern town (Cintas, 1949). The great vault, now tilted like a ship run aground in the shallow waters of the little port, had been known, though not identified for what it really was, since the Roman quarrymen, digging into the surrounding cliffs, had respected it and left it as evidence (figure 54). Since then, emptied of its contents, the monument has not been datable, but Cintas was able to establish that the

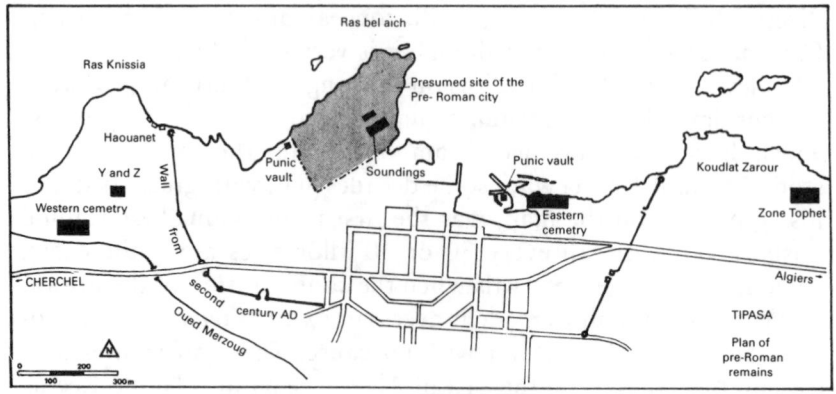

FIGURE 53   *Tipasa: plan of the situation of vestiges of the Punic era, shown in black (S. Lancel).*

small cemetery in which it is situated could be dated to about the fourth century BC, the great vault certainly being earlier. It was therefore permissible to recognize Tipasa as one of those stepping-stones in Punic coastal navigation, established on the westward route and preceding the major landfall of Iol-Caesarea (Cherchell) just before the formidable Cap Chenoua passage.

About twenty years ago I myself followed up these Punic excavations at Tipasa by bringing to light a second cemetery, situated on the other side of the town, towards the west, and nearly two kilometres away from the first (Lancel, 1968). Attic and Ionian

FIGURE 54   *Tipasa: the eastern Punic cemetery, the vault undermined and tilted by the sea in the little fishing port (S. Lancel).*

FIGURE 55 *Tipasa: the western Punic cemetery in 1967 (S. Lancel).*

pottery gathered in these hypogea allow the oldest of them to be dated to the end of the sixth century, the earliest point of a chronology that leads without interruption to the beginning of the first century BC. The most numerous series of objects of Punic tradition can be placed between the fourth and second centuries, and the twenty or so graves excavated, which represent only a small part of a much bigger funerary complex, bear witness to the material importance and wealth of the dwelling area to which they belong, at least from the fourth century (figure 55).

The first question posed by these discoveries is obviously that of the location of that dwelling area, as more than two kilometres separate this cemetery from the one in the east excavated by Cintas. As it is rather unlikely that each of these burial areas related to a distinct settlement or even a distinct dwelling area, the site of the pre-Roman town must be sought between these two deposits, and it is thought to be on the central promontory (the Ras bel-Aich) of a sort of trident formed by the site of Tipasa. At all events, tombs unearthed a short distance from that central spur, found empty but typologically Punic beyond doubt, support the hypothesis of this siting, as does the discovery of numerous sherds of Campanian pottery made during investigations on this promontory, which bear witness to dense occupation at least from the second century BC

(Lancel, 1982a, pp. 746–52). But it is again the material from the excavation of the western cemetery that furnishes both quantitative and qualitative information on the site. Apart from some Greek and Hellenistic pottery, the grave goods are formed basically by common pottery of Punic type, most likely made on the spot, with a faithfulness to the old shapes that reveals a noticeable discrepancy in comparison with the development of this kind of production in the Carthaginian capital – a phenomenon sometimes referred to as 'provincial backwardness'. Various indications make one think that these items of pottery in the Punic tradition may have been influenced by the Iberian world, from which imports are present among the articles (notably grey marl pottery). Such imports, including those of late Attic pottery, disappear almost entirely from the middle of the fourth century, and this break doubtless reflects the consequences of tighter control exercised by Carthage over the Maghreb coasts at the time of the second treaty with Rome, in the period of the Punic Wars. On the other hand, important finds of late Campanian pottery mark the resumption of trade with the Italian world and Sicily from the middle of the second century, that is, after the fall of Carthage. But the Punic forms live on, and numerous black-glazed imitations give evidence of both the flexibility of the adaptations and, at that date also, as in the past with Carthage, a relative economic independence in contrast with what would henceforth be a dominant flow of imports.

Even the best informed archaeology can tell only what it knows. It can provide no more than an outline sketch of what Tipasa may have been between the sixth and second centuries BC. The material size of the town, which is soon perceptible, rules out the possibility that it was simply a trading post. In any case, it is not very probable that it could have provided Carthage with a colony for peopling. The monuments in the cemeteries and the objects in the tombs are of Punic traditions; but the rites – position, reburials, the practice of funerary red make-up – all refer to Libyan or Berber traditions. As in a certain number of other pre-Roman sites in Mauretania and Numidia, at Tipasa a hypothesis may be suggested of a large indigenous substratum at the origin of the nucleated settlement (Février, 1967, pp. 107–23). While not assuring us that Tipasa was a political dependency of Carthage, archaeological data nevertheless bear witness to the cultural preponderance of the Punic mother-city in a territory that was equally open to Iberian contributions and in a city that must have played a role alongside Iol (Cherchell) in forming Mauretanian kingdoms from the third century. After the fall of Carthage Punic influence would remain, at once persistent and restricted. Though the language of Carthage left no written trace there, the shape of the funeral vaults long obeyed Punic architectural traditions, and the frequency of Punic-type votive stelae also bears witness to the clear survival of that influence in the religious domain, right up to the imperial Roman epoch. Moreover, on the Koudiat Zarour, a few steps from what would subsequently become the basilica of Saint Salsa, the supreme holy place when the city became Christian, a small sacrificial area was discovered with uninscribed votive stelae *in situ*, tables for offerings and the burnt remains of substitute victims (animal victims of the rite of *molchomor*) contained in the common pottery of the first century AD; obvious proof, in an advanced phase of Romanization, of the local vitality of the most characteristic religious attitude of Punic tradition (Lancel, 1982, pp. 753–4).

The historical experience of Tipasa can hardly have been an isolated case. Future investigations will probably multiply and undoubtedly clarify evidence of the Carthaginian hold over the northern Maghreb littoral in a number of sites, at least from the fifth century. It is the Punic pottery attributable to this era that the excavations of the 'Joinville islet' at Cherchell (Iol-Caesarea) unearthed about thirty years ago (Vuillemot, 1965, p. 334). The physiognomy of the town of Iol contemporary with this material has yet to be uncovered, but it agrees with the early dating (fifth century) of Greek pottery found before a little farther to the west at Gunugu (Gouraya), a dating recently confirmed by a re-examination of these vessels (Villard, 1959, p. 12; Morel, 1980, p. 61). The recent work of an Algerian-British mission at Cherchell confirms the importance of the pre-Roman city of Iol (Leveau, 1984, pp. 12–13; Potter, 1985, p. 458).

Pushing still farther westward, on the coast of present-day Oran, one meets sites that have provided the earliest material, notably at Mersa Madakh, which appears to have been inhabited as early as the sixth century (Vuillemot, 1965, p. 155). An analysis of the articles brought to light on the site makes it evident that it was in contact with the Ibero-Phoenician colonies of southern Andalusia in that period, and not with the Punic metropolis. We thus find at Mersa Madakh a bowl-lamp decorated with red slip and having a single spout at a period (sixth century) when these two characteristics had long since disappeared from the Carthaginian production of lamps, but survived through 'provincial backwardness' in the Phoenician-influenced area of the Iberian sea. In these parts the earliest settlement is indisputably that of the small isle of Rach-goun, facing the mouth of the Tafna. As well as a cemetery of about a hundred tombs, remnants of a dwelling area and also a little artificial port, a 'cothon', cut out of the rock of a converted creek, are dated from the middle of the seventh century. The temptation to see the isle of Rachgoun – we would gladly recognize the present place-name as a descendant of an ancient *Rusguniae* – as a Phoeni-cian stopping-place properly speaking, must be resisted (Decret, 1977, p. 116). It is more likely that the islet was colonized in the sixth century from the Andalusian shores, which were less than 200 kilometres away.

BEYOND THE PILLARS OF HERCULES

In the middle of the fifth century Herodotus had already heard of the expeditions, no longer of the Phoenicians but of the Carthagin-ians, beyond the Pillars of Hercules (figure 56). He tells us so in a page of his 'Libyan accounts' (IV, 196), which is famous chiefly for what it tells us about silent bartering:

> The Carthaginians still relate the following story. Beyond the Pillars of Hercules there exists a Libyan country inhabited by men whom they visit. They unload their goods and lay them out neatly on the shore edge, then they reboard their vessels and send up columns of smoke to attract the notice of the natives. The latter, seeing the smoke, draw near to the sea, place next to the goods the gold they are offering in exchange, and withdraw. The Carthaginians disembark once more and examine what has been left. If they estimate that the amount of gold matches the value of the goods, they take it away and raise anchor. If not, they return to their ships and wait. The natives, coming back in their turn, add more gold until the Carthaginians are satisfied. Neither side does the other any wrong. The one does not touch the gold before the quantity laid down seems to match the goods. The other does not touch the goods before the Carthaginians have taken their gold.

With due respect to Herodotus, who apparently considered this exchange fair, this text is probably the oldest testimony we have to the one-sided exploitation, in a captive market, of raw materials from the heart of Africa. The natives obviously take no initiative in the progress of the transaction, in which their desire to acquire

FIGURE 56   *The Pillars of Hercules, an aerial view taken on a level with Cap Spartel. In the right foreground, Tangier and its bay; in the background, Mount Abila, one of the Pillars; opposite, on the left, Gibraltar (after M.* Ponsich in *Aufstieg und Niedergang der römischen Welt, 1982, pl. XXIV).*

goods with value added, as we would say, forces them to accept the conditions set by the Carthaginians. It would be nice to have some idea of the goods for which they parted with their gold. It will be remembered that Homer, recalling the trade of the Phoenicians in their 'black vessels', spoke of *athyrmata*, a word which we have seen suggests, if not luxury, at least superfluity, expensive extravagance. The term used by Herodotus is generic: *ta phortia*, he says, that is 'bundles' or 'packages', the cargo of a trading vessel. The reality eludes us, but crockery, probably of simple terracotta, must have formed a large part of it. As some indication one may quote the articles which, according to the *Periplus* of the Pseudo-Scylax (112), the traders (here termed 'Phoenicians') who landed at Cerne offered to the 'Ethiopians' who inhabited the mainland to the right of the island: perfumed oil, 'Egyptian stones' (sardonyx?), Attic pottery and 'vats', terracotta vessels of large capacity. We will ignore the 'wild boar' that the text adds to the list in a very suspect fashion.

To return to Herodotus, the geographic setting is chiefly to be remembered. 'Beyond the Pillars of Hercules' puts us on the Atlantic coasts of Africa and, more exactly, the mention of the gold offered by the Libyans brings to mind no longer the littoral of present-day Morocco, but farther south, the Rio de Oro in Mauretania and even, at a still lower latitude, the land of Bambouk, homeland of the black gold-panners, in the basin of the upper Senegal.

HANNO's *Periplus*

As we cannot recount it at full length, we must here take a glance at the record of *Hanno's Voyage*. This is the name given to an account of Carthaginian journeyings along the Atlantic coasts of Africa which has come down to us, in a rather miraculous fashion, in a Greek version preserved in a Heidelberg manuscript dated to the ninth century. According to this version, a text posted up in the temple of Kronos (that is, the temple of Baal Hammon) in Carthage informed the public of the purposes and vicissitudes of a voyage 'beyond the Pillars of Herakles', entrusted by the Carthaginians to 'King' Hanno in order to 'found Libyphoenician towns'. Hanno is thus supposed to have departed (perhaps from *Gades*, Cadiz) with sixty fifty-oar vessels ('penteconters', long ships), with about 30,000 men and women on board, together with the necessary victuals and equipment.

The account of this voyage, not quoted here because of its length, then begins, using the first person plural. A first part, already covering several days' sailing, shows Hanno's companions touching land several times before reaching the mouth of the River Lixus. In this initial phase they meet the stated objectives by founding colonial towns on the littoral: Thymiaterion to start with, then, beyond Cape Soloeis, Mur Carien, Gutte, Akra, Melitta and Arambys. Up to that point, barring a few details, modern commentators agree fairly well in acknowledging this beginning of the account as 'a report on the methodical survey of an already Phoenicized coast' (Rebuffat, 1976, p. 148). In the first town to be founded, Thymiaterion, they have recognized Tangier, which had already received the Phoenician imprint, as witnessed by the material unearthed which, as we have seen, goes back to the seventh century. One can identify with complete certainty the 'Libyan' promontory called Soloeis with Cap Spartel (cf. figure 56), beyond which the Moroccan Atlantic coast clearly bends southwards, as the text of the *Voyage* says that, once past this cape, navigation was in the direction of the rising sun; now, it is known that in ancient geographic tradition Morocco formed an acute angle, past which the coast led towards the south-east. Gutte would be the Cotta of Pliny the Elder (*NH*, V, 2, 3), perhaps on the site of present-day Ras Achakar. And between this last cape and that of Kouass a series of Phoenician cemeteries have not long been known (Ponsich, 1967) on whose locations some of the place-names still to be identified could well be situated.

Next, Hanno's companions arrived at the mouth of the River Lixus, unhesitatingly identified as the Wadi Loukkos. It is there, as we know, that the town of Lixus was situated, in a meander of the river's estuary, close to present-day Larache and attributed by tradition to a very early date. Archaeology has not as yet confirmed this antiquity, but can instance, on the acropolis of Lixus, traces going back to the seventh century, that is, to an era prior to the passing of Hanno and his companions, or at least contemporary with it (Ponsich, 1982, p. 826). From the *Voyage* we know that on the banks of the Lixus the Carthaginians formed friendly ties with Lixite shepherds (*nomades* in Greek), from among whom they would take interpreters for the rest of their journey. But there is not a word about the famous city, a point that does not fail to surprise. However, as has recently been emphasized, the very fact that Hanno was able to find interpreters among the inhabitants of the place proves at least that both sides spoke a common language, Phoenician. It has been suggested that this silence concerning the ancient city of Lixus in the Heidelberg version may be explained by alterations made to the initial account, which are apparent in the manuscript (Rebuffat, 1978, pp. 77–85).

The next part of the account plunges us into an unknown that allows all manner of explanations. After two days' sailing towards the south, then a day's eastward, the travellers arrived at the end of a gulf, at a small island where they left colonists, after naming it Cernè (figure 57). Very frequently – since the identification enjoys the posthumous authority of J. Carcopino, who affirmed it in an outstanding article – that island is identified with the isle of Herné, in the bay of the Rio de Oro. From Cernè, as from a sort of base camp, Hanno's companions would make a longer incursion that

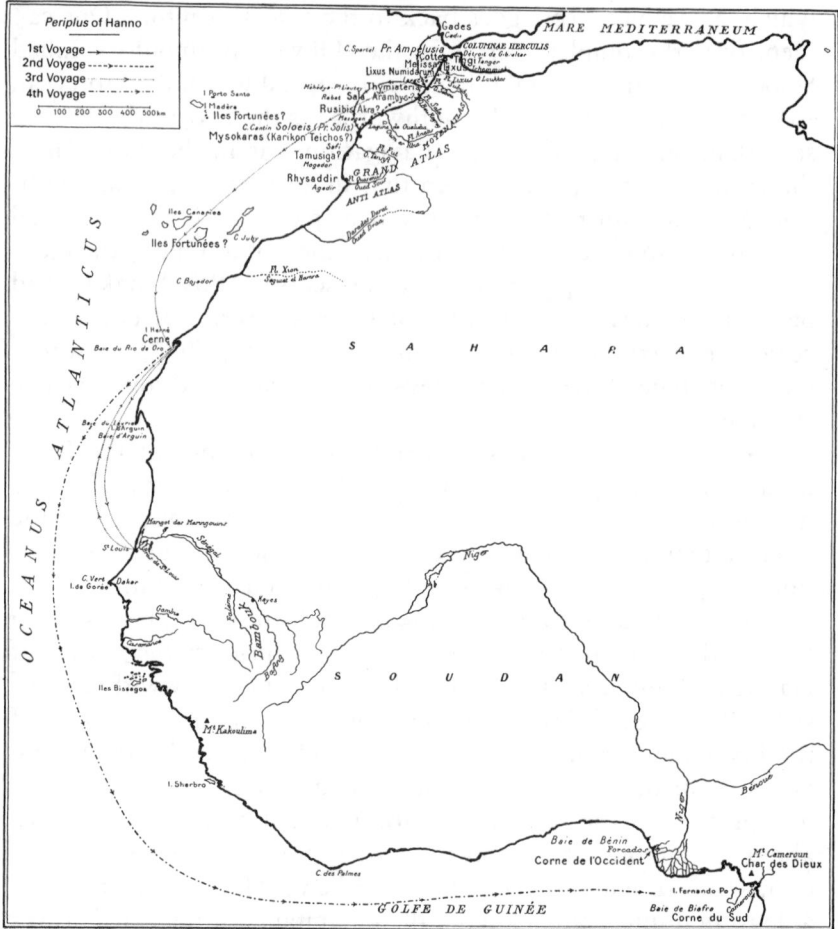

FIGURE 57   *The* Periplus *of Hanno (after J. Carcopino,* Le Maroc antique*).*

would lead them to the mouth of a big river, the Chrétès, where
Senegal is traditionally recognized, then to another watercourse,
full of hippopotami and crocodiles. Returning to Cernè, the
Carthaginians departed southwards, running for twelve days along
an inhospitable coast, peopled with 'Ethiopians' who spoke a language unintelligible even to the Lixite interpreters, before calling at
a port at the foot of high mountains, covered with a variety of
sweet-smelling trees. There has been no hesitation in equating these
mountains with the Fouta-Djalon massif in present-day Guinea.

   Pursuing their journey, Hanno's companions came face to face
with ever-increasing marvels, not least of which were the fires that

blazed with great intensity along the coast at night. At the end of a week, they reached a large gulf which their interpreters pointed out as the Horn of the West (it has been seen as the Bight of Benin), where an island enclosed a lagoon, itself containing another isle resounding with disturbing music and cries that caused them to flee. But what followed was even more terrifying: the land they were by then skirting was as if 'set ablaze with the vapours of fragrant perfumes'. From ground rendered inaccessible by the heat poured burning streams that flowed into the sea.

The writer of the *Periplus* no longer conceals the fear of the voyagers, who are, however, not yet at the end of their troubles and surprises. For four successive days they journey by sea off the coast of a land which, by night, appears to be covered in flames, and at its very heart there is a fire that is unreachable and huge enough to touch the stars: by day they can see a very large mountain called *Theon Ochema*, the 'pedestal' or 'chariot' of the gods. The heights of the Cameroon mountains have been identified with those that the Carthaginians took three whole days to sail past before arriving at the end of their journey, the Horn of the South or, following the same system of identification, the Bight of Biafra, or rather the indentation scooped out of the coast directly below Douala. It was there that the voyagers met with a final adventure, for in the bay there was an island, and on that island (according to a scheme of representation of the geographical space already encountered in this account) was a lake, itself enclosing another island peopled with savages, among whom were women with hairy bodies called 'Gorillas' by the interpreters. Because they could not seize any males, Hanno's companions captured three females whose resistance could be overcome only by killing them and whose skins they brought back to Carthage. For, concludes the writer, 'we sailed no farther, as our supplies had run short.'

It was when they reached this point of return that the real difficulties began for the Carthaginians, to such an extent that they would hardly have had a chance of seeing their homeland again if they had truly reached the heart of tropical Africa. The worst would not have been sailing along the southern coasts of the Gulf of Guinea, but rather, beginning from the shores of Senegal, the long haul back along the coasts of the western Sahara. About thirty years ago, a study of the technical conditions of medieval sea traffic on the Saharan coasts before the discoveries of the Portuguese pointed out their difficulties, which were chiefly due to the system of winds and currents that almost invariably carry everything southwards (Mauny, 1960, pp. 1–22). This is suggested as an explanation for the unwillingness of the people of the Barbary Coast, who held sway in the Mediterranean with well-known success, to venture farther into the Atlantic than Cape Juby. In order to solve the problem of the return journey the Portuguese, thanks chiefly to use of the compass, followed the open sea route by way of the Cape Verde Islands and the Azores. More recently, there have been efforts to minimize these difficulties by observing that, from Cape Verde to Cape Blanc, and at least during summer and autumn, a south-westerly monsoon can favour the return voyage (Lonis, 1978, pp. 147–70). But between Cape Blanc and Cape Juby the situation remains constantly unfavourable. And even though the square sails of Punic ships to some extent allowed them to use the wind to get back, there remained the obstacle of a considerable current, continually against them, and wearisome to fight against with oars in the stifling heat of the day. The discovery of Punic coins made on Corvo, one of the Azores, in the middle of the eighteenth century, albeit suspect and of controversial authenticity (Monod, 1973, pp. 231–4), gave rise to the hypothesis that Hanno's vessels, like those of the Portuguese later, could have returned by way of Cape Verde and the Azores. But the Carthaginians did not have at their disposal the same refinements as the contemporaries of Henry the Navigator, and in particular their penteconters, long and fragile vessels built for sailing coastal waters, were not of a size to confront the high seas (Rougé, 1975, p. 92).

To these negative indications archaeology adds its own silence, which is of course explicable if that far voyage remained an isolated and short-lived reconnaissance exercise, always supposing that its sailors reached the low latitude that is still sometimes claimed. But at least in its first stage, and in a manner acknowledged until the landfall at Cernè, the purpose of the expedition was to found colonies and establish milestones or bridgeheads for future exploitation. It is therefore reasonable to expect to find traces on the ground, if not of the expedition itself, at least of the consequences it must have brought in its wake. South of Rabat, apart from sporadic discoveries of coins along the shoreline, and some signs of a Punic settlement provided by parts of a cemetery near El-Jadida, it is particularly on the tiny island of Mogador that we may instance an early (from the seventh century BC) and durable occupation (Jodin, 1966 and 1967). Now, curiously enough, no one has managed to write Mogador into the setting of the first days' travel of the *Periplus*. Beyond, it appears that late Punic pottery has been

collected at Cape Rhir (Cintas, 1954, p. 32), but there all trace of
the Carthaginians ceases. In the Rio de Oro nothing has been
found, despite careful prospecting, and in the isle of Herné, which
does not seem capable of berthing even small vessels, several investigations have remained negative (Monod, 1979, pp. 15–20; Gran
Aymerich, 1979, pp. 16–19). In any case, the very basis for identifying the Cernè of the *Periplus* with the islet of Herné, because of
their phonetic similarity, crumbles when a study of the different
phases of the region's cartography shows that Herné is merely a
spelling variation of *Herne* (or *Hern*) Island, an English transcription which appeared in 1763 of the French name Heron Island
(*île des Hérons*) given to the site from the beginning of the eighteenth century!

Lastly there remain – and perhaps this is where we should have
started – the doubts and perplexities aroused by philological analysis of the *Periplus* and of the way in which the Greek version
passed on by the Heidelberg manuscript fits into the ensemble of
the traditions concerning this voyage. It has recently been shown
that ancient literature includes certain mentions of the *Periplus of
Hanno*, notably in the *Chorographia* of Pomponius Mela
(around AD 40) and Pliny the Elder's *Natural History*, slightly later
under the Flavians (Desanges, 1978, pp. 45–85). Examination of
these texts reveals that they are dependent on earlier sources, all
contaminated by the cycle of Perseus and the Gorgon, which
ancient mythology had for a long while (already in Hesiod and
Aeschylus) localized in regions vaguely situated in the south-west of
known Africa. Herodotus (II, 91) placed the combat between Perseus and the Gorgon in Libya. In a development devoted to the
islands, Pliny the Elder (*NH*, VI, 198–205) mentions the Gorgades
islands, former haunts of the Gorgons, facing the promontory
Hesperu Ceras, that is, at the south-west corner of Africa. Hanno,
he says, penetrated these islands and had two 'hairy women'
skinned, their hides being put on display in the temple of Juno (or
Tanit) until the fall of Carthage. This contamination by the Perseus
cycle is found in the version of the *Periplus* transmitted by the
Heidelberg manuscript, even if there it appears veiled in that manuscript tradition. One may indeed wonder if the *Gorillas* in this text,
with no other mention elsewhere, are no more than a purely graphic
distortion of *Gorgadas* (in Greek capitals the two forms are graphically very similar) (Desanges, 1978, p. 64). And it may be noted in
passing that gorillas, the large apes of equatorial Africa, derive their
name from this ancient uniquely mentioned name (*hapax*) which

two British naturalists, T. Savage and J. Wyman, who had studied the *Periplus*, used to advantage in 1847! One must therefore beware of regarding the *Gorillas* of the Heidelberg manuscript as monkeys, primates that the Carthaginians were sufficiently familiar with not to confuse them with 'hairy women', who were probably mythical females, as the text says; those captured by Hanno and his companions were three in number, like the Gorgons according to Hesiod (*Theogonia*, 276).

It is thus tempting to conclude, in company with one of the best experts on this text and the whole of the document, that 'once past the mouth of the Lixus, the *Periplus* cannot be divested of its Greek mantle without blurring its outlines into pointlessness' (Desanges, 1978, p. 85). Nevertheless, it is still permissible to believe in the historicity of a real voyage of a real Hanno, accomplished, according to Pliny (*NH* II, 169, and V, 8), in an era when Carthage was at the summit of its power (*Carthaginis potentia florente . . . Punicis rebus florentissimis*). One may hesitate between the end of the seventh century and the sixth (the major period of Punic settlement in the western Mediterranean) and, on the other hand, the fourth century, when Carthage affirmed its monopoly over the Libyan coasts with the second treaty with Rome. If, as we have seen, the voyage encountered no problems as far as Lixus, the difficulty lies in setting what happened subsequently, poetically distorted as it is by the Hellenistic taste for *mirabilia*, in an acceptable geographical frame. A minimal solution has recently been proposed, by which the island of Cernè becomes a river island situated in the lower course of the Wadi Sebou (which would then be the *Chrétès* of the *Periplus*), 24 kilometres from the sea: the Portuguese isle of Santa Maria, upstream of which the 'merjas' would be the lake dotted with three islets described by the writer of the *Periplus* (Rebuffat, 1988a, pp. 198–200).

Some people will surely regret that these stern philologists, these demanding archaeologists, these sensible historians should thus shatter our dreams. Let us not reproach them for doing their job, which lies precisely in allowing dreams their share while at the same time ensuring as far as possible that reality also plays its own part. From the starting-point of a Punic inscription, which we can admit really existed, on public view in the temple of Baal Hammon in Carthage, the Greeks indulged in a great deal of dreaming, embroidering a probably rather dry and factual canvas with their taste for the exotic and using all the resources of their fine mythological and heroic patrimony. Thus was born an incomparable text for Antiquity, which has constantly intrigued and incited modern writers as well to romantic extrapolation, as shown by a *Journal de bord d'Hannon le Carthaginois* ('Shipboard Journal of Hanno the Carthaginian'), published quite recently (Lallemand, 1973).

4

The Means of Power:
From Thalassocracy to State

One of our best experts in Semitic studies warned us not so long ago that it is impossible to retrace Carthage's internal history (Sznycer, 1978, p. 550). And even more recently an eminent specialist expressed his doubts by giving the following title to his address at a large international congress: 'Is it possible to write a history of Carthage?' (G. C. Picard, 1983, p. 279). At all events, the warning and the question have not deterred their authors from making their own attempt, in the wake of some illustrious predecessors. A history must be made, in spite of real difficulties. How, indeed, can a history be written of a city whose archives have disappeared, whose chronicles and annals have not come down to us, in short, whose development and institutions are known to us only through the distorting glass of what we are told by Greek and Latin writers?

As we have seen in the foregoing pages, as regards the activities and attitudes of Carthage in the western Mediterranean basin, we can depend on the near-certainties of factual history. Nevertheless we realize, in the case of Ibiza, that although archaeology may for the most part confirm the data supplied by the ancient texts, it may also invalidate them or at the very least cast doubt upon them. In the field of Carthage's internal history, in particular its political aspects, archaeology can offer us no help at all; nor can epigraphy, which cannot conceal its infuriating poverty beneath the voluminous disguise of a large number of texts. So one is reduced either to resigning oneself to knowing absolutely nothing about Carthage's history or to agreeing to give consideration to the faint echoes found in the classical authors. Not, of course, without subjecting them to critical scrutiny, for they may be suspected of not always having been well informed or of having been mistaken about their sources. It will be seen that not the least of their difficulties stemmed from the fact that of necessity they used words in their own language (Greek or Latin) to speak of institutions or political concepts which for the most part were deeply foreign to them.

A precious note on the 'constitution' of Carthage, included in a chapter of Book II of Aristotle's *Politics*, is due to the good opinion he held of Punic institutions. One may add pieces of information scattered through Diodorus of Sicily and Trogus Pompaeus (or his abridger Justin), as well as in Polybius, Livy and Appian. The 'history' one can build with these *membra disjecta* is necessarily fragmentary. The reducing effect of passing through classical texts seems specially to apply to the names of Carthaginian protagonists in this history: from a wealth of Punic names – but complicated and barbarian for a Greek or Latin tongue – only a tiny number have been preserved, simplified in their transcription. For Livy, everyone was called Hanno or Hannibal, Hamilcar or Mago.

FROM THE MAGONIDS TO OLIGARCHY: THE POLITICAL HISTORY OF CARTHAGE

From this historical wreckage, however, the first name to emerge, after Dido, belongs not to a Mago but to a Malchus. According to Justin (XVIII, 7), this person, a general (in Latin: *dux*), was vanquished in Sardinia after achieving successes in Africa and Sicily. As punishment for his failure in Sardinia, Malchus was sentenced to exile, in company with the remnants of his army. Unable to obtain a pardon, the exiles one day landed in Africa and besieged Carthage. However, Malchus' son Carthalon, a priest of Melqart, returning from Tyre, where he had been to deliver a tithe of the booty gained in Sicily, was urged by his father to join the rebels. Carthalon at first refused, so that he could go into the town to discharge his religious duties, then, having received the people's permission, rejoined his father. But the latter, not forgiving his son's first disobedience, accused him of being an insult to the wretchedness of the exiles and had him crucified, dressed in his priestly vestments, on a very tall cross erected opposite the town. Soon afterwards Malchus seized Carthage, summoned the People's Assembly and, confining his vengeance to those who had advised his exile, ordered the execution of ten senators. He himself was subsequently accused of tyranny and put to death. These events are supposed to have taken place in the middle of the sixth century.

As recounted by Justin alone – neither Herodotus nor Diodorus breathes a word of this strange story – the episode leaves one feeling uncomfortable. One thinks of Macbeth and his definition of life: 'a tale told by an idiot, full of sound and fury, signifying nothing'. In order to give it some acceptable interpretation, a 'decoding' of the account was recently proposed, throwing light on its mythical and religious background. First, it was pointed out that the name Malchus – in any case fairly badly treated in Justin's manuscript tradition – conceals a Latinized form of the root MLK (Phoenician *milk*), meaning 'the king'. So Malchus is not a historical person but 'the king', the king *par excellence*, and the crucifixion of his son Carthalon, tortured while wearing his priestly attire, is the sacrifice of the king or rather of the king's son. Certainly, the pyre on which Dido perished, on which the holocaust of thousands of young victims was practised for centuries, and on which in the city's final days Hasdrubal's wife cast herself, is missing here. But it is true that one reads stories in the Old Testament telling of the sacrifice of royal sons by hanging or crucifixion. The conclusion one is tempted to draw is that Trogus Pompaeus, abridged by Justin, did not use a 'historical' work for this account, but a treatise on Carthaginian human sacrifice (G. and C. Picard, 1970, pp. 54–5). Wishing to turn the 'religious sociology' text he was using back into political history, he was perhaps inspired by a certain amount of knowledge that he, like his contemporaries, possessed about the institutions of Carthage at the time of the Punic Wars. Hence the anachronisms: the mention of 'senators', the 'People's Assembly', whose political role is not reliably vouched for until several centuries later.

PUNIC 'ROYALTY'

This page of Justin, which exemplifies the difficulties of interpretation raised by classical texts referring to the earliest episodes in Carthage's history, is equally revealing about the problems relating to data on the institutions. The attempt above to travel back through this text to the Semitic substratum and religious background rests largely on the recognition in the name Malchus of the Phoenician root of the word for king, MLK. Justin merely says, on two occasions, that Malchus is *dux*, 'war leader', and that what caused his downfall was the accusation levelled against him that he was aspiring to 'royal power': *adfectati regni accusatus* (XVIII, 18). He paid with his life for that ambition and, adds Justin (XVIII, 19), his successor was the 'general' Mago (*Mago imperator*), thus the first of those known as the Magonids, 'who by his talents enhanced the power, territory and military glory of Carthage'.

It happened that classical authors gave the title 'kings' (Greek *basileis*, Latin *reges*), despite their collegial administration, to the supreme magistrates in charge in Carthage from at least the third century – the 'suffetes', who in fact bore a closer resemblance to the Roman 'consuls'. But in the text and for the era with which we are concerned, what clearly comes to the fore is the reality of a military command. Malchus, like his successor Mago, is a war leader, and it is as commanders of armies that we know Mago's descendants. One of his sons or grandsons, Hamilcar, bears the title of 'king' (*basileus*) in Herodotus' text (VII, 165) which informs us that in 480 he commanded the famous expedition to Sicily; but Herodotus adds (VII, 166) that he had become king of the Carthaginians 'by virtue of his valour', thus by selection and not birth. The concept of 'dynasty', often used about the Magonids, must therefore be relativized: 'The Carthaginian king is chosen for his personal qualities from a family who pass on to him a hereditary charisma' (G. C. Picard 1991, p. 388). In any case, Latin texts mentioning certain of the Magonids sometimes describe them as *imperator*, *dictator* and *dux* (Justin, XIX, 1, 3, 7, 8; 2, 5; Pliny, *NH*, V, 8 and VI, 200), all terms which imply the granting of plenary powers, but temporary and probably renewed: one of Mago's sons, Hasdrubal, was invested eleven times with the 'dictatorship'. Regarding the amount of authority vested in the elected occupant of this temporary 'royalty', one can only surmise. Diodorus (XIII, 43, 5 and XIV, 34, 5) says of the Magonids that they were 'kings by virtue of the laws', which presupposes a legal procedure and not an arbitrary seizing of power, but we know nothing more, as political bodies such as the People's Assembly or the Council of the Elders are not attested in that period. It is admitted, however, reflecting what is a known fact from very early times in Phoenician cities in the east, that a Council of Elders must have been in existence from the earliest times in Carthage (Sznycer, 1978, p. 577).

What is certain, at least, is that this 'quasi-royal' power remained in one family for four generations, during which generals and admirals won renown, for instance, like Hanno the Navigator in the third generation who, let it be said in passing, is referred to as 'king' (*basileus*) in the Heidelberg manuscript, which has preserved for us the Greek version of the famous *Periplus*. Carthage was at the time essentially a thalassocracy, whose families of shipowners had to agree to entrust to one of them prerogatives which were apparently not hereditary and which, as we have just seen, bore the risk of being frequently called into question. Naturally the imprecision, not to say the total silence, of our sources makes it hard to pinpoint the chronological end of this dynasty. A distinguished study made about thirty years ago identified Himilco as the last of the Magonids, and doubtless also the last 'king' to emerge from that thalassocracy through a certain consensus whose political instruments remain obscure (Maurin, 1962, pp. 5–43).

At the very beginning of the fourth century Himilco's campaigns in Sicily, marked by sacrilegious acts regarding Greek cults and by some spectacular profanations, notably at Agrigentum and Syracuse, ended in disaster. The Punic army was ravaged by epidemics and an enormous fire destroyed the fleet that was besieging Syracuse. As if struck by madness, Himilco fled to Africa after negotiating a shameful peace and deserting his Libyan and Iberian contingents. Returning to Carthage, he did public penance: clad in slaves' clothing, he went to all the temples in the city proclaiming the wrongs he had committed and then killed himself in his own home. According to L. Maurin, that suicide marked the end of the Magonids, whose family, henceforth accursed, was removed from power for good. It was then, in 396 – in the same year that a cult in honour of the Greek goddesses of Sicily, Demeter and Kore, was inaugurated in Carthage – that the aristocracy is supposed to have set up the tribunal of the One Hundred and Four to run political life. It is nevertheless still possible that a last Mago, in power around 370, may have extended the long reign of this family of 'general-kings'. He was responsible for halting a terrible revolt by the Libyans, who had laid siege to Carthage, and for resuming the initiative in Sicily after the disaster undergone by Himilco.

THE ARISTOCRATIC REPUBLIC

'In the fourth century, then, Carthage presents the image of itself that modern people are accustomed to evoke: that of an aristocratic republic, a sort of ancient Venice, secret and well ordered, where individuals are subject to the harsh laws of the austere and disciplined rich.' This sentence by G. C. Picard (1970, p. 123) suggests the essence of the new countenance presented by the Punic city at that time to its chief partner, the Greek world, which knew it well, if for no other reason than the fierce struggle going on in Sicily.

In fact, the fourth century in Carthage was one of sometimes violent transitions and changes. The 'republic' was not instituted overnight. After the Magonids, a new family took over the running of affairs. Its leader was Hanno the Great, whom Justin (XXI, 4, 1) refers to as *princeps Carthaginensium*, stressing the wealth and power of his house. It was he who, in 368, was appointed general-in-chief and given charge of operations against Dionysius I. The way in which Justin relates his downfall, while he was trying to make use of his fortune to usurp power, clearly shows that he could not be regarded as a 'king' in the manner of his predecessors, and also that he relied on support from brotherhoods, Aristotle's *syssitia*, the Semitic *mizrah*, kinds of societies or 'colleges' whose solidarity was expressed in concrete fashion by banquets. But – apparently a novelty in the public life of Carthage – Hanno had a political rival in the person of someone whom Justin calls Suniatus (perhaps a corruption of the Punic name Eschmouniaton) and who seems likely to have been the leader of the majority in the Council of the Elders: *potentissimus Poenorum*, as Justin says of him. The original form of royalty that the Carthaginians had known for two centuries appears well and truly dead. It died definitively on the cross where, in 308, the general Bomilcar paid for his attempt to seize power by a military *putsch* by taking advantage of the difficulties of the city besieged by Agathocles. But the political bodies which Aristotle knew and esteemed had already been established.

CARTHAGE'S 'CONSTITUTION'

In the view of the Greek philosopher, the Carthaginian institutions must have had an archaic flavour. That may explain why, aside from the analogies he perceived between them, he drew a parallel between the *politeia* of Carthage and that of Sparta or of Crete. It has been shown quite recently (Weil, 1961) that Aristotle's image of the Punic city was by no means inflexible and that, between Book II of the *Politics*, in which the eulogy of Carthage's political institutions is almost without reservation (although Aristotle points out the danger of a plurality of public offices) and Book V (chapters vii, 4 and xii, 12) in which mention is made of attempts to establish a tyranny, notably that of Hanno 'the Great', Aristotle was aware of the upheavals of the first half of the fourth century and brought his information on the subject of Carthage up to date. These subtle variations must be taken into account, but the essential remains the full marks awarded by the Greek philosopher to the Punic political system, and the picture he draws may be judged as reflecting the state of affairs that existed in the second half of the fourth century.

The 'constitution' of Carthage is considered to be one of the 'mixed constitutions', that is to say, those that were deemed to contain the best elements of each of the three great political systems that divided the ancient world among them: monarchic, aristocratic (or oligarchic) and democratic. From the monarchic system Carthage drew a strong executive power, in this particular case the 'kings' (*basileis*), or at least the very special kind of royalty that we have seen, whose power was balanced by that of a deliberative assembly, the Council of Elders (*gerousia*) and controlled by another chamber, a sort of tribunal, the One Hundred and Four, which seems to have been of recent creation and whose importance Aristotle underlines by designating it 'the Supreme Magistrature of the Hundred' (II, xi, 7). In these two bodies lay the simultaneously aristocratic and oligarchic aspect of the Punic system. Aristotle indeed emphasized a feature that seemed to him to be original and completely appropriate in this organization. Among the Carthaginians, he said, it is believed that in the election of magistrates account must be taken not only of merit but also of wealth, for a poverty-stricken citizen cannot be a good magistrate and have the necessary leisure time. So if election according to wealth is an oligarchic principle and choice according to merit an aristocratic principle, the system on which, among others, the constitutional rules of the Carthaginians repose presents a third combination (II, xi, 9–10). According to him, another significant feature of a clear tendency towards oligarchy is the fact that members were recruited by co-option for the 'pentarchies' (that is, bodies each composed of five magistrates, the existence of which we know only through Aristotle), who had sovereign power to make decisions about many important matters (II, xi, 7). As for the democratic aspect of the regime, it was marked by the existence of the People's Assembly (*demos*) and the importance of its role. This role of arbitration seems clearly defined:

> Together with the Elders, the kings have power to decide whether or not to present a matter to the people, when all are in agreement; if not, it is up to the people to decide. Regarding matters presented to the people, the latter are granted not only the right to listen to the decisions of the executive, but also the power to come to a decision of their own with full power; and

every citizen who so desires can put forward counter-proposals, something that does not exist in other constitutions (II, xi, 5–6).

It is understandable that such a subtle political system – when all is said and done – with weights and counterweights, should have aroused the Greek philosopher's admiration. From this exposition, if it really reflected the true situation, it is easier to understand the working difficulties and the number of crises in embryo that such a regime would contain.

Aristotle's text does not deal by name with a magistrature which appears, in an author such as Livy, to be the supreme one in Carthage at the time of the Punic Wars, especially in Hannibal's era, that of the suffetes. Here we are approaching one of the most delicate institutional questions, largely because of the ambiguity of the terms used by classical authors to convey Carthaginian political realities. Formed on the root ŠPṬ, the word *shophet* (more probably pronounced *shouphet* in Phoenico-Punic) is well attested in Punic inscriptions, but it is also to be found in Latin transcription (*suf[f]es*, plural *suf[f]etes*) in authors, and later in certain Latin inscriptions, the magistrature having survived in African cities of ancient Punic culture. On the other hand, hardly any Greek transcription is known: the word used by the Hellenes is the one meaning royalty, *basileus*, the very one employed by Aristotle in the page we have just seen on Carthage's constitution. Hence the problem, with modern scholars forming two schools of thought – those who, following Gsell (vol. II, 1921, p. 194), accept the argument that the terms *basileus, rex* and *sufes* are synonymous, and those who do not think that the suffetes elected for one year in the Carthage of Hannibal's time are comparable with the 'kings' of Carthage known in the sixth and fifth centuries, whom Aristotle identified with the Lacedaemonian *basileis* (e.g. G. and C. Picard, 1970, p. 141). Indeed it seems difficult to decide between this view and that of those (e.g. Sznycer, 1978, pp. 567–70) who consider that, even in the earliest times, Carthage never had 'kings', and that at any time the specifically Semitic reality of the suffetate is what must be understood to underlie the classical terms *basileus* and *rex*.

THE 'DEMOCRATIC EVOLUTION'

The word 'revolution' is to be avoided, with its implication of brutal changes and accelerated processes, even of precise dates, which are not in fact attested. It is still the questions raised by the institution of the suffetes that allow the problem to be posed. Starting from a certain epoch, the testimony of early authors and of inscriptions establishes that there were two suffetes, collegially appointed for one year and eponymous with that year. It is generally agreed that the appearance of the two annual suffetes occurs either about the end of the fourth century or during the third. It has often been thought that the Roman institution of two annual and eponymous consuls may have been copied, but Semitic experts point out that two suffetes conjointly exercising their authority were already known in Tyre in the fifth century (Sznycer, 1978, p. 571). Some have proposed linking the regular institution of the annual collegial suffetate in Carthage with a 'democratic revolution' supposed to have occurred in the Punic city at the outcome of the first Punic War, and the exact date of 237 BC has been put forward (G. and C. Picard, 1970, p. 307). It is no more than a hypothesis, chiefly inspired by a few lines of Polybius, which deserve to be quoted, since they give a good account, from the viewpoint of a Greek in the entourage of Scipio Aemilianus, of the development of political life in Carthage after Aristotle's study.

> Regarding the Carthaginian state, it seems to me that its institutions . . . were well thought out. There were kings; the council of the elders, of aristocratic nature, for its part had certain powers at its disposal and the people were sovereign in matters within their jurisdiction. Taken as a whole, the organization of power in Carthage resembled what it was in Rome or Sparta. But at the time when Hannibal's war commenced, the Carthaginian constitution had deteriorated and that of the Romans was superior. The evolution of every individual, every political society, every human undertaking is marked by a period of growth, a period of maturity, a period of decline . . . The Carthaginians had known power and blossoming some time before the Romans and had gone past their peak just at the time when Rome was in full vigour, at least in so far as its system of government is concerned. *In Carthage the voice of the people had become predominant in deliberations*, whereas in Rome the senate was at the full height of its powers. For the Carthaginians, it was the opinion of the greatest number that prevailed; for the Romans, that of the elite of its citizens. (VI, 51)

Polybius' text thus clearly stresses the preponderance of the People's Assembly, about the end of the third century, and he considered it the result of a warping or debasement of the balance of power extolled by Aristotle slightly over a century earlier. There are historical indications of that growing power of the popular assembly, even stronger some years later at the beginning of the second century, after the unhappy outcome for Carthage of the second Punic War. Livy (XXXIII, 46) tells how Hannibal, on taking charge as a suffete in 196, used the occasion of a disagreement he had with a magistrate whom the Latin historian describes as *quaestor* to settle scores with the powerful 'order of judges' (*ordo iudicum*). This *quaestor* (apparently a magistrate entrusted with financial duties), who belonged to the faction opposed to Hannibal and was almost certain of impunity since, on leaving office, he was bound to enter the order of judges, who were irremovable magistrates, ignored the suffete's summons. Hannibal had him brought by an attendant before the People's Assembly and took advantage of that Assembly's support to put through a law determining that in future the judges would be elected each year, and that no one could be a judge for two consecutive years.

If the facts recorded by Livy are correct, it would seem that the senate, or if preferred the Council of Elders (*gerousia*), was not consulted in what was nevertheless an important matter, and that the control exercised by the People's Assembly led directly to the adoption of demagogic attitudes by the top magistrates. In this particular context, however, Hannibal's personal situation must be taken into account; that he should have done everything in his power to keep the Elders at bay is not surprising. They included those he was then trying to force to make restitution of their ill-gotten gains, in order to lighten the taxes demanded from the ordinary citizens to pay the war indemnity imposed by Rome. They would not hesitate to get rid of him by handing him over to the Romans. Hannibal, as we shall see (below, p. 403), anticipated them by flight and exile.

Convened by the suffetes, at least from the end of the fourth century, the People's Assembly numbered among its responsibilities the election of generals, at least from the time of the first Punic War, until the middle of the third century (Polybius, I, 82, 12; Diodorus, XXV, 8). It is known that in 221 the choice of Hannibal to command the army of Spain was ratified by the popular assembly. One would like to know the composition of this assembly: male citizens, probably, but certain groups of workers may have been excluded. Another question to which there is little in the way of reply is under what conditions could the right of citizenship, and thus the right to take part in this People's Assembly, be acquired in Carthage? In exceptional circumstances, foreigners were able to obtain Punic citizenship. During the second Punic War two of Hannibal's officers, Greek by name and of Syracusan origin, but citizens of Carthage (their mother was Carthaginian) formed part of an embassy addressed to the tyrant of Syracuse, Hieronymus (Polybius, VII, 2, 4; Livy, XXIV, 6, 2). And Hannibal promised his soldiers, in the event of victory, *civitas ex virtute* as a reward.

Below the high magistrates, that is, below the suffetes and judges, other magistrates and functionaries were known in Carthage, sporadically and sometimes rather vaguely. The *quaestor*, subordinate to the suffete, with whom Hannibal was in dispute, as we have seen, was perhaps one of a body of what the inscriptions term the MHŠBM, literally 'accountants', who were doubtless, like the Roman *quaestors*, magistrates concerned with finance (Sznycer, 1978, p. 585). It is tempting to equate with the Roman *censor* – despite the apparent difference in rank, for the *censor* appointed every five years in Rome was a very important figure – a DR RKT, 'chief valuer', known not through a text from Carthage but through a Punic inscription from the isle of Gozo, near Malta (*Corpus Inscriptionum Semiticarum*, I, 132). Similarly, we can mention and suppose that they held responsibility in the Punic metropolis, magistrates known through neo-Punic texts from Leptis Magna, the MHZM, 'inspectors of markets', who may be likened to Roman aediles (Levi Della Vida, 1971, p. 457). While fulfilling their office, all these magistrates had need of what were formerly called 'clerks' in our own administrations: these are the 'scribes' or 'secretaries', *sopherim*, whose appellative, SPR, figures in several Carthaginian inscriptions. One particular problem is that posed by numerous mentions in the Punic epigraphy of Carthage of people bearing the title RB, *rab*, that is, 'chief', if the word is followed by a determiner (e.g. *rab sopherim*, 'chief of scribes'; see Bonnet, 1991, p. 154), or 'notable', 'dignitary' if the title is used on its own in a rather obscure fashion, which often occurs in Carthage.

THE 'EMPIRE OF THE SEA'

At the risk of anachronisms of which one must always beware, it is frequently tempting to make a comparison, as I did earlier, between the destinies of Carthage and Venice, so strongly do the similarities, *mutatis mutandis*, leap to meet the eye. In the sixteenth century the

Doges' Republic had also become a land power, exploiting a vast agricultural territory from Friuli to Lombardy. And, like Mago the Agronomist in Carthage in the third century BC, a Venetian patrician and great landowner, Alviso Cornaro, was the agricultural theorist of the era. The Republic was then at its apogee and approaching its decline, and Carthage was not far from its own end when it affirmed its African anchorage.

To the very last, however, as Venice would be later, Carthage was a city of merchants. Its power remained based above all on trade, on the control of commercial circuits and the resources provided by that control, by the levying of customs duties. It will soon be three-quarters of a century since the great historian of ancient Africa, Gsell, summed up in a few sentences the fundamental direction of the effort constantly maintained by Carthage:

> The republic had, then, a commercial policy which can be expressed like this: to open up markets for the Carthaginians, whether by force, by treaty or by founding colonies; to keep the exploitation of them reserved (for Carthaginians) in areas where it was possible to do away with any competition; where a monopoly could not be established, to regulate transactions by pacts stipulating mutual advantages; to ensure the freedom of the seas, and the continued existence of maritime cities and trading posts against pirates (vol. IV, 1924, p. 113).

This protectionism did not belong to Carthaginians alone in the ancient world, but it particularly formed the bulwark of their economic power. Does this mean that it was not accompanied by the conquest and preservation of markets by Carthage's production and circulation of competitive goods? We shall see that this was the case sometimes, chiefly in the area of that large semi-industrial production represented by pottery.

The chief instrument of this policy was Carthage's fleet or rather fleets: the warships and the trading vessels. To begin with the latter, somewhat paradoxically, there is little direct evidence for the Punic trading ships that criss-crossed the western Mediterranean for centuries.

COMMERCIAL SHIPPING

This is not so for their predecessors of the early Phoenician era, although there is still some hesitation about the specific nature of the ships that biblical texts call 'vessels of Tarsis': either ships specializing in commercial relations with a land called Tarsis, and there is some inclination, as we have seen, to favour identifying this 'land of Tarsis' with the Tartessus of the Greeks, the Andalusian Eldorado; or ships specializing in the transport of metals and their ores, this hypothesis resting on the existence of a root – *-rss* meaning 'to refine metal' – that is to be found in the very name of the town of Tarsus in Cilicia, which was the centre of a metalworking sector. Following this hypothesis, a 'vessel of Tarsis' seems to have been discovered at Cape Gelydonia on the south coast of Asia Minor (present-day Turkey) in a wreck with a cargo composed of ingots of copper and tin and tin ore, as well as numerous bronze tools, with a dating (provided by carbon 14 analysis) of around 1250–1150 BC (Rougé, 1975, p. 152).

Despite the major uncertainty over the interpretation of 'vessels of Tarsis' in biblical texts, various documents from the first millennium BC help to give a picture of the principal type of Phoenician

FIGURE 58 *Phoenician ships with two banks of oars, for war (with rams) or for transport (Nineveh, Sennacherib's palace, after A. Layard, 1849, pl. 71).*

trading ship that the Greeks called *gaulos*, giving it a name that is sometimes thought to reproduce a Semitic word. It was a ship with a rounded hull, two banks of oars, but with no masts and therefore no sails, like the one depicted on the bas-reliefs of Sennacherib's palace at Nineveh, dated to the eighth century, on which it is accompanies warships fitted with a ram, acting as a troop carrier (figure 58). The absence of sails should not be surprising: specialists (Casson, 1971, p. 65) think that the first merchant ships to plough the Mediterranean must have been propelled for the most part, if not entirely, by oars. And even though the use of sail tended to become more general, as the size of vessels increased to match the frequency and volume of trade, the oar-propelled trading ship certainly continued its career on a sea where periods of calm, frequent in the summer, bring sailing to a halt, and where moreover the system of summer winds impedes it in certain directions.

Another type of transport ship, apparently quite small, which seems to have enjoyed a prolonged vogue over the centuries in the Phoenician domain, also figures on Assyrian reliefs: a perfectly symmetrical ship from stem to stern, manoeuvred by oar but provided with a mast, with a figurehead in the form of a horse's head (figure 59). That is why the Greeks called this type of ship *hippos*, and Strabo (II, 3, 4) repeats an anecdote that says much about its career. Recalling an account he had found in Poseidonios of Apamaeus, he tells us that towards the end of the second century BC, in the reign of Ptolemy VII Evergetes, the navigator Eudoxus

FIGURE 59 *The Phoenician 'hippos' in a relief from Sargon's palace at Khorsabad (722–705 BC) (Louvre, Paris).*

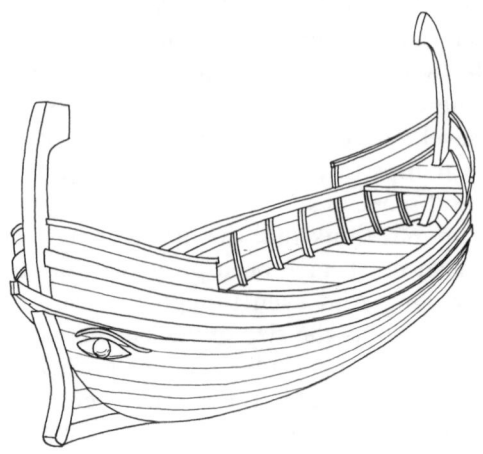

FIGURE 60　*A Punic boat, a descendant of the 'hippos' (after*
P. *Bartoloni in* Rivista di Studi Fenici, 7, 1979).

of Cyzicum made two voyages to the Indies, and on the second he
was driven by a monsoon on to the east coast of Africa, off the
coast of Cape Gardafui. There he found on the shore the wreck of
a ship with a horse's head prow. Having returned to Egypt, Eudoxus enquired about the origin of this figurehead from some captains
of trading vessels from the port of Alexandria, who told him that it
must have come from one of the little fishing boats from the port of
Gades (Cadiz) that went seeking their fortune along the Moroccan
coasts as far as the River Lixus. A certain scepticism is permissible
over the possibility of those fishing boats being able to travel as far
as the Somali coast (Desanges, 1978, pp. 164–5). But what remains
from this story is the longevity of these *hippoi*, attested since the
seventh century as transport ships, until their demotion, with
reduced dimensions, to the status of fishing boats (figure 60) for the
people of Gades, in an era later than the fall of Carthage.

The suggestion that at the beginning of the first millennium BC
Phoenician, then after the foundation of Carthage, Punic trading
vessels were omnipresent in the Mediterranean, to the point where
they could seem to be emblematic of maritime trade, is made in a
poem such as the *Odyssey* which, when it portrays a sea trader,
depicts it as a Phoenician boat. But the description that the swineherd Eumaeus gives of the 'black vessel' of the Phoenician traders
(XV, 415 ff.) must not delude us into seeing in the Homeric epithet
a distinctive feature of their ships. All those boats' hulls must have

FIGURE 61   *A trading ship from the* Tomb of the Ship, *Tarquinia (beginning of the fifth century* BC) *(Archaeological Museum, Tarquinia).*

appeared black, mainly because of the bitumen with which they were coated, as witness the picture of a two-masted ship on a fresco in the *Tomb of the Ship* at Tarquinia, dating from the end of the sixth century (figure 61). But as it happens this picture, which dates from the *belle époque* of the fruitful alliance between Carthage and the Etruscans, may very well have been modelled on a Punic transport vessel.

THE WAR FLEET

As Gsell said, the organization of Carthage's maritime trade relied on treaties, such as the one concluded in 509 with Rome, which essentially concerned the demarcation of their respective zones of influence. In order to ensure that agreements and treaties were respected, and to keep pirates at bay, a war fleet was required, and for a long time that was Carthage's armed force, far more than land troops, which made their appearance later. At the beginning of the third century BC the first conflict with Rome, known as the first Punic War, was chiefly a series of naval battles, the most important in Antiquity.

From the eighth century this war fleet was certainly deployed on many occasions, even if we have to wait until the end of the sixth century to find a historic reference to its engagement, in Herodotus

(I, 166), according to whom 60 Punic ships, combined with a like number of Etruscan ships, confronted 60 Phocaean vessels off the eastern shores of Corsica, at the battle of Alalia. The repetition of the figure might appear suspect if it did not recur in Diodorus of Sicily (XIII, 54, 1), who mentions Carthaginian squadrons composed of 60 and 120 vessels, brought to bear against the Greeks of Sicily at the very end of the fifth century. It is known that this figure of 60 represents a unit in the sexagesimal system, which is still present in our measures of degrees, minutes and seconds. As for the strength mentioned, it does not seem exaggerated. Still according to Diodorus (XI, 1, 5; 20, 2), Hamilcar took 200 ships on his Sicilian expedition of 480. As far as can be estimated, this figure is approaching the probable total of Carthage's naval force, not counting the troop-carriers and small units, the *myoparones*, seen in action chiefly during a phase of the siege of the city in 147. Let us recall that a famous text of Appian (*Libyca*, 96) puts a figure of 220, in the middle of the second century BC, on the number of berths provided in the war port for the shelter and repair of its vessels.

It is known that Rome, unlike Carthage, originally had nothing in the way of maritime power. Generally speaking, credence is given to the story related by Polybius (I, 20, 15) explaining how the Romans turned themselves into shipbuilders. At the start of the first Punic War, around 261 BC, they managed to lay hands on a Carthaginian quinquereme that had run aground as the result of a faulty manoeuvre in the Straits of Messina, and used it as a model for the building of their fleet. There is nothing improbable about the anecdote. Of course, people have not failed to point out that Rome could for at least half a century previously have found carpenters at Syracuse or Taranto capable of building a quinquereme, without any need for a Punic model (Brisson, 1973, p. 48). But at that time the Carthaginian quinquereme ruled the waves and it is understandable that the Romans should have wanted to reproduce the features that gave it superiority over the pentecontors of their Campanian, Italian or Sicilian allies. For us, the question is wherein did that superiority lie? From Polybius' text we know that the Punic vessel was decked: *kataphractos* (figure 62).

The total number of men carried on this type of ship, including the marine infantry who were on deck, is put at about 300. The essential crew members were on the rowing benches, but how were they arranged? The solutions put forward betray the confusion of

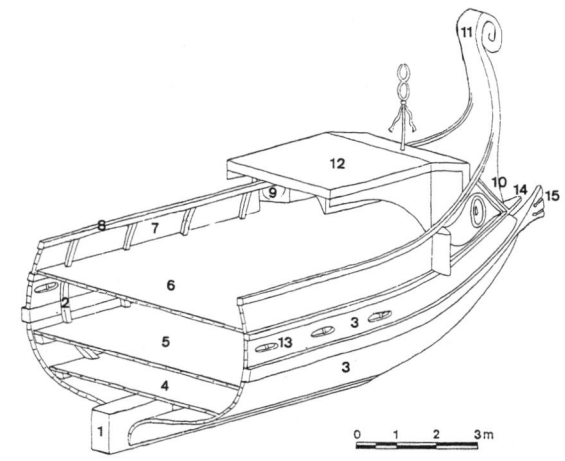

FIGURE 62 *An axonometric reconstruction of the forequarter of a Punic penter: 1 keel; 2 rib/frame; 3 planking; 4 bottom deck; 5 rowers' deck; 6 upper deck; 7 bulwarks; 8 gunwale; 9 hawse-hole; 10 stem; 11 akrostolion/scroll; 12 forecastle; 13 scuttle; 14 proembolon; 15 embolon/ram (after P. Bartoloni in* Rivista di Studi Fenici, 5, 1977*).*

the specialists. The very word 'quinquereme', if one understands it as one does 'trireme', suggests a ship with five superimposed rows of oarsmen: this would seem impossible, for the stability of such a vessel would be more than upset by its height above the waterline, to say nothing of the steep and extremely awkward angle the uppermost oars would create with the surface of the water. On the other hand, if it is envisaged (with Rougé, 1975, p. 113) that these ships were propelled by five rowers to each oar, that is ten to a pair, the oars would have to be disproportionately long and of necessity excessively wide. The solution arrived at is that of ships with two superimposed benches of oarsmen, one with two rowers per oar, the other with three (Casson, 1971, p. 105; Rougé, 1975, pp. 103–4).

Though it was the large warship in fleets of the Hellenistic epoch, together with the quadrireme, the quinquereme had not, however, supplanted the vessel which formed the basic unit of war fleets, starting from at least the end of the seventh century, and which is generally agreed to have been a Phoenician invention, even though the Greeks contributed to its improvement: the trireme. Numerous illustrated monuments have made its outline familiar; but they do not show the interior, so that the problem posed by the arrangement of the oarsmen in this case as well has provoked the questions of researchers and excited the imagination of naval architects. Under the Second Empire one of them built a trireme for Napoleon III: but once in the water on the Seine at Asnières, and although provided with good rowers, it needed a tug to make it move forward (Basch, 1987, pp. 39–40). And not too much faith should be put in the reconstructions of this or that famous film: the triremes in Ben Hur moved forward only on the screen.

A passage from Aristophanes (*The Frogs*, line 1074), clarified by scholiasts, clearly establishes that the classic trireme, a boat about 35 metres in length by 5.5 metres wide, carried oarsmen placed at three levels. Following an article published in 1941 by J. Morrison, it was commonly admitted that the trireme was technically an extrapolation of the ship with two rowing benches set one above the other, the bireme, to the gunwale of which was added a small platform that hung slightly outwards over the hull of the ship. It was in this additional openwork superstructure that the oarsmen of the top level, the 'thranites', took their place, and this arrangement explains why they alone are visible in side views of these vessels (figure 63), for the oars of the two lower tiers passed through scuttles made in the hull which hid the oarsmen from view.

It is known that naval warfare at that time, even if it could include attacking manoeuvres and thus hand-to-hand fighting by soldiers

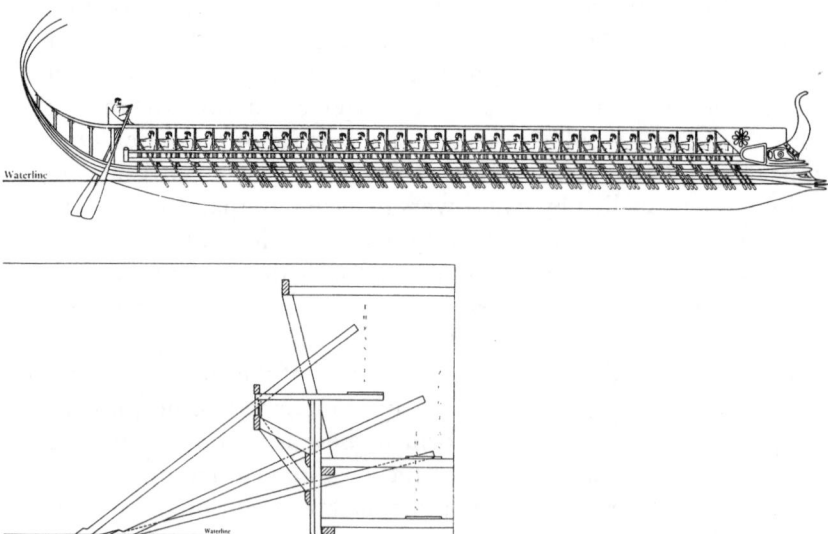

FIGURE 63 *Plan of a trireme of the fifth to fourth century* BC; *general side view and detail of the arrangement of the rowers' benches (after L. Casson).*

FIGURE 64   *The prow of a warship on a Punic coin from Spain (end of the third century). The ram in the form of a trident can be clearly seen and, above and slightly behind it, the* proembolon.

on board, consisted above all in ramming the enemy vessels. Propelled through the water by its crew, like a projectile, the trireme or quinquereme would impale itself in the side of the enemy ship, which took in water and foundered because of the breach thus opened. Coinage issued in Spain by Hasdrubal about 228–221, just

FIGURE 65   *A Phoenician warship with two tiers of oars, on a relief from Sennacherib's palace in Nineveh (705–681* BC) *(British Museum, London).*

like the stelae of the tophet of Carthage dating from about the same era, show that the Punic quinquereme, following the example of boats in other Hellenistic fleets, possessed a ram in the shape of a trident (Basch, 1987, pp. 396–7) (figure 64). Simpler rams with a single point were also used: these were the one-pointed rams that are to be seen on the reliefs at Nineveh (figure 65) and, in a later period, on a shipwreck raised in the last few years by Honor Frost off the coast of Sicily, not far from Marsala, a study of which has contributed much to our knowledge of the Punic battle fleet in the third century, the approximate date of the Marsala wreck. This ship belongs to the category of what would be called 'monoremes' in the

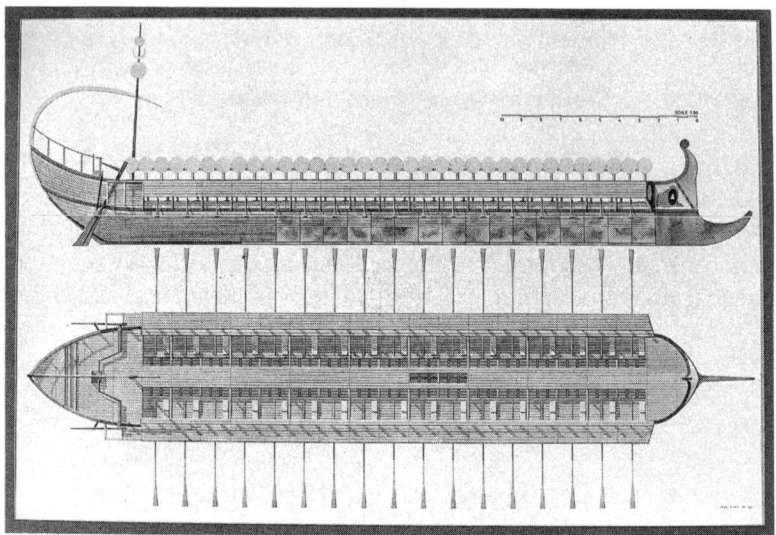

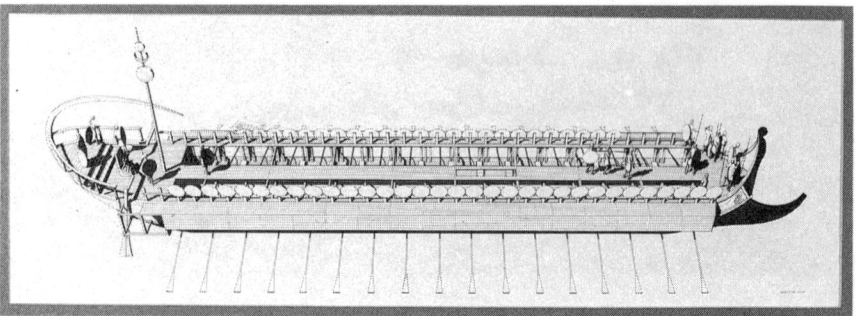

FIGURE 66 *The Punic warship from Marsala (Honor Frost).*

Byzantine era, boats with a single rowing bench, but in this case there would have been two rowers to an oar on each side. It was thus a 'galley-slave crew' of about seventy oarsmen who drove into the side of the enemy vessel a ram, in this case curved back like an elephant's tusk, of which only the point showed above the surface of the waves (figure 66).

THE MARSALA WRECK

The Marsala wreck has also allowed some valuable observations to be made on the construction techniques of Punic carpenters. We know that in our traditional type of shipyard, once the keel is laid, with the stem and stern-post in position, the carpenter first puts the skeleton in place, that is, the ribs, beams and beam-clamps, before building the planking of the sides, which are moulded to some extent around the external curved parts of the skeleton. In Antiquity the normal sequence of operations was different. Along the line formed by the keel, stem and stern-post, next came not the skeleton but the sides, within which, once they were built, the skeleton was put into position. The Carthaginian dockyards generally employed this technique, known as 'shell first': it was noticed very recently on the wreck of a Punic trading vessel of the third century BC, lying in several metres of water in the Binisafuller inlet, south of the island

FIGURE 67 *The stern and keel of the Marsala ship (Honor Frost).*

of Minorca (Guerrero, 1989a, pp. 120–1). But the study of the Marsala wreck lets us see that the builders resorted to a complex and very elaborate mixed technique. On the keel (figure 67) the carpenter first used tenons to fix the garboards forming the first layer of planks of the hull; next came the eleven lines of planking forming the sides below the waterline; only then were the floor timbers introduced into the hull that was taking shape, attached to the layers of planking by dowelling pins and nails. Then entire sections of the sides were laid to the level of the gunwale and lastly this wall of wood was made rigid by positioning half-couplings alternating with the floor timbers. Minute examination of the planks forming the sides has revealed traces of painted markings (alphabetic signs) which facilitated assembly and speeded up the work of the carpenters, who thus had veritable prefabricated components at their disposal (Frost, 1989, pp. 127–35). With such methods, it is easier to understand how in 147, at the height of the siege, Carthage's arsenals were able so speedily to build several dozen triremes and quinqueremes (Appian, *Libyca*, 121).

Lastly, the Marsala wreck presented the chance to observe an unprecedented detail about the conception of the hull which says a great deal for the technology of Punic naval architects. In Antiquity the planks were assembled 'freeboard', that is, placed alongside one another edge to edge. It seems that the other method, 'clinker building', where each higher plank overlaps the lower, was unknown in very early times in the Mediterranean area, where it was introduced in the Middle Ages, having come from Nordic countries. There is an obvious advantage in the latter form of assembly, in which the overlap acts as a deflector for trickles of water and spray. A section through the sides of the Marsala wreck (figure 68) has revealed that, starting from the twelfth line of planking, on a level with the waterline, the pinewood planks of the side are fashioned so as to present, even when constructed freeboard, a sort of protuberance next to the lower joint that functions just as efficiently as a deflector at high speeds. That would have been an element of comfort greatly appreciated by the marines who could thus keep dry while on deck.

We have seen how, at the beginning of the first Punic War, in the vicinity of the Straits of Messina, the Carthaginians were victims of what we now call industrial espionage and technological warfare. Rome placed an astonishing capacity for adaptation at the service of its dawning imperialism by equalling, then outstripping in the space of a few years, the descendants of the Phoenicians in a field

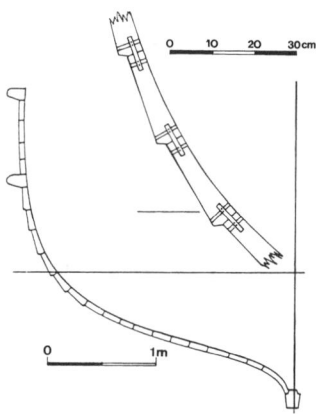

FIGURE 68   *The Punic ship from Marsala: a cross-section of the hull showing the method of construction (Honor Frost).*

in which they had been pioneers. It is also known – to cap this disgrace – that in order to compensate for their inferior manoeuvrability the Romans then had the idea of adapting for their warships a machine, 'the crow', which allowed the consul C. Duilius to transform naval war into hand-to-hand fighting and carry off the victory of Mylae in 260 BC. Polybius (I, 22, 4) described this 'crow' in a few evocative lines: in the bows of the vessel, a sort of tilted derrick which could become a gangway, placed horizontally, by means of a system of pulleys allowed a heavy iron weight ending in a point resembling a crow's beak to be dropped on the deck of the enemy ship, smashing the wood and securing one ship to the other. The marines then had only to rush across it on to the enemy vessel immobilized in this way.

The history of this 'crow' is characteristic of an era when Rome's emulation of the powers of the Hellenistic world, and above all its increasing ambition, caused more progress in the techniques of maritime war in the space of a few years than throughout the whole of Antiquity. 'Iam in mari . . . deleta Carthago,' concluded Florus (I, 18, 35), who knew what the outcome would be. The truth is that Carthage emerged the loser from this confrontation, which would lead it to transfer its hopes to the formation of a powerful land force. With Hannibal at its head, the gamble came within an ace of succeeding; but it was really the beginning of the end.

5

The Development of the City Between the Fifth Century and 146 BC

Much has been written about the 'fifth-century crisis' in Carthage, on the supposition that the defeat of Hamilcar, son of Mago, beaten by Gelon of Syracuse at Himera in Sicily in 480 BC, had marked the moment of the Punic city's first decline. Let us consider it. This opinion was based on a belief that there was a dearth of imported, mainly Attic pottery in the grave goods datable to this era, but it has not held good in the light of reviews of Carthaginian collections undertaken in recent years. In fact, many more black-glazed, undecorated Attic vases, and even those with red ornamentation, are to be found than had been believed (Morel, 1980). And recent excavations, in particular those of the French mission, have appreciably increased the amount of evidence of those imports (Morel, 1982 and 1983). The impression of impoverishment was also derived in part from the supposed rarity of fifth-century tombs, which are curiously absent from the cemeteries and very sparse in content when they *are* recognized. The truth is that people have not always been able to recognize the burials of that period, which only occasionally form homogeneous ensembles in Carthage, unlike what happened in other centuries (Lancel, 1990, pp. 23–5).

It had long been known that Carthage had compensated for the setback in Sicily by building up an African territory for itself and breaking free of the annual tribute paid to the Libyans since its founding. These two events, which were certainly more or less concomitant, are customarily dated to the second quarter of the fifth century, that is, a few years after the Himera defeat. With somewhat less precision, the excavations recently carried out in Carthage also place in this era a decisive stage in its urban development.

FIFTH- AND FOURTH-CENTURY CARTHAGE

The German mission's excavations along the shore, in the Avenue de la République, opposite the former Bey's palace, have in fact provided evidence for the establishment of a whole dwelling area, built on backfill from the archaic era and making an advance towards the sea of several dozen metres in comparison with the former shoreline (figure 69). Farther to the east, on the sea side, a very deep stratum is formed by sea sand absolutely devoid of any archaeological material. It is therefore certain that occupation of the terrain in the archaic era had halted well behind the line of the present shore even though, as we shall see, the sea level was at that time perceptibly lower than it is today.

In a very rich stratigraphic zone, continuously occupied from the fifth century BC until the Byzantine era, the German excavations could not be carried out over an 'open area' but were effected in the form of large and deep sondages, which do not allow complete units to be uncovered and necessitate extrapolations. With these

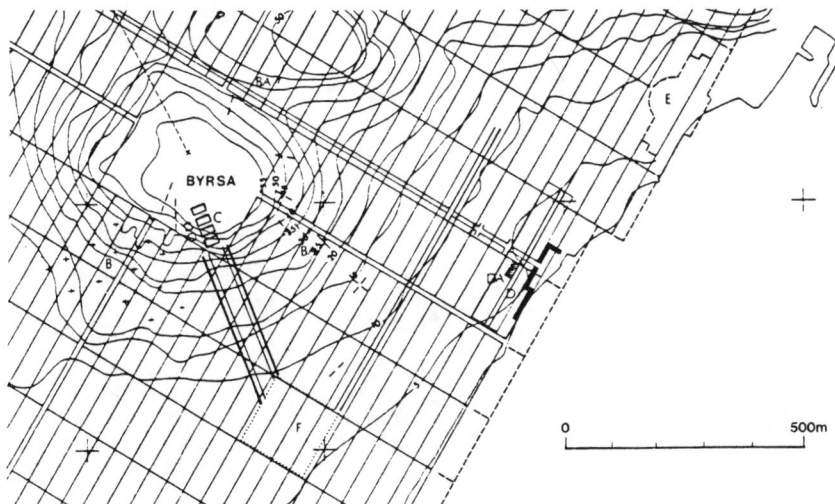

FIGURE 69 *The site of the sea-front area excavated by the German mission. DA debris from the archaic period; D sea wall and gate (plan made by the German Archaeological Mission on the basis of a Roman survey).*

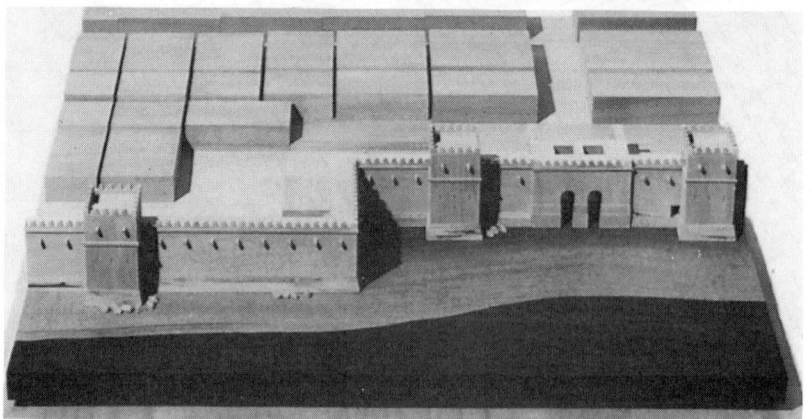

FIGURE 70   *The sea-front area from the fifth century to the beginning of the third. A is the street leading to the monumental sea gate, flanked by two towers. Note the space left clear between the blocks of houses and the city wall overlooking the sea (model by the German Archaeological Institute, Rome).*

reservations, the excavation and meticulous observation of the surroundings permit a distinction to be drawn between several stages of occupation in this zone. At an early date, in the fifth century, units of habitation of fairly modest size, with varied and atypical layouts, having no peristyle, were built in such a way as to leave between them and the wall bordering the shore, erected in the same period, an open space estimated at 60 cubits (or about 30 metres) (figure 70). The street serving this quarter, which lay at right angles to the shore and on a roughly east-west axis (and would more or less become the *decumanus I north* of Roman Carthage) led on to a monumental gate in the sea defence wall, flanked by towers. It goes without saying that only the foundation of this structure was brought to light, and the reconstruction of its elevation is even more hypothetical than that of its plan (figure 71). The use of a pump during the excavation allowed the discovery, at the base of the foundations, of the horizontal groove hollowed out by the incoming tide during the period prior to the positioning of the breakwater (Rakob, 1984, p. 8). Now, this mark is situated 50 centimetres below today's sea level. This means that at the foot of

FIGURE 71 *The large stone slabs of the base of the sea wall in the fifth century. The big blocks visible in the foreground served as breakwaters; in the background the axial drain of the Roman* decumanus I north *can be seen (German Archaeological Institute, Rome).*

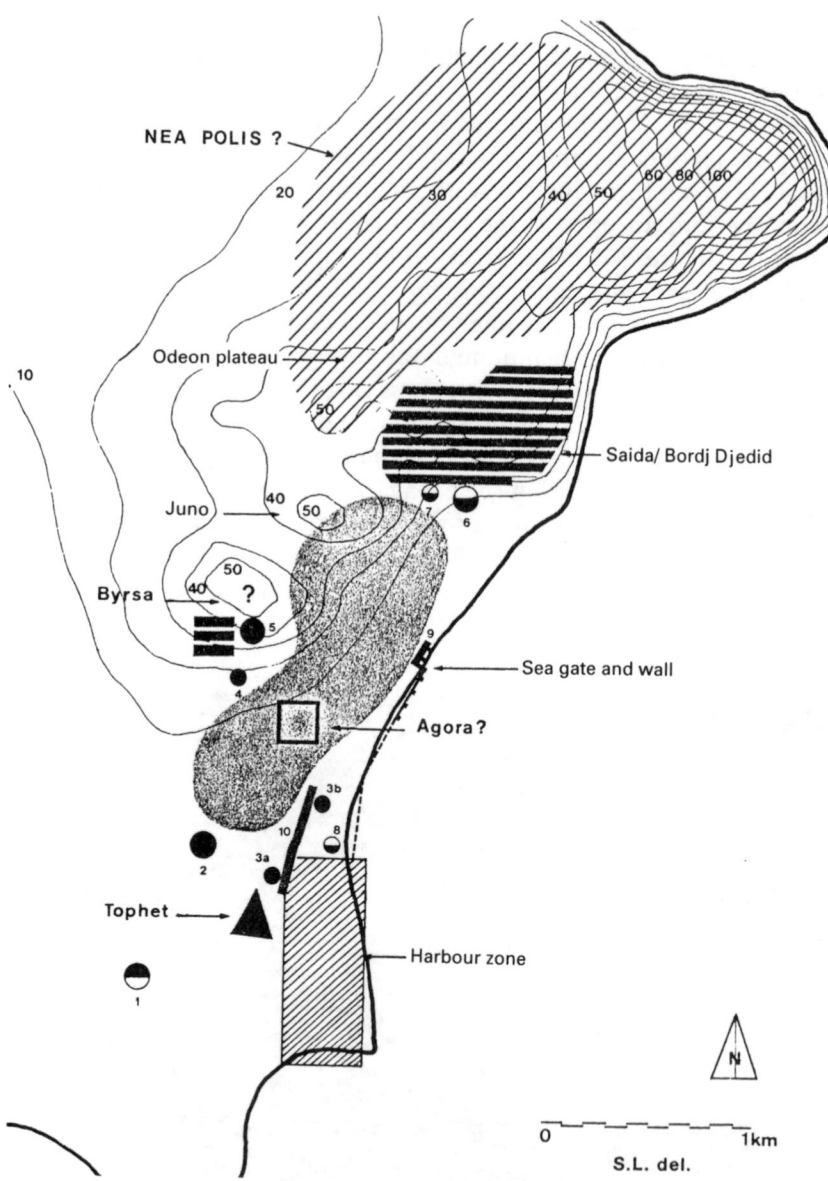

FIGURE 72 *The site of Carthage (end of the fifth to the beginning of the third century BC). In the middle and on the sea-front, in light grey, are dwelling areas, bounded to the north by the cemeteries of Saïda-Bordj-Djedid and to the west by that of the south-west slope of Byrsa. The peripheral industrial zones are shown by circles: all black for metal workshops, white over black for potters, black over white for a fuller's workshop (plan from S. Lancel, 1985, p. 737).*

the fifth-century wall there was then a flat, sandy shore, flattened by the waves and suitable for future extensions. Farther south at different points along the shore, findings of either coping blocks or even foundation or plinth blocks enabled Rakob to suggest that this sea wall followed a more or less continuous line at least as far as the environs of the circular lagoon, that is to say, what would later be Carthage's military port (figure 72). There indeed, very close to the present shore, the foundation of a wall structure was discovered that could well have belonged to one of the wall's towers or bastions (Rakob, 1987, p. 335).

Only extensive surface excavations, which are extremely difficult in view of the current built-up state of the area, would enable us to establish the boundaries of the fifth-century city. But observations made earlier, notably by C. Saumagne, lead one to think that the town of that period could not have extended southwards to any great degree. It even seems more than likely that, until the Hellenistic era, part of the ground situated lower than the present-day 5-metre contour mark, set back from the sea wall built in the fifth century, remained if not totally unused at least not included in the systematic overall town plan. Between the sea and the sector where, hypothetically, the agora might be sited, there seems to have been a marshy area that was extended farther southward by the lagoon zone, where the inner ports or 'cothons' would be established (Saumagne, 1931, p. 654; Lancel, 1990, p. 13). We will return later on to this situation when discussing the difficult problem of the port installations of Punic Carthage.

In various other sectors of the town, the spread of dwelling zones in the fifth and fourth centuries can be approximately mapped out from what recent sondages, coupled with earlier discoveries, have revealed about the siting of small industrial and artisanal zones, especially those involving activities incompatible with living areas, such as metal workshops. The information thus provided adds to that from the identification of cemeteries actively in use then, and helps us to mark out the space devoted to urbanization at that time (figure 72).

So we find that to the north and west, except perhaps towards the so-called hill of Juno, the primitive town gained only very little ground from the oldest cemeteries. This is especially the case in the north-east, below the heights of Bordj-Djedid, around the Roman site of the Antonine Baths, where former excavations had revealed fifth-century tombs and perhaps even fourth-century ones in some instances, scattered among still earlier burials (Lancel, 1990, pp. 24–5). These cemeteries nearest to the city of the living were themselves bordered on their earliest fringes – which were no longer in use for funerary purposes – by artisanal zones clearly marking the limits of dwelling areas: for example, to the north, potters' kilns discovered previously by Père Delattre and P. Gauckler on the lowest slopes of Dermech and Douimès (points 6 and 7 on figure 72). To the west, on the middle and lower southern slopes of the hill of Byrsa, the ground is densely filled, at the edge of a cemetery which is still in use, by vestiges of metal workshops, which the French mission in its recent excavations was able to date to between the end of the fifth and the end of the third centuries (points 4 and 5 on figure 72). Towards the south, the industrial sites recorded seem to imply that, for the period under consideration (up to the middle of the third century), the dwelling area could not have extended as far as the tophet, even in that part of the site above the 5-metre contour mark, set back from the lagoon shore zone.

In this sector several areas of metal workshops have been brought to light in the last few years, with a chronology sometimes extending down to the end of the third century. A notable example was a workshop unearthed by Tunisian archaeologists (point 2 on figure 72), while in the environs of the future trading port, as well as within the circular zone of the future war port, American and British teams similarly discovered indubitable traces of metal workshops (points 3a and 3b on figure 72). We may also recall that, previously, excavations for the foundations of the marine biology laboratory, situated between the two lagoons on the sea side, had enabled a potter's workshop to be recognized (point 8 on figure 72). And Cintas had subsequently quite justifiably used that potter's kiln as a basis for his argument refuting the contemporaneous existence of the two harbour basins (Cintas, 1976, p. 206). We shall see further on that the argument lost its validity, at least for the last half-century of independent Carthage.

The very latest developments in current excavations, not yet known at the time I write, will doubtless confirm the great effort of systematic town planning and the establishment of a coordinated street layout undertaken in this period in the central part of the town, chiefly between the hills of Juno and Byrsa and the shore. It was then, and very probably from the fifth century onwards, that Carthaginian town planners did their best to harmonize the orientations which subsequently governed the urban development of the city, in particular by adapting the almost regular and orthogonal

grid pattern of the low town to the fan-shaped districts of the south
and east slopes of the Byrsa hill. The agora, which should be
discovered one day, must have acted as a hub. To this vigorously
expanding central urban nucleus the sea defence wall discovered by
the German mission provided a frontage that was spectacular and
indeed dazzling, when one remembers that its huge blocks of
El-Haouaria sandstone, surmounted by cornices decorated with
mouldings, were clad with fine white stucco which sparkled in the
sunlight.

Confined on the south by an area of lagoons in the context of
which, to the east of the tophet, the harbour installations are still
hard to discern, the town of the Magonids saw the horizon of its
potential expansion to the north and north-east restricted by a belt
of cemeteries that had yielded hardly an inch of ground since the
archaic era. As far as they can be dated, the traces of habitation
(cisterns and floor levels) brought to light in the present park area
of the Antonine Baths, above the oldest burial levels, seem to be no
earlier than the third century (Lancel, 1990, pp. 28–9). And it will
be seen that in the Saïda sector (formerly known as Sainte-
Monique) the funeral zone which Père Delattre had called 'the
cemetery of the Rabs' was virtually never out of use right up to the
last days of the city. In that period, in order to spread north towards
the heights of Sidi-bou-Saïd, the city of the living had to straddle the
domain of the dead, by way of fairly narrow passages.

We are certainly steered in this direction by the sole text which we
can compare with archaeological data for this period. I am speaking
of the detailed account left to us by Diodorus of Sicily (XX, 44) of
the *coup d'état* stirred up in Carthage by a general named Bomilcar
(= Bodmelqart) when, appointed together with another military
chief to operate the city's defences at the time of Agathocles' expedition in 308, he attempted to seize power. Diodorus shows us
Bomilcar reviewing his troops in a locality called *Nea Polis* (the
'New Town'), 'situated a short distance from old Carthage'; then,
keeping 4500 soldiers with him (or 1500, according to a variation
in the manuscript tradition), he divided them into five columns,
which made their way towards the agora through the streets of the
old town. There, however, resistance was formed to the 'putschists'
and Bomilcar and his supporters were forced to fall back through
the 'narrow streets' towards the 'New Town', where they took
refuge in a 'high place'. Without being truly precise, the topographical data of the text are unequivocal: the *Nea Polis* locality,
the point of departure and retreat for Bomilcar and his men,

comprises heights in comparison with the agora, which we know from descriptions relating to a slightly later era (Appian, *Libyca*, 128) to have been situated in the small littoral plain a little to the north of the harbours. This locality also includes open spaces adequate for the assembly and manoeuvres of several thousand men: in short, a sort of suburb, with dwellings as yet scattered.

Stéphane Gsell had already stressed that these data fitted in well with 'the region lying to the north of the cemetery zone' (*HAAN*, vol. II, 1921, pp. 14–15) and, let it be said more precisely, with the present 'plateau of the Odeon' and the ground which, from there, rises towards Sidi-bou-Saïd (Lancel, 1984, pp. 39–40). Whatever the problems posed by the name *Nea Polis* used by Diodorus (let us remember that the name Carthage 'Qart Hadasht' already means 'New Town'), it has to be admitted that at the very latest around the end of the fourth century the urban development of the city, among others, materialized in the form of a 'Newtown-by-Carthage' beyond the line of the cemeteries, that is, beyond the arc formed by the heights of Byrsa and Juno and the lower slopes of the plateau of the Odeon and Bordj-Djedid. It was the beginning of the vast suburban quarter, a veritable town bordering on, and to some extent surrounding, the old one – but probably with a different occupation of the ground and a more loosely woven urban fabric – later known under the name of *Megara* (Sznycer, 1986, pp. 123–31).

CARTHAGE IN THE PUNIC WARS (MIDDLE OF THE THIRD
CENTURY TO 146 BC)

Punic epigraphy is very repetitive and of little documentary value outside the religious field since it is basically made up of ex-votos, in particular the votive inscriptions from the tophet, which are dry and stereotyped in form, with a few rare exceptions. One of these exceptions is represented by a text of several lines engraved on a slab of beautiful black limestone (figure 73), discovered about a quarter of a century ago in Carthage, in a layer of rubble above the ornamental floor tiling of a house of the late Roman era, bordering on the present-day Avenue de la République. This means that the text was not found *in situ*, but had been removed from the archaeological context to which it alludes, and therefore that as an aid in its interpretation no argument can be drawn from the spot in which it was discovered.

FIGURE 73   *The 'urbanistic inscription' from the Avenue de la République in Carthage. The text is incomplete on the left (Musée national de Carthage).*

The inscription, which is truncated on the left, has been the subject of various translations. I quote the one rendered by A. Dupont-Sommer:

> . . . this street was opened and constructed, leading to New Gate square, which is in the southern wall (?), by the people of Carthage, in the year of the suffetes Safat and Adonibaal, in the time of the magistrature (?) of Adonibaal, son of Esmounhilles (?) son of B (. . . and of . . . son of Bodmel)qart, son of Hanno and their colleagues. Those in charge of the work (were): 'Abdmelqart (son of . . . , son of . . . , in the capacity of foreman[?]); Bodmelqart, son of Baalhanno, son of Bodmelqart, as road engineer; Yehawwielon the brother (of Bodmelqart, as quarryman [?]). (And there worked on it all) the tradesmen, porters, packers (?) from the plain of the town, the weighers of small change (?) and (those) who have neither (silver [?] nor gold [?] and also those who do, the gold-smelters, the craftsmen who make vessels (?), and (those employed) in working the furnaces, and the makers of sandals (?), (all) together. And (if anyone effaces this inscription) our accountants will punish that man with a fine of one thousand (shekels of) silver, over and above (X) measures (?), (for the price of the inscription [?]). (1968, pp. 116–33)

The inscription had not been obliterated, but the large number of question marks with which the Semitic scholar peppered his interpretation shows that the text is by no means clear. At the very least one gathers that it commemorates the achievement of a major work of construction, and more precisely, it seems, the driving through of a street, unless, as has also been suggested, it concerns the opening of the city wall and building of a new town gate (Sznycer, 1978, p. 560). In any hypothesis the text confirms the distinction, implicit in the passage from Diodorus that we have just seen, between a 'low town' and a 'high town', in so far as it situates in the 'plain of the town' the artisans' corporations and guilds that have, somewhat unexpectedly, contributed to the operation. Apart from the continuing uncertainties about the nature of the work in question, the fact that the inscription was not found *in situ* greatly limits and even virtually forbids any speculation on its topographical context. Nevertheless, there remain its purpose, even if uncertain – new street or new gate – and its date. The text is dated by reference to the suffetes who are themselves unknown, and so can be placed only by palaeographic criteria, probably in the third century. Thus the sole epigraphic text on which one can call at least confirms the archaeological information, in that the latter underlines important activity in urban expansion and renovation during the last century of Punic Carthage.

All the reports of recent excavations published to date in fact tally in giving the impression of a very noticeable acceleration in the process of the city's development at the time of the Punic Wars, and of a prosperity which, paradoxically, seems to reach its apogee in the aftermath of the second war against Rome, although the outcome of that was ruinous for Carthage.

The phase plan that can now be proposed for this period illustrates these facts well, even though it must be added that the traces of habitation presented are not all strictly contemporaneous. We have here a picture, still only partial and incomplete, of the town at the beginning of the second century (figure 74). Let us add that the very frequent imprecision which occurs in the earlier publications is of little help in plotting old discoveries, which are located approximately, and even less in establishing their orientation, which the plan can only suggest very approximately. Both chance discoveries made during the period prior to the recent programmed excavations, and the location in the central zone of the investigations entrusted to various missions at the time of the international campaign sponsored by UNESCO, explain why the littoral plain, north of the harbours, has benefited especially from this enrichment of the archaeological landscape. It must be borne in mind that, in the international campaign to safeguard the site, the choice of the various working areas was largely determined by the threats posed

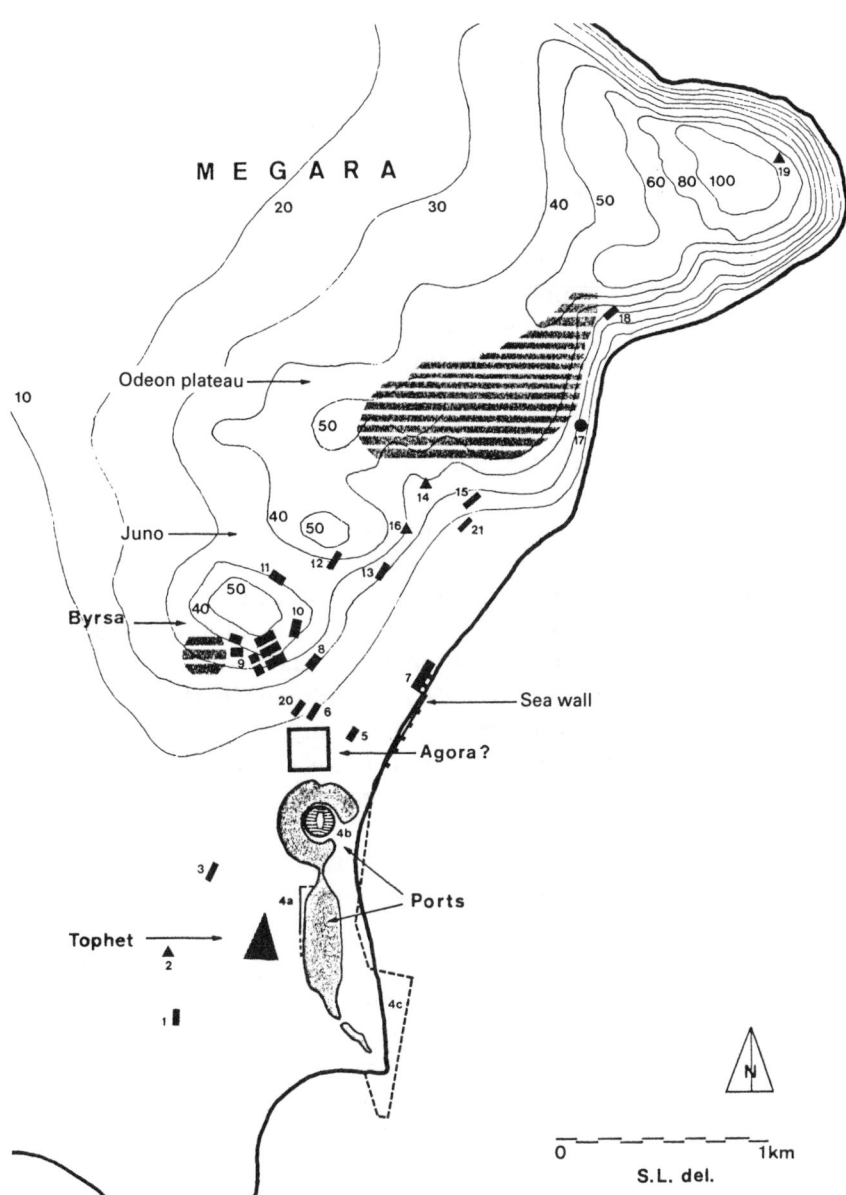

FIGURE 74   *The site of Carthage (beginning of the second century* BC*). The small black rectangles indicate the orientation of the traces of dwellings that they represent; they are replaced by a triangle when the orientation is unknown, for example, the 'Carton chapel', point 2 (plan from S. Lancel, 1985, p. 744).*

by galloping urbanization. But, as regards the urban expansion of late Punic Carthage, one may note the very southerly position, about 400 metres south-west of the tophet, nearly 300 metres south of the 'Carton chapel' (point 2 on figure 74), of the traces of late dwellings brought to light opposite the Kram stadium in rescue excavations. These traces (point 1 on figure 74) are not precisely dated, but their superposition over a fuller's (or dyer's) workshop and the overall features of the material associated with these structures allow them to be dated to between the second half of the third century and the beginning of the second. At the present stage of research, we have here the most southerly non-funerary structures that have so far been discovered (Lancel, 1984, p. 47).

THE LINES OF DEVELOPMENT

In the middle of the urban site or, to be more exact, on the hills known today as Byrsa and Juno, and between these hills and the sea, what characterizes the layout (or, if you will, the choices made for the establishment of a street network), in so far as the structures discovered allow their orientation to be mapped, is the contrast between an axis roughly parallel to the shore line in the lower parts of the site and a polygonal or radiating system of varying directions that take into account the constraints of the contours, on the slopes of the hills and particularly on the south, north and north-east sides of Byrsa.

In the lower town, at heights below the 20-metre contour, one may note the uniformity, except for minor variations of alignment, of an orientation for which the surest testimony has been supplied by late Punic dwellings unearthed under the Roman levels in the German mission's excavations bordering the shore (point 7 on figure 74). There the foundations of pre-Roman walls, as well as a section of the street serving the quarter, on a north-west/south-east axis, and emerging on to the sea defence wall, give certain evidence of an orientation used since at least the middle of the third century and probably, though in a less systematic and less precise way, since the first siting of the quarter in the course of the fifth century, as we saw earlier. This orientation, inclined at 30 degrees north-eastwards, was adopted and subsequently extended to the whole of the urban site by the Roman surveyors in charge of the Augustan survey. In fact, one can see in the German excavation, where there is no break in the archaeological continuity, that the axes of the walls in the imperial Roman era were superimposed on those of the Punic walls.

Different structures recently found in the same sector reproduce this orientation either almost exactly, in the low-lying areas (as is the case for a section of wall underlying palaeo-Christian levels along Avenue Bourguiba); or with a slight deviation, in the vicinity of the 20-metre contour, for example, a cistern brought to light during investigations near the track of the TGM, below what is today Rue Kennedy (point 8d on figure 75). But there, at the foot of the south-east side of Byrsa hill, and almost on the same axis as that of the future Roman Carthage's *decumanus maximus*, the Punic orientation tends to return to that prevailing on the plain. In contrast, the lack of precision of the publications and especially the absence of location maps do not allow one to be so positive when dealing with the traces found in old discoveries. This is so for elements of late Punic dwellings excavated in the 'Clariond plot' (point 5 on Figure 74), for structures uncovered by Cintas at the foot of the east slope of the hill of Juno, near Carthage station (point 13 of figure 74). The uncertainty that surrounds old observations does not allow us to affirm that a regular, perfectly uniform, town plan had governed the whole area of the urban site since the third century, even less since the fifth. What is true is that corrections in angles and amendments to orientations that have been recorded, from the fifth or fourth century onwards, in the modifications to the layout of a single building or group of buildings, show that the orientation revealed in the German excavations beside the sea was tending to become generalized all over the low-lying zone (Niemeyer, 1990, p. 51).

As for recent observations, among those that can be made, not without some risk if one goes by the orientation of cisterns of elongated design underlying the houses (if they are contemporary with the walls they are dug out on the same axis, but they may have been re-used in a later building), there is no shortage of examples which reveal a certain liberty taken with that favoured orientation. The axis of the house of the 'Clariond plot' just mentioned seems to show a divergence of about 15 degrees, and not far from there and slightly higher, Punic cisterns underlying buildings of the late Roman era, known as the 'House of the Greek Charioteers', excavated by the second American team, show a nearly comparable divergence (point 20 on figure 74). To the north of the small plain, in the ancient archaic funerary complex of Dermech now contained in the bounds of the archaeological park of the Antonine Baths, the orientations of cisterns belonging to late Punic houses found by Gauckler in his excavations of the plots of Ancona and Ben Attar appear very free and varied (point 21 on figure 74). Lastly, slightly north of the Ben Attar plot, Saumagne noted under the Roman levels of the 'House of the Peacock' a long, narrow cistern, absolutely characteristic of the latest Punic times, that shows an angle of more than 20 degrees compared with the Roman layout and whose axis thus marks a clear break with the orientations of the littoral plain (point 15 on figure 74) (Lancel, 1990, pp. 29–30).

What can be affirmed at the very least is that the orientation parallel to the line of the shore, which is 'natural' to some extent, had been preferred everywhere in the central zone of the Punic city except where the constraints of the area's relief affected it, where it could thus be established without the necessity for vast terracing or dealing with differences in levels by means of steps. The resumption of this orientation by Roman surveyors (but this time applied to the entire urban site, including the hills) does not necessarily mean that they had taken note of the regular layout, effected as they say in Latin *per strigas*, in the ensemble of the littoral plain. But the town planners of the Augustan age could not fail to be struck by the obvious advantages of that axis inclined at 30 degrees north-eastwards, even if they did not always find it carried out systematically. The systematic mentality was their own, since in order to make it work equally on the slopes of the hills they had no hesitation in undertaking a veritable remodelling of the upper parts of the site, as can be noted in particular on the hill of Byrsa.

THE HILL OF BYRSA

Indeed, on those slopes, such an effort at urban development had not been made by the Carthaginians, who were nevertheless thoroughly imbued with Hellenistic culture in an age when, in nearby Sicily, for example, we see that it was the rule to adopt regular and uniform overall layouts even when the natural relief of the area imposed large-scale remodelling and earthworks, as at Selinunte and Soluntum. On the hill of Byrsa (figure 75) the lesson we learn from the French mission's recent excavations, confirming and appreciably clarifying the information provided by old investigations, is that flexible solutions prevailed in the late Punic era (this sector was not, in fact, urbanized before the beginning of the second century), solutions that took account of the natural relief of slopes

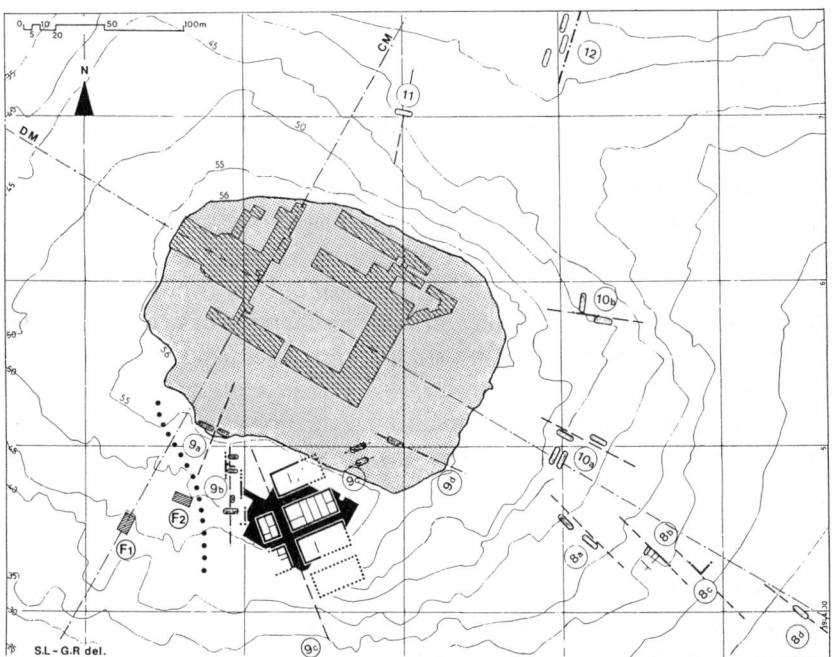

FIGURE 75 *Punic traces on the hill of Byrsa and its approaches. To the south-west (left) F1 and F2 are burial deposits (the 'common graves' excavated by Père Delattre). With the exception of the 'Hannibal quarter' (orientation 9c) excavated by the French mission, vestiges of habitation are confined to cisterns and sometimes a few sections of wall which indicate the orientations. The grey zone shows the plateau at the summit, razed in the Roman era, because of which its archaeological situation in Punic times remains unknown (plan by S. Lancel and G. Robine).*

and contours. The result was a polygonal system comprising small areas within which orthogonal lines were laid out, with alterations in the axis from place to place, the differences in angle between one little quarter and another being very nearly the same, in the region of some 20 degrees.

It must be added that exploration of these slopes is incomplete, so the real facts about the Punic levels on the west and north-west sides are still unknown, and it emerges from old investigations mid-slope on the south-west side (Père Delattre's excavations at the end of the last century) that part of this face continued to be used as a cemetery virtually until the destruction of the city in 146. I will return later, when recalling the end of Carthage, to the two great 'common graves' brought to light by Père Delattre a few dozen metres to the west of the south side dwelling area (F1 and F2 on figure 75), where skeletons of victims of the last days of the siege were discovered in their hundreds.

In contrast, to the east of the future line of the Roman *cardo maximus*, at about 180 degrees, as far as the pass separating the hill of Byrsa from that of Juno, the situation of the late Punic levels is now quite well known. Three distinct orientations, 9a, 9b and 9c, were pinpointed in the recent excavations of the French archaeological mission; they are provided not only by the axes of the cisterns but also by the walls and, especially in the case of 9c, as will be seen a little further on, by streets and several blocks of houses (figure 75). On the east slope, 8a is the axis of two cisterns unearthed by the Swedish mission about a dozen years ago, just below the Reine Didon hotel. Orientations 8b and 8c, identical, and thus like 8a inclined 45 degrees to the east, are provided on one hand by the extremely interesting late Punic structures (end of the third to the beginning of the second century) revealed during a rescue excavation in Rue Astarté (Chelbi, 1984, p. 213), and on the other, by a more limited examination dealing with a few sections of walls, carried out slightly lower down in the same sector, in Rue Kennedy. Continuing north-eastwards, on a slightly higher level, 10a and 10b are the two different axes, in the form of cisterns and wall structures, found by Saumagne during excavations made earlier in this sector (Lancel, 1979, pp. 35–8). Finally, in the pass separating the two hills, to the north-north-east, orientation 11 emerges from the uncovering of a late Punic cistern during recent (1980) work by the Swedish archaeological mission.

Of course, as I said earlier with reference to the littoral plain, it must be stressed that these varying orientations are not all attested in equally certain fashion. Although experience has shown that in these late Punic houses cisterns of elongated rectangular shape are generally dug out following an axis corresponding with one of the two axes of the walls, orientations relying only on the position of a cistern cannot be regarded as firmly established: this is the case with axes 9a, to the south-west, and opposite, 11, to the north-east. Similarly, an isolated cistern may seem aberrant; for example, the axis 9d, marked by only one of these water-tanks. But the material form of most of these axes is sufficiently firmly established to make the reality of a 'radiating pattern' beyond doubt. What about the time-scale? Was there, in the setting up of this polygonal system, some sort of planning strategy, some coherence that datings can reveal?

The answer to this question suffers from the very special archaeological situation of what we call, very probably with good reason, the hill of Byrsa. When, at the beginning of the emperor Augustus' reign, more than a century after the destruction of the Punic city, the decision was taken to found the *colonia Iulia concordia Karthago* on the old town site, a radical course of action was chosen for what was to become the monumental centre of the Roman colony, one that would obliterate any trace of the past still remaining: a gigantic levelling operation – a remodelling that is almost unimaginable for us without the help of our powerful earth-moving machines – resulted in the flattening of the entire summit of the hill, over an area of about three to four hectares (indicated in grey on figure 75). The ground thus removed, without doubt more than 100,000 cubic metres, was thrown and pushed down the slopes; this first deposit, which was itself superimposed on the layer of destruction *in situ*, was complemented by other contributions, as the stratigraphy of the embankments revealed at the time of the excavation. The whole accumulation was contained by strong retaining walls, some pieces of which still survive. 'Beulé's apses' in front of Carthage's museum are the best examples; their semicircular convex surfaces, acting like a barrier, effectively withstood the thrust and pressure of the soil. A rectangular platform thus replaced the summit of the original hill: in fact, a large, flat, orthogonal surface, orientated according to the axes retained for the street layout of the new town, was more suitable for the erection of large-scale monumental buildings such as a basilica, forum and temples.

The archaeological consequences of that operation are obvious. With a thickness of about four or five metres of historical material – at least in the centre of the razed zone – having been dispersed in this way, there is no chance of finding even a trace of what, by all accounts, constituted the strength of Byrsa's citadel: the enclosing wall that surrounded it and turned it into a kind of impregnable keep, the temple of Eschmoun, which was its very heart and soul, the famous stairway of sixty steps leading to it – everything has vanished, walls, floors, the foundations themselves. At the very most, on the fringes of the razed area, some cistern bases dating from the Hellenistic era may be retrieved.

Not the least of these irremediable consequences is that one is reduced to unverifiable hypotheses when trying to assess the role played by the hill in the site in every period, especially the archaic, and its relationship with the remainder of the urban site on the littoral plain. Keeping to what excavations have firmly established, it will be recalled that at the present stage of research, in the earliest times, there is only the evidence of burials on the hill slopes. We have seen that, from the beginning of the seventh century, all the south and south-west slope was occupied by a cemetery which was maintained on its western fringe up to the latest Punic times. On the east side, facing the sea, the tombs recorded by Saumagne in the deep levels of his excavations, around the 45-metre contour, are doubtful, but no non-funerary structure has ever been found for the archaic era. As far as it is known, the situation hardly changes from the fifth to the third century, except that on the south face metal workshops occupy part of the grounds of the earlier cemetery, before making way themselves for a dwelling quarter, from the beginning of the second century. And on the east face, the vestiges of habitation located (orientations 8 and 10 on figure 75) are not significantly earlier. It is therefore certain that in the late Punic era the slopes facing the sea were built up following radiating lines of orientation, but this polygonal system does not appear to have any earlier antecedent. The fact that at one point, an orientation pro-vided by a small section of archaic era wall at the foot of the south-east slope (8d on figure 75) is similar to later orientations is not sufficient justification for stating that the radiating orientations on the slopes are of archaic origin (Rakob, 1987, pp. 337–8). Nevertheless, even if they lie at the bottom of the east face, the discovery of these archaic traces, modest as they are, on a favoured axis which will later become more or less that of the Roman town's *decumanus maximus*, is very interesting. If it was con-firmed by other findings of traces of habitation belonging to the same period further up the same slope, on the same alignment, it could signify that in the earlier period there had been at least a connecting corridor between the oldest nucleus of the lower town, now well attested, and the summit of the hill, where – always hypothetically – the citadel must have been located in the city's earliest days (Lancel, 1990, pp. 20–1). Indeed, what could be done with a citadel cut off from the lower town by a continuous belt of cemeteries?

TOWN PLANNING AND ARCHITECTURE IN CARTHAGE IN THE LAST
YEARS OF THE PUNIC CITY

Setting out the problem just mentioned gives some idea of what still remains to be achieved in our archaeological knowledge of

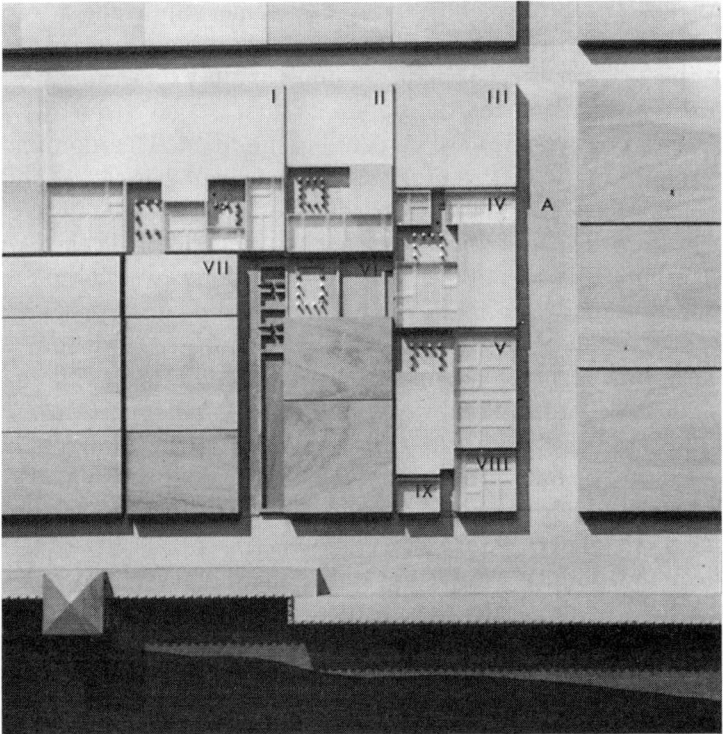

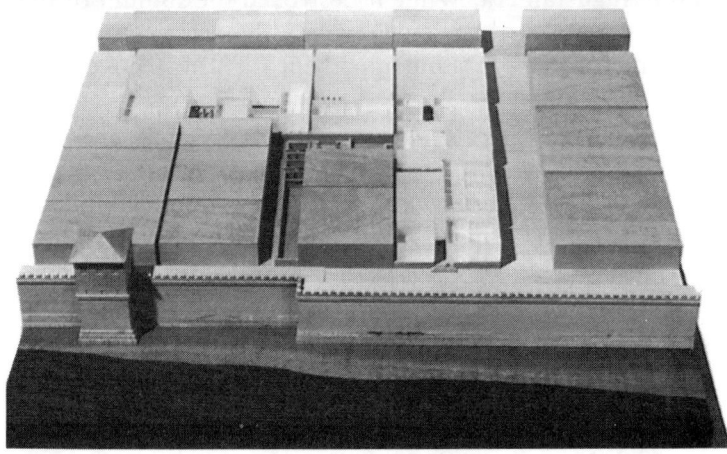

FIGURE 76   *The sea-front area in the first half of the second century. The monumental sea gate has disappeared. The demand for habitable space is shown by the encroachment of the wall on the shore and by the buildings on ground formerly open. Note the more ample layouts of the houses, ventilated by peristyles (model by the German Archaeological Institute, Rome).*

Carthage. There have, however, been some important advances, particularly with regard to the final half-century of the city.

By the sea, on the German mission's main excavation site, the features of the quarter dating in its first stages from the fifth century (above, p. 135) are perceptibly modified. The monumental gate opened in the fifth-century sea defence wall was closed and the new line of the wall shows a clear advance on to the shore (figure 76). The large open space which extended between the fifth-century wall and the built-up areas of the same period is done away with. On the ground thus made available, the former dwelling units grouped in a compact type of arrangement give way to much richer, better ventilated houses, centred around true peristyles (figures 77 and 78). The stucco decoration and variety of floors in *pavimenta Punica* of all kinds are in keeping with this enrichment of dwellings, starting from the end of the third century, which was doubtless matched by sociological developments in the quarter, about which we are unfortunately completely ignorant.

The archaeological conditions of the site, however, are such that, in the field of domestic architecture, what we now know best in detail is not the patrician or at least the opulent quarter, but the dwellings grouped in *insulae* on the south slope of the hill of Byrsa. I mentioned above the operation of flattening the summit carried out in the Augustan era. While it destroyed the summit of the hill, it was the salvation of the sides, where the vestiges surviving the destruction of 146 were submerged beneath a protective mantle of

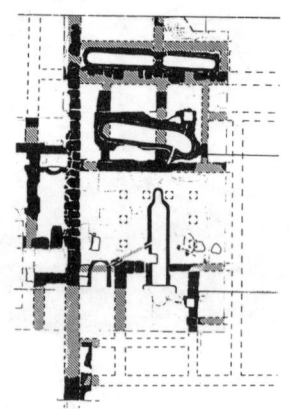

FIGURE 77   *The German archaeological mission's excavations: 'House IV', the state of the Punic structures after excavation (survey and drawing by G. Stanzl, German Archaeological Institute, Rome).*

FIGURE 78 *'House IV', its state at the beginning of the second century BC restored at floor levels (German Archaeological Institute, Rome).*

thick rubble. When excavated, the underlying Punic structures, where they are not destroyed by the substantial Roman foundations set deeply into the embankment, still show elevations sometimes reaching three metres (figure 79), enough to cause journalists in search of the sensational, some dozen years ago, to claim that the French mission then working on the site was proving that, despite old Cato's maledictions, the Romans had not succeeded in destroying Carthage. What *is* certain is that, after burning the town, they did not raze the remains to the ground or plough them in and sow them with salt, whatever a tenacious though fairly recent legend may say.

FIGURE 79 *The Punic quarter of Byrsa. The northern extremity of 'Block C' below foundations of the Roman era (S. Lancel).*

THE 'HANNIBAL QUARTER' ON THE SOUTH SLOPE OF BYRSA

Excavation has allowed us to retrace the brief but full history of the whole of the late Punic quarter on the south slope of Byrsa. In the fifties some of its elements, excavated on too small a scale by Père Ferron and his architect M. Pinard to be set in a coherent overall plan, had suffered from erroneous dating. At the time it was thought possible to infer a correspondence (which in any case was only an approximation) between the orientations of a few discovered walls and the axes of the centuriation in operation in the time of the Gracchi (122 BC), when a small colony, the *colonia Iunonia Karthago*, had been founded, very fleetingly, on the borders of the accursed site of Punic Carthage destroyed in 146. It seems, in fact, that traces of this Gracchan centuriation had been found on the edge of the town, in the neighbourhood of what would later be the Roman circus (Saumagne, 1928–9, pp. 648–64). It was but a step – too hastily taken – to date the similarly orientated traces on the south face of Byrsa to the era of the Gracchi. In fact, all of what had been unearthed in the fifties clearly belonged, not to the end of the second century BC, but to the late Punic period, its cultural stamp undeniably proclaimed not only by the typology of the walls and floors (*pavimenta Punica*) but also by all the material gathered at floor level, notably coins and pottery.

Recent excavations have allowed us to refine a chronology which even then was not doubtful. All the sondages carried out under the floors yielded that yellow-fabric and smooth black-glazed pottery, known to the specialists as *Campanian A*, which can hardly have reached Carthage before the first years of the second century or, at the earliest, before the very end of the third, when Hannibal returned with the ruins of his army from his famous Italian adventure. It is this pottery, so characteristic with its brilliant, most frequently bluish and metallic glaze, that is to be found in profusion on the floors of houses and in the refuse layer in the streets. Even more than Punic bronze coins, which are unfortunately of uncertain date, the stamps on Rhodian amphorae provide interesting chronological confirmation (figure 80). The fairly well-dated stamps on these amphorae, which brought wine to Carthage from the island of Rhodes, at the other end of the Mediterranean, assure us that the second century had already begun when those blocks of dwellings arose, inhabited only a mere fifty or so years between the last

FIGURE 80   *A stamp on an amphora from Rhodes bearing the name
(Nysios) of a trader, around 180 BC (S. Lancel).*

magistracy of Hannibal, his 'suffetate' of 196/195, and the city's
destruction in 146.

This mention of Hannibal's last magistracy before his enforced
departure into exile is not inspired only by the chronological coincidence. We have seen that these *insulae* on the south slope of
Byrsa have no antecedent, although it has such a good exposure and
is so well placed on the site, facing the harbours and the Lake of
Tunis. And this new quarter, in the first years of the second century,
appears to be the product of concerted town planning marked, as
will be seen from examination of the overall plan and the layout, by
an evident concern for standardization (figure 81). Often repetitive,
modest in size but executed with great care, the layout of the plots
seems to meet the need to house a homogeneous population, social
categories that one would be tempted to identify as public officials,
officers or priests.

These little islets or blocks are separated and served by streets
crossing at right angles, having the average width of urban roads of
the Hellenistic period, between five and seven metres. But, unlike
what may be seen in comparable Mediterranean cities, for instance
in Sicily, they were not paved streets, but simple footpaths of beaten
earth that required frequent restoration. As there was no axial
drain, liquid waste was collected in soakaways or wells, hollowed
out of the natural sand or clay ground underlying the street levels,
their walls lined with small stones. A drain, most often summarily
constructed from amphorae fitted into one another, linked the
soakaway with the small gutter in the axis of each entrance passage.
It was thus, so to speak, an individual mains drainage system: half

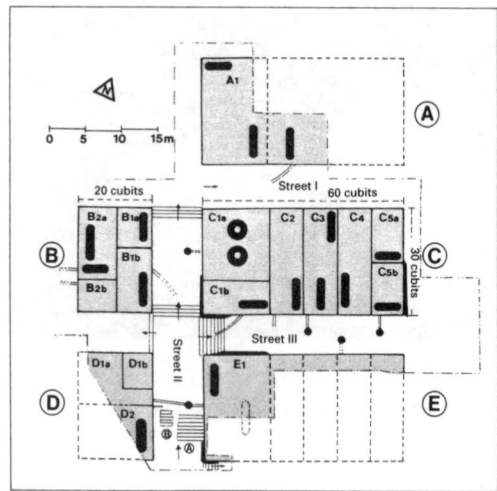

FIGURE 81   *The late Punic quarter on the south slope of Byrsa: plan of the streets and the distribution of living quarters. The black dots in the streets indicate the position of soakaways collecting liquid waste (S. Lancel).*

a dozen of these soakaways were discovered in streets II and III of this quarter. As for rainwater, it ran away down the hard-packed surface of the streets and collected most often in a central depression, a sort of gutter that formed naturally along the line of the street.

Although they lacked paving and constructed drains, these streets on the south side of Byrsa were enlivened here and there by flights of steps and stairways that were made necessary by a fairly sharp difference in levels, the average slope of the streets, notably street II, on a north-east/south-west axis, being of the order of one in seven. Because of this, the streets were used by pedestrians and were unsuitable for carts, but not necessarily for beasts of burden. At the crossroads of streets II and III the steps placed on the upward slope turned this crossing into a sort of tiny square, open towards the downhill slope, that is, towards the harbour area. Excavation has shown evidence that the little square so formed must have provided an animated centre of public life in the last decades of the Punic city; at the foot of the first step of the stairway in street II, a jeweller who used cornelian, obsidian and coral as his raw materials had set up his workshop-cum-stall, exposed to the elements (figure 82). But these streets were rubbish tips just as much as souks, and the steps

FIGURE 82   *The west corner of the crossroads of streets II and III. At this corner of the small central square in the quarter, excavation brought to light the jeweller's workshop. The two bottom steps indicated by the arrow had been covered over by the raising of the road level in 146 (S. Lancel).*

of this crossroads had not escaped the raising of the level resulting from public refuse dumping; the lowest step just mentioned was no longer visible in the few years preceding the destruction in 146. The situation brought to light, there too, by the excavations can without doubt be attributed to the difficulties experienced by the town during the three years of the siege's duration (149–146). It is thanks to them that we have acquired such a good knowledge of the types of crockery used by Carthaginian housewives over those years. In normal times Carthage must have had its municipal domestic garbage collectors, its *koprologoi*, just like several cities of the ancient world that we know about, Athens, for example.

The slope was steepest mainly downhill from the crossroads and so some adjustments were necessary. That was the function of a stairway of several steps between Block D and Block E, divided

FIGURE 83   *The two stairways A and B in street II, between blocks D (left) and E (right) (S. Lancel).*

down the middle by a depression hollowed out of the footpath and acting as a central drain. Looked at more closely, the two flights of steps are not alike on both sides. On the side of block E, on the right as one ascends, the first stairway (we will call it stairway A) comprises eight fairly low steps, very much worn (figure 83). On the left, on the side of block D, stairway B at first glance seems symmetrical: in fact it is very different, both in its steps, which are high and narrow, and for the amount of wear they show – much less than for stairway A. Let it be added that these steps are not in line and are not extensions of one another. Furthermore, A has eight steps, B only six. In fact, the two flights of steps are clearly distinct from each other: stairway B, the more recent – and in fact better preserved – is a modification of the road system in connection with the building of block D, at the time of a final phase of urbanization in this sector.

These remarks, confirmed by other observations (chiefly in relation to the modules of the blocks, mentioned below) allow us to propose a chronological framework for the laying out of the quarter as a whole. In an initial phase, the very first years of the second century, blocks A, C and E were constructed, and were separated

FIGURE 84 *The north-west corner of block C. The white arrow shows the level from which the last plastering of the reinforcing course was carried out (S. Lancel).*

and served by streets I, III and V. There followed several stages of modification without any new building. During these the blocks, notably C, acquired at the foot of their façades a substantial reinforcing cushion, probably with the function of protecting the houses against the undermining action of running water in these steeply sloping streets (figure 84). Similar structures were observed in the American excavations of a third-century Punic site at Morgantina in Sicily and, curiously enough, these same thickenings may still be seen today protecting the bases of house walls in Sidi-bou-Saïd. In the same period the street layout was organized, with flights of steps being put in position to compensate for the slopes, in particular the steps of stairway A, just mentioned. Lastly, in a fourth phase, the construction of blocks B and D demarcated what then became street II, at right angles to the direction of the streets already in existence, the broadest in the zone and also the most monumental, with stairways and steps punctuating it here and there. Probably that last stage, around the middle of the first half of the second century, also saw the erection of the structures lying on orientations 9a and 9b (figure 75, above), which ongoing excavations

reveal as far more ruined and disrupted and which mark the farthest westward thrust of that domestic habitat, a short distance
from what remained until the end of the city the domain of the
dead.

Perhaps just as much as the constraints of the site, connected with
the sloping terrain, this chronological view can throw light on the
differences disclosed by the overall plan between one and another
of these blocks. The differences are very noticeable in the case of the
two wholly preserved blocks, B and C. To start with the second, it
was found to measure 15.65 metres in width by 31 metres in length,
which expresses a ratio so close to 1:2 that it is reasonable to
suppose this ratio had been sought by the architect, the margin of
error in its execution being negligible. If one tries to convert these
metric measures by reference to a unit of measurement probably
used in that era, one is led to give consideration to the large cubit,
with a value of around 52 centimetres, frequently observed on
Punic sites in the west. Among the conversion calculations effected
on this basis, one catches the eye: assuming a cubit of 52.18
centimetres, the rectangle of block C becomes a surface area of 30
by 60 cubits, in other words, with a unit of measure commonly
attested in the Punic era, the ratio of 1:2 observed in the overall
plan would have been sought on a base of 60 (figure 81, above).
Such a result in unlikely to have been due to chance, for it is known
that in Semitic lands the sexagesimal system of numbering of Baby-
lonian origin (still preserved in measuring time, for seconds and
minutes, and angles, for degrees) was commonly employed for
measurements: for example, one reads in the Bible (I Kings, 6:2)
that King Solomon's temple was 60 cubits long, 30 cubits high and
20 cubits wide. And we shall see that those values appear again in
texts relating to the town's ramparts. Even in a Carthage profoundly Hellenized at the time, but in many respects faithful to its
original culture, it would not be surprising for the Punic architect
to resort to the sexagesimal system for his plans. Block B presents a
different overall dimension: for a depth of 30 cubits matching
the small side of block C with which it is aligned, it has a breadth
equal to 20 cubits. There are thus two distinct overall layouts
coexisting in this quarter. It seems well established by the excavations that the construction of the rectangular layouts in the ratio of
1:2 (blocks A, C and E) pre-dates that of the more 'compact'
layouts (blocks B and D), subsequently adopted for reasons perhaps
related to the natural constraints of the site, in other words the
slope of the terrain.

THE ARRANGEMENT OF THE DWELLING UNITS

Within the blocks, findings reveal if not a standard layout for the dwelling units, at least one for the plot, repeated several times in block C with slight variations, which gives every indication of having been chosen as the base unit. The clearest illustration of this

FIGURE 85   *House 4 of block C (S. Lancel).*

design is provided by dwelling unit C4 (i.e. house 4 of block C) (figure 85). This occupies a plot equal in depth to the width of the block (15.65 metres or 30 cubits) by a width equalling one-sixth of the length of the block (31 metres or 60 cubits), that is, 10 cubits (about 5.20 metres). The fairly modest total surface area (about 75 square metres) is diminished even more by the inevitable constraints of providing access and using space in a layout of an elongated rectangular form, in a ratio of 1:3. Note the access from street III, provided by a hallway 6 metres long by 0.90 metres wide, leading to the inner courtyard. Secured from the street by a door, this corridor is also shut off from the yard by wooden shuttering, so the privacy of the house is well protected. The flooring of the passage, like that of the courtyard, is of a type very frequently used: an agglomerate consisting of a grey concrete base containing numerous sherds of pottery, chiefly in greenish and yellowish shades, and ornamented with a fairly evenly distributed scattering of white marble fragments. Along the corridor, a depression fashioned in this paving serves as a gutter carrying the house's liquid waste to discharge outside into one of the soakaways located in the roadway.

The courtyard is both the source of light (we shall see that a question will arise as to how many storeys there may have been) and the centre of this tiny dwelling unit. It is likely that in an earlier period it was bordered by a portico along one side, in the earliest stage when the access corridor extended the entire length of the house and perhaps held one or two stairwells (figure 86). In its first state the house would have comprised only two rooms, of appropriate size (7 and 8 on figure 86b). The fitting of partitions on to the original floors and the superimposition of pavements establish that in a second period the already modest space of the 'portico' (5 on figure 86b) was divided into three, one of the tiny rooms thus obtained, in the extension of the access corridor, being a washroom, as the traces of a vertical water-supply pipe and the waste-water drain bear witness. Its floor tiling is a mosaic composed of small-cut terracotta squares, a speciality of this type of premises, also found elsewhere (7 on figure 86a). At the back, added partitions on floors of beaten earth formed a little group of windowless rooms, which might be storerooms (8 on figure 86a). On the other side, giving on to the courtyard, but also perhaps opening on to street III (the destruction caused by huge Roman foundations does not allow positive affirmation on this point), a room of slightly more generous dimensions could be what was called an *oecus*: a living-room,

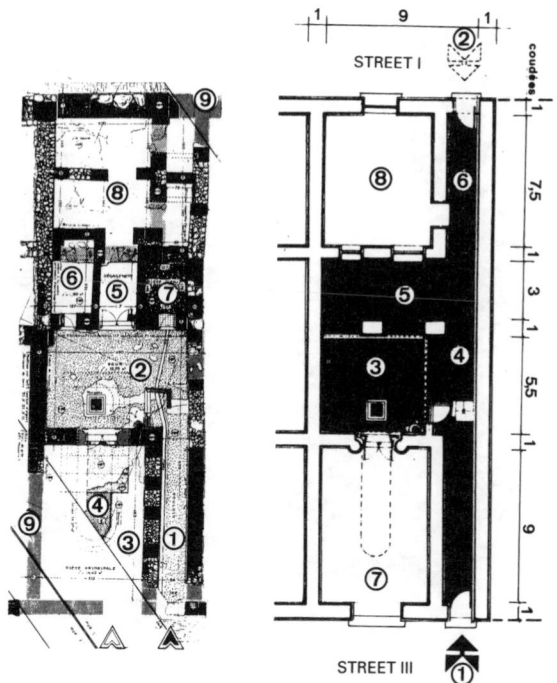

FIGURE 86   *The late Punic quarter on the south slope of Byrsa: house 4 of block C. On the left, its present state: 1 corridor; 2 courtyard; 3 oecus; 4 water tank; 5 passage; 6 room; 7 shower-room; 8 storerooms; 9 area destroyed by Roman foundations. On the right, its hypothetical restored state: 1 access from street III; 2 access from street I; 3 courtyard; 4 and 6 staircases(?); 5 portico; 7 oecus; 8 room overlooking street I (survey and drawing by G. Robine).*

perhaps. Identifying this as a grander room seems justified by the quality of the broad limestone threshold linking it to the courtyard through a double door, and by that of its floor surface, a mosaic of white marble tesserae preserved in fragments.

A certain number of dwelling units on the ground floor of these blocks seem to have been laid out according to this central courtyard plan, in particular houses 2 and 3 of the same block C, although the plan is less obvious because the middle part of the block was largely destroyed by Roman foundations, and the restoration of the internal layout is partly hypothetical. A clear example of this arrangement is in any case provided in the excavated part of block E, a good three-quarters of which still lies buried under the depths of the Roman backfill that reaches a height of about a dozen

FIGURE 87   *The mosaic-floored central courtyard of house E1. In the
centre, the circular opening of the* impluvium *of the underlying cistern
and the wide threshold of the* oecus *of house E1 (S. Lancel).*

metres in that spot. When excavation has been completed there, it
will yield a fine dwelling unit in its entirety, perhaps the finest and
best preserved in this quarter of Byrsa. We already know that it is
disposed around a central courtyard, itself bordered on three sides
by a portico whose sloping roof rested on pillars or columns of
stuccoed sandstone (figure 87). In the centre of the yard, which has
a pavement ornamented with a regular pattern of white marble
tesserae, is a small circular *impluvium* to collect rainwater destined
for the cistern. A broad threshold of white limestone, flanked by
engaged half-columns in white stucco, opens wide on to a reception
room (*oecus*) still for the most part covered by the backfill. Let me
add that in this house a washroom was also discovered, opening on
to the vestibule, of small dimensions but remarkably well
preserved, with its vertical water inflow in a stuccoed conduit,
niches built into the wall, and its typical mosaic of tiny terracotta
squares.

The evidence of this architectural arrangement has been stressed since, before the recent excavations, both at Byrsa and on the sea-shore site of the German mission, there was an unwillingness to admit that this type of construction with a peristyle (more spacious on the plain than on the hillside where there was no room to spread out) had been prevalent in Carthage as it had in the majority of cities in the Hellenistic world, in Delos for instance. But it must be added that in these dwelling blocks on Byrsa the plan with the central yard coexists with other styles of room plan. Thus, at one of the extremities of block C (west side), a large plot C1 is in fact subdivided into a small lodging, C1b, comprising four tiny rooms on either side of a small access passage leading on to street III, and a large cruciform whole, C1a, to which there was access from street II by an entrance hall flanked by two rooms, themselves overlooking street III; these have no communication with the rest of the house and may therefore be considered as shops (figures 88 and 89). This last example particularly highlights the limited habitability of these premises which, even apart from the two shops, were largely used as passages and corridors for people to move around. Is it possible that so many walls were erected (and such thick ones: the large cubit – about 52 centimetres – is the usual thickness of the

FIGURE 88   *The west extremity of block C. In the foreground, plot C1b (S. Lancel).*

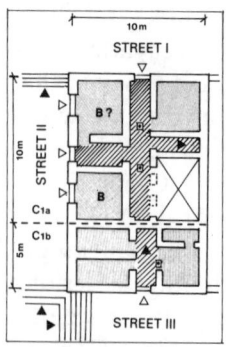

FIGURE 89   *Plan of plots C1a and C1b. The hatched areas show the arrangement of corridors. The arrows in the corridors indicate the probable locations of staircases giving access to the upper storeys; B = shops. Note the position of the openings for drawing water from the cisterns in the cross corridor in C1a and on the right of the entrance in C1b (drawing by G. Robine and S. Lancel).*

load-bearing walls) and so many cisterns hollowed out (and of such capacity: we shall return to this subject) for such limited possibilities of accommodation at ground-floor level? This raises the question of storeys.

The famous passage of Appian springs to mind (*Libyca*, 128) which describes the advance of Scipio Aemilianus' troops from the agora towards the acropolis in the final phase of the siege in spring 146. It shows them making their way along the three roads and taking by storm, one after the other, houses that were six storeys high. We will return later on, in the pages devoted to the end of the city, to the significance of this text relative to the identification of our quarter. Let us recall Appian's reference – his source was Polybius, an eyewitness in his role of companion to Scipio Aemilianus – to the existence at that time in Carthage of houses (let us understand residential blocks, exactly like ours today) several storeys high (the figure six must not be taken too literally). But mention of storeys implies staircases in order to reach them: nowhere have excavations been able to find any trace of them whatsoever, either in rough stone or masonry. The layouts discovered or restored, however, show evidence in several dwelling units of ends of corridors whose sole plausible function can only have been to house wooden staircases, which naturally were completely obliterated in the fire that followed the capture of the town. Oblique marks left on the coating of walls by such flights of wooden stairs were observed at Delos. Poorer preservation of the internal surfaces of walls in these houses in Carthage has prevented a similar observation. But the large number of flooring fragments recovered in excavations among the debris above the ground-floor pavements, therefore necessarily coming from higher levels, allows us to affirm the existence of upper storeys without being able to state their exact number.

The number and capacity of the water tanks, as has already been indicated in passing, also suggest that not so much care would have been taken to plan water supplies only for the very limited population of the ground floors. In the cleared area of the quarter, with a surface of less than half a hectare, sixteen large-capacity cisterns have been counted, some measuring about twenty cubic metres (figure 90). Two of them, in plot C1a, are shaped like bottles deeply fashioned in the clay of the subsoil. All the rest are uniformly constructed on the same model: an elongated rectangle finished off like a bathtub by two semicircles; with a width close to a metre and a length somewhere between three and five metres, the depth may reach and exceed four metres. A double layer of internal cladding

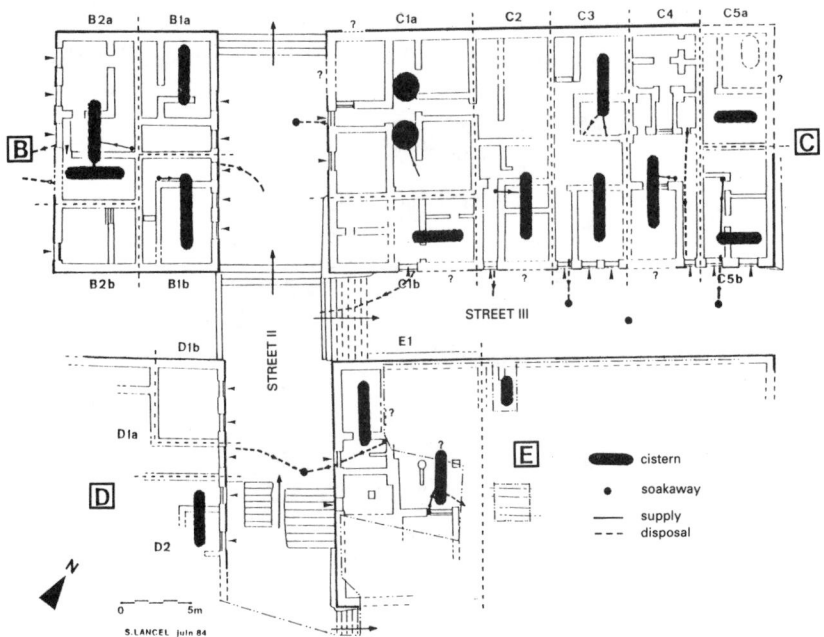

FIGURE 90 *Plan of the supply and disposal of water in the Punic quarter of Byrsa (plan by S. Lancel, based on a survey by G. Robine).*

FIGURE 91   *A cistern cover in block C, with 'pitched' slabs (S. Lancel).*

made of grey concrete mixed with ash ensured that they were effectively watertight. Two methods chiefly prevailed for their covering: most common is a pitched roof made of small slabs of

FIGURE 92   *A cistern without its cover in block B. Note the channel bringing water to the cistern (S. Lancel).*

sandstone (figure 91); a well attested variation consists of large slabs lying flat and juxtaposed (figure 85, above). More surprising and more rare – but observed twice – is a cover made of the bodies of amphorae fitted into one another and secured with concrete. In that period and context the body of the amphora takes on the guise of a multi-purpose material; we have seen, when speaking of the disposal of waste water, that they were used to make pipelines, but they are also to be found acting as sanitation drains. Rainwater reached these tanks, in at least one instance, by way of an *impluvium* made in the centre of a courtyard (figure 87), but most often it came from terraces by means of vertical pipes, then gently sloping channels that are sometimes partly preserved (figure 92). It is interesting to note the positions of the openings for drawing water: they are sometimes in the central yard, but more often in a corridor, and particularly in the masonry of a low wall giving on to the vestibule; such a location would facilitate communal use of the cisterns by all the inhabitants of the quarter.

This word 'quarter' would not be fully meaningful for us if it were deprived of its commercial resonance (figure 93). We saw earlier the

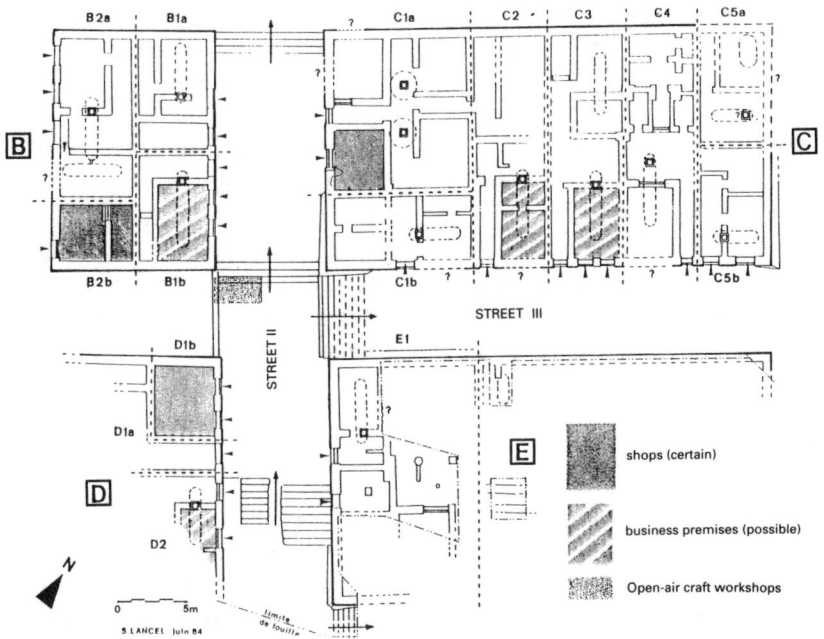

FIGURE 93 *Plan of commercial establishments in the Punic quarter of Byrsa (plan by S. Lancel, based on a survey by G. Robine).*

reasons for regarding as a souk the small square, together with its steps, formed by the crossroads of streets II and III. Being the undoubted centre of public life in the quarter does not diminish its commercial aspect. Two rooms opening on to street II and framing the entrance to lot C1a have already been identified as shops, but the destruction wrought in that spot by the Roman foundations prevented a specific designation of their use. Nevertheless, the excavations of one particular space in the vicinity of the crossroads clearly suggest its intended purpose. It is a fairly large room situated at the north corner of block D (lot D1b), without any communication with the rest of the block, but opening on to street II by way of two entrances of equal width. The function of these premises could be shown from the discovery on the floor of two parts of a rotary grain mill (the fixed part or *meta*, shaped like a cone, and the movable part or *catillus*, shaped like an hourglass), worked by muscle power by means of large wooden shafts engaged with the moving part. It was therefore a mill.

The dwelling area brought to light on the south side of the Byrsa hill thus illustrates the last decades of an urban development extending over more than six centuries, if we assume the traditional date of the Punic city's founding. Together with the large-scale construction of the military port, which will be examined below, these blocks of collective dwellings (shortly afterwards to be known in Latin as *insulae*) are the clearest possible testimony to a vitality which the harsh conditions of the treaty imposed by Rome in 201, after the defeat at Zama, had not really worn down. And one of the most important lessons learned, in the international campaign recently carried out under the aegis of UNESCO, is that Appian's hints about the rediscovered prosperity of Carthage on the eve of its downfall have been fully verified – a prosperity of which the famous fig brandished by Cato was but the most perishable emblem.

CARTHAGE'S HARBOURS

A good many cities in the ancient world lived by and for the sea – Tyre, Corinth, Massalia (Marseilles), Ampurias and others may be cited. Carthage belongs eminently to their number. Its prosperity and power, at least until the fourth century BC, long rested almost exclusively on its capacity for mastery of maritime communications, a fact which presupposes – and the reality is unchallengeable, as we saw earlier – the maintenance of a large trading fleet and naval forces, and therefore harbours to shelter them. Now, the question of Carthage's ports ranks precisely among the most irritating problems that can face the archaeologist or historian. Let me sum it up straight away in a few words: for the first five centuries of the city's history the location of the ports is unknown, as is *a fortiori* their configuration. For the period in which something appears to be known of their organization – and this knowledge is fairly new – this is very late, since recent work on the islet of the circular lagoon does not allow us to go further back in time than the beginning of the second century BC as regards the military port. In other words, our only tangible reality relates to a mere half-century of the city's history out of a total of over six centuries.

Of course it must at once be added that nothing on an ancient site can disguise itself as successfully as a port. In archaic times, and in many instances for a fairly long while afterwards, boats were hauled up on dry land amid port installations whose specific details are not easy to detect or which were profoundly disturbed at some later stage. Ports constructed in the Classical, then Hellenistic and Roman eras were frequently buried under alluvial deposits, concealed – to a point at which they totally disappeared – by changes in the shoreline and its environs, even in sites not occupied after the end of Antiquity. With even greater cause, they are still more difficult to discern in those places where urban development never ceased. It needed the Bourse excavations at Marseilles, some twenty years ago, to reveal at long last the topography of ancient Massilia's harbour basins, at least in part.

But, the objection will be raised, at Carthage everyone can see these ports; there they are, in the shape of two lagoons, a picture that has hardly changed from the Greek historian Appian's celebrated description, taken from a vanished writing of Polybius – the eyewitness of the siege of 148–146 – which must be presented to the reader:

The harbours were connected to each other, and access from the open sea was obtained through a channel 70 feet wide, that could be closed by iron chains. The first basin gave shelter to trading vessels and contained all kinds of ships' tackle. In the middle of the interior basin lay an islet and this, as well as the basin, was partitioned by large jetties. These jetties were occupied by berths made for 220 ships, and by stores connected with the berths, for fitting out triremes. Two Ionic columns rose in front of each berth, giving the periphery of the basin and the islet the appearance of a portico. On the islet stood a pavilion for the fleet commander, from which the trumpeter would give signals, the herald orders, and the fleet commander himself could keep an eye on everything . . . The docks were not fully visible at first approach, even for merchant ships entering, as they were enclosed by a double wall, and there were gates which allowed traders to pass from the first harbour into the town without traversing the docks (*Libyca*, 96).

At first sight, the text seems completely to match the landscape which, even these days, bare and perfectly legible, seems to have bridged time to illustrate it, minus the walls and ships (figure 94). All the more so since the reader of Appian's account of the final stages of the siege in spring 146 comes across details confirming that description, in the changing view of the advance of Scipio Aemilianus' troops. Having established a bridgehead (several months earlier) on the *choma* (we shall see that this was an artificial platform reclaimed from the sea of an outer harbour for which the big north-south jetty served as a pierhead at the entrance to the interior basins), they burned the docks that lay behind the east quay of the merchant harbour along the *choma* and, taking advantage of

FIGURE 94   *The two lagoons at the end of the nineteenth century (ND Photograph).*

this diversion, took by surprise not the merchant harbour but the military one, which was linked to it but separated from it by a double wall (Appian, *Libyca*, 127). Thence the Roman soldiers would gain a foothold on the nearby agora, where they would camp for one night before launching the final assault on Byrsa.

Here we find a good example, however, of the difficulty sometimes encountered at certain stages of research in the field, in matching textual and archaeological sources. Before the discovery of the tophet in 1921, the only known vestiges of the very earliest Carthage were the cemeteries, disposed in an arc from south-west to east, from the hill of Byrsa to the slopes of Bordj-Djedid, to the boundaries of the present park of the Antonine Baths. And the city corresponding with these cemeteries, which was assumed reasonably, though not yet known, to be sited between them and the shoreline, seemed far too distant (over a kilometre) from the lagoons for the latter to be easily envisaged as the ancient harbours, even with Appian as guide. At that time, one of the most careful (and most intuitive) observers on the site of Carthage, Dr Carton, had the idea of locating the port of archaic times in the concavity that he had already guessed lay at the site of the Antonine Baths, which we now know to have been built on land subsequently reclaimed from the sea (Carton, 1911, pp. 230–4). We shall see that this hypothesis still merits consideration. Sixty years later, another

FIGURE 95 *The circular lagoon (military port). The arrows indicate the site of the British excavations (1974–9) (Combier, Mâcon).*

expert on the site, P. Cintas, was still refusing to accept the identification of the lagoons with the ancient ports. In a statement published with some ado at the commencement of the first operations in the international campaign sponsored by UNESCO, he emphasized the reasons for his scepticism. He chiefly drew attention to the existence, revealed by former excavations in the immediate vicinity of the lagoons, of installations that had been active in certain periods of the Punic city (notably potters' kilns), and were apparently hardly in keeping with a harbour environment (Cintas, 1976, p. 206). The British (figure 95) and American excavations, which were then beginning on the islet of the circular lagoon and on the west border of the other one, would soon prove him both wrong and right.

THE CIRCULAR OR MILITARY HARBOUR

The investigations of the British archaeologists in fact resulted in the certain recognition, on the islet of the circular lagoon on one hand, of quays around its perimeter, their lowest foundations dating probably to the late Punic era (figure 96), and on the other, a series of graving docks and winter berthing, in the form of ramps, of which a few remains were identified with great difficulty. By projecting some of the measurements that are certain, the vestiges

FIGURE 96 *The remains of the quays of the circular island (British archaeological mission).*

discovered allow us to reconstruct the layout, with the greatest probability, of an ensemble of thirty docks, arranged symmetrically and slightly fan-shaped, on either side of an axis formed by a central open area of an elongated hexagonal shape, on the short south side of which would have stood a watch tower: in this may be recognized the fleet commander's building mentioned in Appian's work. On the packed earth floor of these ramps, inclined at about one in ten, wooden cross-pieces were arranged transversely and kept in place by a masonry construction, thus forming a slipway, of which carbonized remains were found. Excavation of one of these ramps obtained indications of their chronology, in the form of broken pieces of amphorae (an Italian Dressel 1a and an African Dressel 18) which would provide a *terminus post quem* of even later dating than the fragments of Campanian A pottery also found in this context (Hurst, 1979, pp. 27–8). If these potsherds do not date a later rebuilding of this ramp, but its original state, it means that the second century BC was already fairly well advanced when these port installations were put into service (figure 97).

Only thirty docks could have occupied the space on the islet, with lengths somewhere between thirty and fifty metres, which makes it possible for at least thirty ships to have been berthed there, depending on their size. To this number must be added berths arranged in

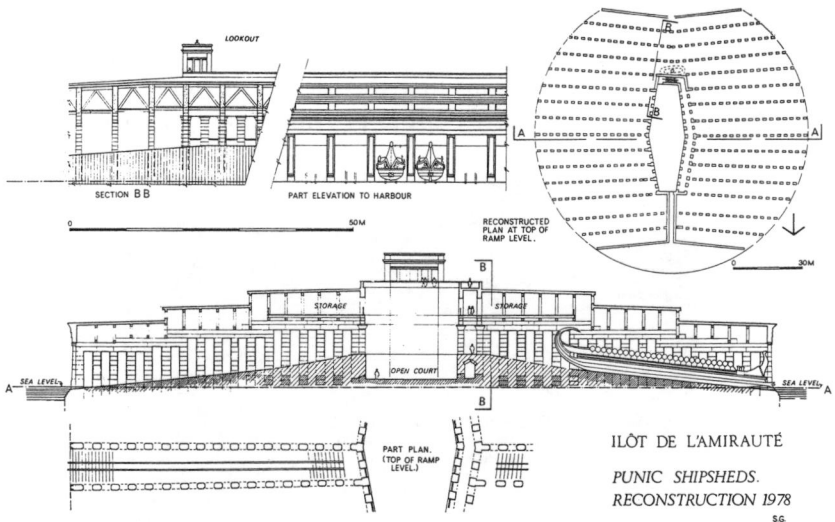

FIGURE 97 *A graphic reconstruction of the installations on the circular island, as it was at the beginning of the second century* BC *(British archaeological mission).*

a radiating pattern on the perimeter of the circular port. A limited excavation on the north bank allowed five of these ramps to be discovered, of a length of forty metres, and an extrapolation based on the average width of the ramps reveals that over the whole of the perimeter there must have been 135 or 140 docks. That is, together with those of the islet, a total of 165 or 170 docks, able to house somewhere between 170 and 180 vessels, or in other words, a fleet whose number of units approaches the figure of 220 indicated by Appian as representing the berthing capacity of the military port.

THE MERCHANT HARBOUR AND OUTER HARBOUR

Going by the same author, it is known that the two harbours were connected by a channel not brought to light by recent excavations, but there is no doubt as to its location. An American mission retrieved a portion of the merchant harbour's west quay (figure 98). The stratigraphy relating to the lowest courses of this quay justifies the dating of its original elements to the second half of the third century BC (Stager, 1978, pp. 27–30). An extension of the excavations along this quay northwards permitted the discovery of its north-west corner – not a right angle, as might have been expected, but a very wide angle, identified as a later reworking. This reworking, which turned an initial rectangular shape into one that is hexagonal, would be datable to the second century AD, and perhaps attributable to the alterations linked with the creation of the great grain-carrying fleet specially built to provide Rome with fresh food

FIGURE 98   *The western quay walls of the rectangular basin of the commercial harbour (American archaeological mission).*

supplies, the *Classis Commodiana*. What is certain is that, despite being silted up on successive occasions, the present-day lagoon still recalls that elongated hexagonal shape.

From this originally rectangular basin the outside was reached by way of an access channel, the existence of which in its last outline, Roman or Byzantine, was recently still marked by a small, oblique, egg-shaped lagoon now filled in (point 2 on figure 99). Did the course of this channel vary between the last Punic era and later times? Certainly very little, but the impossibility of examining this area, which is still a military zone as it was in the time of the protectorate, does not allow us to be absolutely precise about it. In fact, the problem is to discover what linked this passage with the outer harbour, still revealed in material form by the shallowly submerged structures of what has always been called 'the quadrilateral of Falbe' since the first prospection carried out at the beginning of the nineteenth century by the Danish scholar; we also need to

FIGURE 99 *Carthage's outer harbour: 1 commercial harbour; 2 access channel; 3 half-submerged platform of Falbe's quadrilateral. The arrow indicates the probable access to the interior harbour basins (after J. Baradez, 1959).*

know the nature, function and chronology of this quadrilateral. On the latter point, a Punic dating for these structures is suggested at least for their northern part by the fact that on this side the pier going more or less at right angles to the shoreline seems to meet it at the point where, as we shall see later, there is good reason to suppose that the sea defence wall of the second century BC lay. Falbe had already observed that the structures of the imperial Roman epoch, situated in front of the late Punic coastline and now submerged – these are the substructures of what Saumagne (1960, p. 157) had called the 'lungomare' of Roman Carthage – run up against this north mole of the quadrilateral and are therefore of a later date. Such dating to the Punic era must also be allowed for the other structures that go to make up the quadrilateral, which forms a coherent whole.

Recently this ensemble was the subject of careful examination by a British team. Although unable to obtain a stratigraphy, obviously nonexistent in a marine environment, a certain number of observations on construction materials and techniques, as well as traces of the removal of blocks in the central part of the quadrilateral, led the authors of this 'offshore survey' to suggest that the quadrilateral in its entirety had very probably been a platform (Yorke and Little, 1975, pp. 94–8). This could in fact be questioned. Thus Colonel Baradez, in whose view the two interior harbours formed the military port – which necessarily presupposed an external stretch of water for the trading port – wanted to regard the quadrilateral both as a harbour basin (though of very slight capacity, as people objected) and as the *choma*, restricted in his hypothesis to a very meagre surface area (Baradez, 1959, pp. 59–60). Certainly too meagre to leave enough space for the developments and fortifications (built by both sides at the time of the final stages of the siege of the town in 147–146) spoken of by Appian (*Libyca*, 123–124) in texts that find their full significance if the irregular trapezium of the quadrilateral is seen as a vast platform for manoeuvres, unloading and storage, with its southern tip acting as a pierhead and effectively affording wind protection to the access passage to the interior harbours (figure 100). As for the passage itself, its seaward extremity, protected by the pierhead, followed a curving line partly re-established by its south quay. A large segment of this quay was found in earlier days: this is the 'Mur Pistor' (point 6 on figure 100), and the flying buttresses of its concave side must have acted as supports to the end of the rampart, on the south side.

The picture thus obtained of Carthage's ports in their final phase may be considered satisfying as regards the coherence of the installa-

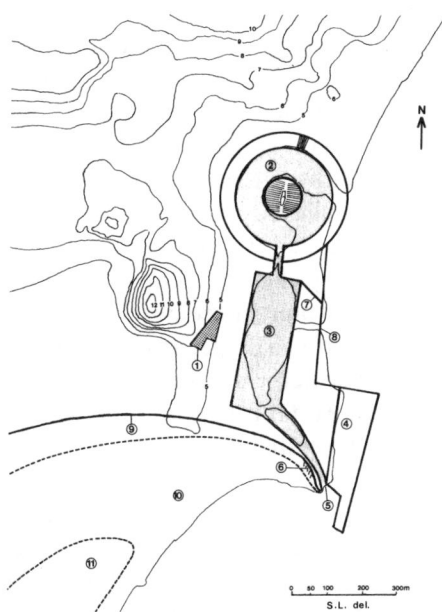

FIGURE 100   *Carthage's ports in the first half of the second century* BC:
1 the tophet; 2 the military harbour; 3 the commercial harbour;
4 'Falbe's quadrilateral', platform; 5 access passage; 6 'Mur Pistor';
7 wall separating the two harbour basins; 8 second-century sea defence
wall; 9 southern city wall; 10 access channel to the lake of Tunis;
*11 extremity of the littoral band (*taenia*) (S. Lancel).*

tions and their appropriateness to requirements. Of course, the
stretches of water in these basins are fairly cramped: with a depth
of about 2 metres, the circular port offers slightly more than 6
hectares of usable surface, and the rectangular port 7 hectares, with
a depth of about 2.5 metres. There has been no little astonishment
at the constraints imposed on warships – which must in any case
have been very confined in their navigable channel around the
island if, as Appian would have it, they were 220 in number – as
they would have had to make their way through the rectangular
port cluttered with trading vessels in order to reach the sea, going
along the one and only passage. And in fact, when Scipio Aemilianus blocked access to the ports by building a barrier from the *taenia*
(coastal spit of sand) in 147, the Carthaginians had no other
recourse but to open a breach in the sea wall on a level with the
circular harbour in order to break the blockade. But that entirely
exceptional circumstance must not be generalized: in normal times,

the docks in the military port must have chiefly served the purpose of shipbuilding yards, for repair and refit operations that would not have simultaneously affected the entire squadron. All or nearly all of the warships would be there together only in the over-wintering period. As regards merchant ships, one forgets that Punic Carthage, like Roman Carthage subsequently, had other harbours at its disposal that would have relieved the strain on the principal harbour, the rectangular port. We shall return to this later.

The main difficulty, very clearly, is chronological. One of the very harsh conditions set by Rome in the peace imposed after the defeat of Zama, in 202, was that Carthage, after being forced to hand over all its war vessels and watch them being burned at sea, must limit its fleet to ten triremes. And it is known that the Roman Senate, still mistrustful, quite regularly dispatched commissioners charged with the task of verifying that the Carthaginians were fulfilling their commitments (below, p. 410). It is hard to imagine that Carthage could have deceived such close surveillance by launching clandestinely into vast harbour works which could scarcely pass unnoticed. On their own, the fashioning of the artificial island and the installation of its monumental setting, as well as that of the circular port's surrounds, assuredly figure among the great achievements of the time in the Mediterranean world. It is true that the dating maintained by the British archaeologists on the basis of pottery collected would tend to place these works in the years shortly preceding the fall of Carthage, in a period when recent excavations show us to what extent the city had recovered its prosperity and how it could have fooled a Roman vigilance that had perhaps relaxed, thus presenting Rome with the *fait accompli* of its naval rearmament. In the middle of the second century there would therefore have been something better than Cato's famous fig to rouse the Roman Senators. It remains to say that this dating, arrived at thanks to a few fragments of amphorae from a stratum which may have been modified, is still shaky, and some uncertainty still hangs over the chronology.

CARTHAGE'S HARBOURS PRIOR TO THE HELLENISTIC PERIOD

Alas! Uncertainty increases as one goes back in time. The Americans thought they could date the most ancient foundations of the west quay of the merchant harbour to the middle or end of the third century, while Henry Hurst, taking into account the coherence he

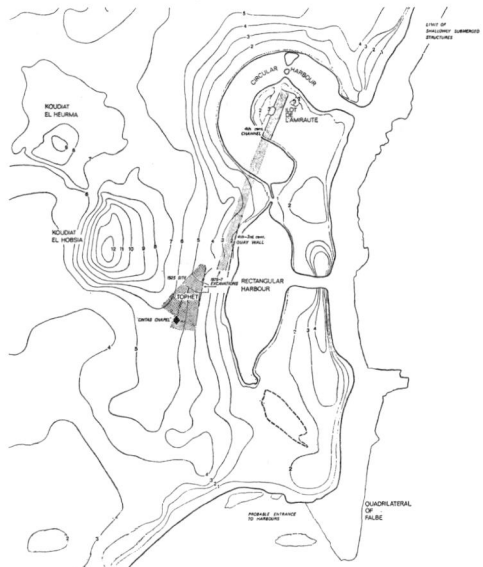

FIGURE 101   *The fourth-century channel (British archaeological mission).*

sees in the fashioning of the two basins, tends to believe them contemporary, thus dating them both to the first half of the second century. But beyond that?

On both sides, in their excavations both Americans and British recognized the course of an almost rectilinear channel that may be followed by extrapolation over a distance of about 400 metres (figure 101). A natural fold in the ground could have provided its origin, but it has been observed that the banks of this channel were built and levelled by the hand of man. Its width was between 15 and 20 metres, and its depth about 2 metres. Its definitive silting-up is dated by the pottery finds from the middle, or at the latest the second half, of the fourth century, whereas no precise date can be put forward for when it was dug out or adapted (Hurst and Stager, 1978, pp. 338–9).

What can its function have been? The sediments and remains of molluscs collected from the mud that filled it in suggest a stagnant marine environment, saturated with hydrogen sulphide (Hurst and Stager, 1978, p. 339). A connection with the Lake of Tunis is thus more probable than with the open sea. It is seen (figure 101) to be orientated along a south-south-west/north-north-east axis, perceptibly parallel with the line of the present-day shore. It may also be seen that it is situated slightly outside the area of the future rectangular harbour, running alongside the eastern edge of the tophet, which must have existed before its construction, and extended north-eastwards (its terminal point is not certain) crossing the zone subsequently occupied by the island of the circular port (a fact which, let it be said in passing, undeniably establishes the purely artificial nature of this island). Two different hypotheses have been put forward regarding the intention of this channel; one would make it a drain put in place to dry out and clean up a marshy area. But its dimensions lead one to prefer the other hypothesis, which sees it as a navigable channel, the more so since Lawrence Stager, in one of his reports, recorded finding at the bottom of this channel, to the right of the tophet, a block of sandstone from El-Haouaria, possibly intended for the sanctuary, and found placed on a piece of wood (Stager, 1979, p. 31). One is thus led to relate this channel to an organization of the harbour prior to the second half of the fourth century (the time of its final silting-up), which unfortunately remains unknown.

Bearing in mind the various data, it is possible to suggest a reconstruction of a certainly hypothetical but not unlikely landscape (figure 102). Recent work has drawn attention to the nature and formation of Carthage's lagoon coast. It is observed that the *taenia*, the sandy littoral band that forms the coastal substratum from La Goulette in the south as far as the present-day township of Le Kram, is near enough aligned with the axis of the equally sandy coast of present-day Carthage north of Le Kram. Admittedly this formation is due to the alluvial deposits of the Medjerda carried by the dominant currents, which come from the north-east, and it is known that these alluvial additions, aided by the development of agriculture, were accentuated at the beginning of historical times, contributing to a rapid thickening of the original beaches (Paskoff, 1985, pp. 613–17). It is noticeable, moreover, that the tip of the present bay of Le Kram, extended by Falbe's quadrilateral, juts out to the east of that alignment, and the hypothesis may be made that natural rocks there could subsequently have been used as a base for the constructed foundations of the *choma*. The fact remains that the laying down of this belt of sand is the geological origin of the lagoon situation characterizing this sector of the coast as it may be pictured at the dawn of its history. There the first dated human installation is the tophet, starting from the second half of the eighth century.

What did the immediate environs of the tophet look like at that time? There is general agreement in siting the line of the seashore

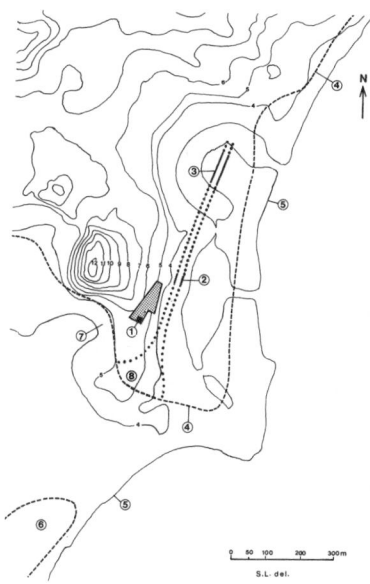

FIGURE 102 *A hypothetical reconstruction of the harbour in the archaic era: 1 tophet; 2 and 3 verified sections of the channel; 4 shoreline in the archaic era; 5 present-day coastline; 6 north-west extremity of the taenia; 7 hypothetical site of the cove of the archaic harbour; 8 hypothetical outlet of the channel (S. Lancel).*

appreciably farther back then in relation to its present line (which, for the south part of the urban site, at the level of the harbours, is more or less that of the second century BC). After the observations of Dr Carton, those made by Saumagne in the thirties, at the time of sondages carried out on the northern edge of the circular lagoon, revealed that this zone was a little polder reclaimed from the sea. He was tempted to think that, in Carthage's earliest days, the shoreline in this sector lay very far back from the present seashore, to the extent that it had to follow the western curve of the circular lagoon (Saumagne, 1931, pp. 654–9). To fix the line of the coast there in the most ancient times would be to push it back excessively, if one keeps to more recent findings – those of Henry Hurst who, in a deep sondage carried out on the islet of the circular lagoon, discovered a deposit of silt-laden clay in contact with the virgin sand, bearing traces of sediments of marine origin. That place must therefore have had a lagoon bottom rather than a marine bottom. An additional difficulty is raised, however, by the records of the level of that deposit. It lies 50 centimetres above the present sea

level, which is itself situated 40 centimetres above our chief indic-
ator of the level of the sea in the Punic era: the groove made by the
backwash at the base of the 'sea wall' identified by the German
mission in its excavation sector beside the former Bey's palace; now,
this wall is dated to the fifth century BC (Rakob, 1984, p. 8). There
is therefore a difference of almost a metre between the lagoon level
recorded in the substratum of the circular port's island and the
water level in the fifth century, lower by 90 centimetres. Can one
admit the possibility of such a drop in level between the archaic era
and the fifth century, that is, in the space of three centuries? It seems
difficult. What we know of the sea level in Carthage in Antiquity is
that it dropped during Punic times, certainly reaching its lowest
point at the time of Carthage's fall and in the next century, and that
it began to rise again in the Roman era and became stabilized at
more or less its present-day level in the Byzantine period (Paskoff,
1985, pp. 613–14). The (very high) level recorded by the British team
in the deep strata of the islet might be prehistoric and should therefore
not be taken into consideration as a relevant fact in the hypothetical
search for the line of the coast and a possible port installation in the
archaic era. Amid these uncertainties, if one extrapolates southward the situation recorded by the German mission in its sector,
several hundred metres farther north, one is led by hypothesis to
situate the archaic shoreline not in a position cutting across the
island in the circular lagoon, but back on average by about a
hundred metres from the recognized line of the city wall on the sea
side in the second century BC (dotted line 4 on figure 102). And it
must not be ruled out that at certain points – as in the sector
investigated by Saumagne – this shore could have held little coves
lying farther back than the general line. Even with this hypothesis,
the space available at the time between the tophet and the sea seems
limited, and hardly suitable for the construction of port installations.

   However, it is still in the vicinity of the tophet that one is ultimately led to look for the oldest port for, as we know better now, the
town in the archaic era reached its southern limits at more than a
kilometre to the north of the sacrificial area (above, p. 44): if the
port had not been close at hand, why should the tophet have been
put there, so far from the town? All the more so since it is observed
that, most frequently, the tophet is not situated to the south of
Phoenician or Punic townships: if this is the case in Carthage, there
must be a reason. Therefore the earliest harbour installations will
be sought in the neighbourhood of the tophet, not to the east
(where they will be later) but rather to the south or west.

When a map of Carthage is examined with special attention to the contour lines, one thing catches the eye. Setting aside the hillock of Le Koudiat el-Hobsia, whose purely artificial nature Dr Carton had already proved (1913, p. 59), it is found that the 5-metre contour turns northward very far back from the shoreline of the Lake of Tunis, as it has been known until lately and as it figures on old maps (figure 102). Now, all the sondages carried out recently in the lower zones complement and confirm former findings showing even then that the thickness of the stratigraphic accumulation subsequent to the Punic era, due as much to erosion as to human contributions, reached and sometimes exceeded four metres. So it seems permissible to locate the shore of the lake, in the archaic era, virtually at the present-day limit of the 5-metre contour line. Not only the greater part – if not the whole – of the present locality of Le Kram, but also a large part of the Douar Chott locality, must then have been covered by the waters of the Lake of Tunis, the Sebkha el-Bahira.

That northern curve of the lake which extended at the time alongside the hill of Byrsa and towards the north-east could well have housed Carthage's oldest harbour, to the west and south-west of the tophet. It will be noted that the most ancient part of the sacrificial area, the 'Cintas chapel' (below, p. 241), lies on the south-west edge, on the lake side, and not on the side of the archaic city opposite. It was by sea, and thus first of all to the quays – or quite simply to the shores – of the archaic era port that the heavy blocks of sandstone came, quarried in El-Haouaria, at the tip of Cap Bon, and destined to become the cippi retrieved from the level of Tanit I. At the present stage of research, the hypothesis for the siting of the oldest harbour seems reasonable, though it needs to be supported by sondages and drillings.

In favour of this hypothesis, perhaps we also have a better understanding of the role that may have been played by the channel skirting the tophet to the east, established at a date which unfortunately cannot be pinpointed. We have seen that it must have been connected, not directly with the open sea but with a lagoon type of ambience. It is conceivable that, opening on the south into the Lake of Tunis, not far from the first port installations which I would date to at least the fifth century, it could have allowed penetration as far as the outskirts of the city which, as I have said, at that time lay several hundred metres farther north. The filling in of this channel did not necessarily take place simultaneously along its entire length. In the middle of the fourth century, it appears to have been filled on the site of the future circular port's island. Several periods of wooden structures have been noted there, especially docks that were exactly parallel with one another, unlike the fanned-out ramps of the beginning of the second century (Hurst, 1978, p. 23). Post holes, clearly visible on the sandy surface of the channel infill, might mark the traces left by the wooden props supporting the hulls being built: in short, the phase of the 'timber structures', from the second half of the fourth to the end of the third century, could have been that of a dockyard, connected with the old harbours, the still water-filled south part of the channel allowing the boats to put to sea once they had been built. On this subject let us recall something written by Diodorus of Sicily (XV, 73, 3–4), which tells us that Carthage's arsenals (neoria) burned down in 368 BC: the link between this text and the wooden structures seems to thrust itself upon us. Let it be added that not so long ago, among other arguments put forward to reject placing the ports on the site of the lagoons (though we now know that he was obviously wrong as far as the final period of Carthage is concerned), Cintas had recalled the former discovery in that zone – to be more exact, on the site of the present marine biology laboratory – of potters' kilns datable to the fourth and third centuries, which would certainly have been incongruous in a purely harbour context, but completely in the right place as an addition to a zone of dockyards (Cintas, 1976, p. 206).

The portion of the channel recognized on the site of the American excavations along the west quay of the rectangular port seems to have been filled in at the end of the fourth century, when the activities of the shipbuilding yard appear to have continued on the site of the future island of the circular harbour. How was that yard reached then, and where was its outlet? The British excavator, Henry Hurst, was tempted to suppose the existence, at some intermediate stage, of a second channel more or less parallel with the first, but slightly to the east, thus crossing the present area of the rectangular harbour and, like the first, ending up in these dockyards. This archaeologist noted, in the layers of intermediate fill between these various phases of arsenals, the existence of deposits resulting from dredging, which seem to postulate in practice the digging out of this second channel, which would to some extent have been a prelude to the fashioning of the future rectangular harbour. It was also found that the long axis of the future rectangular harbour ran parallel to that of the first channel and to the line of the shore.

If one wants to sum up the development of this whole southern sector of Carthage over nearly six centuries, the following schema may be advanced as plausible. Originally, the harbour would have been arranged in a broad indentation in the Lake of Tunis going northward and eastward at least to the level of the tophet, which is known to have been active since the middle of the eighth century (figure 102, point 7). To the north-east of the sacrificial area, the zone where the circular port would later be built, at that time a northern extension of the sandy littoral belt of La Goulette – probably cut by small lagoons – was occupied at least until the end of the fourth century (and perhaps right up till the construction of the ports in their final appearance) by shipbuilding yards linked to the Lake of Tunis, rather than the open sea, by a first channel whose line can be partly recognized, then by a second, merely assumed, which may have been the rough outline of the future rectangular port. In this phase, which spread over several centuries, the city remained enclosed within the perimeter defined by the fifth-century city wall, well established some hundreds of metres farther north, bordering on the shore, and apparently leaving *extra-muros* the tophet, the ancient harbours and their building yards. The square tower discovered by Rakob, slightly back from the present sea edge a short distance to the north-east of the future circular harbour, must have marked the southern extremity of that enclosure (Rakob, 1987, p. 335; Lancel, 1990, pp. 10–11).

In the first half of the second century (though we have seen the problems posed by that dating), when the two ports were constructed in their probably contemporaneous final version (including the forming of the platform or *choma* of Falbe's quadrilateral), additional segments of surrounding walls were added to the fifth-century wall to enclose them. It is this second-century wall that was recently discovered, in the form of a few coping stones found *in situ*, in the breach opened to bring circulation to the stagnant waters of the rectangular port (below, figure 244); in this spot it can be seen to lie more or less on the line of the present-day shore. Sections of walls parallel to the shore, discovered at the time of early excavations, seem to follow the same alignment (Cintas, 1976, p. 158; Rakob, 1984, pp. 9–12). Opposite the circular port, the extent of the docks, estimated at forty metres, implies, even if they abutted on the enclosing wall, that this wall – perhaps here quite simply confused with the rounded structure closing the docks (figure 100) – must have lain some dozen metres out from the present-day shore, which means that its foundations are now submerged. A fragment of wall lying obliquely in relation to this second-century sea defence wall, discovered by chance at the beginning of the fifties, is possibly part of the wall that separated the trading port from the military port, according to the disposition described by Appian (point 7 on figure 100); it must be contemporaneous with the ensemble of these constructions (Lancel, 1990, pp. 14–18). Lastly, the very clear traces of the wall, first recognized by Dr Carton on the north border of the Lake of Tunis and partly uncovered during both land and lake excavations effected in this sector by the army at the beginning of the fifties, must also belong to the period of those last modifications (Lancel, 1989, pp. 260 and 274–7). This new south wall followed the line of the lake's north shore, a shoreline that was very noticeably farther to the south than it had been in earliest times, and gives the full measure of the ground gained there by the Punic city for its development. Let it be added that this is an ongoing history, and in the course of very recent years the process of 'polderization' has speeded up before our very eyes.

In a text too often forgotten (*De lege agraria*, II, 32, 87), Cicero says that Carthage was destroyed although it was 'fortified with walls, surrounded by harbours': *succincta portibus*. The assessment set out above, in which hypothesis has an all too generous share, concerns only what must be regarded as the Punic city's main harbour sector. Other harbours or moorings were used, thus affording some relief to the port installations on the south of the town, on a scale that varied according to the direction of the winds. We have a sure testimony at the end of the fourth century AD, in the text of the moving account given by Saint Augustine of his departure for Rome in 383 (*Confessions*, V, 8, 15). As his mother Monica could not bring herself to watch him leave, he pretended to accompany to the shore a friend who was embarking for Ostia, and persuaded his mother to spend that night in the chapel of Saint Cyprian, which was very close to the vessel; while she was praying there, he boarded the ship. We now know that this *memoria Cypriani* is to be identified with a basilica brought to light some decades ago on the heights overhanging the gully and cove known as Hamilcar. Here we are outside the wall of Theodosius of the beginning of the fifth century, thus outside the Roman city and, in all probability, to the north of the main urban nucleus of the Punic city. But we have seen that, in the south, before the last developments of the final phase, the ports had for a long time been outside the defensive circuit of Punic Carthage. Between the gully at Hamilcar and the little promontory of Bordj-Djedid, Dr Carton, confirming the observations of the naval officers Courtet and Roquefeuil, had shown that constructed and relatively well protected harbour basins existed in the Roman era (Carton, 1911, pp. 230–4). His observations on the vestiges of moles and jetties that he had patiently observed and the comparisons he had been able to make between these remains and clearly Punic segments of walls found on the north edge of the Lake of Tunis gave a strong suggestion, if not actually providing proof, that the port installations used under the late Empire, as witnessed by Augustine's embarkation in 383, had pre-Roman antecedents.

We are again indebted to Dr Carton for an intuition whose truth has been verified by the most recent research. This last observation concerns the sector situated immediately to the south of the preceding one and the little promontory known as Bordj-Djedid, which now houses the presidential palace of Carthage and its annexes. In the middle of the second century AD it was on this spot that one of the most imposing edifices of Roman Carthage was constructed – the Antonine Baths.

Investigations have revealed that these baths and their adjuncts had been erected on made ground, the ancient shore, as it would have appeared in the Punic era, backing on to a small cliff still clearly visible when one returns from the Baths with one's back to the sea towards the present-day archaeological park of the Antonine Baths. In earliest times, therefore, there had been a small cove, certainly shallower than Dr Carton believed, but well protected from the north-east winds by the strong mole of 'Roquefeuil's quadrilateral', which acquired its name from the naval officer who, at the beginning of this century, had recognized the structures now generally agreed to be attributable in their earliest state to the Punic period (figure 103). The profound modifications undergone by this entire part of the site, beginning in the Roman era, rule out any hope of ever finding some trace of harbour construction, but it may be maintained without much risk of error that this indentation in the shoreline, to the north of the urban site of the archaic Punic era and bordering the cemeteries used until the fifth century BC, must have formed a very valuable landing point.

Lastly, knowing how much toponymy reveals the enduring nature of the use to which places have been put through the centuries, we

FIGURE 103   *'Roquefeuil's quadrilateral', protecting an ancient cove,*
several cable-lengths from the Antonine Baths (P. Cintas).

must remember the broad, sandy shores of La Marsa. There, over
three kilometres to the north of earliest Carthage, but on the sea
front of what would later be the suburban area of Megara, and
within the great encircling wall of the Punic city, a gently sloping
shore, very negotiable when the winds are in the south or west,
offered coasters and little trading vessels facilities whose durability
is illustrated by the present name of La Marsa ('the port').

6

Religion

It would certainly not have been unreasonable to give the religious aspects of Punic civilization equal ranking to the navy among its means of power. For the Carthaginians, perhaps more than for the other peoples of the classical world amid whom Carthage evolved, reference to their religious universe constituted the principal binding force of a unity which their scattered presence around the periphery of the western Mediterranean could not have made easy to preserve. It is significant to note that, in a State increasingly penetrated by Hellenism, two fundamental elements of their cultural identity were able to put up an effective resistance: their language first, and their religion.

We shall see that, right up to the fall of Carthage, this constancy manifested itself to a great extent through loyalty to a terrible practice in which families pledged allegiance to their gods in flesh and blood by the device of sacrificing their children. But this practice, unparalleled elsewhere, is merely the most lurid aspect of the religious manifestations of a State that may be called theocratic, whose embassies went regularly to pay homage to the Melqart at Tyre, the mother-city, and whose generals offered solemn sacrifices to the gods before any engagement. It was a State where worship was regulated by public authorities, where sanctuaries were erected by them, where, when foreign divinities were introduced into the city, it was done in official fashion – as happened when the Sicilian goddesses Demeter and Kore (Persephone) were installed in Carthage at the beginning of the fourth century (Diodorus, XIV, 77, 5). And the Carthaginians seem to have been no less religious in private: to be persuaded of that it is enough to note the abundance of 'theophoric' names given to children by parents, marking relationships of dependence, or at the least protection, between gods and men, no equivalent of which is to be found in the onomastics of classical cultures. Even though history remembers one above all, the annals of the western Semites swarm with people named Hannibal ('he who enjoys Baal's favour'). Similarly, Hasdrubal is 'he who has Baal's help'. Behind the numerous Hamilcars of classical texts is hidden an Abdelmelqart, 'pledged to the service of Melqart'. And Eschmoun and Astarte also figure largely in the make-up of many Punic names.

This study of Punic names, based mainly on the votive inscriptions of the tophet, is even one of the sources of our knowledge of Carthage's 'pantheon'. But it is a source that should not be used without some precautions. Although the large majority of these votive inscriptions date from the last stage of Punic Carthage (third century and the beginning of the second), the onomastic material they contain appears very conservative, if not archaic. The divine elements predominating are the names of old Phoenician divinities who were most honoured in Tyre: Melqart, Astarte and Eschmoun. While the dedications of these ex-votos reveal the overwhelming predominance of Tanit and Baal Hammon in Carthaginian devotions at this time, only four instances of the former's name have been found among the names of the dedicants. As for Baal Hammon, he is completely absent from the list, in the full form of his divine name, even if it is tempting to see him – with the Hannibals and Hasdrubals just mentioned – in the abbreviated form of the impersonal Baal (Halff, 1965, p. 65).

Even if permissible, the hypothesis is not certain. In Semitic languages Baal meant – and still means – 'master' 'lord', sometimes 'citizen', in the political sense. The word thus covers a very broad semantic range, from the divine register to secular and non-religious usage. In the religious sphere, various determinatives pinpoint the attributes of the 'Baalim' in Semitic pantheons: Baal Shamin, the 'lord of the heavens' (the *dominus caeli* of Saint Augustine, who knew of his existence) or possibly the Greek Zeus whose name is invoked first in Hannibal's famous oath, to which we shall return. Baal Magonim, the 'lord of the shields', perhaps Ares, also figures in the text of the oath. Another document on which I shall touch later, a tariff for sacrifices found in Marseilles but originating from Carthage (*Corpus Inscriptionum Semiticarum*, 165), concerns the temple of a god called Baal Saphon, who was not unknown to the Phoenicians of the orient.

BAAL HAMMON

In Carthage, however, none of these 'lords' enjoyed the omnipresence and apparent omnipotence of Baal Hammon, for whom, together with his feminine counterpart Tanit, the thousands of ex-votos in the tophet were intended. These attestations are not confined to the Punic capital: the god also figures frequently on the stelae and dedications of Punic Africa, from the territory of present-day Tunisia to Constantine in Algeria. Outside Africa, Baal Hammon appears on inscriptions in Sicily, Sardinia and Malta, in other words, those territories which from the very earliest times had been subject to the Carthaginians. This clear and well-defined geographical distribution assures us of its Carthaginian identity over a long period, even though the Syrio-Phoenician origin of the god has long been known and was confirmed by recent discoveries of new evidence in Tyre, Carthage's mother-city (Bordreuil, 1986, p. 71).

Despite so many instances, however, the divinity remains somewhat mysterious. Thus, the personal part of his 'theonym' (Hammon: ḤMN) continues to raise problems. Most often agreement is reached in connecting it with a root *ḥmm, which in Semitic languages expresses the idea of heat. So it has been suggested that Baal Hammon may be seen as the 'lord of the perfume altars' (G. C. Picard, 1954, p. 59). In a completely different direction, a toponymic explanation has been sought in this determinative. This long-established hypothesis rests on the discovery of two texts, which belong to two distinct explanatory records, one at Massoub, near Tyre, including the words BᶜL ḤMN (which should perhaps be translated rather as 'the citizens of Hammon', the last word indicating a place-name), the other having revealed in 1902, at Zincirli, in south-east Turkey on the Gulf of Alexandretta, an ancient god Baal HMN (the inscription is dated to the end of the ninth century), who was at once associated with Mount Amanus, which rises in this region. But what would have predestined the 'Lord of Amanus' to become the divine lord of Carthage? The objection has not surprisingly been raised of the distance and the lack of contact between Carthage and that area situated beyond Antioch, on the northern border of the classic Semitic world (Le Glay, 1966, p. 440).

We do better if we return to that root *ḥmm, 'hot' or 'burning being', already mentioned. And, if he is not the 'lord of the perfume altars', Baal Hammon could well be the 'lord of the furnaces', a possibility which has gained much ground since, with the discovery of the tophet in 1922, the name of the god has been especially associated with the ritual of immolation by fire, which we shall encounter elsewhere. And as solar symbols are also often associated with Baal Hammon, both on certain stelae of the Punic era and on

stelae of the Roman era devoted to Saturn, his successor, the idea is
acceptable that the determinative discussed above could, in an
ambivalent manner, refer to both the fire of the sun and the fire of
the sacrifices.

Nevertheless, other solutions may be envisaged, inspired not least
because of an unwillingness to link the great god of Carthage with
these sinister pyres. Very recently a distinguished Semitic scholar
proposed a re-examination of the determinative which is based in
particular on the Carthaginian stelae *CIS*, I, 404 and 405, where
the masculine counterpart of Tanit is designated only under the
name ḤMN, which makes it less easy to identify him as 'furnace'
and seems to rule out a toponymic origin for this name used on its
own. That being the case, if the three letters are broken down into
two components, ḤM-N, a form meaning 'to our protector' is
revealed (Fantar, 1990, pp. 74–5). This ingenious suggestion is not
certain to win over the specialists and put an end to an argument
that has been further complicated by the hypothesis – old, but
sometimes still reactivated – that Baal Hammon should be identified with the Egyptian god Ammon, whose worship had spread, by
way of caravan routes and the oases of Cyrenaica and Tripolitania,
among the Libyans before the Phoenician colonization, probably
owing to an assimilation of the Theban divinity, whose totem
animal was a ram, with an indigenous Libyan ram god. In fact, an
example of syncretism could have occurred between the Egyptian
Ammon and the Phoenician Baal Hammon, who are both sun gods,
and especially in Tripolitania, where the establishment of the Egyptian divinity and his confusion with an indigenous god went back a
long way in time (Amadasi-Guzzo 1984, pp. 195–6). With the
gradual weakening of the strong guttural of the initial H in the
Punic language, confusion reigned over the pronunciation, which
had at first been quite distinct, and then over the transcription of
the two divine names. In this connection, let us note that for
modern people the usual way of writing Baal Hammon (instead of
Hamon) is itself influenced by the doubling of the labial in our
transcriptions of Zeus or Jupiter Ammon.

Has the last word on Baal Hammon been provided by a recently
published monograph? On completion of a rigorous analysis of the
literary and epigraphic data relating to the god, and in particular
his appellative HMN, the author rejects earlier interpretations of
this part of the theonym: it is neither Amanus, nor any other place,
nor 'furnace', nor 'perfume altar'; ḤMN would seem to mean
'baldaquin' or, metonymically, 'chapel' or 'small temple' (Xella,

1991, pp. 222–34). By agreeing to settle in this type of abode made for him by men, his faithful believers at State as well as domestic level, the god assumes the figure of a royal and paternal deity, the protector of government but also the guarantor of the issue and durability of families. Alongside Melqart, 'the god of Phoenician expansion, the divinity who continually extends the horizon, who opens the way to the enrichment of human experience', Baal Hammon is the guarantor of continuity, the guardian of eternal values.

Baal Hammon, together with Tanit, must truly have answered many expectations and fulfilled a great many hopes to have warranted so many sacrifices in the tophet. The ritual phrase that the dedicant had engraved on the stele, always the same ('for having granted his prayer') unfortunately gives us no exact information about the god's virtues and powers. That he was the last resort of the city in its days of misfortune we may gather from a text of Diodorus, which tells us that at the time of Agathocles' expedition, at the end of the fourth century, the Carthaginians resolved to sacrifice, officially and collectively, several hundred sons of leading families in order to get back into the favour of the god whom the Greek historian calls Kronos (XX, 14, 4). The fact that archaeology has not so far confirmed in the field the reality of these collective sacrifices does not totally invalidate this testimony. The god is mentioned here under his Greek name. Somewhat paradoxically it is in his Greek version and even more, after the fall of Carthage and the extraordinary survival of the god in his Roman version, with the features of African Saturn, that we are best able to grasp the attributes and powers of Baal Hammon (cf below, p. 435). To his function of protector and guarantor of the city's prosperity was added that of regeneration and fecundation which belong to a *frugifer* god. Baal Hammon's divine personality was rich and complex.

For a long time the iconography of Baal Hammon remained uncertain. How he was represented nevertheless exercised men's imagination, even in Antiquity, since in the text just referred to Diodorus suggested a portrayal, flamboyantly taken up by Gustave Flaubert in his *Salammbô* and bound to ensure its popularity among modern people: the bronze statue, whose open palms let the bodies of the sacrificed children slide into the trench filled with burning coals. It is useless to add that no archaeological document has provided the slightest support for this imagery. We had to wait until the middle of this century before a discovery by Cintas in the tophet at Sousse provided a representation from the 'classic' Punic era (it dates approximately from the fifth or fourth century BC) of Carthage's great god (Cintas, 1947, pp. 14–16). This fragment of a stele, which since seems to have disappeared, shows the divinity in right profile seated on a throne flanked by winged sphinxes. On his head the god wears a tall, oriental-style, conical head-dress, and both his beard and his long robe also recall a typically Phoenician iconography. In his left hand he holds an upright spear, while with his right he appears to be making a gesture of blessing to a worshipper (or a priest?) represented, on an obviously reduced scale, standing before him (figure 104). The scene seems to be placed in the setting of a chapel or temple, in which one can recognize parts of a colonnade and, on a beam, a winged disc flanked by *uraei* emphasizes the 'sun' aspect of Baal Hammon. In this iconographic tradition can be placed a little terracotta statue from the Roman era (first or second century AD), found at the beginning of this century in the ruins of a temple at Thinissut, near Bir-bou-Rekba, in Cap Bon. The god is similarly seated on a throne flanked by two sphinxes. He too is bearded, but in place of the tall conical head-dress there rises from his head either a high crown of plumes or a sort of fluted cylindrical tiara, and his long and loose-fitting tunic is in oriental style (figure 104).

FIGURE 104 *Two images of Baal Hammon: on the left, the stele from Sousse (P. Cintas); on the right, the terracotta from Thinissut (Musée national du Bardo, Tunis).*

Apart from a few differences, which from the point of view of form mark its distance from more faithfully oriental representations, such as the Sousse fragment, the statuette bears witness to the persistence of the worship of this god in one of the most beautiful provinces of the former Punic territory.

TANIT

The little monument of Thinissut was discovered in the ruins of a sanctuary dedicated to Tanit, who had become *Caelestis*, and to Baal. Epigraphic fragments in Latin found at the site of the tophet of Salammbô lead to the belief that in the Roman era a temple to Saturn stood in this sector, near, if not on, the site of the temple to Baal Hammon which is justifiably supposed to have been there. According to the famous Heidelberg manuscript, it was in Baal Hammon's temple – but was it the one in the tophet? – that Hanno is presumed to have placed the long inscription giving an account of his memorable expedition along the western shores of Africa (above, p. 102).

On the dedication of the neo-Punic temple of Bir-bou-Rekba, the name of Tanit follows that of Baal. But on the ex-votos in Carthage's tophet, and on thousands of texts spread over two or three centuries, the female divinity takes precedence, under the name TNT PN BᶜL, a title usually translated as 'Tanit face of Baal', with some uncertainty as to the vocalization of this theonym, which appears with the same consonantal skeleton Tnt on an ostrakon from Sidon datable to the beginning of the fifth century; this is more or less the time when Tanit began to make an appearance in Carthage. In fact the most likely vocalization of TNT would be *Tinnit*, as is shown by a Greek transcription found at El Hofra, near Constantine; the customary vocalization Tanit owes a great deal to Flaubert's novel. As for the qualifying 'face of (or facing) Baal', it recalls the one that in certain Phoenician cities unites another divine couple formed by Baal and Astarte. But the fact that Tanit, on Punic monuments, should have her name first is an arrangement peculiar to Carthage.

For want of any evidence of Tanit in the Orient, it was long believed that the oriental Astarte became Tanit in Carthage (Harden, 1962, p. 88). This opinion was strengthened by the rarity and late date of Carthaginian documents relating to Astarte, which nevertheless record a temple to that goddess and mention a priestess of the Astarte of Eryx, the future Erycine Venus of the Latins. For all that, if the two goddesses have similar natures, both appearing as principles of maternity and fertility, the identification of Tanit in classical cultures – as Hera for the Greeks and Juno Caelestis for the Latins – assures her of a truly distinct personality.

An effort has been made recently to establish a connection, no longer between Tanit and Astarte, but between the goddess of Carthage and another great Ugaritic goddess, Anat (Hvidberg-Hansen, 1979). This argument rests on a philological analysis whcih leads its author to recognize in the theonym Tanit the name of the Ugaritic goddess, preceded by the Libyco-Berber prefix *ta- which indicates the feminine gender in the native tongues of North Africa. Thus Tanit would be the product of cultural assimilation, the Africanization of a Phoenician divinity. But Tanit did not bestow her favour on the author of these ingenious hypotheses for, at the very time when he was developing them, a discovery was made on the Phoenician site of Sarepta, about fifteen kilometres south of Sidon, of an inscription datable to the end of the seventh century or the beginning of the sixth, mentioning *Tnt-ᶜstrt*, or the name of Tanit associated with that of Astarte (Pritchard, 1978, pp. 131–48). In the present state of knowledge this inscription on ivory, which is older than the ostrakon of Sidon already mentioned, is the earliest oriental evidence of Tanit and by its very date decisively rules out a North African development of the name and personality of the goddess.

In a field which is still not well known, any new document gives a fresh impetus to the game of investigation and hypothesis. Such is the case with the engraved ivory from Sarepta, which is the dedication of a statue 'for the Tanit of Astarte', for it would seem that the juxtaposition of the two divine names is to be understood in a genitive sense. By joining the name Tanit to a Semitic root meaning 'to weep, to lament', it has recently been suggested that the term should be interpreted as signifying 'worshipping weeping woman' (Lipinski, 1987, pp. 29–30). The 'Tanit of Astarte' of Sarepta would (originally) have been 'the weeping worshipper of Astarte', but the title would afterwards become a divine hypostasis. This would explain why Tanit was associated with Astarte in the religious cult celebrated in the sanctuary of Tas es-Silg, in Malta, and why a sanctuary in Carthage itself was dedicated to Astarte and Tanit of Lebanon (*CIS*, I, 3914). Keeping to this line of explanation, *Tanit pene Baal* ('Tanit facing Baal') may first have designated the priestess lamenting before Baal, before the religious title became a theonym referring to a hypostasis of Astarte under the name Tanit. And it will be seen that by way of an unexpected detour and a few additional justifications we come back to the intuition of those who formerly held that there was a strong link connecting Astarte and Tanit.

THE 'SIGN OF TANIT'

Are we on firmer ground with the iconography of the goddess? Unlike that of Baal Hammon, which is little documented but clear, the iconography of his divine consort is abundant but problematical. Here we touch on questions relating to the 'sign of Tanit'. This is the name given to a symbol found by the thousand, chiefly on stelae but also on very diverse objects: figurines, amulets, mosaic floors (figure 105), and even on pottery fragments, where it appears scratched, like a graffito (figure 106). With numerous variations in detail, it reproduces a simple design of a triangle (more rarely a trapezium) on the tip of which rests a horizontal bar (sometimes with the ends lifted), itself surmounted by a circle or disc. The whole suggests the frontal view of the stylized shape of a feminine figure with its arms extended. And there are instances – fairly rare, however – where the addition of significant details compels an anthropomorphic interpretation.

The origin of the 'sign of Tanit' has provoked much discussion. It has sometimes been seen as a deformation of the *ankh*, the loop-topped Egyptian cross and symbol of life, and in fact it is not impossible that the Egyptian ideogram underlies the stylization of

FIGURE 105 *The 'sign of Tanit' on a mosaic pavement from Kerkouane (S. Lancel).*

FIGURE 106   *The 'sign of Tanit' cut on the base of a black-glazed bowl
(Campanian A) (French archaeological mission to Carthage, S. Lancel).*

the 'sign of Tanit' (Bisi, 1982, pp. 62–5). There is now general
agreement in believing that the sign derives from a schematization
of the realistic portrayal of either the Syrio-Canaanite image of the
goddess in full frontal nudity, pressing her breasts, or of the hiero-
dules with extended arms, both forms frequent in the Orient at the
end of the Bronze Age (Moscati, 1972, pp. 371–4; 1981, pp. 107–
17). There remains the difficult problem of the development of this
representational design and its chronology. People were led to
consider that this abstraction met the need to express a multiplicity
of religious meanings or understandings in one simple but very
polysemous symbol. The 'sign of Tanit', from one variation to
another, is simultaneously the emblem of a praying man or woman,
or that of the divinity intended to receive the prayer; one can see in
it the shape of a cippus-altar (the lower part) and the symbolization
of the crescent moon and solar disc (the upper part) (Cintas, 1968,
pp. 9–10). There was the temptation to see in it an original creation
of the priestly elite of Carthage, with a proposed dating of the early
fourth century BC (C. Picard, 1968, pp. 77–87). But apart from the
difficulty of imagining a religious brotherhood in Antiquity, whatever it may have been, getting together – as one of our modern
advertising firms might do – to come up with what we would call a
'logo' to symbolize both a religion and a goddess, such a hypothesis, which assumes that the first appearance of the sign occurred
in Carthage, could not survive the recent discoveries of indisputable
'signs of Tanit' in the Orient, notably in 1972 off Akziv in Israel, of
two figurines bearing the sign and datable to the fifth century BC
(Benigni, 1975, pp. 17–18). It will be noticed that another Semitic

scholar ventured to conjecture that Carthage might have adopted the Sidonian Tanit, the hypostasis of Astarte, when it passed from monarchy to oligarchy and thus distanced itself from Tyre, where Melqart continued to rank first, as Baal Hammon formerly had in Carthage (Garbini, 1981, pp. 34–6). Now – if it is possible to speak of 'monarchy' in Carthage, knowing that the matter is arguable – this political evolution, as we have seen, took place in the Punic city around the end of the fourth century or the beginning of the third, in other words at a time appreciably later than the first appearances of the 'sign of Tanit'. But (this is not the least of the problems raised by the symbol when attempts are made to place it more precisely in the Punic religious context) it is not certain that the sign should be specifically and exclusively linked with the goddess. And it must be added that other no less schematic symbols, with variations equally open to differing interpretations, also figure on stelae dedicated to Tanit and Baal Hammon. In particular let us note the 'sign of the bottle', which could be the symbolic representation of the child become hero after its passage through fire in the *molk* sacrifice (figure 107). Apart from this symbolism which is fairly directly connected with the goddess, Tanit's iconography also includes representations in which the similarity with the Egyptian Isis is very

FIGURE 107 *The 'sign of Tanit' (left) and the 'sign of the bottle' on stelae from Carthage (after* Archéologie vivante, *1, 2).*

FIGURE 108   *Tanit on a stele from the tophet of Hadrumetum (Sousse)*
(P. Cintas).

noticeable, for example, on a stele from Sousse (Cintas, 1947,
pp. 20–2), dated to the fifth century (figure 108).

MELQART

Tanit and Baal Hammon engage the attention of anyone interested,
even if fleetingly, in the Punic pantheon, by their pre-eminence and
the massive number of testimonies to them – to the point where
they seem to eclipse other deities from an older Semitic religious
background.

It would be wrong, however, to think that a god like Melqart,
associated with Carthage, as he had been at Tyre and Gades, in the
episode of the founding of the city, completely disappeared from the
horizon of Punic piety. What is true is that the 'King of the Town'
(the meaning of the theonym Melqart), whose worship was part of
the symbolism of royal power, could not but be affected by the
political developments emerging at Carthage around the end of the
fourth century in a 'democratic' direction. Melqart none the less

preserved a prime position in the Punic pantheon. It is known that he had a temple in Carthage, though its site has not been determined (*CIS*, I, 4894 and 5575); together with the god Sid in the city he formed a divine couple, whose servant is indicated in an inscription (*CIS*, I, 256); in the form of Milkashtart, he was associated with Astarte there as in the rest of the Phoenico-Punic world (*CIS*, I, 250, 2785, 4839, 4850, 5657). We have seen that his place in Carthaginian onomastics bears witness to his durability in popular devotion, even taking into account the conservative nature of the use of names and the lapse of time it implies.

At Tyre, the principal ceremony in the worship of Melqart was what was called in Greek sources the *egersis*, that is, the 'awakening' or resurrection of the god, preceded by his cremation on the pyre. Such a rite presupposes the participation of officiating priests, at the head of whom in Tyre itself, one may surmise, came the person of the king in his capacity as heir and substitute for the god (Bonnet, 1988, pp. 174–9). Now, though there are no occurrences of this in the Phoenician city, the title 'resurrector of the divinity, husband of Astarte' appears several times in inscriptions in Carthage, with indications arguing in favour of linking this title with the cult of Melqart (*CIS*, I, 227, 260–2, 377, etc.: Amadasi-Guzzo, 1967, app. 4). Several suffetes and high priests are numbered among his officiants, a sign that in Carthage the ceremony of the god's resurrection was surrounded with pomp and was a source of prestige.

At the end of the second century AD Tertullian, a Carthaginian writer in Latin who is one of the witnesses to the persistence of Punic culture in North Africa, tells of having seen someone burnt alive at a theatrical performance while playing the role of Hercules (*Apologeticum*, XV, 5; *Ad nationes*, I, 10, 47). It has been suggested that this dramatic scene could be interpreted as Melqart's cremation rite before his regeneration, while the difficulty may be emphasized of making a distinction at this late date between attributes of the Phoenician god and of Herakles-Hercules, whose deeds also included mounting a funeral pyre on the Oetan mountain (Bonnet, 1988, pp. 172–3). Of course, both the mythical and the actual history of Carthage are punctuated by these fiery immolations, from Dido-Elissa, at the founding of the city, to Hasdrubal's wife, on its last day in the spring of 146 BC (Appian, *Libyca*, 131), by way of the Magonid Hamilcar, the 'king' vanquished at Himera in 480. But it would probably be wrong to reduce all those ritual suicides by fire to a single common denominator.

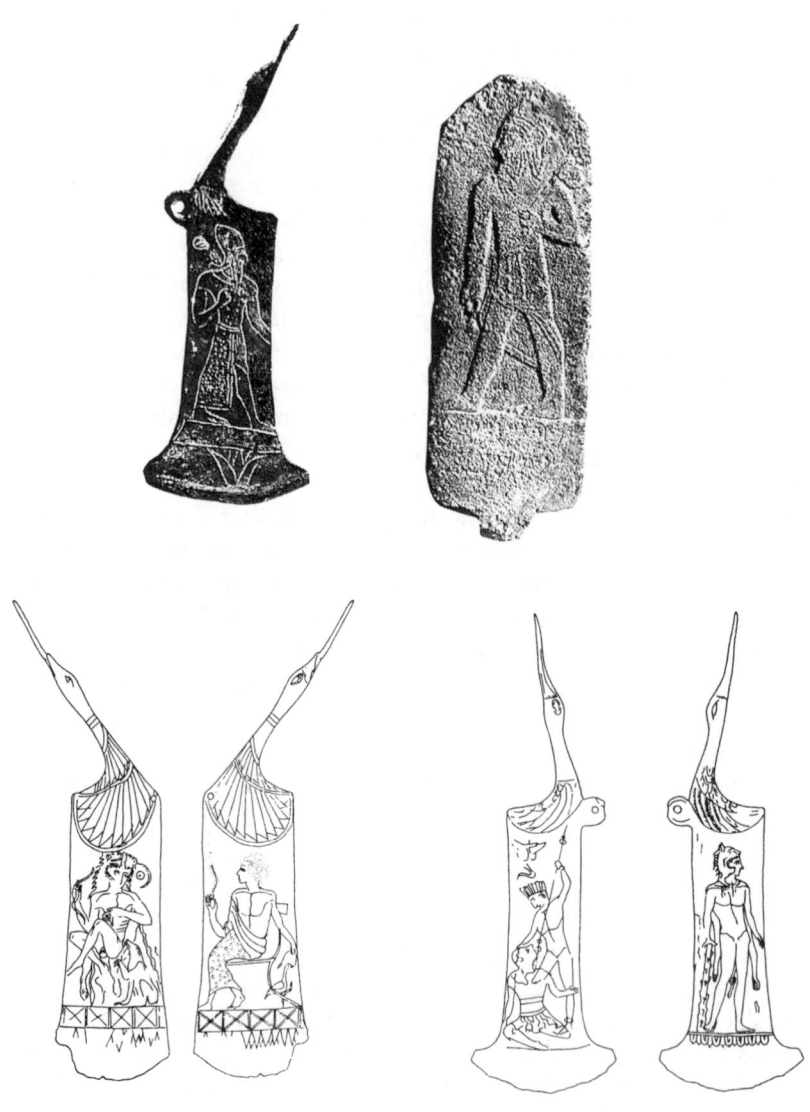

FIGURE 109 *Images of Melqart; top right, the stele of Alep (after C. Bonnet, 1986 and 1988).*

Melqart's iconography in Carthage, though not very plentiful, is highly representative of the cultural cross-breeding that is one of the Punic city's characteristics, particularly in the last two centuries of its existence (figure 109). In fact, we see here the coexistence of the oriental tradition and the adaptations introduced by Hellenism with the similarity of Melqart to Herakles. This coexistence of two iconographic types in the same period – approximately the third century BC – can be observed in a category of ritual objects which probably originated in New Empire Egypt (Vercoutter, 1945, pp. 302–3) with an admixture of Minoan and Hellenic elements (Picard, 1967, p. 80; Acquaro, 1971, pp. 186–7) which makes it an original component of tomb assemblages from as early as the end of the seventh century right up to the last days of the city. These are the bronze 'hatchet-razors', most frequently ornamented with incised and engraved designs, unlike their Egyptian equivalents. Thus a hatchet-razor of the Barcid era, coming from the Sainte- Monique cemetery (figure 109), shows the god standing on a sort of podium, which itself surmounts a lotus flower, wearing a tiara or conical head-dress and a long slit garment, and holding in his right hand a 'perforated axe' which rests on his shoulder: the same features (including the lotus flower, symbol of resurrection) are to be seen on a much older stele found near Alep (end of the ninth century BC), where the image of Melqart is identified as such by the inscription that figures on the lower part (Lemaire, 1984, pp. 337–49). In the same era, two other razors originating from the same cemetery bear witness to the accompanying Hellenization of the representation of the god. On one of them a standing Herakles-Melqart, naked under his lionskin – one of the attributes of Herakles – leans on his club. On the other side the hero, wearing a plumed tiara and grasping a kneeling warrior whom he is piercing with his spear, is none other than Şid, another Punic god whom we have seen connected with Melqart in Carthage itself, which assures us that the god in the lionskin is not only the Greek demi-god but also a Hellenized Melqart (figure 109). On the second razor Herakles-Melqart, equipped with his club against which he rests his right shoulder, is seated crosslegged, wearing the lion's head on his own (figure 109). On the reverse side is the seated figure of Iolaus, associated with the god in the legend of the Tyrian Herakles. If it is true that it was the coinage of Croton and Tarentum which seems to have supplied the iconographic type of the Herakles in repose depicted in a sitting posture, that is really only an 'Italianate veneer' on the Carthaginian god (Bonnet, 1986, pp. 220–2).

THE DIVINITIES OF 'HANNIBAL'S OATH'

These representations of Melqart from the cemetery known as Sainte-Monique are more or less contemporary with Hannibal. Specialists in Carthaginian religion happen to have at their disposal for this period a key document, but one which most clearly shows how difficult it is to penetrate a culture of which the evidence is filtered down to us through classical writings. Polybius (VII, 9, 2–3) provides us with what seems likely to be the Greek translation of a Punic version of the treaty concluded in 215 BC between Philip V of Macedonia and Hannibal. To support their oath, Hannibal and the Punic leaders present with him invoke divinities grouped in triads – under their Greek names: Zeus, Hera and Apollo; the *daimon* of the Carthaginians, Herakles and Iolaus; and lastly Ares, Triton and Poseidon. There is still argument about the identification of most of the gods mentioned in this text, and the first question, which is whether they represent the pantheon of Carthage or the personal pantheon of the Barcid leader, has some effect on the proposals that may be made. So the first-named, Zeus, according to the second hypothesis, would rather be Baal Hammon, Carthage's principal male deity in Hannibal's time, but some specialists prefer to think he is Baal Shamin, the traditional *dominus caeli*, as we have seen (Huss, 1986, p. 223). Hera could be Astarte, who corresponds to her in the *interpretatio Graeca*, but could just as likely be Tanit, who forms a pair with Baal Hammon as Zeus does with Hera. Apollo raises a problem because, if he is traditionally likened to Reshef, the Semitic god is not attested in Carthage; but Appian (*Libyca*, 127 and 133) mentions, at the time of Carthage's fall in 146, a temple of Apollo in the vicinity of the agora. In the second triad there is general agreement in recognizing Tanit in the *daimon* or tutelary deity of the Carthaginians, which rules out seeing her as the equivalent of Hera in the first triad. Herakles is obviously Melqart, and for Iolaus there is a choice between the god Sid and Eschmoun, as both are closely connected with Herakles-Melqart. Eschmoun, still interpreted in Greek as Aesculapius, must be left out, but the difficulty is patent: how can one accept the absence from that solemn oath of a divinity whose temple, on the hill of Byrsa, was the largest in Carthage? The last triad poses fewer problems: Ares must be Baal Haddad, Triton, Baal Malage and Poseidon, Baal Saphon. It appears that this third triad matches one invoked in the seventh century BC in the treaty concluded between the king of Tyre and Asarhaddon (Bonnet, 1988, p. 182). From this one may draw the conclusion that Hannibal's list was conservative in nature, as it repeated the divinities invoked in a Tyrian treaty of four centuries earlier, and also that it referred to the official pantheon of Carthage rather than to the dynastic pantheon of the Barcids.

THE CARTHAGINIAN PRIESTHOOD

If we speak of gods we must also speak about places of worship, religious practices and priests. The preceding sections give us a glimpse of how much social weight was carried by priests (*kohanim*) in Carthage. Of this clergy, which seems to have been large in number, we have the picture left to us by inscriptions (epitaphs, ex-votos); as for their physical image, we shall look at the stelae further on. The genealogies provided by some inscriptions reveal that religious dignities remained the privilege of aristocratic families and that they were passed on from one generation to the next, like certain civil offices: a stele from the tophet mentions seventeen generations of priests of Tanit. This hereditary character is also attested in the Orient, where it must have existed, as in Carthage, side by side with the co-optation, albeit very restricted, of new families into the priesthood. Despite the prestige enjoyed by the clergy, it does not appear that they constituted a caste in the State machinery, and even less that they played a role in the political field. But at the head of the serving priests in each temple was a 'chief of priests' or head of the sacerdotal college (*rab kohanim*) with important prerogatives: the erection or restoration of sanctuaries, the fixing of sacrificial tariffs. Such entitlements inevitably had a quite noticeable effect on the economic life of the city.

We have seen that the Carthaginian pantheon was relatively numerous, and was both conservative and evolving, without even taking account for the moment – we shall come back to it later – of the introduction of foreign divinities, such as the Sicilian *Cereres* or corn goddesses at the beginning of the fourth century. In that respect Carthage was no different from other cities in the Phoenician world, in which the immortals' order of precedence and their role in the city varied from one town to another. It may be imagined, in the unfortunate absence of any documentation about it, that such a complex religious life fed theological debate in sacerdotal colleges. It has even been suggested that the clergy may have been charged with the task of preserving and passing on a whole literature – probably mostly oral – relating to the most ancient traditions, and notably the deeds of the founding queen, Elissa-Dido (G. C. and C. Picard, 1982, pp. 76–7). We must admit that we know almost nothing about the functioning of intellectual life in Punic Carthage. But if one reflects on the ways in which Punic culture survived in Romanized Africa, where the survival of the language was accompanied by that of certain religious cults, one can agree that the priests in Carthage could well have played a fairly important cultural role.

Luckily we are better informed about their specifically religious role. The documentation that has been preserved mentions restrictive liturgies, whose detail calls to mind the finicky meticulousness of the instructions in Leviticus. Accomplishing the rites required the services of an entire staff to assist the priests and attend to a multiplicity of duties: scribes, first and foremost (and they in particular were the guarantee that the written language could hold out againt too much erosion; see Bonnet, 1991, p. 158) but also those taking part in worship in the strict sense: cantors and musicians – whose presence is postulated in a famous description, by Diodorus of Sicily, of the holocaust ceremony in the tophet – attendants who looked after the lights, sacred barbers and also, above all, butchers whose task was to slaughter and cut up animals for the sacrifices and prepare their meat. In the image of the *mageiros* in classical Greece, who was nearly always a public official, the Punic sacrificer combined in his person the sacred and the profane, being simultaneously butcher and cook, but also priest (Ribichini, 1985, pp. 34–5). The sacrificial tariffs of Carthage testify to a strict organization of the ritual of sacrifices, carried out on the initiative of the faithful, sometimes on other occasions than public festivals, and their food-control function at that time was very obvious.

The main one of these texts, known under the title of the 'Marseilles Tariff' – from the place where it was discovered: in actual fact it was posted up in the temple of Baal Saphon in Carthage – has as its heading the Semitic term b^ct which the contents of the document have caused to be translated as 'tariff', but which – its etymology remains obscure – could just as well mean 'collection' (in the sense of tax) (Xella, 1985, pp. 40–1). This text makes distinctions between the various sorts of offerings, especially animals; they can be classified in five categories, taking account of their size and thus of their food value: fully grown cattle, calves, fully grown sheep, lambs and lastly birds. There is dispute about the meaning of the word ʾyl, found in these lists, which may indicate not a ram but a stag, and indeed just recently the German mission's discovery of a deer-hide in a foundation deposit dated to the third century confirms the likelihood of members of the deer family being used as sacrificial victims. Not all the offerings were meat: the 'tariff' mentions, among others, flour, oil, milk and pastries. The justification for calling these documents 'tariffs' is the precise detail they provide about the share allocated to the priest and dedicant respectively, according to the type of animal offered and the nature of the sacrifice. 'For an ox as an expiatory or communion sacrifice or as a holocaust,' states the Marseilles Tariff, 'to each of the priests ten (shekels) of silver. And, for an expiatory sacrifice, over and above that, meat weighing 300 (shekels). And, for a communion sacrifice, the breast and the right leg. The hide, ribs, hooves and the rest of the flesh belong to the one ordering the sacrifice.' The document also makes provision for possible abuses on the part of the priests: 'Any priest levying a tax other than the one fixed by this table will be fined.'

The physical aspect of these priests is known to us through their representations on the stelae. First their garment, a long 'talar' robe or tunic falling to their feet, apparently worn over a loincloth, and which must have been linen: this is how the 'priest with child' appears on the famous grey limestone stele preserved in the Bardo Museum in Tunis (figure 122, below), the sight of which decided François Icard to undertake the excavation of the tophet on Christmas Eve 1921. On another stele, also from the sacrificial area, the priestly garment of distant Egyptian origin worn by a person in an

FIGURE 110 *Two representations of priests on stelae from Carthage (after A. M. Bisi, Le stele puniche, 1967).*

attitude of prayer, bare-headed, his uplifted palms facing forwards, is embroidered with a 'sign of Tanit' in which it is tempting to recognize a specific cultic character (figure 110). The two people mentioned above are both beardless and shaven-headed, which does not seem to be generally the case, if we are to judge by another representation, also from the tophet, of a man who is marked out as a priest by virtue of the oenochoe and patera he holds to make a libation, who has a good growth of beard and hair, the latter visible under a veil that falls to his shoulders like a *klaft*.

THE TEMPLES

What we would like to know more about are the temples where these priests officiated. The most celebrated one from literature is the sanctuary of Eschmoun, regarded as the richest, situated on the summit of Byrsa Hill, very probably facing the sea, and reached from the coastal plain by a stairway of sixty steps: it was the last resort of resistance in the final phase of the siege of Carthage in the spring of 146 BC (Appian, *Libyca*, 130). It was during the burning of this temple on the last day that the wife of Hasdrubal – the commander who had already surrendered to Scipio – deliberately chose to perish, thus symbolically recreating Dido's act, so many centuries later (ibid., 131). Unfortunately, as we have lately come to know (one of the negative results of recent French excavations), there is no chance of finding the slightest trace of this temple, whose foundations themselves must have vanished in the gigantic work of levelling the hill carried out in Augustus' time (Lancel, 1982, p. 363). Still according to Appian (*Libyca*, 127), the temple of Apollo – perhaps the Semitic Reshef (cf. above, p. 208) – situated on the edge of the agora near the merchant harbour, contained a religious statue of gilded bronze, itself enclosed in an edifice with walls covered with leaves of gold, which Scipio's soldiers plundered by detaching them with their sword-points. This unfortunately throws no light on the layout of the sanctuary.

It is agreed that the prototype of the Phoenico-Punic temple was the one constructed by King Solomon at Jerusalem at the beginning of the first millennium BC, with the help of builders from Phoenicia. As no vestiges of that 'First Temple' remain, the description of it given in the Old Testament (I Kings: 6–7) allows us to recreate its arrangement with some degree of probability. It was an oblong edifice, composed of three linked parts: a vestibule (*Ulam*), the

great hall of worship (*Hekal*) and last, at the very end, the Holy of
Holies (*Debir*), wherein lay the Ark of the Covenant. The façade of
the porch, on the east side, its entrance framed by two free-standing
or engaged pillars, gave on to a vast open area. Archaeology has
sometimes been able to find on Punic sites this tripartite design
characteristic of Semitic religious architecture, for example, at
Monte Sirai in Sardinia, where a sanctuary certainly goes back to
the sixth century. Still in Sardinia, at Cape San Marco, near Tharros, an archaic temple shows these same three linked parts: vestibule, main hall consecrated to worship and, at the back, a *cella*.

In Carthage itself during the twenties, Dr Carton excavated a
little sanctuary of the Hellenistic era, traces of which had appeared
on the southern edge of the modern built-up area, about 500 metres
west of the tophet, when work was in progress to lay the electric
railway (Carton, 1929). The building comprised a very simple
rectangular *cella*, divided lengthways by partitions of hard-packed
earth. Against the rear wall of the *cella* stood an altar surmounted
by a canopy supported by half-columns resting *in antis* on walls
of clay. The architectonic fragments of stuccoed sandstone that
have been preserved have enabled us recently to present a plausible hypothesis for the reconstruction of this canopy in cross-
section and elevation, with Ionic-order columns (Ferchiou, 1987,
and figure 111).

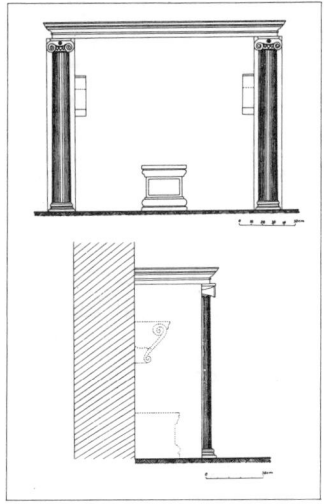

FIGURE 111 *The 'Carton chapel': proposed reconstruction of the
'canopy' in cross-section and elevation (after N. Ferchiou).*

Here the opportunity arises to present both sides in a debate that is certainly not over. Many Carthaginian votive stelae show an architectural motif composed of two columns, most often Ionic, more rarely Doric, supporting an entablature sometimes crowned by a pediment. In the wake of Gsell (cf. chiefly *HAAN*, vol. IV, p. 204) it was generally considered that this type of decoration provided a scaled-down picture of Punic temples in the Hellenistic period, prostyle distyle *naoi* of which the Sicilian monuments appeared to be the model (C. Picard, 1976, p. 99: Fantar, 1984, p. 437). Alexandre Lézine differed, and proposed seeing them as only a reproduction of the canopies – like the one from the 'Carton chapel' we have just seen – situated inside the *cella* (Lézine, 1959, p. 248). Thus, according to one man who for a long time was chief architect for historic monuments in Tunisia, the architectural decoration on the stelae could not be used to support the argument that latter-day religious architecture in Carthage purely and simply adopted Greek models. What in fact characterizes a Greek temple and best differentiates it from oriental sanctuaries is its method of roofing, with two sloping sides, expressed by the triangular pediment on the façade of the *pronaos*.

Now, even in Hellenized late Carthage, nothing attests the existence of this type of roof. The *naiskos* found at the beginning of this century at Thurburbo Maius, not far from Carthage, with figurative motifs – notably the pig – suggesting a cult of Demeter (cf. below, p. 313), may be taken as a fairly representative model of the stage reached by the development of religious architecture in Carthage on the eve of its fall. The building with a *cella* that it reproduces, preceded by a porch with two columns, the whole thing resting on a plinth, includes a flat covering with a pediment-less entablature whose rich and heavy decorative mouldings I shall describe later (figure 181). The entire edifice derives from the distant model of an Egyptian-style *naos*, modified by the addition of a porch and thus transformed into a distyle building. Pretty well contemporary is a possible funerary chapel found in the vicinity of Thizika, still in the region of Carthage, and Naide Ferchiou recently put forward a suggested reconstruction (figure 112). Here the reconstruction is also of a flat-roofed building, its *cella* preceded by a porch supported on Doric columns; this order is repeated in the engaged columns flanking the entrance to the *cella*, but – a revealing sign of architectural cross-breeding – coexists with the Egyptian-grooved cornices of the entablature (Ferchiou, 1987, p. 27).

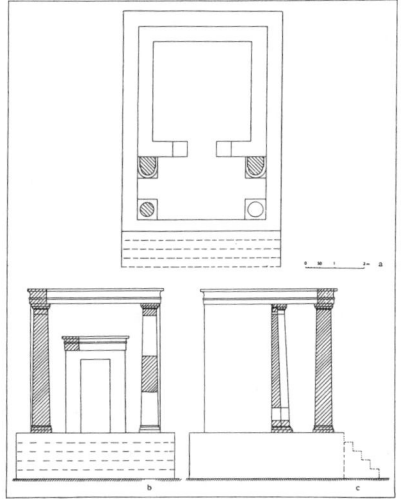

FIGURE 112 *The 'hawthorn chapel' (Zaroura) near Thizika (after N. Ferchiou).*

Does that mean that the old tripartite layout of the oriental temple, of which King Solomon's was the prototype, had by then disappeared from Carthage? Perhaps it still survived, at least if one is to judge by the interior arrangement of a very small 'chapel', now destroyed, brought to light in 1919 on the slopes of Sidi-bou-Saïd, in the northern suburb of Carthage. It was possible to distinguish in it a porch, a room for worship and a 'holy of holies', linked together, the three pieces on a very small scale, as if the desire had been to reproduce in this building a far larger monument, whose reduced image one had here (Lézine, 1959, p. 251).

ATTITUDES TOWARDS DEATH AND THE DEAD

When at the start of this book I emphasized the invaluable contribution to the knowledge of earliest Carthage provided by the cemeteries, I raised the question which must be posed by the presence of grave goods in the tombs. The very composition of even the simplest (receptacles for solid and liquid foodstuffs, drinking vessels, plates) presupposes at least some concept of material survival, or perhaps less clearly the analogical or symbolic provision of the material conditions for survival; to these objects a lamp is added to give light to the dead person and guide him in the shadows. Could it be to guide him in the next world? That would already be to answer a question that is just being formulated. What motivations of conscious piety did these practices in fact satisfy? For lack of any written document dealing with what was believed in Carthage about the dead man's ways of survival, his life after death, the whole body of ideas and doctrines that the classical world called eschatology, one can only examine with caution clues of an archaeological kind.

They at least bear witness to the belief – common to the majority of civilizations in the ancient world, apart from a few variations – that the dead person must be installed in his 'eternal home' (BT^cLM in Phoenician, and tombs were also referred to in this way by the ancient Egyptians) in the best conditions for 'physical survival' but also of comfort and protection. Hence, over and above the articles mentioned earlier, those to be seen in Carthaginian inhumations surrounding the defunct, the presence of those called in Phoenician the *rephaim* (Caquot, 1981, pp. 344–57), a title which seems to evoke simultaneously the languor of an absence of life but also a nearly divine status, like the Greek *makaroi*.

The protective function surely belongs to the amulets and figurines in terracotta whose presence in tombs of the archaic era I mentioned before. Slightly later, from the end of the seventh century almost up to the last days of the city, we frequently see those objects so typical of Carthage and its area of direct influence (Sardinia, the Balearics) which I have already referred to in connection with the iconography of the god Melqart: the hatchet-razors. About a hundred of these bronze razors were collected from the cemeteries at Carthage, generally placed near the dead person's head and often wrapped in a bag made of plaited or woven esparto grass. Their elegant elongated shape was established from the fourth century, with the long handle like a bird's neck, and on both faces it became usual to have an engraved design, first executed by stippling and later by line drawing. It is precisely the subjects of this decoration which throw a little light for us on the reasons for the presence of these objects with the dead, since their use for the requirements of a 'material' toilet is not the whole of their significance: they have been found in the tombs of women, who would have had no use for them in daily life, since they removed their unwanted hair by plucking. These razors, which were probably used by the living to perform a ritual toilet – we have seen that in Carthage temple staff included 'sacred barbers' (*CIS*, I, 257–9 and 588) – feature essen-

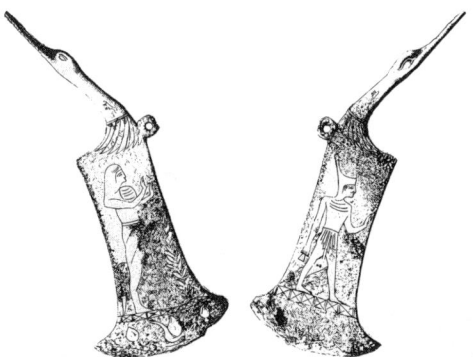

FIGURE 113 *A hatchet-razor from Carthage (front and back). On the right, the crown of Lower Egypt and the ankh sign held by the man in his right hand are in Egyptian style. On the left, the lotus flower at the foot of the design is enough to Egyptianize this representation of a praying woman (after J. Vercoutter, 1945, plate XXVII).*

tially religious themes: scenes of prayer, representations of divinities (Egyptian and Phoenico-Punic, as in figure 113) and mythical figures, like those we have seen illustrating the deeds of the god Melqart. The razors placed in the tombs are therefore protective talismans in so far as they are connected with acts of piety formerly accomplished by the deceased and which the decorative picture renders eternally present and effective (C. Picard, 1967, pp. 112–15).

In discussing the archaic tombs I referred earlier to the terracotta masks, the purpose of which was obviously apotropaic, above all when they were grimacing or grotesque. I emphasized that they hinted at ritual disguises, and their relatively small number permits the inference, as suggested, that those found in the tombs belonged to initiates. In the more recent tombs these terracotta masks developed into what is generally agreed to be the most brilliant expression of Punic artistic craftsmanship: pendants in polychrome glass. These pendants, fashioned on a core, are not unknown elsewhere and their production in the Orient is ancient, but the specimens from Carthage, where they must have been manufactured on the spot from at least the fourth century, derive their success from the perfect chromatic blend of the material (in which blues and yellows on a white background predominate) with the iconographic detail of these little masks (figure 114). Are they, as a specialist has recently proposed, representations of protective deities? In the

FIGURE 114   *Three glass pendants fashioned on a core (Musée national de Carthage; after* The Phoenicians, *Milan, 1988).*

female faces, which are rarer, Tanit could be identified, and in the more plentiful range of masculine masks Baal Hammon might appear with the features of an old man with an abundant beard, whereas perhaps Melqart or Eschmoun should be recognized in the younger-looking masks, where the beard is less full (Seefried-Brouillet, 1982, pp. 59–62). Whatever the truth of these suggestions, emphasis has chiefly been laid on a characteristic common to nearly all these little objects – the disproportionately enlarged size of their bulging eyes, with the iris dilated, which gave them a magic power. They thus preserved in the tomb the protective function ascribed to them throughout the life of the deceased, who would have worn them round their necks, as is evidenced by the little ring allowing the masks to be linked to other amulets forming a necklace. That was not the case for another category of masks, for which there is no hesitation in recognizing a strictly funerary intention – the faces, always female, suggested rather than actually drawn, on ostrich-egg shells, a choice of material which should cause no surprise. In Carthaginian burial places, but also in the Punic cemeteries of the Balearic Islands to which they were exported, there are numerous instances of articles, often goblets or bowls, made of these shells, evidence of a time when the North African fauna was of a richness and diversity that would soon be impoverished by man the predator. On these shell fragments, where

FIGURE 115 *Fragment of an ostrich egg painted in the form of a mask (Carthage, fifth century* BC*) (after* The Phoenicians, Milan, *1988).*

three spots of red colour – vermilion – place the mouth and the two rouged cheekbones (figure 115), most noticeable are two immense eyes, often with clearly shown lashes: the gaze of magic dolls, eyes wide open in the darkness of the tomb to put evil spirits to flight.

The egg is a universal symbol of life, and it comes as no surprise therefore to find the ostrich egg present in Punic funerary tradition in another form, where it is immediately recognizable: cut, either in two halves or, more frequently, to three-quarters of its length, with the edges notched, possibly to accommodate a lid. The deceased could therefore drink from a choice receptacle which in itself imparted a potent regenerative power to the beverage it contained. The red-painted designs ornamenting the surface reveal the taste of the decorator in carrying out compositions arranged in vertical and horizontal sections determined by geometric motifs in which various animal or plant themes are used, but with the almost constant presence of Phoenician-style subjects: the palm frond, the lotus flower, the tree of life (figure 116). Very much present in Carthage from the seventh century, decorated eggs were found fairly frequently along the west Algerian littoral, at Tipasa and Gouraya. But it was in Spain, notably Villaricos, and on Ibiza that the finest and most numerous collections were found (Astruc, 1951 and 1957). They provide an excellent example of the favoured connections maintained between both sides of the Iberian sea, since the decoration was obviously carried out on the spot using raw material exported from Africa. And the similarity of the ornamentation might suggest that, once their decoration had been painted on, the

FIGURE 116   *Decorated ostrich eggs from tombs in Carthage, Gouraya (Algeria), Ibiza and Villaricos (Spain) (after M. Astruc).*

eggs made the return journey to sites on the Algerian coast, with a heavy added value. One might hesitate about the provenance of eggs unearthed in the archaic tombs of Carthage. It cannot be ruled out that they were imported in their natural state from the upper valley of the Nile and decorated on the spot, like those discovered in the oriental-style tombs of central Italy (Cerveteri, Tarquinia, Vulci) (Gras, 1989, p. 142).

INHUMATION AND CREMATION

On the subject of the cemeteries at Carthage in the archaic period, I pointed out earlier that the rite of cremation coexisted with that of inhumation, even if it was then very much a minority practice. As the convergence of several indications would suggest, cremation would have been carried out in Carthage at that time by a population that had remained faithful to a Phoenician practice where, nevertheless, inhumation was not unknown. Let it be said clearly: the distinctions laid down by archaeologists over half a century ago between those who interred and those who cremated are no longer acceptable. In the very early period in Carthage, grave goods from cremation burials, although coming down to us in poorer condition because they had been at least partly subjected to the cremation fire, were no less well supplied than those of the inhumation tombs. This suggests that at least in that era the recourse to cremation was not accompanied by a spiritualization of beliefs relating to the afterlife. But the fact that the material fate of the corpse was of little import, that at the same time and in the same cultural context it could equally well be consigned to earth or fire, is in itself an indication of spirituality.

Excavators of Carthage's cemeteries have noted that the practice of cremation became generalized from the end of the fifth century. In the Hellenistic period (from the fourth to the beginning of the second century) the most frequent form of burial was in a little casket of limestone, covered with a lid like a sloping roof, in which the cremated remains were collected. From that time on a greatly diminished number of objects – sometimes to the point of being totally absent – accompanied these remains. Remarking on this fact, the inference was sometimes drawn that there had been an evolution, a refinement, in religious beliefs (Fantar, 1970, pp. 12–13; Decret, 1977, p. 149). But it must not be forgotten that funeral practices cannot be separated from the conditions of urban development. In the great cities of the ancient world urban growth took place at the expense of the cemeteries, which were taken out of service and pushed farther away as fast as the town expanded. Carthage reclaimed the territory of the dead to the advantage of the living, for instance, at Dermech and Douimès to the north of the littoral plain, as well as on the southern slopes of the hills of Juno and Byrsa, at the same time allowing burial enclaves to persist for a long while in its urban fabric, for instance, on the Odeon plateau and in the Sainte-Monique or Saïda locality (Lancel, 1990, pp. 18–25). This partial coexistence of the living and the dead, certainly a nuisance for the former since it limited their expansion, was for the latter also necessarily translated into a smaller individual possession of the soil (or subsoil) they continued to occupy, all the more since, in its size of population, the Carthage of the fourth century had nothing in common with the city of Dido and her first descendants. Demography by itself, and even more when linked with that original cohabitation of living and dead on part of the city's territory, could account for the method of burial most often adopted from the end of the fifth century. In this new funeral situation, a greater caution in the inclusion of grave goods was linked to the great restriction of space allotted to the dead.

OUTLINES OF A PUNIC ESCHATOLOGY

Around this same time, however, outside Carthage but in the near-by Punic domain, it is possible to find traces of a veritable eschato-logy in certain funerary iconography. In Cap Bon, to be more precise at Djebel Mlezza, the cemetery of a city destroyed in the middle of the third century, Kerkouane, contains burial chambers with mural paintings. In one of them, Tomb VIII, the pictures represented on the side and rear walls seem to follow on from one another as if recounting in pictures the stages in a symbolic history. On one of the side walls, beside a mausoleum with a pyramidal roof, a type very common in the Africa of that period (fourth to third century), a sacrifical altar is depicted with its fire lit (figure 117); on another wall, on the other side of the mausoleum, is a cock with a broad comb but most noticeably with multiple and dispro-portionately enlarged spurs, a detail which is most unlikely to be there by chance and might well have an apotropaic value (figure 118). The same cock, with the same probably significant distorted shape, appears on the rear wall of the tomb above the repres-entation of a town protected by a wall with towers, which its rounded merlons allow to be interpreted with certainty as an en-closing wall (figure 119). This wall is semicircular, like that of Kerkouane, and there is some reason to believe that it was this small coastal town nearby which was thus schematically depicted (Lézine, 1968, pp. 187–8). But it may just as well be an 'ideal' city, repre-sented in this way from a character common to towns in the

FIGURE 117 *Tomb VIII of the Djebel Mlezza: south-east wall (Istituto per la civiltà fenicia e punica, Rome).*

FIGURE 118 *Tomb VIII of the Djebel Mlezza: north-west wall (Istituto per la civiltà fenicia e punica, Rome).*

Phoenician world, which were almost all coastal, open to the sea and at the same time protected by a wall on the land side. From that it is but a step, sometimes boldly taken (Fantar, 1970, pp. 36–7; Decret, 1977, pp. 150–1), to interpreting this picture as the 'Kingdom', the celestial city towards which the soul of the deceased, here

FIGURE 119 *Tomb VIII of the Djebel Mlezza: north-east wall (Istituto per la civiltà fenicia e punica, Roma).*

in the form of a cock, is making its way. If, for want of convincing parallels, a certain amount of scepticism is permissible over the eschatological significance of the city with the crenellated ramparts in Tomb VIII at Djebel Mlezza, more sustained attention will be given to the cock, the more so because it also figures twice, perched on the pyramidal roof of a two-storey mausoleum painted on the walls of a *hanout*, i.e. a burial chamber hollowed out of rock, in the region of Séjenane in the north-west of Tunisia (Longerstay, 1990, p. 130). And it will be recalled that the inscription in verse in one of Roman Africa's most beautiful mausolea, that of the Flavii at *Cillium* (Kasserine) notes, in the description of the monument, a detail that has now disappeared, the 'quivering wings of the cock on the summit of the edifice' (*CIL*, VIII, 211b). It would therefore seem that the association of the cock and the mausoleum has an ancient African origin, which one may hesitate to identify as Punic; it might just as well be Libyan, i.e. indigenous or Libyco-Punic, and demonstrate that cultural mix of which there are plenty of other examples. The symbolism remains to be assessed. Recognizing the cock as the soul of the departed, or the dead in general, roaming near the tomb, watching over the tomb, or on its way to the ideal city, would certainly – though not without the risk of over-interpretation – impart a strong consistency to the representations in the Djebel Mlezza tomb.

The delicate question of funerary symbolism in this Libyco-Punic world cannot be approached without mention of the figures painted on the walls of another *hanout*, at Le Kef el-Blida in the Mogods mountains. These frescoes, which have been frequently written about since their discovery in 1900, include one enigmatic scene in particular. We see a ship sailing, with an elevated stern-post and its sail hoisted half-way up the mast, seemingly about to make a landfall (figure 120). It is possible to recognize it as a warship of Phoenician type, perhaps an *eikosore* or boat with twenty oarsmen, which would be datable to the archaic era, according to a recent estimate which seems to me a little early (Longerstay, 1990a, p. 42). Seen frontally, seven (or eight?) warriors line the deck, each with a spear held upright in his right hand, a round shield in his left hand allowing his head, clad in a pointed helmet, to be seen above it. On the prow, or rather, poised on the *akrostolion* – which places him on a clearly superior level – is another person, bearded and in profile, holding in his left hand a round shield bearing a raised V, his right hand lifted high in the air brandishing a *bipennis* or double-headed axe with which he seems to be threatening a third

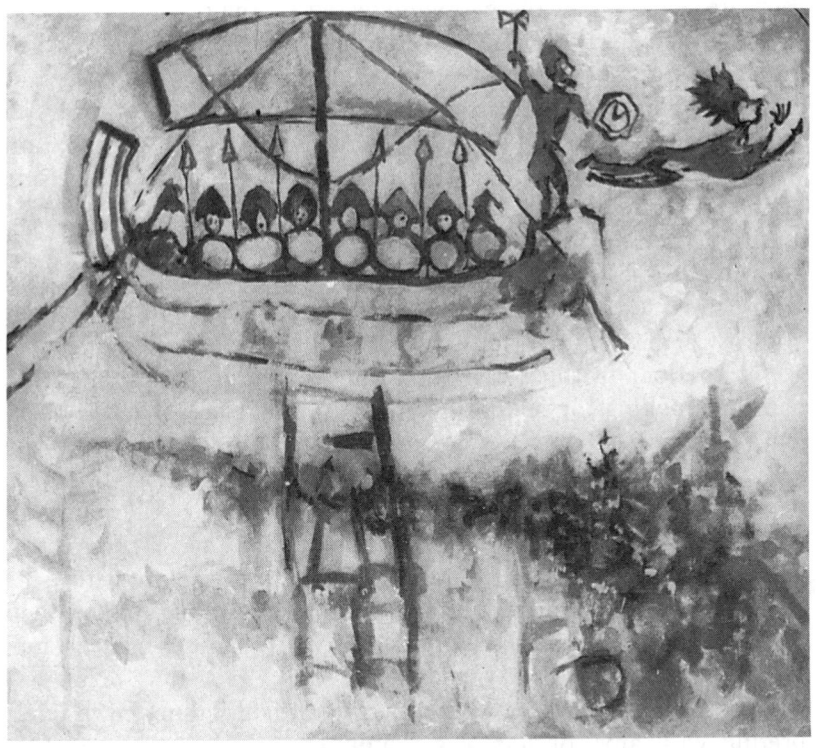

FIGURE 120   *The painting in the Kef el-Blida* hanout *(after J. Ferron, in* Archéologia, *no. 20, January–February 1968).*

figure, stretched out horizontally outside the ship and apparently floating in the air rather than on the surface of the water. This person wears a sort of spiky helmet, unless it is a plumed head-dress.

To describe this scene is a start towards interpreting it, if only in the relationship between the figures that one articulates by doing so or in the importance given to certain attributes that seem to be recognizable. If, for instance, a helmet with a 'cock's comb' is to be seen in the headgear of the horizontal figure, connection with the symbolism of the cock, just mentioned, will suggest the identification of this person with an image of the deceased (let us not forget that the *hanout* is a tomb) 'flying in celestial space or sailing in the higher ocean' (Bisi, 1966, p. 100). In a funerary context, the representation of a ship has since earliest Antiquity been able to evoke the voyage undertaken by the dead person in the afterlife. But what, then, do we make of the people depicted on the boat? If there are seven of them, as they were first counted, they may be seen as seven indigenous divinities, seven minor gods associated with the great god Baal Hammon-Saturn, as indeed they frequently appear on stelae (Camps, 1961, p. 105). If, as a more careful examination would seem to allow, there are actually eight – four on either side of the central mast – it is proposed to recognize them as the eight *kabirim*, the Phoenician gods of sailing (Ferron, 1968, p. 54). In both hypotheses the figure with the menacing *bipennis* is credited with the same identification: he must be Baal Hammon, the great god of Carthage. But what is his relationship with the figure who seems to float in the air, if the latter represents the soul of the departed making for celestial realms? In order to resolve this problem, Jean Ferron (ibid.) conjectures that the god features in the scene in the role of psychopomp or conductor of souls. To give a better explanation of its threatening attitude, while still maintaining the figure's function as psychopomp, another commentator alters radically the perception of the person stretched out before the ship: this would no longer be the dead man's soul but a malevolent spirit 'wishing to thwart the propitious voyage of the funeral ship' (Fantar, 1970, p. 30).

Such different views clearly reveal the difficulty inherent in interpreting with any confidence a monument which is unique of its kind, with which therefore nothing can be compared. The eschatological context, which remains probable but could be clarified only by comparable discoveries, seemed reinforced and rendered more exact, in the view of the first commentators, by their perception of a ladder beneath the boat, with a figure apparently climbing the rungs; and the symbol of the ladder, that link between the lower world and the higher spheres, is in fact present in the Roman era on many a stele to Saturn, Baal Hammon's successor in the *interpretatio Romana*. But this drawing on the lower section of the Kef el-Blida *hanout* is now so faint that one hesitates to distinguish its subject, and in any case if it *is* a ladder, the connection with the vessel and its occupants is in itself an enigma. It must be added that, if the archaizing features of the ship's representation are evident, to the point where it seems difficult to put a later date on it than the sixth century, the 'ladder', which refers to a corpus of beliefs belonging to an appreciably later time, confuses the chronology.

To return to the firmer ground of funerary rites, one last finding urges caution as regards any eschatological interpretation one may be tempted to make. Though it is true that in Carthage the rite of

FIGURE 121 *The interior of a tomb at the cemetery of Djebel Mlezza (P. Cintas).*

cremation appears to have been dominant (but not exclusive) in the Hellenistic period, it has been found that this was not at all the case in the same period in the big cemeteries of the Tunisian Sahel and Cap Bon, where space for the dead was not restricted as in the Punic metropolis. At Djebel Mlezza, the cemetery for the town of Kerkouane, mentioned above, the underground tombs hewn out of the rock, which were reached by staired *dromoi* or shafts, were spacious chambers where excavations revealed the dead – often two to a tomb – lying stretched on their backs, surrounded by plentiful grave goods (figure 121).

THE TOPHET OF CARTHAGE AND THE PROBLEM OF CHILD SACRIFICE

Although the term 'tophet' does not appear in any Phoenician or Punic inscription, it is customarily used to designate an open-air sacrificial area characteristic of many a Phoenician or Punic site: at Motya in Sicily, at Tharros in Sardinia, at Hadrumetum (Sousse) in Tunisia, to quote only the most important and earliest known of these areas. The term tophet is encountered on several occasions in the Old Testament, especially in prophetic passages, when the 'high place' of the tophet in the valley of Ben-Hinnom, where boys and girls were sacrificed by fire, is associated with the idolatrous worship of Baal condemned by Jeremiah (Jeremiah, 7: 31–2; 32; cf. also II Kings, 17: 17). At the end of the seventh century BC King Josiah had the tophet (furnace) of Ben-Himmon destroyed, but we do not know whether that destruction was final (II Kings, 23: 10).

There was nothing like that at Carthage, where the sacrificial area shows clear evidence of a continuity of use over nearly six centuries: it was there, as we have seen (above, p. 31), that the oldest vestiges of the Tyrian colony, datable to the middle of the eighth century, were brought to light, and there is nothing to suggest that its use was interrupted at any time until the last days of the Punic city. Moreover, if we are to believe the first African Father of the Church, Tertullian, these sacrifices of children to Saturn (the name given to Baal Hammon in the *interpretatio Romana*) continued under Roman domination, but apparently in another place than the tophet of Salammbô (Tertullian, *Apologeticum*, IX, 2–4). That continuity in time and the size of the Punic metropolis make the tophet at Carthage the largest of the known sacrificial areas. Its exact boundaries, in the quarter abutting on the western edge of the rectangular harbour, cannot be fixed with certainty, and the erection of villas surrounding the parts already excavated will probably never allow them to be determined. But at the height of its development, in the third century, one may estimate at almost a hectare the enclosure into which votive offerings were crammed, forming a stratigraphic complexity that we shall see later.

THE DISCOVERY OF CARTHAGE'S TOPHET

As often happened in archaeology in a period when findings did not stem from a planned programme drawn up by a team of well-informed specialists, the discovery of the tophet was due both to chance and the good luck of enthusiastic and tenacious amateurs. The circumstances of the discovery – on Christmas Eve in 1921 – contribute still further to turning it into a story and ensuring its star position in archaeological legend.

The tale was told by the chief discoverer of the site, François Icard, a former NCO in the infantry who had become a police inspector in Tunis. With Paul Gielly, a minor public official in

Carthage, he shared a taste for seeking out antiquities that was aided by remarkable intuition. Icard, in particular, is typical of those years before the regulations set up by Louis Poinssot, the real creator of the Tunisian Department of Antiquities, when, notably in Carthage, archaeological research was a somewhat marginal activity, in the pursuit of which scientific curiosity and the enrichment of personal collections often went hand in hand. It would be wrong, however, to criticize those pioneers – among whom was Dr Carton, very frequently cited in these pages – forgetting that at the beginning of this century legislation regarding excavated articles was limited or nonexistent. To return to François Icard, his publications and, even more, his unpublished notebooks, reveal that his personal interests melted away in the fire of the feverish search he and his friend Gielly carried on in the tophet of Salammbô.

For some time the two comrades had been intrigued by the goings-on of a Tunisian – one of those stone-hunters whose activities had for centuries been devouring the subsoil of Carthage – who more and more frequently would offer them stelae, heavy and sometimes stuccoed, in sandstone, or long and tapering in a fine limestone; these had been known since their discovery, in large batches, at various points in Carthage, as early as the middle of the

FIGURE 122 *The tophet of Carthage: the priest stele (Musée national du Bardo, Tunis).*

nineteenth century (cf. below, p. 444). One of the last stelae he had handed over made them determined to get to the bottom of the affair. That was the 'priest stele', now kept in the Bardo Museum, a veritable talking image of a sacrificial area: it shows a man wearing the robe and head-dress of the *kohanim*, his right hand raised in a gesture of prayer, holding in the crook of his left arm a swaddled infant whose fate, in such a context, seems evident (figure 122). On a clear night at the end of December 1921, Icard and Gielly were on the lookout for their supplier whom they surprised while, with the help of a few workers and the complicity of the owner of the land, he was in the act of extracting stelae from the depths of a piece of ground situated not far from the rectangular harbour (now Avenue Hannibal).

THE EXCAVATIONS OF ICARD AND GIELLY

Icard and Gielly jointly bought the piece of land and set to work, devoting their Sundays and the little spare time they had to excavation. As early as the first weeks of 1922, the archaeological reality of the tophet of Salammbô was beginning to appear fairly clearly. It consisted of the superimposition, in uneven strata, of votive ensembles, each made up of a stele or a cippus that surmounted the deposit, in the form of a terracotta urn containing calcined remains of bone, sometimes accompanied by jewels or amulets (figure 123). Icard was a correspondent of the North African Commission of the Comité des Travaux Historiques et Scientifiques and, in a letter of 31 December 1921, had immediately communicated his discovery to the president of the Commission, E. Babelon, the curator of the Cabinet des Medailles of the Bibliothèque Nationale (cf. *Bulletin Archéologique du Comité des Travaux Historiques*, January 1922, pp. XXIII–XXIV). At the latter's request, he submitted a report to the Director of Antiquities, Louis Poinssot, and that marked the beginning of a frequently stormy collaboration, since Icard was offended by the communications, more carefully elaborated than his own, which Poinssot and his second-in-command, Raymond Lantier, drew up on the basis of the information he passed to them.

It is nevertheless a pity that some of Icard's observations were not taken up in the official reports, since he was an excellent excavator for the period. I should like to quote this, addressed to E. Babelon in an (unpublished) letter dated 7 February 1922:

FIGURE 123 *The tophet of Carthage: the Icard and Gielly excavation on 1 March 1922, with Icard on the left and Gielly on the right (Icard papers).*

While carrying out a fuller examination at a depth of 5.50 metres, we encountered a uniform layer of viscous yellow clay three centimetres thick. This layer which extends horizontally under the ground is well packed and is pierced here and there by blocks of raw tufa that emerge like small menhirs. Under these blocks of tufa we made the most curious find. When we freed one of the menhirs we found a kind of subterranean dolmen under which was a two-handled urn, elegantly shaped and painted with reddish circles. This little dolmen, about 0.50 metres tall, was made with blocks of tufa that doubtless came from the vicinity of Carthage, probably the edges of the lake.

Impressed by the extreme antiquity of his findings in the lowest part of his excavations, Icard added that they might belong to 'such a distant era that they could be attributed to an Egyptian colony'. Poinssot's report, published shortly afterwards (*BAC*, meeting of 14 February 1922, pp. XLII–XLV) refuted such naïve remarks, but regrettably it omitted the excavator's stratigraphic details – that uniform 'carpet' of viscous yellow clay, covering the layer that

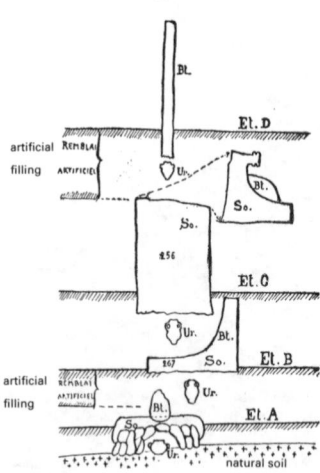

FIGURE 124 *The tophet of Carthage: the four levels of the stratigraphy (A, B, C, D) of the Icard and Gielly excavation (drawn by Charles Saumagne, October 1922).*

would later be known as 'Tanit I', subsequently observed separately by Donald Harden and Pierre Cintas.

Confronted from day to day with the complexity of this excavation where – with the exception of the separating 'carpet' of yellow clay at the bottom – monuments were superimposed in a somewhat overlapping position, Icard had taken care not to propose too rigid a stratigraphy. Poinssot's report which, reworked and developed by his own pen and that of Lantier, would a little later become the first scientific article on the tophet (Poinssot and Lantier, 1923) presented a four-stage stratification, from stage A at the base of the excavation to stage D, the most recent, situated at about 2.5 metres below modern ground level (figure 124). An attempt at absolute dating accompanied this distinction between the levels, with stage A set back as far as the end of the sixth century, whereas B was dated to the fifth century and C to the fourth. We shall see that subsequent excavations perceptibly modified that view of both stratification and chronology, but essential points had been established a year after the discovery of the tophet, although the excavation had touched only a small surface area, chiefly at the deep level.

The formulae invariably repeated on the inscribed stelae, especially starting from the fourth century BC, confirmed something that the study of stones sporadically discovered at Carthage had already indicated since Ernest Renan's first works: the dedicants, who in an oriental manner mentioned their forebears as far back as the second preceding generation, sometimes beyond, for the most part devoted their vows jointly to the Lady Tanit, *pene Baal* ('face of Baal') and Baal Hammon, and sometimes to Tanit alone. Beyond the somewhat artificial distinction between the four stages, the excavation revealed the unusual nature of the first level of deposits, inserted in a layer of black marshy clay just above the virgin soil and contained in urns with a red-glazed surface or decorated with red bands, which were carefully closed – this would not always be the case subsequently – and protected by kinds of stone cists (Icard's 'little dolmens'), surmounted occasionally by a carved and sculpted cippus and more commonly by a crude *sema* or baetyl. Last and most important, the first serious analyses of the urns' contents, notably those of Paul Pallary (1922), established beyond doubt the presence in most of them of the calcined bones of young children.

On this subject Icard's notebooks and two illuminating articles, one by Eusèbe Vassel, the other by Charles Saumagne, both in 1923, reveal the dawning doubts and hesitations and the polemic that was to develop. The first practitioners to be consulted were loath to identify the calcined residue as the bones of children and preferred to see them as the remains of goats, lambs, dogs – even monkeys! But they had to yield to the evidence and admit, alongside the minority presence of kids' and lambs' remains, the major presence of human remains, generally those of extremely young infants, aged from a few days to a few months. The controversy revealed how difficult it was to appreciate the reality of a practice which the Old Testament bore witness to while condemning it, just as later it provoked the horrified condemnation of the classical world. We shall see that this very human reaction still underlies the interpretation sometimes given even today to a reality that no one tries any longer to deny. Furthermore, Pallary's analyses (1922), although at the time based on an insufficient number of pieces of evidence, already revealed that, compared with animal remains, there was a higher proportion of infant remains in 'level C' than in 'level A'. The most recent excavations fully confirm the finding, which at first sight appears paradoxical, that from the earliest times onwards the number of substitutions declined, and thus that the harshness of the sacrifical rite was greater in the fourth and third centuries BC.

Icard and Gielly's excavations were suspended on 4 November 1922 for lack of funds, and also because of the disagreements between the authors of the discovery and the management of the Antiquities Service. With very few resources, hundreds of stelae and hundreds of urns had been brought to light, but the majority were lost from a scientific viewpoint because they had not been recorded precisely. The bad luck that has been attendant since then on the tophet excavations was already showing itself: the publication of the results by no means matched the importance of the discovery and, badly protected, the enclosure of the first excavations was looted.

THE EXCAVATIONS OF FRANCIS KELSEY AND DONALD HARDEN

At that point an unexpected person entered the scene, who could be described as highly colourful had he not always been impeccably clad in white, displaying in the photographs of the period the elegance of a dandy of the 'roaring twenties'. 'Count' Byron Khun de Prorock, of Hungarian origin but an American citizen, combined a pronounced penchant for archaeology with a New World practical sense and a spirit of enterprise. He bought the unfortunate Icard's land from him, restored it to order and, by means of lectures and thanks to a clever public-relations exercise – all recorded in his little book, *Digging for Lost African Gods*, published in 1926 – he succeeded in interesting a Franco-American team in the development of the tophet excavations (figure 125).

French scientific support was chiefly represented by the Abbé Chabot, publisher of the *Corpus Inscriptionum Semiticarum.*

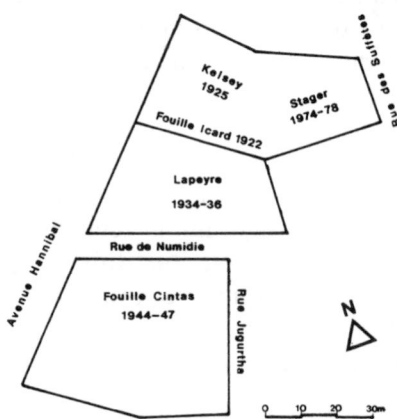

FIGURE 125   *The tophet of Carthage: plan of the excavated plots.*

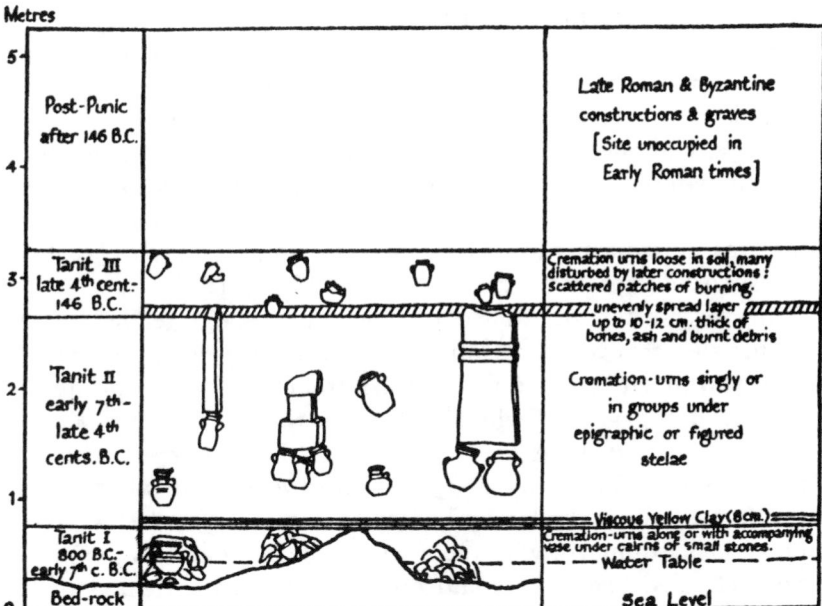

FIGURE 126   *The Harden and Kelsey excavations of the tophet of Carthage: Donald Harden's stratigraphic plan.*

Alongside the mission's director, Francis Kelsey, of the University of Michigan, the name chiefly recalled will be that of a young British man, Donald Harden, who was to end his career as Director of the London Museum and rank among the greatest experts on the Phoenician and Punic world.

It is to Harden that we owe a decisive improvement in the stratigraphic perception of the tophet, based on works carried out in 1925 on a plot of ground that abutted the first trench to the north. We still make use today of his definition of three major periods (figure 126). The earliest, which he called Tanit I, corresponded with Poinssot and Lantier's level A; but a superior comparative knowledge of pottery in the oriental tradition allowed Harden to place that first period of the tophet more exactly between the end of the eighth century and the middle or, at the latest, the end of the seventh: over one century, at the most, the votive deposits, which at that time were not very numerous or thickly laid down, had occupied a wide space. The second period, Tanit II, covered a far longer time span, which it was proposed to extend to about 300 BC, the last period, Tanit III, lasting very nearly a century and a half, until the destruction of Carthage in 146 BC. It was greater awareness of the shapes and techniques of Phoenician, then Punic pottery that had enabled the young assistant lecturer from Aberdeen University to propose a stratification destined to last because, without being too ambitious, it rested on a strict analysis of that material. And indeed, his classification of plates and saucers, used as lids on the urns, has never been amended, and his study of the urns subsequently formed the basis for more elaborate classifications worked out by Cintas (Harden, 1927 and 1937).

An adverse fate continued to dog undertakings related to the tophet. Its excavation was abandoned after the death in 1927 of Kelsey, who left behind only a slender preliminary report promising a fuller 450-page one which never saw the light of day (Kelsey, 1926, p. 11 note 1). A few years later Dr Louis Carton, who had been interested in Carthage for over thirty years, with what success we know, bought the land adjacent on the south to the two plots previously examined, with the intention of doing his own exploration. He died before he could do so but, at the entreaties of his widow, a White Father, G. G. Lapeyre, excavated the ground in 1934–6 with financial support from the French Institute. Thousands of cippi, stelae and urns then emerged from the ground, but there is no information on the conditions of their excavation other than a few pages in two communications from Père Lapeyre published in the reports of the Académie des Inscriptions et Belles-Lettres in 1935 and 1939. A great deal of material was thus amassed for epigraphists and specialists in the sculptured decoration of these monuments, but it was just objects unfortunately removed from their context. Understanding of the tophet in its function of a sacrifical area had not advanced one iota. The Second World War was then looming perilously, and the site remained dormant for several years.

THE EXCAVATIONS OF PIERRE CINTAS

The resumption of the excavations, after the war, was the concern of Pierre Cintas, acting under the aegis of the Antiquities Department whose new head was Gilbert Charles Picard. Cintas was the last and most accomplished of those archaeologists who rose from the ranks – in his case the Customs – self-taught but compensating for that handicap by dint of a passion for the work, very quickly grasping the evidence on the ground; in Tunisia they were among

the greatest contributors to the advancement of knowledge of antiquities and Antiquity itself. We are indebted to Cintas for a major
book, *Céramique punique* ('Punic Pottery'), which appeared precisely mid-century (1950) and truly laid the foundations for the
study of pottery in this particular domain. This ample study was
born from numerous preliminary works; the author had done his
training in the field with an experienced and exacting practitioner,
Dr Gobert, who, during those years in Tunisia, was to pre- and
proto-history what Dr Carton had been to Punic and Roman archaeology. By the standards of the time, Cintas had been well
taught. But it can also be said of him that he excavated with a magic
wand, an instrument that does not usually figure in the panoply of
the perfect archaeologist; hence jealousy was provoked and suspi-
cions awakened. In a brief mission to Tipasa, in Algeria, he applied
by instinct, so to speak, a few parameters for researching sites, later
formally theorized, and was able to lay hands on the first known
pre-Roman traces of the 'Punic stepping stones'. It is but a step
from that to talk of sleight of hand, but it would be wrong to do
so. Cintas did not produce his sherds from his hat. This great
enthusiast had other weaknesses and we shall soon see what they
were.

The plot in the shape of a trapezium involved in the new excavations, starting in July 1944 – the 'Hervé property' (*terrain Hervé*)
between Avenue Hannibal on the west, the Rue de Numidie on the
north and Rue Jugurtha on the east – was close to the site of the
preceding explorations but of quite a different character (cf. figure
125). Its substratum was also different (if one excepts part of the
vaulted substructure in the Kelsey-Harden excavation) because it
soon revealed itself to be cluttered with walls and, deep down, with
Roman foundations which had disturbed the depositional strata,
thus making the excavators' task much more complicated. Taken as
the basis for a three-dimensional system of coordinates, these walls
were used in drawing up the detailed survey and one, a thick widely
curving wall following an approximately east-west axis, served to
divide the excavation into two sectors, north and south.

The first, 'northern excavation', a band between eight and ten
metres wide lying east-west, was at first very disappointing. Begun
on the west side, starting from Avenue Hannibal, the examination
revealed, even at a depth of four to five metres, nothing but stelae
and late Punic pottery. Further eastwards the stratification seemed
to fill out, with the appearance at a depth of between five and six
metres of cippi in stuccoed sandstone, but the archaic level was

FIGURE 127   *The north excavation of the tophet of Carthage by Pierre Cintas, showing traces of a surrounding wall (P. Cintas).*

nonexistent. The explanation for this disconcerting situation came with the discovery, shortly afterwards, while still advancing eastward, of a row of vertical slabs forming a wall, on a north-south axis (Cintas, 1970, pp. 313–14). It seemed that they had in fact discovered one of the boundaries of the sacrificial area, or at least part of its first enclosure, on the west side, before the accumulation of deposits in a period that cannot be precisely dated (perhaps around the fourth century) forced its infringement (figure 127). In fact, within the row of slabs, in the eastern part of the dig, Cintas and his assistant G. Feuille found the stratification described by the preceding excavators. At a depth varying from 6.5 to 7 metres below the present ground level, the first votive deposits were buried in the layer of black clay which extended over the concreted surface of the natural subsoil to a depth of between 40 and 60 centimetres. In earlier pages dealing with the harbours, we saw that this layer is a relic of 'prehistoric' times when the whole area was lagoonal and marshy (above, p. 184).

At this depth the archaeologists ended their excavation in water, which is explained by the rise in the sea level – to the east the sea is very close – of about just under half a metre in comparison with what it had been in the Punic era. As in preceding explorations, these archaic deposits of the 'Tanit I' period seemed fairly widespread and protected in little constructed vaults (figure 128). Also similar to the observations already made by Icard in 1922, Cintas noted above this first level the fairly regular layer of sand mixed

FIGURE 128   *A small pit or* pozzo *in Cintas's excavation (P. Cintas).*

with yellow clay, of a thickness varying between 5 and 20 centimetres, which clearly separated it from later levels. The latter themselves were not superimposed in any strict way, as Poinssot and Lantier suggested with their levels B and C – which would have implied a planned and regularized use of the space available in the area – but in a rather anarchic fashion, with undulations and overlappings, 'like fish scales', as C. Picard well described them (1990, p. 78). So if Harden's division of the periods into three eras (Tanit I, II and III) was to be preserved as a broad chronological framework (quite precisely dated as regards Tanit I), it would be necessary to note stratigraphic aspects that varied from one mini-sector to another.

The Tanit I level of the north part of the 'terrain Hervé', which was excavated over a surface area of about 80 square metres, produced invaluable observations. Although for the most part the urns contained the calcined bones of very young infants, remains of birds were also found mingled with them. There were Egyptian-style beads and amulets in abundance, which were virtually absent from the level above. Particularly noteworthy alongside the urns of this low level and, like them, protected by little caskets or vaults made of assembled stones, was the discovery of male or female campaniform statuettes, examples of which Père Lapeyre had already published ten years earlier, in his excavation of the 'terrain Carton' (Lapeyre, 1939, p. 295). Were they in place of a votive deposit, as Père Lapeyre suggested? There is still argument as to their significance (cf. above, p. 163).

As the different parts of the tophet do not constitute a homogeneous whole, it is not surprising that certain disparities should be

Religion

FIGURE 129 *Stele number 5780 from the* Corpus Inscriptionum Semiticarum *(P. Cintas)*.

revealed between one plot of ground and another by excavations carried out at the same level. Thus one of G. C. Picard's preliminary reports, confirming Cintas's excavation notes, remarks on the abundance at the intermediate level (the beginning and middle phases of Tanit II) of hollow altars, 'kinds of *bothroi*', holding the stelae (G. C. Picard, 1945, pp. 448–50). If one compares these hollow altars with the round holes pierced in the concreted ground on which the stelae of the Tanit III level lie in the north sector of the 'terrain Hervé', one is led to suggest that the various orifices were intended to receive libations. In support of this hypothesis of funerary worship celebrated in the tophet itself came the discovery, on 12 July 1945, of a stele with a pediment (stele Cb 687 b: *CIS*, 5780) showing a woman clad in a long pleated tunic, half kneeling near a mound on which she rests her left hand; in her right she holds a vessel with a handle (figure 129). This representation has been much commented on, but it is agreed that it shows a scene of libation. It was thought that it might be a cult of Dido, given heroic status after her suicide by fire, or perhaps a funereal rite celebrated in honour of victims of the sacrificial ritual, equally rendered divine. We shall return to this later, in connection with what is known as the 'Cintas chapel'.

THE 'CHAPEL' AND THE FOUNDATION DEPOSIT

From 1946, for two short seasons, the excavations moved to the other side of the 'curved wall', into the south part of the plot. There Roman structures superimposed on the Punic remains took the form of large square foundation piers, arranged in staggered rows, and the excavators used their tops as the starting-point in determining the depth of the levels, the other marker being, at the very bottom, the level of water noted from day to day. This 'southern excavation', and more especially the small rectangular sector situated between pillars V, VI, XIII and XIV, aroused Cintas's strongest emotions. It was there that in the spring of 1947 he discovered what, on first examination, seemed to him to be not one of the first deposits in the sacrificial area, part of Tanit I, but an even earlier

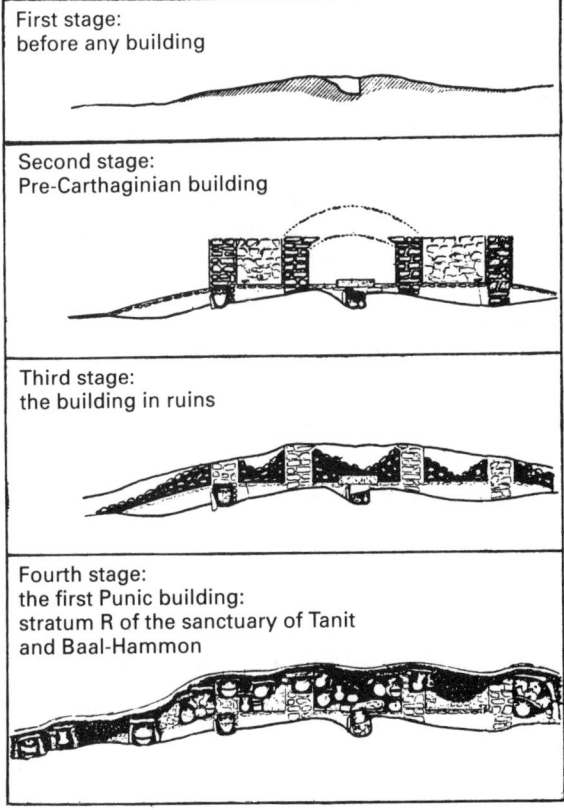

First stage:
before any building

Second stage:
Pre-Carthaginian building

Third stage:
the building in ruins

Fourth stage:
the first Punic building:
stratum R of the sanctuary of Tanit
and Baal-Hammon

FIGURE 130 *The tophet of Carthage: the 'Cintas chapel' (after* Revue tunisienne, *1948).*

FIGURE 131   *The 'Cintas chapel' just after its excavation (P. Cintas).*

monument, a 'pre-Carthaginian sanctuary', to use the title he gave
his discovery in an article in the *Revue tunisienne* (1948). From the
debris of collapsed walls, in the crevices of which many votive
deposits of Tanit I had become lodged after their destruction, he
reconstructed, by a process of reasoning in reverse from effect to
cause, a primitive 'chapel', a kind of small vaulted chamber of tiny
dimensions, surrounded by low walls marking out little corridors
(figures 130 and 131). The whole thing was centred on a geological
cavity in the ground, a sort of natural tomb whose rich contents
were revealed by the excavations.

I have already mentioned this in the pages dealing with the dating
of Carthage's foundation, for the arguments relating to that chronology revolved around these objects for a long time and still do
today. Apart from a lamp with two spouts and an amphora, which
occupied the upper part of the 'vault' (and which were identified as
the signs of later re-use), there was an apparently homogeneous
assemblage covered by hardened mud that had filled the cavity
(figure 132). To name only the most diagnostic pieces: an askos in
the shape of a bird, three oenochoi and two cotyles with geometric
decoration were found. In addition to this, another find was made
at the base of one of the enclosing walls of this 'chapel': an apparent
foundation deposit of two objects that called for a very early
dating, a bowl-lamp in the Phoenician tradition with a single spout
(the lamps from the archaic tombs have two) and, most important,
an egg-shaped amphora with twisted handles, in the geometric
decoration of which Cintas wanted to see Mycenaean charac-

Religion 243

FIGURE 132   *The objects from the 'Cintas chapel' (P. Cintas).*

teristics. It seemed to him possible to date the assemblage of these
objects, from both the 'foundation deposit' and the 'vault', to the
end of the second millennium (Cintas, 1948, pp. 29–30). Thus he
believed he had discovered, right beside the shore where the first
arrivals from the Orient must have set foot, an archaeological sign
of the legend, mentioned in the fourth century by Philistos of
Syracuse and in the same period by Eudoxus of Cnidus, according
to which Carthage was founded at the very end of the thirteenth
century BC, before Utica.

For an archaeologist there is nothing more irresistibly intoxicat-
ing than the very earliest dates. At the bottom of the tophet Cintas
had experienced the rapture of the deep. Not particularly sobered
afterwards by the dating corrections that the expertise of Pierre
Demargne (1951, pp. 44–52) made it necessary to apply to this
material, which could not be earlier than the middle of the seventh
century, Cintas went off to Utica to search for what Carthage had
denied him, the longed-for meeting-point of archaeology and legend.

In the evening of his life, publishing in 1970 the first volume of
his *Manuel d'Archéologie punique* ('Manual of Punic Archaeology') – in fact a manifesto supporting the earliest datings for
Carthage – this lucky but dissatisfied excavator deliberately

destroyed 'his' chapel. Returning to the documentation of his excavations in the forties, he pointed out archaeological situations
that were, if not completely similar to those of the 'chapel', at least
comparable in principle. Other 'little chambers' existed, inadequately described at the time of the excavation, similarly sheltering
little *pozzi* which themselves did not hold sacrificial deposits but
votive objects: baetyls, cippi, various pottery articles (Cintas, 1970,
pp. 318–19). Yes, but there still remained the exceptional nature of
the collection of objects contained in what Cintas, at the time of the
discovery, had called the 'holy of holies'. One cannot help the
feeling that the author of *Céramique punique*, disappointed at
having to acknowledge that the items of Greek pottery in the
'chapel' were not of the desired antiquity, chose to make a common-
place of the archaeological context of this discovery, using arguments that are not all compelling.

This hypothesis did not fail to weigh heavily on the definitive
publication of these excavations, on which its author was working,
though prevented by his premature death from bringing it to a
successful conclusion. It is a great pity, because the archives left by
Cintas, which are unfortunately incomplete and virtually unusable
without him, demonstrate that he had perfectly understood the
special demands of the visual reconstruction of extremely rich and
complex archaeological situations. Probably the most up-to-date
techniques of computer-aided drawing would today be the only
method capable of grasping the realities and displaying them in an
all-round view. His quite rare qualities of draughtsmanship had

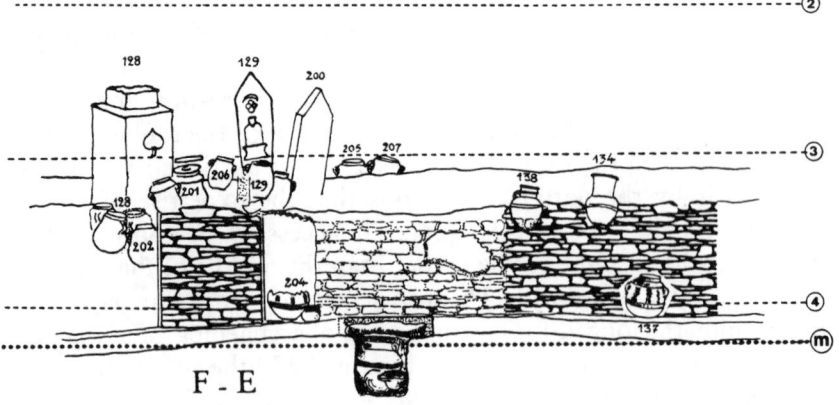

FIGURE 133   *A cross-section prepared by Pierre Cintas of a sector of his
excavation in the vicinity of the 'chapel'.*

allowed Cintas to record the data of his plot three-dimensionally, as faithfully as manual techniques would allow. He intended to show them graphically by complementing the reconstructions in plan with numerous cross-sections that might almost be termed 'histological'. The sample given below (figure 133) will revive the regret that an unfinished work always arouses.

RECENT INVESTIGATIONS

The year when, together with Cintas, all prospects of the publication under his own care of the details of his excavation of the tophet disappeared, saw the opening of the international campaign to protect the site of Carthage, under the sponsorship of UNESCO. For four years, between 1975 and 1979, a team from the American School of Oriental Research, led by Lawrence Stager, resumed exploration where it had been abandoned half a century before by another American team, that of Francis Kelsey, or to be more precise, on the eastern boundary of that plot (cf. figure 125).

As I write this, over ten years after the end of the excavation, the publication of the entire findings has still not appeared, but partial reports and a few articles allow its principal contributions to be stressed, clarifying the preceding observations on essential points. The new team thought they could define nine stratigraphic horizons, perhaps in a slightly artificial way and in any case valid only for a restricted sector of the tophet. But they preserved the overall differentiation between three major periods, proposed by Donald Harden, and more careful observation now enabled their appearance to be established more precisely (figure 134). If, for the beginnings of Tanit I, there is still a reluctance to go back earlier in time than 730 BC – which leaves a yawning gap of three generations between then and the legendary founding date of 814 – its end has been brought forward to 600 BC, which means perhaps overextending that first period, which is well characterized by its stratigraphic clarity, by the placing of votive deposits in constructed 'vaults' or *pozzi* occupying the lowest level quite sparsely, and also by its pottery content. Thanks to recent excavations on the south slope of Byrsa, we now have a better knowledge of the pottery from the second half of the seventh century: it is not to be found among the material from Tanit I.

A votive monument which is common from the Tanit I period, alongside the baetyls and crude pyramidions or obelisks, is an

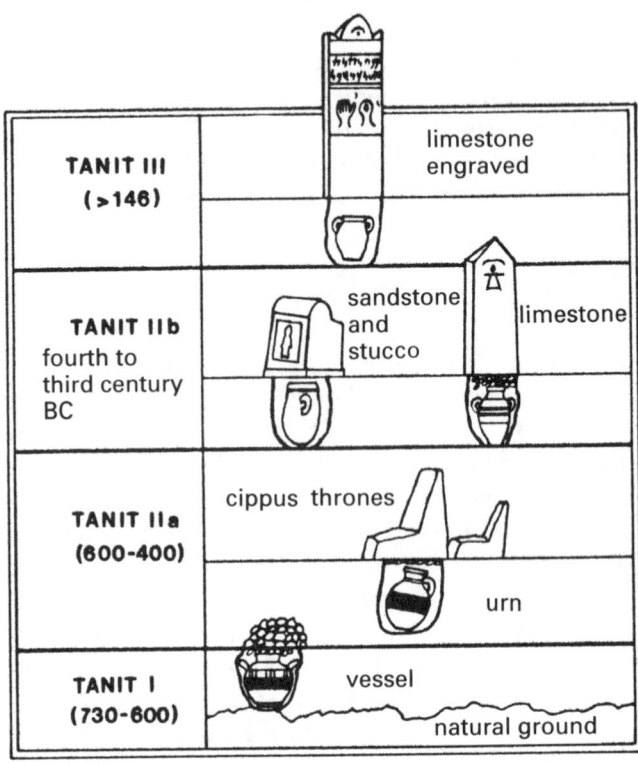

TANIT III **(>146)**		limestone engraved
TANIT IIb fourth to third century BC		sandstone and stucco limestone
TANIT IIa **(600-400)**	cippus thrones	urn
TANIT I **(730-600)**		vessel natural ground

FIGURE 134   *The tophet of Carthage: a schematic stratigraphy of the excavation by the American School of Oriental Research (American mission)*

L-shaped cippus, often labelled 'throne-cippus', cut out of sandstone from the quarries at the tip of Cap Bon (El-Haouaria). It is still present in the Tanit II stage, at least in the earliest phase, which can be dated to the middle or end of the fifth century. These 'throne-cippi' were then replaced by heavier monuments, still hewn from El-Haouaria sandstone, but frequently coated with white stucco on the surface of which traces of brilliant colouring sometimes still survive (yellow, red, light blue). Representations in bas-relief can be seen on the front of these little monuments: often a stylized baetyl, and also frequently a female divinity in whom it is permissible to recognize Tanit, standing full-length, sometimes holding a drum in her arms folded on her bosom, in a temple portal shown in the Egyptian manner (figure 135). It is from the second phase of Tanit II (fourth to third century) that grey limestone stelae rival, then

FIGURE 135   *Cippi from Tanit II, in sandstone from El-Haouaria; the
one on the right, representing a baetyl, is coated with stucco (after
P. Bartoloni, Istituto per la civiltà fenicia e punica, Rome).*

supplant the sandstone cippi. Ending in a triangular pediment, they
show different symbols, at least two of which are divine symbols:
the disc and the crescent (without doubt Baal Hammon) and the
'sign of Tanit', a triangle surmounted by two raised forearms. It is
also on these stelae from the final phase of Tanit II that the name of
Tanit 'face of Baal' (*pene Baal*) first appears, on inscriptions which
become increasingly frequent but always in a desperately dry and
repetitive form. At the Tanit III level, where the topmost layers were
disturbed and decapitated by Roman constructions, these limestone
stelae became more and more fine and slender. In most cases
acroteria flank the terminal triangular pediment. The incised and
sculpted decoration is different. Beside the ever-present religious
symbols (for example, the raised right hand with opened fingers
symbolizing prayer) an iconography emerges that is very varied in
its repertoire and remains one of the best sources of our knowledge
of Punic art (figure 136). In this regard the harvest from recent
excavations has merely added examples to the already impressive
collection coming from the old excavations, notably those of Père

FIGURE 136 *Stelae from the level of Tanit III, showing the open right hands on the pediments; note the 'sign of Tanit' between caducei on the centre stele (after C. Picard).*

Lapeyre and Cintas. The collection has given rise to studies devoted to the characteristic imagery of this late period of Carthage, when oriental and Semitic features had not been completely obliterated by the decorative themes of the Hellenistic Koine (see particularly C. Picard, 1967a, 1976 and 1978). This persistence of the original features of its culture gives Carthage a very distinct image, even in the late period, and in all fields, notably the artistic one, as we shall see below.

ANALYSIS OF THE URNS AND THE REALITY OF SACRIFICES

The most novel contribution of the American excavations in the seventies was the care given to an internal examination of the votive deposits. Of some 400 urns brought to light by this mission, 130 were subjected to a meticulous analysis of their contents (Stager, 1982, p. 159). In the main they belong to two chronological groups, one dating to the seventh century (Tanit I) and the other to the fourth (end of Tanit III). In this last period, the former Tyrian colony had been broadly and, one might suppose, even deeply Hellenized: had it not adopted the worship of Demeter and Kore at the beginning of the fourth century? Now, astonishingly – perhaps the most surprising of the confirmations provided by the latest investigations – it is in the group of votive deposits datable to the fourth century that the lowest proportion of 'substitute sacrifices' or, to put it more objectively, remains of young animals compared with the remains of young children, are to be found: roughly one urn out of ten, whereas the proportion had been nearly a third in the seventh-century group. We saw earlier that the first findings, of Pallary in 1922, were already tending in this direction, but with less chronological precision.

Such a conclusion obviously poses a basic problem. Everyone remembers chapter 22 of Genesis, in which Abraham, *in extremis*, sacrifices in place of his son Isaac a ram he notices caught by its horns in a thicket. Among other meanings, this famous passage retraces in a symbolic summary the evolution leading from a 'barbarous' ritual practice of human sacrifice to a gentler 'civilized' version of the ritual, the sacrifice of a substitute victim. Using the language of the votive inscriptions, it is the transition from the *molk* sacrifice to the *molkomor* sacrifice. One would expect that this development would be historically attested and irreversible. We see that it was nothing of the kind.

How can this be explained? The first step is to try to account for it while remaining in the religious sphere and looking at it in relation to the historical evolution of the city. Carthage's first defeats do not date from the fourth century, but it is true that the first great dangers it encountered in its African territory, to the extent of seeing its very existence in peril, occurred at the end of that century, when Agathocles' Sicilian expedition came within inches of causing its downfall and seriously weakened the political structures of the city, with Bomilcar's *coup d'état* in 309–308. It was then that the collective sacrifices mentioned by Diodorus of Sicily in a passage used many times (XX, 14, 4–7) are assumed to have taken place. Hundreds of children of aristocratic families were consigned to the holocaust and placed, as Diodorus specifies, in the arms of a bronze statue of Kronos (the Baal Hammon of the Carthaginians, the future Saturn of Romanized Africa), which precipitated them into a pit filled with burning embers. We know what dramatic capital Flaubert made of this evocation in *Salammbô*.

Unfortunately – or fortunately! – archaeology does not confirm the truth of such collective sacrifices. But, as well as giving evidence for the reduction of substitute sacrifice in the classical period, it fixes the identity of the holocaust victims. In early times they were for the most part either newborn or stillborn babies: the condition of the bony remains, barely ossified, does not allow a distinction to be made with any certainty. In the group datable to the fourth century, the remains are largely those of children aged between one and three years, rarely more. Above all, one out of three urns contains the remains of two or even three children. In the latter case, examination of the teeth would allow the statement that of the three (two being twins, either newborn or stillborn) the third child was aged between two and four years. This difference in age between the baby (or the stillborn infant) and the child of between two and four seems to indicate that they were children of the same family – as is already suggested by the fact that their remains are collected in the same urn, under the same votive monument – for that age gap is the average natural interval between births in societies that do not practise birth control.

A difficulty then arises if one recalls the biblical commandment about first fruits: 'The firstborn of thy sons shalt thou likewise give to me' (Exodus, 22:28), which precludes the principle of dual victims. One of the classical authors who makes reference to the Phoenician practice of sacrificing infants, the Greek Kleitarchos, in the fourth century BC, says only that in particular the Carthaginians, in order to obtain a great favour from Kronos (= Baal Hammon), pledge *one* of their children to the holocaust. To reconcile the single victim in the religious commandment with the duality often found in actual fact, it may be imagined (Stager and Wolff, 1984, p. 49) that the parents pledged a child yet to be born. In cases where the child pledged to the holocaust was stillborn, or died shortly after birth before the day appointed for the sacrifice, the family had no other recourse than to redouble its sacrifice by the offering – more agreeable to the god – of a living child, aged between two and four years, as shown by analysis of the bones collected in the urns.

Considerations other than strictly religious ones may have intervened, both paradoxically to restrict the practice of animal substitution by comparison with the archaic period and to multiply the number of votive deposits (the American team estimated the number of urns that the tophet may have received between 400 and 200 BC at around 20,000) and frequently to double the offering in each deposit. In the fourth century Carthage had become a 'megalopolis' on the scale of the ancient world. This was the time when Diodorus of Sicily, recounting the manoeuvres of General Bomilcar during his attempted putsch, talked of a new town (a *nea polis*) beside the old city: this would be the Megara of texts of the

Hellenistic period. Unlike archaic Carthage, when the sacrifice of children could easily have rendered an insufficient population even more fragile, a special form of Malthusianism might have been able to reconcile demographic imperatives with religious requirements. Ritual infanticide might also have played the role of a means of birth control, even if our minds refuse to accept the idea; perhaps, too, it was a system of economic control. Study of the votive inscriptions (Mosca, 1975) reveals a fairly clear predominance of the rich classes (represented by traders, but also by priests and magistrates, *shofetim, rabbi*) among the dedicants of these ex-votos. For these families, limiting their offspring was a way of avoiding the dispersal of inheritances, even if the rule of primogeniture already limited the risk of their being dissipated. And, from yet another viewpoint, fewer mouths to feed doubtless saved families of more modest means from poverty.

THE FUNERARY HYPOTHESIS

Specialists in the civilizations of the Semitic world have long been divided over how to interpret the irrefutable fact of the presence of very young infants' calcined bones in the votive urns found in the tophet. For the modern conscience, there has not indeed been automatic acceptance of a sacrificial rite involving such victims. Thus for the excavator of Ras Shamra-Ugarit in the middle of this century, C. F. A. Schaeffer, the deposits revealed in these areas should be regarded as belonging to cemeteries of a very special kind, reserved for children, and installed on the fringes of a sanctuary (Schaeffer, *CRAI*, 1956, p. 67; *Ugaritica*, IV, 1962, pp. 81–3). It is not surprising, therefore, that the explanatory hypotheses just mentioned, developed from the American mission's important work on the tophet at Carthage, should have aroused reactions, in particular those of a very eminent Semitic scholar, Sabatino Moscati. Recalling that in the thirties Otto Eissfeldt had demonstrated brilliantly that the famous god Moloch – with all due respect to Flaubert – was merely the product of a misunderstanding over the sense of the term *molk*, which actually means an offering ritual, Moscati fifty years later wished to give the support of his celebrated name to the refutation of the argument, accepted by the majority, that *molk* consisted of a ritual and bloody sacrifice of young children. Like the word *mtnt*, which appears in the stock phrases of votive inscriptions, the word *molk* would mean 'gift' or 'offering'.

And even if it may allude to passing through fire, it would not imply that the victim was previously killed; the tophet would thus be a sacred area in which, rather than children in general, stillborn babies or those who died shortly after birth would be burned and then buried in urns (Moscati, 1987, pp. 3–15).

The arguments of these 'revisionists', of whom the Italian scholar is the leader, are of two kinds. The first derives from a re-examination of literary sources. It is pointed out that the major historians of the ancient world, from Herodotus to Thucydides and Polybius to Livy, did not breathe a word about a practice which could not have failed to horrify them, had they been aware of it, and which they would not have hesitated to blow up out of all proportion, in the polemical context that they most frequently created in their presentation of the Phoenicians and then the Carthaginians. It is thus a matter of an argument *a silentio*, the least convincing of all for a historian; but that silence clashes loudly with the concert of accusations of impiety and perfidy which are usually directed at the Carthaginians by classical authors. There remains the passage from Cleitarchus, which I mentioned, and especially the one from Diodorus of Sicily (XX, 14, 6), if it does not derive from Cleitarchus, as there have recently been attempts to demonstrate (Simonetti, 1983, pp. 95–8). It must be emphasized that Diodorus is here referring to a practice which he presents as exceptional, that of the collective sacrifices which the Carthaginians were said to have offered in order to obtain divine favour when besieged in 312 by Agathocles' soldiers.

To that may be added observations of an archaeological kind. It is known that infant mortality was very high in the cities of the ancient world, especially in the neonatal and prenatal stage. Data obtained from a cemetery of the Roman imperial period at Setif (ancient *Sitifis*) in Algeria, are revealing in this respect: almost 17 per cent of infants did not reach full term or died at birth, and almost 40 per cent did not reach the age of one year (Février and Guéry, 1980, pp. 119–20). That mortality rate could not have been any lower in Punic Carthage, some centuries earlier. A recent study of Carthage's Punic cemeteries revealed the great rarity in the old excavations of tombs identified as those of children, especially of a tender age (Bénichou-Safar, 1981, pp. 6–7). This quasi-lacuna or rarity in the findings is explained to a certain extent by the scant attention paid in former times by excavators in a hurry – and frequently absent from the excavation sites – to modest burials that may have passed unnoticed (cf. Lancel, 1982, p. 333, for an example of a cremation burial of a child aged several months). But the fact remains solid enough for the suggestion to have been made that the tombs of very young children which were not being found in the cemeteries were actually in the tophet (Ribichini, 1987, p. 3). The sanctuary would thus have afforded shelter to the remains of young beings whose death on the very threshold of life had left them, even more than the *ahoroi* of Greek tradition, on the fringe of adult society. Excluded also from the society of the dead in the cemeteries, they would have been 'pledged' or 'offered' to the divinity and gone through fire in ritual fashion in the hope of entering another life or being reincarnated (Bénichou-Safar, 1981, p. 8; Moscati, 1987, pp. 9–10).

The explanation is attractive, coherent from a sociological and religious point of view, but it does not take account of all the data. For what are we to make of the young children of between two and four years who, even if not in the majority – at least at an early date – are also attested in analyses prior to those carried out by the American mission (Richard, 1961, pp. 115–16: analyses carried out on the contents of urns from the Cintas excavations in the tophet of Carthage and at Sousse)? Will it be claimed that they too were 'offered' *post mortem*, i.e. after a natural death, and not ritually sacrificed like the young animals whose remains sometimes lie with theirs in the same urns? Perhaps the day will come when more expert osteological analyses will allow us objective certainty about when and how the death of these young children occurred. That will put an end to the argument which in its present state does not permit a categorical denial of the reality of Carthaginian human sacrifice.

THE 'MOLK' SACRIFICE IN ACTUAL FACT

Even if they are neither romantics in the style of Flaubert nor sensation-mongering journalists, historians have nevertheless sometimes felt the temptation to reconstruct the *molk* sacrifice in its concrete form. Two approaches are possible. The first is the textual one already used by the author of *Salammbô*. The passage on which it is based is of course the famous page from Diodorus of Sicily, and to these references will be added details from Cleitarchus and Plutarch (*De superstitione*, 13). Combining these scattered data and drawing from Isaiah (30:31–3) the sonorous accompaniment that Plutarch also evoked, and borrowing the nocturnal backdrop from the reference made in Latin (*sacrum magnum nocturnum molchomor*) in the substitution ritual from the stelae of Ngaous in Algeria, a French Semitic scholar, James Février, has suggested a gripping overall tableau of the ceremony:

> It is night . . . The scene seems to be lit only by the fire burning in the sacred pit, the tophet: its reflections rather than its glow can be seen. But the great bronze statue of Baal Hammon, standing on the very edge of the sacred pit, to which its hands are outstretched, takes on a reddish hue from the flames. In front of the statue . . . are the flute and tambourine players, creating a deafening din. The father and mother are present. They hand the baby to a priest, who advances alongside the pit, cuts the infant's throat in a 'mysterious' (*mystikos*) fashion . . . then places the little victim on the outstretched hands of the divine statue, from where it slips into the furnace. Meanwhile the crowd, crazed by the noise and the odour of burnt flesh, sways rhythmically in time to a wild tempo that the beats of the tambourines make ever faster. The offering of each new victim will increase the collective frenzy. (1960, pp. 183–4)

As we can see, the philological approach, especially if it proceeds as it does here by an uncritical overall inclusion of heterogeneous data, tends to re-create a picture that for us is sinister, highly coloured, with a wealth of sound, assuredly very 'oriental' in tone. A century after Flaubert, only Flaubert's rhetoric is missing – all the theatrical props he used are there.

A generation later, deaf to the flutes and tambourines, leaving the famous bronze statue to the props men, specialists favour the archaeological approach. Using as their basis expert analyses that tend to calculate with some precision the age – between a few days and three or four weeks – of the animal victims (lambs and kids), born in the spring litters, which accompanied the remains of human child victims in the burial deposits, Italian specialists working on the material from Tharros in Sardinia fix the date of the *molk* sacrifice around the month of March, which would thus appear to make it a fertility festival similar to those celebrating the first fruits and to Passover (Fedele and Foster, 1988, pp. 29–42). For her part, supporting the painstaking analysis of the contents of the urns with observations from what might be termed experimental archaeology, a very careful student of Punic rituals has proposed the following trial reconstruction:

On the area of the tophet, or in its immediate proximity, a small pyre of intermingled resinous branches is erected in the open air . . . A baby or very young child (more rarely two) is laid on its back directly touching the branches, or perhaps separated from them by a piece of wickerwork. The child is clothed or wrapped in a cloth held together by two fasteners. There is nothing to indicate whether it is alive or dead, but in the first eventuality its limbs are doubtless bound since it does not change its position. The pyre is set alight. Before the process of cremation gets under way, sometimes only afterwards, part or the whole of a newborn animal is placed alongside the infant. The fire is not poked but fanned to ensure complete combustion. When the calcination is deemed sufficient, a handful of earth or sand is used to extinguish it. An instant beforehand, however, a little wild animal – sparrow, lizard, rodent or batrachian – has been thrown on to it, but its skeleton generally does not have the time to be attacked by the flames. The moment comes to fill the urns. Ashes and embers are, if necessary, cooled down with water and, after the maximum amount of fuel has been removed, they are tipped from the pyre's support into the urn. Bones that are too long may be

FIGURE 137 *The part of the tophet of Carthage preserved as a crypt under vaulted foundations of the Roman era (S. Lancel).*

broken if the need arises; following which, a few jewels, chiefly bead necklaces and amulets, are spread on the surface of the ashes, then the urn is closed with an inverted piece of pottery or a plug of clay. (Bénichou-Safar, 1988, pp. 66–7)

Far from romantic flamboyance, this is without doubt all that may only be suggested, with caution, after a meticulous and modest examination, leaving the actors in the shadows while it concentrates on the essentials, the physical realities of the holocaust which will remain in the memory when one visits the part of the tophet now preserved underground beneath the vaulted foundations of Roman date (figure 137). It will be noticed that a painful question remains unanswered – was the infant alive or dead? Perhaps, in order to rise above those pyres which will be a problem for a long while yet, emphasis should be placed in this debate on the frequently insoluble difficulty encountered by the historian of the ancient world when he attempts to make textual sources and archaeological data agree, and to complement the one with the other.

7

Expansion into Africa

It sometimes happens that History compensates those it has otherwise penalized. In 400 the defeat suffered at Himera had forced Carthage to restrict its horizons in the western Mediterranean. Of course it would still fight for every inch in Sicily for more than two centuries and keep the essential part of its commercial positions throughout the entire basin. But the phase of triumphant expansion was over (G. C. Picard, 1970, pp. 87–8).

Compensation came to it in Africa itself. We know that seemingly since the origins of the city Carthaginians had agreed to pay a yearly tribute to the Africans, who had remained in possession of a country on the borders of which Dido had founded her town (Justin, XVIII, 5, 14). With a few interruptions, notably in the sixth century, that obligation had been maintained. It was only in the second quarter of the fifth century, a few years after Himera, that the Carthaginians were able to free themselves from it, or rather, as Justin puts it in an unfortunately very summary fashion (XIX, 2, 4), that the Africans were forced to grant them remission.

CONQUEST OF AN AFRICAN TERRITORY

It is probably this hard-won emancipation that is meant in a much later passage, from the Greek rhetor Dion Chrysostom (*Discourse*, XXV), which mentions a Hanno who 'had transformed the Carthaginians from the Tyrians they had been into Libyans' (as we know, the ancient authors used that word in its widest sense). Even if it is open to various interpretations, that sentence probably refers to the conquest of the African hinterland, the work of the Magonids. But in that 'dynasty' *which* Hanno was it, among the many bearers of the name? He is most often identified with a homonym, with the probably altered surname 'Sabellus', mentioned in the summary of Book XIX of Pompeius Trogus, and would be none other than the son of Hamilcar, vanquished at Himera. 'To him that hath . . .': following Meltzer, a leading specialist on Carthage reckoned that this policy of conquering African territory is due to the same Hanno who, as we have seen, is credited by a famous text with the exploration of Africa's Atlantic coasts (G. C. Picard, 1970, pp. 88–9). But we also saw earlier that the beginning of the fifth century is not the best chronological slot in which to place the famous *Periplus*, whatever the reality may have been.

Nor is it easier to define with any exactness the territory that, in successive stages, Carthage built up for itself in Africa. To avoid any misunderstanding, perhaps it is as well to make the distinction between territories that were administratively controlled and, in the broadest sense, Carthage's African sphere of influence. The latter was certainly very extensive, since it is possible to include first, to the east, in present-day Libya, the Phoenician *Emporia* of the Syrtis Major: Leptis Magna, Oea, Sabratha (the three cities that originally formed the basis of what would afterwards become Tripolitania). That Carthage should have controlled this region as early as the end of the sixth century is an undeniable consequence of its intervention to drive the Greek Dorieus from his colony of Cinyps, east of Leptis Magna. At the beginning of the second century BC those cities of the Syrtis Major were still paying tribute to Carthage (Livy, XXXIV, 62, 3). But it does not follow that they were administratively dependent on it, and the geographical distance from the Punic metropolis, from which they were separated by the semi-desert stretches bordering on the Syrtis Minor, did not facilitate close connections. To the west, on the shores of present-day Algeria, cities where Punic culture and crafts predominated were spread out at fairly regular intervals, as we have seen, from east to west. But – and this appears to be more particularly the case with Tipasa – there is no evidence to suggest that these towns, placed as Carthage had been originally on the coastal border of indigenous kingdoms, were in any way politically subject to it. And as I remarked earlier, even the westernmost of those towns lived in symbiosis more with southern Spain than with Carthage.

Obviously we must seek the limits of the Carthaginians' African territory in the northern regions of present-day Tunisia and the Algerian east. Classical texts give us scant help, whether it is Appian (*Libyca*, 57) claiming that Carthage was mistress of more than half of Libya, or Strabo (XVII, 3, 15), according to whom the Phoenicians (by which we understand Carthaginians) 'had finished by annexing all the lands that contained no nomads' and 'possessed

300 towns' in Africa at the time of the third Punic War. From Strabo's writing one may, however, retain the fact that Carthage had chiefly applied itself to gaining control of fertile lands, where the settled Libyans were living. It would not be mistaken to suppose that Thevesta (present-day Tebessa) was the Punic stronghold farthest into native territory towards the south-west, since it must be identified with the Hecatompylos which another Hanno would seize in the middle of the third century, according to Diodorus of Sicily (IV, 18, 3; XXIV, 10, 2) (Desanges, 1978, p. 187). From there the route, heading north-west, led to Cirta (Constantine) across the high Numidian plateaux, and passed through the *Macomades* locality, whose name in this Latinized form conceals a Punic Maqom Hadash, the 'new village'. This must be seen as evidence of Punic cultural influence in Numidian lands, rather than as an advanced bastion of Carthaginian administration. We shall see in the pages dealing with Carthage's survival that the whole of the Algerian north-east was lastingly impregnated with that influence, especially as regards language.

Set well back from this region of strong Punic influence, Sicca Veneria (Le Kef), some 170 kilometres south-west of Carthage, was nevertheless one of the outposts set up in depth and it housed a large camp where, notably, the mercenaries assembled on their return from Sicily following the disastrous end of the first war against Rome. But there is no positive proof that the traditionally Numidian country lying immediately to the east of the town (which belonged to the Massylian Numidians) was under Carthage's direct control.

THE PAGI OF CARTHAGE

The territory administered by Carthage is known in broad outline, together with its subdivisions, at least as it seems to have been constituted from the fourth century onwards. This follows a familiar historical process which it is worth examining since it will help to throw some light for the reader on the difficulties already encountered in writing the internal history of a city of which in many cases we have only the reflection, distorted by classical cultures, or the traces it has left after its disappearance (figure 138). A quarter of a century ago, in the Roman forum of Makthar, in the Tunisian Dorsale, a dedication to the emperor Trajan was discovered, mentioning the sixty-four *civitates* of the *pagus Thuscae et Gunzuzi*. It obviously concerned one of those territorial districts which the Romans, with their remarkable pragmatism, had preserved within the framework of their own administrative control, while maintaining

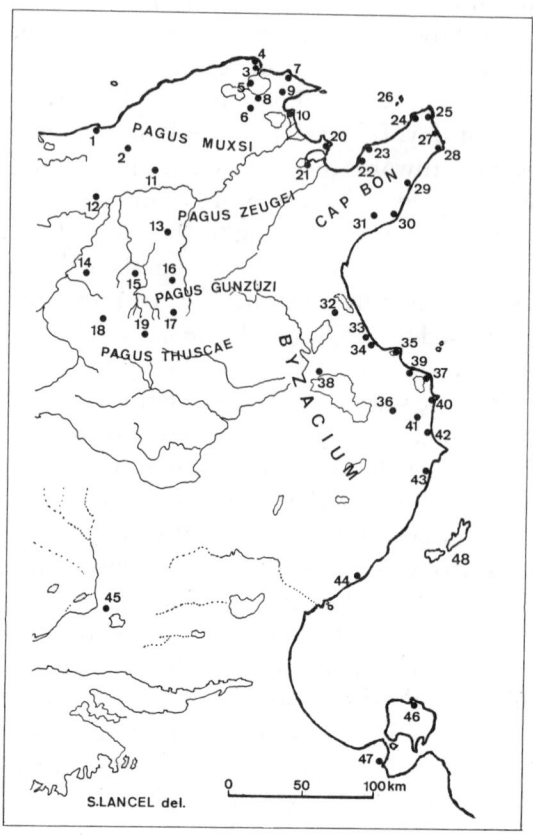

1. Tabarka (*Thabraca*)
2. Kef el-Blida
3. Bizerta (*Hippo Dhiarrytus*)
4. Cap Blanc
5. Tindja
7. Ras Zbib
8. *Theudalis*
9. *Uzalis*
10. Utique
11. Béja (*Vaga*)
12. *Bulla Regia*
13. Dougga (*Thugga*)
14. El-Kef (*Sicca Veneria*)
15. La Ghorfa
16. Zama

17. Makthar (*Mactaris*)
18. Medeina (*Althiburos*)
19. Henchir Meded (*Mididi*)
20. Carthage
21. Tunis
22. Sidi Reis (*Carpi*)
24. El-Haouaria
25. Ras ed-Dreck
26. Zembra
27. Kerkouane
28. Kelibia (*Clupea*)
29. Korba (*Curubis*)
30. Nabeul (*Neapolis*)
31. Bir-bou-Rekba (*Thinissut*)
32. *Gurza*

33. Sousse (*Hadrumetum*)
34. El-Kenissia
35. Monastir (*Ruspina*)
36. Smirat
37. Ras Dimass (*Thapsus*)
38. Sidi el-Hani
40. Mahfia
41. Ksour Essaf
42. Salakta (*Sullecthum*)
43. *Acholla*
44. Bordj Younga
.   (*Macomades Minores*)
45. Gafsa (*Capsa*)
46. Djerba (*Girba*)
47. Bou Ghrara (*Gighti*)
48. Kerkennah (*Cercina*)

FIGURE 138   *The territory of Carthage (map by S. Lancel).*

their designation. It is easy to make a connection between this *pagus Thuscae* and the reference to its Greek equivalent *chora Thusca*, which comprised fifty towns, and which Appian tells us (*Libyca*, 59) Massinissa seized from the Carthaginians in 152, taking advantage of their weakness. Better still, this *pagus Thuscae* or *chora Thusca* could be paralleled with the two Punic words of an inscription discovered earlier on a mountainous ridge some 25 kilometres north of Makthar, where it was one of the boundary markers for what the Carthaginian text calls ᵓRṢT TŠKᶜT, 'the lands (or territory) of Tiskat'. To the north and mainly the east, this district of which Makthar might have been the centre or chief town was bordered by the Numidian kingdom. The *pagus Gunzuzi* linked with it on the Latin dedication to Trajan must have bordered it on the north-east, in the direction of Carthage (G. C. Picard, 1966, pp. 1257–62). Using this solid core as a starting-point, one must proceed by analogy, in order to reconstruct Carthage's administrative landscape, with the help of Latin epigraphic texts of the Roman period in which the names of other districts appear like fossils. Thus, besides Gunzuzi and in the same way, two other *pagi*, Muxsi and Zeugei, appear in a dedication in Utica made to a Roman quaestor in the first century BC. Admittedly, the last-named, which is probably the beginning of the appellation Zeugitana given to the province of Proconsularis under the Late Empire, must have applied to a vast territory next to the Punic metropolis, between the Medjerda and the Wadi Miliana. As for Muxsi, in which Picard was inclined to see the northern part of Carthage's territory, it has been ingeniously likened to the name of the Libyan subjects of King Hiarbas, whose attentions, as we know, had driven Elissa-Dido to suicide. Maxitani, we read in the works of the Latin abridger Justin. But one group of manuscripts of this text proposes the reading 'Muxitani', which the closeness to Muxsi makes preferable (Desanges, 1967, pp. 304–8). It is remarkable that a native principality, probably that of the mountain-dwellers settled north of the Medjerda, should eventually become one of the administrative regions of the town founded by Dido, at the edge of its African base.

The most important of these districts was what the Greek authors called Byzacium, which would become the Byzacena of the administrative system of the Late Roman Empire. 'A region in the vicinity of the Syrtes,' says Polybius in a text passed on by Stephanus of Byzantium, 'rounded in shape, with a circumference of about 2,000 stades' or, for us, the equivalent of about 360 kilometres' circumference or a radius of about 60 kilometres. If the compass point is placed a little west of Thysdrus (El Jem), an approximate determination of the boundaries of this district can be made, the curve of the coast of the Tunisian Sahel forming the sea front, from Ruspina (Monastir) in the north to Taparura (Sfax) in the south. This region, which was not, however, nearest to the Punic metropolis, must have had to pledge allegiance to it in much earlier times, even before the period (the middle of the fifth century) when Carthage was concerned to create a vast African glacis, at least if, like the majority of historians, we stick to 509 BC as the date of the first treaty concluded with Rome, as indicated by Polybius (III, 23, 2). Indeed, at the time of the first treaty, we have seen that if the Carthaginians, according to the Greek historian, did not want the Romans to sail with their 'long vessels' southwards beyond the 'Beautiful Promontory' (i.e. Cap Bon), it was in order to avoid their making contact – particularly of a commercial kind – with that territory which was already Carthage's own preserve at the least. We shall see later that the coastal cities of this region and their immediate hinterland rapidly developed a rich and original mixed Libyphoenician culture.

North of Byzacena, going up towards Cap Bon, the autonomous territory of Hadrumetum (today Sousse) was perhaps interposed between these two great regions. That would be the *pagus Gurzensis*, which is also known to us through a document of the Roman era, a *tabula patronatus*, or deed of patronage, linking it with the proconsul Domitius Ahenobarbus in 12 BC (*CIL*, VIII, 68). In fact, a city named Gurza (Kalaa Kebira) was known in the Roman era, about a dozen kilometres from Sousse, and tombs of the Punic period have been excavated there. But it is not certain that the Roman district concealed a Punic ꜥRST.

Still farther north, beyond the broad curve known as the Gulf of Hammamet, the mighty promontory of Cap Bon, the territorial district nearest to Carthage and the richest from an agricultural viewpoint, extended to the north-east. From their houses rising in tiers up the hillsides, from Byrsa to Sidi-bou-Saïd, the Punic landowning aristocracy looked out to the east, to the other shore of the Gulf of Tunis, on those lands between two seas which were both the granary and the advanced lookout post for Carthage.

CARTHAGE'S LAND DEFENCES

From the beginning of the second century AD, Rome would protect its African territories on the south and west sides by a *limes*, or fortified frontier, about which – following the recent work of Pol

Trousset, complementing that of Jean Baradez in the middle of the century – we now know that it was not a linear barrier, like Hadrian's Wall between England and Scotland, but a system of structures set up at variable intervals and serving as much for controlling passage as for defence needs. Fragments from a Greek-speaking historian, Eumachos – doubtless one of Hannibal's historiographers – mention a ditch dug by the Carthaginians all around their African territory. The existence of the 'Phoenician ditches' is confirmed by Appian (*Libyca*, 54), according to whom, by the terms of the treaty that in 201 put an end to the war waged by Hannibal against Rome, Carthage was allowed to keep the territory lying within the 'ditches', but had to withdraw the garrisons it had beyond. But the archaeological reality of that fortified frontier remains unknown, and even its course raises problems.

It seems that this course, to the north, embraced the 'great plains' (*Magni Campi*) of the middle basin of the Medjerda, to the east of Bulla Regia, and surely also the region of Thugga, to the south-east of these great plains, then that of Zam and Makthar, in the centre of the *chora Thusca*, to continue from there almost in a straight line towards the south of Byzacena, where the 'ditches' rejoined the shore probably at Thaenae (Henchir Thina), on the edge of the *Emporia* of the Syrtis Minor, which did not strictly form part of Carthaginian territory. There also the famous *fossa Regia* ended at the sea, and within its bounds, just after the destruction of Carthage in 146, Scipio Aemilianus confined the newly acquired *provincia Africa*, isolating it from the Numidian kingdoms. For all that, with the exception of where it jutted out westward towards Bulla Regia and Makthar, the 'Phoenician ditches' and Scipio's *fossa* – well known in several sectors thanks to the boundary stones set up along its restored course under Vespasian in AD 73–74 – are in many places conterminous (Di Vita-Evrard, 1986, pp. 31–50). One may suppose that, like Scipio's *fossa*, the 'Phoenician ditches' originated at right angles to the north coast at Thabraca (Tabarka).

On its south and west African frontiers (Tripolitania, Numidia, Mauretania), Rome would later maintain permanent garrisons of *limitanei* intended for their defence. As well as walls and ditches, large camps have been found on the edge of the pre-desert serving as outposts; these were the quarters of the frontier guards, whose number and role became increasingly important as pressure from the 'barbarians' grew. On the *limes* of the Punic period our information is unfortunately scantier. I said earlier that no trace of the south and west frontiers of the Carthaginian State had been brought to light.

FIGURE 139 *The promontory of Ras ed-Drek, seen from the Punic fort. At the top the arrow indicates the substructure of a little temple(?); in the foreground, the fort (Istituto per la civiltà fenicia e punica, Rome).*

FIGURE 140 *The Punic fort of Ras ed-Drek (Istituto per la civiltà fenicia e punica, Rome).*

FIGURE 141 *Kelibia: below right, foundations of the Punic fortress at the foot of the Hispano-Turkish fort (Gallimard, 'Univers des Formes').*

All we know is that Carthage had established permanent garrisons in front of those defences, as at Sicca Veneria (Le Kef) and perhaps at Thevesta (Tebessa). Though solid evidence for these defences on the side of the African heartland eludes us, we can fortunately form some idea of them from defence and lookout structures of the Punic period which have been identified in recent years at Cap Bon. The fortifications confronting the Numidians in the west must have differed from the small forts of Cap Bon only as regards size.

At the end of the sixties, an Italo-Tunisian team prospecting at the north-east tip of Cap Bon recognized one of those little defensive installations that had until then gone unnoticed (Barreca, 1983, pp. 17–28). It is a place called Ras ed-Drek, 'Cape Terror', a name that assumes its full meaning in bad weather and reminds anyone who had forgotten that the very name 'Cap Bon' is nothing but a euphemism. A spur towering several dozen metres above the rocky coast bears a construction comprising two main ranges at an angle, provided with five large-capacity water tanks (figures 139 and 140). Examination of these structures allows us to affirm that they were in use from the end of the fifth century to the fall of Carthage. Surface excavations have collected cast terracotta slingshot and catapult ammunition: this small fort could have housed a garrison of several dozen men, perhaps about fifty (Barreca, 1983–4, p. 43), and its position enabled it to maintain visual links with another fortress situated about thirty kilometres away as the crow flies, at Clypea (Kelibia) on the south-eastern horn of the promontory. Unlike the Ras ed-Drek fort, which must have acted chiefly as a lookout post, what remains of the fortress at Kelibia, the vestiges of which were used as foundations for the Hispano-Turkish fort that still dominates the region (figure 141), suggests a plan that was far more ample and at least originally complex, almost tentacular. But a precise report has yet to be made and a recent preliminary study simultaneously challenges the observations made in the sixties on the original layout and the very existence of defensive elements that can be dated as early as the fifth century (Gharbi, 1990, pp. 187–98). In a rearrangement that is datable to the beginning of the second century BC, a more compact, quadrilateral plan was adopted (figure 142, 2). One may still see the first courses of square towers, the foundations of which were positioned in the rock that had previously been cut so as to provide a base (cf. figure 141). As well as a view over Ras ed-Drek to the north, the site of this fortress guaranteed it visual control of the entire south-east coast from Cap Bon as far as Neapolis (Nabeul).

Roughly midway between Kelibia and Ras ed-Drek, on the rocky coast of the tip of the promontory, excavation has been going on for some decades at the place known as Kerkouane of a city discovered in the middle of this century, whose ancient name is still unknown. The ancient town was adequately defended seaward by a small cliff that plunges steeply into the sea and protected on the landward side by a semicircular defence or, more exactly, by a double enclosing wall (figure 143). A first wall, extending over a kilometre, is flanked by towers (figure 144) and has two gateways, of which the western one, angled and inserted parallel with two curtain walls, themselves parallel, seems to be related to an old Syrio-Palestinian layout (Fantar, 1984, pp. 144–50). Difficult to date, this inner enclosing wall belongs to the first period of organization of the city (sixth to fifth century). Beyond a wide avenue, an outer wall was

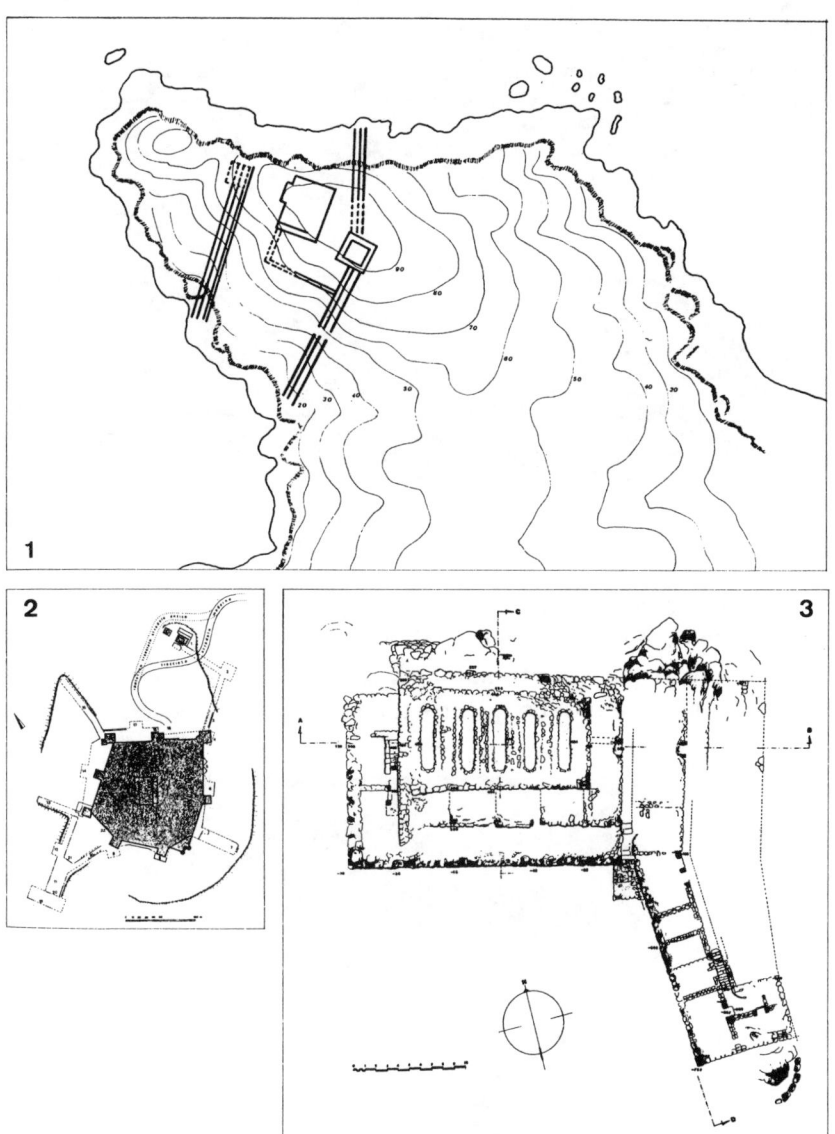

FIGURE 142 *Punic fortifications at Cap Bon: 1 Ras Fortass; 2 Kelibia; 3 Ras ed-Drek (after* The Phoenicians, *Milan, 1988).*

FIGURE 143   *The site of Kerkouane in 1958 (Armée de l'air française).*

erected at a later time, perhaps after the experience of the destruction
committed by Agathocles during his expedition and short occupation
of Cap Bon at the end of the fourth century. Despite these precautions, the town was subsequently taken and its impressive defence

FIGURE 144   *The (square) north tower of the city wall at Kerkouane
(P. Cintas).*

system was razed at a date that has been estimated around the middle of the third century, for excavation of the city has come up with nothing that can be dated later than that period; in particular, none of the series of Campanian pottery imported on such a large scale into the Carthaginian world from the end of the third century (Morel, 1969, p. 474). The hypothesis that springs naturally to mind is that if Kerkouane's defences managed to withstand Agathocles' expedition, they did not do so against that of Regulus, in one of the episodes that we know of the first war with Rome, when the Roman consul occupied Cap Bon in 256–255 BC.

This cape was no less protected on its western flank, which looks towards the Gulf of Tunis. In particular, the promontory of Ras el-Fortass, which locks in the gulf on this side as does Cape Carthage on the west, was the site of a vast fortress on a spur around 100 metres in height; in its entirety this fortress formed a trapezium 250 metres broad by 300 metres long (figure 142, 1). Walls over three metres thick, flanked by towers, were found there recently (Barreca, 1983, pp. 13–15). Judging by the construction techniques, the inclination is to date them to the fifth century BC. It will be noted that this eminently strategic site has never been abandoned. The fortress destroyed when Carthage fell was rebuilt in Roman imperial times and used again, after some adaptation, in the Muslim Middle Ages.

CARTHAGE'S RURAL AREAS AND CARTHAGINIAN AGRICULTURE

At the end of the fourth century BC Carthage directly administered and exploited economically in either direct or indirect fashion more than half of present-day Tunisia, including the richest or most fertile regions, from Tabarka and the forests of Kroumiria in the north-west to the olive groves and fishing-grounds of Sfax in the south-east. If this is compared with the very limited size of the *ager Romanus* in central Italy in the same period, and even if that is combined with the territories of the Romans' allies, the disproportion appears glaring and the comparison very much in favour of the Carthaginians. Although its positions were increasingly difficult to hold in the Sicilian west and it had to compromise with Rome in Sardinia, and its trade in the western Mediterranean had to compete with that of Marseilles and southern Italy, Carthage had become the front-rank agricultural power in the Mediterranean West, thanks entirely to its African lands. In the ancient world, that was an essential dimension. It has often been said of Carthaginian trade that it was a commerce of redistribution. It is indeed likely that the aristocracy of great Carthaginian merchants had grown richer from generation to generation, thanks to the organization and operation of a trading network in which the products distributed were most frequently not Punic in origin. In the main, chiefly up till the fourth century, it was an activity of intermediaries run by families of shipowners. It will be seen, notably, that in the field of pottery, Antiquity's only semi-industrial product whose preservation permits clear locations and fairly sure analyses, the Carthaginians took a long time to develop and then to circulate a product (black-glazed) of a quality comparable with the Greek and then Campanian articles with which they were inundated. But one forgets that Punic agriculture provided large food surpluses, for the most part exported: exports that have left no archaeological traces, except for the amphorae holding oil and wine, as we shall see later when examining the map showing the distribution of Punic amphorae, particularly those stamped with the name Mago in Greek letters.

Anyone travelling today through the little 'Mesopotamia' that extends along a south-west/north-east line between the course of the Wadi Miliana and that of the Medjerda (the *Bagradas* of the Ancients), then, beyond its confluence with the Siliana, in the region of the middle basin of the Medjerda, as far as Simitthu (Chemtou), not far from the Algero-Tunisian frontier, can gather some idea of the richness of this soil, which more than twenty-five centuries of intensive farming have not exhausted. Over this spread of gently rolling plains, formerly less attacked by erosion than they are in our day, the average annual rainfall is sufficient to produce fine cereal harvests, without the need for crop rotation or letting land lie fallow. Looking at the political map of the region in the Roman period (figure 145), it is noticeable that the greatest density of urban settlements is situated there, unequalled in Antiquity, even in the Greek Orient. Every ten kilometres at the most, often every four or five, a village or small town makes its mark on the landscape and, with a few rare exceptions, their *raison d'être* and means of existence can only have been agricultural. As the exclusively indigenous place-names indicate, and as is sometimes suggested by municipal epigraphy where there are many Punic survivals, these townships were not originally of Roman creation, or at least the majority were not. It is here that we must seek a good number of

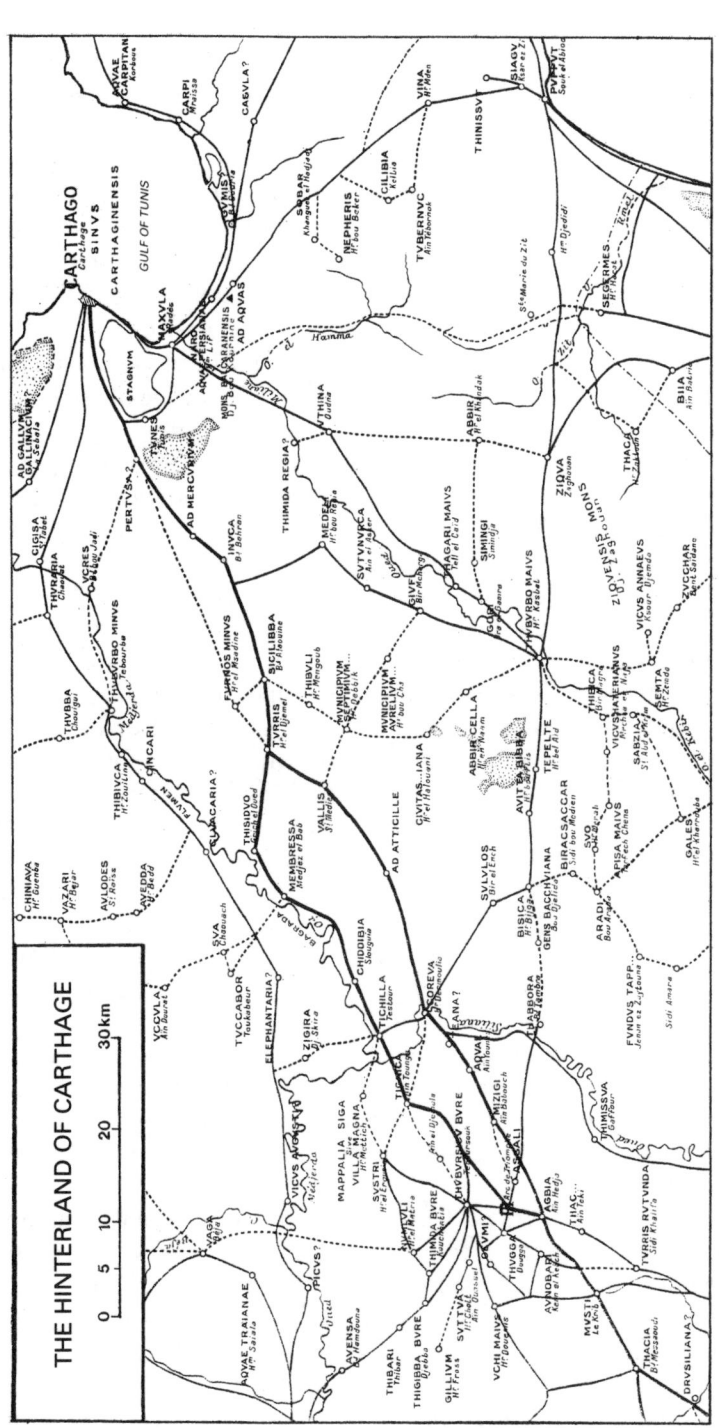

FIGURE 145 *Carthage's hinterland, between the Medjerda and the Wadi Miliana, in the Roman period. Many of these townships emerged from pre-existent Libyco-Punic nuclei (map by P. Salama).*

the '300 towns' – a round figure, not to be taken too literally – which Strabo (XVII, 3, 15) credited the Carthaginians with possessing at the time of the third Punic War. Whenever local archaeological study probes beneath the Roman monumental stratum, the Libyco-Punic substratum comes to light. Prospecting recently carried out between the basin of the Wadi Miliana and the bottom of Cap Bon has revealed vestiges of many small indigenous towns, often fortified, which have remained anonymous (Ferchiou, 1990, pp. 43–86). What a pity that we have not discovered here the pre-Roman equivalent of the great texts engraved on stone of Ain el-Djemala, Ain Ouassel or Henchir Mettich, which gave us a knowledge of territorial organization during the Roman Empire, but we need not doubt that this organization was largely inspired by the Carthaginian legacy.

It is very likely that Carthaginian masters had already put into practice the recipes for agricultural exploitation in relation to the Libyans, the first occupants of the land, which the great landowners of the Roman era would apply with Romanized natives. We shall see later that cereal crops were not peculiar to the Punic agriculture whose merits were extolled by Latin agronomists. And among the extracts from Mago's works that have come down to us, there is nothing that relates directly to the growing of wheat or barley. In the 'fertile crescent' which I mentioned, and farther south in the plains scattered all along the Tunisian Dorsale, between Dougga and Makthar, cultivation was carried out by Libyans operating as sharecroppers, from the time that Carthage had taken possession of the land. We catch a few echoes of this agricultural labour force, to which must be added a few serfs, in the riots that shook Carthage on several occasions, and were all the more dangerous for the Punic metropolis because African soldiers enrolled in the Carthaginian armies sometimes joined in, as in 396 when, taking advantage of the disaster suffered by Himilco at Syracuse, 200,000 insurgents, according to Diodorus of Sicily (XIV, 77), marched on Carthage after seizing Tunis. That figure, it must be said, appears somewhat exaggerated: ancient authors frequently yielded to the intoxication of large numbers.

Those African farmers on Carthaginian territory used ploughing implements that owed nothing to the Phoenicians and are still employed almost unchanged in the present day by the Berber peasants of North Africa, exactly as they were conceived in the Neolithic Age, after an even earlier initial phase of working the ground with a hoe (Camps, 1986, pp. 177–80). Pictures of primitive swing ploughs on Punic stelae from Carthage could serve to illustrate them. The slanting shaft, ending in a handle held by the ploughman, is extended horizontally by a stock in front of which is fixed the ploughshare, the only metal part of the whole implement, which in the Iron Age probably replaced a piece of flint; behind the ploughshare, and on both sides, an 'ear' – actually a little board going across the stock laterally – acts as a harrow. A harnessing beam is attached to the shaft by a system of pins.

Simple, easy to make and repair, relatively light and manageable, this tool obviously gave a fairly modest performance as a plough. But that is precisely where its advantage lay, in that it dug only shallowly into the arable topsoil and did not exhaust the underlying ground. In the light and sandy soil of the Sahel, donkeys were adequate for pulling the plough, as two or three centuries later authors such as Columella (VII, 1, 2) and Pliny the Elder (XVII, 41) bore witness. Pliny even adds that with his own eyes he saw in Byzacium a plough harnessed to a small donkey on one side and an old woman on the other, a sight that would not be unknown even today. On heavier ground oxen were harnessed, according to the Carthaginian agronomist Mago, quoted by Columella (VI, 1, 2–3). Another implement which was in common use in ancient times in the Orient and is recorded in the Late Roman Empire as being traditionally used in North Africa (Augustine, *City of God*, I, VIII, 2; *Enarrationes in Psalmos*, 92, 5) has come down through the ages and is still included in the usual tools of the Tunisian peasant. This is the *tribulum*, used for threshing grain, a kind of tray of hard wood, the underside of which is spiked with flint fragments that have been embedded in it; it is moved over the sheaves, weighed down with a heavy weight or the body of a man standing on the top of the tray. Another threshing implement is attested by Varro in his *Res rusticae* (I, 52, 1), the 'Punic cart' (*plostellum Punicum*), which was used, says Varro, chiefly in Spain, where the Carthaginians must have introduced it at the time of the Barcid kingdom, in the second half of the third century BC. That was also a tray, but underneath it had rows of little toothed rollers set in a wooden frame. It was still being used not so long ago in the Tunisian Sahel for threshing barley.

MAGO AND PUNIC AGRONOMY

As I said earlier, it was not cereals that brought Punic agronomy its renown, but tree crops and vines. Like the fig tree and the almond tree, the grapevine is indigenous to North Africa. In the Carthaginian

domain, its favourite ground was the light sandy soils of the
Tunisian north-east, north of Utica, and the calcareous terrain of
the Cap Bon peninsula, particularly its base, in the Mornag and
Grombalia region, where decent wines are still produced. Passages
from Mago that have survived in the form of quotations bear
witness to the Carthaginians' experience in the matter of viticul-
ture. According to Mago, vineyards must be planted on hill slopes
facing north, Columella tells us (III, 12, 5), remarking that this
precept applied to the climatic conditions of a hot country. Mago
further advised letting air get to the roots by placing a few stones at
the bottom of the trenches in which the vine stocks are planted
(Columella, III, 15, 4) and also, to encourage the vine to thrust its
roots downwards, only to half-fill the trench at first, a precaution
that Columella (V, 5, 4) stressed was excellent in dry ground and
thus in Africa. Other helpful hints, also reported by the Latin
agronomists, relate to fertilizers and enriching agents and to prun-
ing, which Mago recommends should be done in the spring, a piece
of advice not shared by Columella, who suggests that it should
rather be done in the autumn in countries where the winter is mild.

Modern readers would like to know the Carthaginian procedure
for the production of what we would call table wines. We shall have
to console ourselves for Mago's silence on this subject by reading
the recipe for making a syrupy kind of wine with raisins, passed on
to us by Columella (XII, 39, 1–2):

> Pick well-ripened early grapes, rejecting those that are mouldy
> and spoilt. Sink forks or stakes into the ground, four feet
> apart, connected by sticks or poles; on top of these place reeds,
> on which the grapes are spread out in the sun. They must be
> covered at night so that the dew does not dampen them. When
> they are dried, pick off the grapes and put them in an earthen-
> ware jar or pitcher; add must, the best possible, until the
> grapes are just covered. On the sixth day, when the grapes
> have absorbed the must and are swollen, place them in a bag,
> put them through the press and collect the liquid. Next, press
> the marc, adding fresh must made from other grapes that have
> been left in the sun three days. Mix well and put through the
> press. Immediately put the liquid from this second pressing
> into stoppered receptacles, so that it does not turn acrid. Then,
> after about twenty or thirty days, when fermentation has
> ceased, clarify in other containers: at once smear the lids with
> plaster and cover them with a skin.

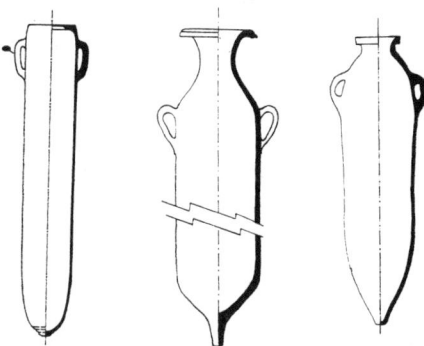

FIGURE 146 *The three principal types of large Punic amphorae of the Hellenistic era (fourth to second century* BC*).*

This recipe for wine made from sun-dried grapes continued with equal success under the Empire: it was the *passum* of the Latins (Pliny, *NH*, XIV, 81) and is still the Italian *passito*.

Was this high-class wine a speciality export of Carthage? There is a strong likelihood, even if we cannot be positive about it. A very large number of Punic amphorae having a mouth with a wide flared rim, by far the most common shape in the third and early second centuries, have been found very widely on western Mediterranean sites: on many coastal sites of North Africa, but also in Andalusia, Catalonia, at Marseilles, Ventimiglia, in Corsica, at Rome and even Athens. These amphorae, it is true, could have contained oil as well as wine (figure 146). With regard to this type of amphora, known as Cintas 312/313 after the archaeologist who was the first to catalogue them (Cintas, 1950), it is necessary to say a word about the few examples which bear a stamp, not in Punic characters – as is most often the case – but in Greek. Recent excavations by the French archaeological mission in Carthage have enriched the small series by bringing to light several stamps with the names Aris and Mago – two very Carthaginian names, both very common, which makes the tempting *a priori* hypothesis of identifying the famous agronomist with the Mago of the stamp rather risky. But the transcription into Greek of the names of Punic merchants on these stamps can at least be taken as inspired by their concern to facilitate the circulation of their products in the Mediterranean market, where Greek was used as the commercial language in international trading, as English is now (Thuillier, 1982, pp. 15–20). Exoticism had not yet been invented and Semitic characters on a label ran the

risk of being more off-putting than attractive. The accident of
discovery has until now confined the finding of such stamps in
Greek to Carthaginian soil; the hypothetical perspective just developed will be confirmed when these stamps appear outside
Carthage. And if they are on amphorae found intact, particular care
must be given to analysing their residual contents.

Nevertheless, a fair amount of the wine produced in Carthaginian
territory was consumed on the spot. Carthaginians' attraction to
wine, and even their propensity for abusing it, are indirectly evidenced by Plato who, in his *Laws* (674, a–b), mentions the legal bans
in Carthage relating to wine, affecting soldiers on campaign, male
and female slaves, magistrates in the discharge of their duties, pilots
and judges. But was that law applied, especially in the army? From
Diodorus of Sicily (XIV, 63, 3) we learn that the Carthaginian
general Himilco, besieging Syracuse in 396, set up stores in his
camp for wine as well as corn. For all that, we know that the
Carthaginians were not content with their domestic production. In
the period prior to the fourth century, when their vineyards were
not yet greatly developed, they imported wine for their own consumption, especially from Agrigentum in the fifth century, according to Diodorus (XIII, 81, 4–5). But they remained importers
subsequently, doubtless for reasons of taste and a desire for variety,
and their purchases of wine from Rhodes are well attested by the
numerous remains of Rhodian amphorae, with stamps on the right-
angled handles, retrieved from archaeological levels in Carthage
dating to the late third and early second century.

Oil or wine? As we have seen, there is a question as to the
contents of the amphorae, for oil was one of Carthage's major
agricultural products. Like the vine, the olive tree grows spontaneously in North Africa, or at least the wild olive, but one needs only
to graft it to have a tree that can produce oil, and Pliny the Elder
(*NH*, XVIII, 129) describes for this grafting operation a process
that was peculiar to Africa. Was it a process attributable to Mago?
'To him that hath . . .' At all events, the Carthaginian agronomist is
again quoted by the Naturalist (XVII, 93 and 128) on the subject of
rules to be followed when planting olive trees, with guidance on the
seasons which differed according to the nature of the soil, and
instructions for the spacing of the trees (from a minimum of thirteen metres to a maximum of twenty-three) that are still in force
today (as regards the maximum) in the region of Sfax. The Carthaginians eventually managed to cover their needs in this domain
too, but certainly later than in the case of vines: in the fifth century

they imported large quantities of oil from Sicily (Diodorus, XIII, 81, 4–5). A legend recorded by a later Latin author, Aurelius Victor (*De Caesaribus*, 37, 3), has it that Hannibal, fearing the pernicious effects of idleness on his soldiers, set them to a mass planting of olive trees. He may indeed have done this during the year between his return from Italy in the autumn of 203 and his engagement against Scipio at Zama, at the end of 202, when he had his headquarters at Hadrumetum (Sousse), or better still, in the years that elapsed between the peace imposed on Carthage after Zama and his suffetate of 196, which was swiftly followed by exile. In fact, according to the author of the *Bellum Africum* (97, 3), a century and a half later Byzacium was producing oil in great abundance. A century later still, Juvenal's spiteful tongue would joke about the poor quality of African oil, widely imported to Rome, but in his view fit only to be burnt in lamps.

However, what most impressed foreigners travelling through Carthaginian country regions, whether peaceful visitors or enemy soldiers on an expedition of war, was the picture of a green paradise that they presented. At Cap Bon, in particular, where the regulatory effect on the climate of the ever-present sea was allied to the fertility of the soil, Diodorus (XX, 8, 3–4) has recounted the wonder of Agathocles' mercenaries when they landed there at the end of the fourth century BC. The Sicilian tyrant's army crossed a land watered by streams and irrigation channels, full of gardens and orchards where all sorts of fruit trees grew. A century and a half later Appian (*Libyca*, 117), describing the contryside near Carthage as Polybius had seen it during the long siege of 148–146, used the same words to evoke Megara. He speaks of orchards separated from one another by drystone walls or living hedges, and watered by numerous channels.

The writings of the agronomists, as well as the popular images on the stelae, inform us about what grew in those orchards. In the first place was the pomegranate or 'Punic apple' (*malum Punicum*) as the Latins called it. Originating in western Asia, introduced into Africa by the Phoenicians, the pomegranate tree had flourished magnificantly (figure 147), but also the almond and, above all, the fig tree. The latter grows spontaneously in North African, but it was probably the Phoenicians who very early on introduced some good varieties. The renown of figs from Punic territory grew very quickly. In his treatise on farming (8, 1). Carthage's implacable enemy, the aged Cato, mentions the African fig tree (*ficus Africana*) which had been introduced to Italy, where it had become acclimatized very

FIGURE 147   *Durum wheat and a pomegranate tree on Punic stelae from Carthage.*

well. One can only marvel the more at the cunning of the man who, in order to make senators more alert to the danger to Rome that he thought the Punic metropolis represented in the middle of the second century BC, one day brought into the Senate House a plump, fresh, smooth, ripe fig, adding that the fruit had been picked three days earlier in Carthage. It is now generally believed (Meijer, 1984, pp. 117–24) that Cato had picked the fig in his own garden and that his colleagues were not deceived.

Did this factor weigh heavily in Rome's decision to have done with Carthage? After the destruction and looting of the town, what was left of its libraries was handed over to the Numidian kings. We shall come back to that. But Greeks and Romans were impressed by the treasures of agronomic science and economic wisdom contained in Mago's books and had undertaken to translate them. It is reckoned today, at least as regards the Latin translation, that this rescue operation was carried out *in extremis* and was due to the influence of a few aristocrats in Rome, who opposed the clique around Cato advocating the 'final solution' for Carthage (Heurgon, 1976, pp. 447–51). We are indebted to the instigators of that operation – who no doubt included another Scipio, Nasica, *princeps senatus* in 147 – for having preserved, if not the whole of the work, which has unfortunately been lost in its two translated versions, at least fairly large extracts or quotations that appear in the later Latin agronomists, Varro and Columella, and even an encyclopaedist like Pliny the Elder (Speranza, 1974, pp. 75–119). The time in which Mago lived and wrote is not indicated by our sources, but it is generally thought that it was about the end of the fourth century (Martin, 1971, p. 45). Thus, over a hundred years before Cato, who lived and wrote in the first half of the second century, the Carthaginian agronomist had developed not only a corpus of detailed and technical instructions on numerous areas of agriculture and breeding, but also a sort of summary of rural economy which, well before Cato and his followers (Varro, for instance), laid down that the owner should live permanently on his land, even going as far as urging him to sell his town house in order to busy himself with his estate, in a direct and personal fashion.

RURAL RESIDENCES

Of course, he was talking about *latifundia* whose farming implied the involvement of sharecroppers or free farm labourers, and equally numerous slaves. Piracy probably, or war as the surest and most substantial way, supplied this servile labour force employed in the fields. In 310, when Agathocles defeated the Carthaginians near Tunis, he found in their camp thousands of handcuffs intended for the prisoners they had counted on taking; and in fact, the following year, when the luck of battle had turned, the Greeks from Sicily who had been taken captive were set to cultivate lands that had lain fallow or been devastated by the war (Diodorus, XX, 13, 2; 69, 5). The inevitable social instability arising from such a labour force by itself necessitated the permanent residence of masters in their rural homes. Diodorus (XX, 8, 3–4), relating the progress of Agathocles' soldiers, describes the Cap Bon peninsula as dotted with these country houses. Half a century later, at the time of Regulus' expedition in the same region, the Roman soldiers, writes Polybius (I, 1, 29), 'destroyed many magnificently appointed houses, seized a great quantity of livestock and carried off to their ships more than 20,000 slaves'.

To render them less vulnerable to attack, both from outside and from domestic rebellions, these farms were often fortified and were then named *castella* ('castles') in classical writings or *turres* ('towers' or 'keeps'). Thus Hannibal had his *turris* on the coast of Byzacena, between Thapsus (Ras Dimass) and Acholla (Henchir Botria), and it was there that he broke his journey before leaving Africa in 195, when his enemies in Carthage in collusion with the Roman ambassadors forced him to go into exile forever (Livy, XXXIII, 48, 1). We must be careful not to see in this 'tower' one of the *diaetae* belvederes which were to enjoy such popularity in imperial Roman estate architecture. It may well be that the 'tower' of Punic rural houses was a souvenir of an oriental tradition well illustrated by the pictures of Persian paradise gardens and Palestinian orchards (Grimal, 1969, p. 261). But the term should rather be understood as a name for the whole of the fortified rural residence, referring to the architectural feature which particularly ensured its defence and was most characteristic. A dozen years after Hannibal's departure into exile, his great rival and the victor of Zama, Scipio Africanus, was himself forced into exile, as a price for having accumulated too much personal power and glory. He retired to Campania to live in a *villa*, and we are indebted to Seneca, who made a pilgrimage there, for a detailed description of it in one of his letters to Lucilius (*Letters*, 86, 1–5): defence towers flanking the entrance gateway, walls sourrounding the grounds, reserves of drinking water for numerous staff (a 'small army', says Seneca); it was not 'La Boisserie' but a veritable stronghold.

We lack a comparable description of contemporary African equivalents of Scipio Africanus' *turris*. And though there is a great temptation to proceed by analogy and picture them in the manner of the great rural dwellings (to which they certainly relate in part) that figure in late African mosaics (I am thinking chiefly of the domain of the 'Dominus Julius'), it is wise to wait and hope for more exact details from a Punic rural archaeology that is only just beginning. Meanwhile we can take note of the fortuitous discovery of a suburban, rather than rural residence at Gammarth, in a recently published report (Fantar, 1985, pp. 3–18). On a site at the north tip of the peninsula of Carthage and near the shore, the plan of the remains shows a bipartite layout, with the *pars rustica*, as the Latins would have called it, being represented by an oil-works: the counterweight of the press, tanks, the *dolium* embedded in the floor. The dwelling part, of fairly modest size, is revealed by the quality of its decor: moulded stucco surfaces, columns with Ionic capitals in sandstone finished with stucco, *pavimenta Punica*. It was one of those well-kept homes, surrounded by gardens and orchards, of Carthage's green suburb known as Megara. Very probably situated within the big defensive wall, it was not fortified, and all the signs are that it was destroyed during the siege of the city, between 149 and 146.

KERKOUANE, THE AGRICULTURAL TOWN OF CAP BON

We must return to the little town of Kerkouane, encountered in the discussion of the defences of Cap Bon, for what is well known about it now illustrates precisely how this prosperous region developed between the fifth and third centuries BC. Situated on the sea's edge, but lacking a true port – boats equipped for coastal fishing were hauled on to dry land in a small cove – it was a substantial agricultural village, deriving the bulk of its resources from a rich and well-farmed hinterland, and it probably had a smaller population than Clypea (Kelibia, the *Aspis* of the Greeks) and Neapolis (Nabeul), farther south. Unlike both these towns, which are well known through literary sources but whose archaeological record, for the Punic period, is confined to funerary remains (figure 148), we still do not know Kerkouane's ancient name. It is a good example of the situation, unfortunately all too frequent in ancient history, where the data supplied by texts cannot

FIGURE 148 *The cemetery of Kelibia (M. H. Fantar's excavations, 1985). There is a stairway down to an underground tomb. Above the entrance doorway to the funeral chamber is the schematic representation of a mausoleum with a pyramidal roof, bearing the inscription in cursive script: S (possessive particle) MGNYM or 'tomb of Mago'. The representation of the mausoleum here acts as a symbolic sema for a monument that is, in fact, invisible (M. H. Fantar).*

be made to tie up with those provided by study of evidence on the ground. Without doubt the important part of what excavations at Kerkouane have contributed is the revelation, in a small rural town of slight political importance, of carefully worked out town planning and attention to domestic living conditions that give material proof of its prosperity. The double defensive wall which I mentioned encloses a built-up area of between seven and eight hectares, which is modest but within the norms of the time, if one bears in mind the way of life and social organization of those little towns in a predominantly agricultural economic context. To take an example that is well known, Tipasa, on the Algerian coast, was no more extensive in the same period. In addition to these somewhat restricted townships there was a great swathe of farms, where the masters and their workforce lived. And although some farmers may have dwelt *intra muros*, the town was home chiefly to artisans, apart from a few sea fishermen and employees in a very limited distribution trade. These craftsmen were mainly connected with the place's maritime activities: salting, makers of garum and also apparently, to judge by the piles of murex shells unearthed near the site, makers of purple dye. But at Kerkouane they made pottery and cut stone too (Fantar, 1986, pp. 504–30).

The plan of what has been uncovered of the town, whose excavation is far from complete, reveals a well spaced-out settlement of blocks of dwellings, served by streets of differing widths but averaging about five metres (figure 149). The roadways are not generally paved, any more than they were in Carthage, as we have seen, and include stone drains built to act as an axial sewer. What characterizes these streets, which cut one another approximately at right angles, at least in the town centre, is a certain irregularity in alignment, which can be partly explained by modifications. One is led to suppose – though the hypothesis is not for the moment sufficiently supported by a stratigraphy established from small trenches – that the town passed through two great periods in its history: before Agathocles went through it in 310 and after the rebuilding necessitated by the ravages his passage must have caused (Fantar, 1984, pp. 212–14). If this plausible historical outline is verified, it is clear that the rebuilders of the little town at the very end of the fourth century did not impose too many constraints on themselves. The inhabitants thereby gained a pleasing layout, with breaks in alignments and even the creation of small public squares.

FIGURE 149 *An aerial view of the northern part of the site at Kerkouane: a group of exposed sectors; in the foreground, the avenue between the two defensive walls (after* The Phoenicians, Milan, 1988*).*

What most surprised and delighted the discoverers of Kerkouane were the hydraulic arrangements of the houses, and first of all the bathrooms, with their hip-baths. Thanks to the exceptional quality of their finish, made of a very resistant tile-fragment concrete, they appeared to the first excavators exactly as they had been when the inhabitants of Kerkouane had performed their last ablutions in the middle of the third century BC (figure 150). I am talking of baths with seats and often elbow-rests, placed in a sort of cloakroom generally giving on to the courtyard, into which the waste water drained. Such facilities were already known, for example, at Delos, in homes datable to the middle of the second or the beginning of the first century. Kerkouane's baths thus have the advantage of their earlier date and, let it be said, superior execution.

The courtyards or patios played a large part in the attractiveness and charm of Kerkouane's houses. One reached them coming from the street along a long, narrow, vestibule corridor, situated laterally,

FIGURE 150   *Kerkouane: a hip-bath at the beginning of the excavation in the 1950s (C. Poinssot).*

that protected the privacy of the house's inhabitants (figure 151 and 152). The living quarters gave on to this central courtyard, in which

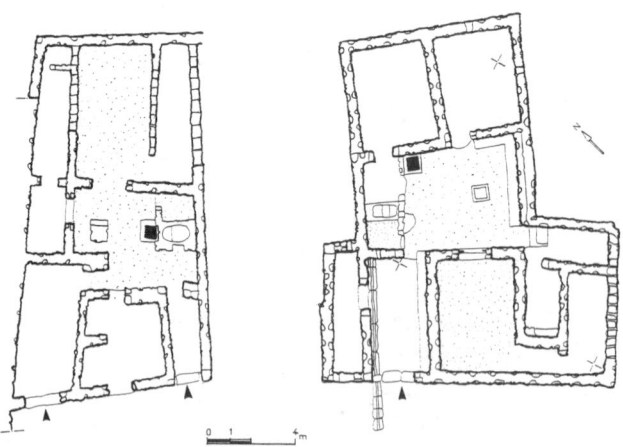

FIGURE 151   *Two plans of houses at Kerkouane. The dots indicate areas covered with* pavimenta Punica *(after M. H. Fantar,* Kerkouane, *vol. II, Tunis, 1985).*

FIGURE 152 *Courtyard of a house with a single column at Kerkouane. In the right background is the bathroom (P. Cintas).*

lay the opening, nearly always edged with a coping, of the well that supplied water for domestic uses. A characteristic that deserves emphasis is that a cistern was an exception in Kerkouane: the underground water level was not very deep and yielded water of acceptable quality, which is surprising in view of the sea's proximity. Also of note in these courtyards is the frequent presence of a pillar or column, on which might have rested an awning set on two sides at right angles. In several houses true porticoes, resting on four or six columns (figure 153), have even been found. At least two of these houses with peristyles seem to belong to the town's first period, prior to Agathocles' expedition (310 BC). That would be an early borrowing from Greek domestic architecture, doubtless by way of Sicily, where the Carthaginians had had plenty of opportunity to appreciate this layout.

Apart from domestic living conditions, of which the excavations have given us more than a glimpse, there is still a lot to discover at Kerkouane, first of all what, besides its defence walls and road system, turns even a modest town into at least a political and religious, if not a monumental centre. The beginning of this

FIGURE 153 *A house with a peristyle at Kerkouane. On the horizon is
the escarpment of the tip of Cap Bon, ending in the point of Ras
ed-Drek (P. Cintas).*

discovery seems already to have been achieved with the finding, in
a central position in the town, of a large religious complex, of
which the area already exposed has reached 400 square metres. The
architectural arrangement of the building, with its benched room
adjoining the vast hall, its courtyards, on to which open the podium
infrastructures of rooms that are now unfortunately razed, allows
us to identify it as a temple. But its precise purpose still eludes us.
It was joined to a small bathing complex which it is reasónable to
suppose was directly connected with the religious buildings.

I cannot leave Kerkouane without stressing the value of the site's
contribution to our knowledge of the Carthaginians' art of building
before the middle of the third century. That *terminus ante quem*
must be emphasized as an important factor, since the evidence from
the site complements, at a slightly earlier date, that provided by
recent excavations at Carthage, especially the French excavations
of Byrsa which cover the last half-century before the destruction in
146. And if there is a difference in scale between the block plans,
the conception of the road layouts, as is to be expected when one
passes from a metropolis to a small provincial town, it must be
noted that there is hardly any difference when it comes to materials,

FIGURE 154 *Kerkouane: a pavement of large sandstone slabs (P. Cintas).*

techniques and details of execution and finishing. Pierre Cintas, to whom, with Charles Saumagne, the honour is due for having discovered the site in the middle of this century, had hinted at its richness, in two communications unfortunately published in far too concise a form (*CRAI*, 1953 and 1958). Let us pay homage to the first finder by reproducing images that he discussed then in all their beautiful freshness (figures 154 to 157). Cintas particularly stressed the strong presence of Hellenism in Kerkouane: not surprising in that small town which, at the tip of Cap Bon, thrust out like a figurehead towards nearby Sicily. This site that reveals so much and whose marine charm captivates every visitor was not neglected subsequently, and the results of the excavations carried on by the

FIGURE 155 *Kerkouane: various types of walls (P. Cintas).*

FIGURE 156   *Kerkouane: pieces of terracotta paving, diamond-shaped and hexagonal, with rabbets for interlocking (P. Cintas).*

Tunis National Institute of Archaeology and Art have lived up to the promises of the first investigations (figure 158). At the close of his monumental monograph on Kerkouane, M. H. Fantar rightly stresses the considerable mass of information furnished in particular on the architectural decoration of a Punic provincial town in Carthage's heyday, and shows that a special place must be reserved for the stuccoes, moulded and painted in simple colours, in which blacks, greys, reds and pinks predominate (Fantar, 1986, pp. 550–1).

THE PUNIC SAHEL

South of the Gulf of Hammamet the low, sandy coast of Byzacium begins. Bordering on the steppe-like expanses of present-day Tunisia, it was Carthage's most beautiful province, rather as the Tunisian Sahel (= 'littoral'), from Sousse in the north to Sfax in the south, is to modern Tunisia: not only a prosperous agricultural region but also the cradle of enterprising and active men, often in political and economic competition with the elite of the capital. Though it is not completely certain whether Byzacena was in the strict sense of the term a district of Carthage's territory, the Ancients seemed to recognize that it had an ethnic or cultural particularity. Describing the region, Pliny the Elder notes that the inhabitants of Byzacena were called 'Libyphoenicians' (*NH*, V, 24). Before him, Livy (XXI, 22, 3) defined these Libyphoenicians as half-breeds of Carthaginian and African stock. For want of a more exact definition, we should probably consider the originality of

FIGURE 157   *Hellenism and the Orient at Kerkouane: 1 a gargoyle in the shape of a bull's head; 2 and 3 terracotta altars with gryphons fighting, comparable to similar monuments from Motya, in Sicily, kept in the Palermo Museum; 4 altar with a stylized Atlas; 5 a Hellenistic bowl with palm fronds; 6 a head-shaped lamp; 7 and 8 black-glazed lamps with negroid subjects (Cintas papers).*

Punic Byzacium as resulting from that mixture of ethnic and, chiefly, cultural backgrounds. For all that, archaeology has produced evidence of a very strong Libyan component in the region, the indigenous substratum being revealed particularly in the funerary domain, with megalithic cemeteries, such as the one of Bir-el-Hadjar, about twenty kilometres south-west of Hergla. These dolmen-like tombs, which are difficult to date, coexist with tombs of Phoenician tradition having a burial chamber cut deeply into the ground. But in these tombs the body is often found lying on its side with its legs drawn up, as is sometimes the case in the cemeteries of

FIGURE 158 *Kerkouane in 1980 (S. Lancel).*

FIGURE 159 *The cemetery at Kerkouane on the Arg el-Ghazouni: shafts with stairs going down to the tombs (sixth to third century* BC) *(after* The Phoenicians, Milan, 1988).

FIGURE 160 *The cemetery at Kerkouane showing the dead laid on benches. The skeleton at the right is crouched on its side (P. Cintas).*

Kerkouane (figures 159 and 160) and the skeleton often bears plentiful traces of a red pigment. Even if it is not completely absent, this funerary red paint is rare in Carthage, and a supine extended position is the rule for Carthaginian burials.

I would not hesitate to say that the Sahel, even more than Cap Bon, is the promised land for Punic archaeology in Tunisia (figure 161). The difficulty is that, on the large sites on the coast, human occupation has never stopped, and there has been a marked and rapid increase in population and building over the last thirty or so years. At Hadrumetum (Sousse) there has been no interruption in the continuity of urban life since the seventh century BC. The Roman town, then the Islamic city, have thus hidden the first settlement, whose citadel must have been located at the summit of the slopes overlooking the sea, to the south-west, like the Casbah today. The city wall of the pre-Roman town has not been found and there is no way of establishing with any precision the extent of Hadrumetum in the Punic period. However, the tophet was discovered under the church built at the end of the nineteenth century and its excavation brought to light five levels of votive deposits, dating from the

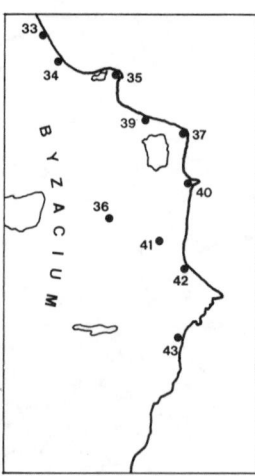

FIGURE 161   *Punic Byzacium: 33 Hadrumetum (Sousse); 34 El Kenissia; 35 Ruspina (Monastir); 36 Smirat; 37 Thapsus (Ras Dimass); 39 Leptis (Lemta); 40 Mahdia; 41 Ksour Essaf; 42 Sullecthum (Salakta); 43 Acholla (Ras Botria).*

seventh to the first century BC (Cintas, 1947). From that deposit came the stele bearing an effigy of the god Baal Hammon sitting on a throne flanked by two winged sphinxes, which is taken to be the surest representation of the god that has come down to us (above, p. 198, figure 104). Numerous tombs have been unearthed at Hadrumetum, but none seems earlier than the fourth century. One of them, explored at the end of last century, left its excavator, R. de La Blanchère, with an apparently unforgettable scented memory:

> Since the start of our excavations, only one chamber has been found closed, and not with potsherds but with a rough slab 0.15 metres thick . . . This closure and the filling in of the grave had produced so perfect a seal that, when the slab was displaced, the tomb released a perfume in which I found it easy to recognize myrrh and perhaps balsam wood (aoud el khmari for our Arabs). This fairly strong and extremely pleasant scent lasted for several hours in the chamber, and faded only slowly. We sought its origin in vain; none of the objects, bones, vases or utensils that were in the room had any odour at all. However astonishing it may seem, the probability is that myrrh resin and balsam wood, no doubt made into tablets as is still

done today, were left burning in the sepulchre. Their ashes had disappeared into the dust of the ground, where rubble fallen from the ceiling and formations of saltpetre had joined them; but the smoke, hermetically imprisoned, had left in the air a perfume that thousands of years had hardly faded. (1888, p. 152)

There is in fact, we know, an archaeology of smells (Bénichou-Safar, 1982, pp. 270–1).

Roughly twenty kilometres east-south-east of Sousse, on the coast, Monastir bears witness by its very name to the enduring quality of human habitation in this part: its present name is clearly derived from the Latin *monasterium* and indicates Christian settlements in late Antiquity. The former name, Ruspina (perhaps 'Corner Cape') was given more precisely to the promontory off which lies a group of islets; the largest, Sidi el Rhemsi (otherwise known as 'la Tonnara', in memory of a fishery of the last century), must have accommodated the first dwellings of the sailors who made landfall here. The *Stadiasmus* (115) indicated a mooring in the vicinity. A gate cut in the rock and excavations where cisterns have been seen are perhaps vestiges of that occupation. The smallest islet, known as the 'Quarantaine' (djeziret el Oustania) has cells cut in the rock which are probably *haouanet*. In fact the ancient town seems likely to have been established, as early as the pre-Roman period, fairly well back from the shore in the place known as Henchir Tenir. It was there, at the beginning of 46 BC, that Caesar set up his camp against Pompey and his troops (*Bellum Africum*, XXXVII, 2–4), and recent surveys have noted traces on the plateau of an urban settlement from at least the fourth century BC. The surrounding countryside was doubtless as flourishing as it was in the time of Pliny the Elder (*NH*, XV, 82), who extolled the quality of the figs that came in casks from Ruspina.

Still following the coast southwards, we find another celebrated site, equally well known from texts and archaeological research: Thapsus, a headland site (Ras Dimass) with a typically Phoenician name (the 'crossing' or the 'ford'). The Punic city fell at the time of Agathocles' expedition in 310, and marked its farthest thrust south, and here also Caesar achieved his decisive victory over Pompey's party in 46. The ancient town has yet to be discovered (Fantar, 1978, pp. 59–70) and attention has been given chiefly to the port installations in their Roman state. But the famous mole (figure 162) seems to have been constructed, at least in part, on infrastructure of the Punic era.

FIGURE 162   *The mole of Thapsus (P. Cintas).*

Lower still, on the point of Cape Africa, huddled in its ramparts of the Fatimid period, the little town of Mahdia even today presents a picture of what the Punic town, whose name eludes us, must have looked like. Perhaps it was *Gummi*, a place-name known through documents of Roman date, which the name of an area lying outside the walls, Gemma, may reflect. At the tip of the peninsula, on its southern edge, a little harbour basin, cut out in the fashion of a cothon, very probably belongs to the Punic period. Not far away there are lines of rock-cut tombs whose dating has been much discussed: Punic for some (Cintas, 1970, p. 261), Fatimid for others. We shall see that at Mahdia, as elsewhere in the region, the ancient cemetery must in fact be sought at an appreciable distance from the coastline.

The real good fortune for Punic archaeology in the Tunisian Sahel lay in the systematic exploration, resumed a few years ago (Ben Younès, 1981), of the littoral band of tufa, formed along the length of the coast by the consolidation of dunes of quaternary date. A short distance (between a few hundred metres and several kilometres) away from the towns, the tomb-diggers found a subsoil ideal for hollowing out hypogea, rock that was easy to tackle with a pick and that hardened quickly on contact with the air. It is chiefly thanks to these vast burial deposits, whose exploration was started as early as the end of last century, that we know about Punic civilization in Byzacium. And in many instances these sites are still available for investigation.

From Thapsus (Ras Dimass) we must go back a little towards the north to find a good example of this at Lemta, formerly *Lepti*, with *Minus* added in the Roman era to differentiate this *emporium* from *Leptis* (or *Lepcis*) *Magna*, the large city in Tripolitania. It was there in 203 that Hannibal set foot in Africa once again, after fifteen years spent in Italy. Nothing has been found of the defences, certainly of Punic date, which are mentioned at the time of Caesar's African campaign (*Bellum Africum*, VII, 2). But numerous tombs of the cemetery established in the consolidated dunes behind the coastline escaped the attentions of clandestine excavators (the heights of this coastal barrier bear the evocative name of Ghiran er Roum, 'the holes or caves of the Roumis'). Most noteworthy of these early excavations are those carried out in the place called Henchir Methkal on the eve of the First World War by the Abbé de Smet, then parish priest of Mahdia. Without any illustrations apart from a few diagrams (figure 163), but with the help of graphic and precise comments, the excavator began to bring to life in his report (1913, pp. 327–42) the ordinary Libyphoenicians who had taken their place *post mortem* in the hundred or so tombs that he had explored. These were single- or double-chambered tombs, access to which was gained by a stairless shaft (sometimes a few steep steps hewn in a side wall of the shaft served the purpose). Skeletons were often found with their legs folded, even crouched, but the vermilion used

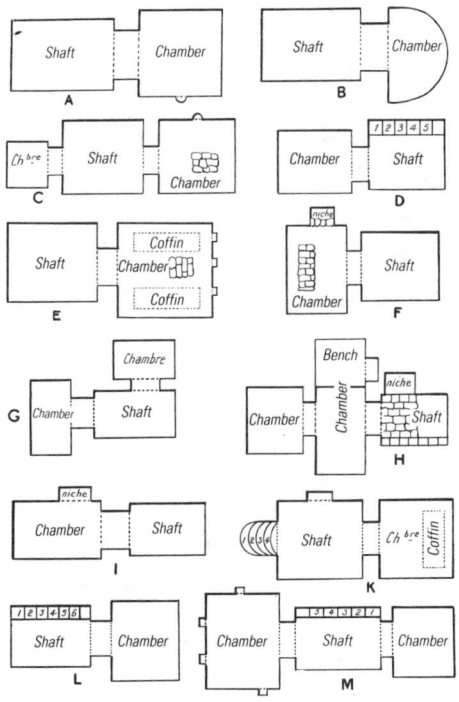

FIGURE 163 *The Abbé de Smet's excavations at Henchir Methkal near Lemta: type plans of the tombs.*

as a funerary ornament appears to be absent here. On the other hand, the excavator noted the great frequency of deposits of clay in the bowls or dishes arranged near the deceased. Were they perhaps 'geophagi', wondered the Abbé, who had his anthropological moments. We shall see these bowls and their clay contents later, for more careful observation uncovered their secret.

As luck would have it, this same cemetery of Bou Hadjar, which had been amply studied, provided Cintas with the opportunity of complementary excavations in the middle of this century. His account in a few notes, which have remained unpublished, confirms the Abbé de Smet's descriptions. Cintas adds some interesting variations to the typology of the hypogea drawn up by his predecessor, and in particular an account of some tombs whose carefully smoothed and coated walls had been decorated with red bands painted horizontally halfway up. An even more remarkable one had an angled ceiling simulating a pitched roof, whose supporting beam would have been placed on the capital of a pillar left projecting, opposite the entrance to the funeral chamber; on the two sides of the sloping ceiling red bands painted at regular intervals represented the joists of a mock framework (figure 164). As the Abbé de

FIGURE 164 *The cemetery of Bou Hadjar (Pierre Cintas's excavations). Top: a painted tomb with a pitched roof and simulated carpentry; bottom: an overturned wooden casket in another tomb, and pottery grave goods spread on the floor of the tomb (P. Cintas).*

Smet had noted previously, Cintas remarked on the presence in some tombs of wooden caskets which had served as sarcophagi. In one tomb the casket appeared to have been overturned and pushed against one of the walls, while all the pottery articles of the grave goods were found piled in a corner of the chamber, on top of a thick layer of rubble that had fallen from the wall (figure 164): an obvious sign that this disturbance, perhaps caused by an earth tremor, had occurred long after the placing of the corpse in the tomb. Cintas also observed skeletons, if not in a crouched position, at least lying on their sides with their legs clearly bent (figure 165, 1), a characteristic of Libyan funeral rites, and – a no less clearly indigenous feature – the abundance among the grave goods of moulded pottery, most often in the form of calyciform goblets (figure 165, 2 and 3), while imported pottery, very much in the minority (figure 165, 4), indicated dates for the burials somewhere

FIGURE 165 *Bou Hadjar (Pierre Cintas's excavations): 1 a skeleton on its side, with bent legs; 2 grave group, with calyciform goblets peculiar to these tombs of the Sahel; 3 a kernos made of three goblets; 4 a black-glazed scyphus with painted decoration (P. Cintas).*

between the end of the fourth and beginning of the second century. Unlike the Abbé de Smet, Cintas noted the wide use of cinnabar as funeral make-up.

It was at Smirat, a little farther inland (point 36 on figure 161), that the cemeteries of the Sahel were first subjected to rigorous archaeological study by Cintas in collaboration with Dr Gobert, on the eve of the Second World War. The two archaeologists showed on this occasion that, in a discipline where one rarely has large numbers at one's disposal, quality of observation can greatly compensate for the quantitative weakness of the archaological material. The twenty-two Smirat tombs, excavated in the spring of 1939, and carefully studied, provided a harvest of information about the populations of the Punic Sahel that subsequent investigations have only confirmed, sometimes fixing details more precisely (Cintas and Gobert, 1941, pp. 83–121). Observations made on funeral rites, often rather hesitant in the reports of preceding excavations, were affirmed and clarified. The red make-up colouring the skeletons, notably the faces of the dead, was certainly cinnabar, which had settled on the bones after the flesh had decomposed; there was thus no cause to speak of the prior removal of the flesh from the corpse. Sometimes, however, instead of cinnabar, clay with a very heavy ferrous oxide content, the *rubrica* of the Latins, was also found in receptacles. Under the lumps of compacted clay filling the bowls, which had intrigued the Abbé de Smet, careful observation discovered the mineral residue of a sort of granular preparation, very probably a food offering; at the same time, certain bowls contained grains of wheat and others grape-pips. Lying on their side, their legs bent (the famous flexed lateral decubitus), the dead were ensconced in their last home in a sleeping position, and the excavators retrieved from under the bodies tatters of a thick woollen fabric: 'Seen under a magnifying glass,' they pointed out, 'this fabric reveals an extremely regular weave. Twisted from left to right, all the threads, when one frays them, have the sinuous appearance of those of modern serges, marked by catches and skips. Certain parts of the material, the best preserved, reveal that it must have been dyed in alternate red and yellow stripes' (Cintas and Gobert, 1941, p. 92).

Less frequently, the bodies had been placed in wooden caskets that were most often equipped with hinged lids, in other words

FIGURE 166 *A wooden casket with feet, from a tomb in Gightis (Bou Ghrara) in the Tunisian south (G. L. Feuille's excavations)*

domestic furniture re-used *in extremis* to act as sarcophagi. Analyses reveal the use of Aleppo pine for the main members and juniper wood for the side planks. The climate in this region, even more favourable in the Tunisian south, has allowed several of these caskets, in well-protected tombs, to remain in a remarkable state of preservation (figure 166). This same quality of the air allowed the Smirat excavators to lay hands on exceptional anthropological documents. In the casket of Tomb XIV were a pair of corpses which had retained a fair amount of their hair; the man's was short, curly, almost woolly; the woman's skull was crushed, but nevertheless clearly revealed slender plaits of the type still to be seen adorning the heads of young Bedouin women in the interior of Tunisia, especially in the south (figure 167). The grave goods in the tombs

a b

FIGURE 167 *A male cranium (a) and the tresses of a female hair-style (b) from tomb XIV in Smirat. The black areas on the male skull were dyed with red make-up (Cintas and Gobert excavations).*

FIGURE 168   *The graffito vessel from Smirat and its inscription (P. Cintas).*

were sparse, exclusively pottery, and anything superfluous (jewels, amulets) was excluded. Only water amphorae, jugs and sometimes lamps were in wheel-turned pottery, while the platters, goblets and bowls shaped like flattened cones were hand-made. But among these dozens of objects in common use one stood out by virtue of a crude schematic human figure engraved on the side before firing (figure 168). The vessel also bore an inscription of a few signs that is still waiting to be deciphered. What does this enigmatic figure represent? Could it be the deceased transformed into a hero, as was suggested not so long ago (Camps, 1961, p. 324)? A symbolic representation of victory over death was put forward more recently, stressing the person's warlike attitude, following a stylization in which several set features of Libyan funerary iconography are to be found (Ben Younès, 1987, pp. 17–32). The text – the undeciphered graffito – might perhaps throw light on the picture; but we shall see how difficult it always is to read 'neo-Punic' writings, above all when, as here, they are freely drawn with the point of a stylus.

One last subject for wonder, then, before we leave Smirat: those Libyphoenician peasants of the Sahel, of very limited means, probably invested much more in the fitting out of their 'eternal dwellings', dug deep in the rock, than in the homes they lived in. But, since we have just talked of eschatology, that was already the first victory over death. We know in any case that such a concern was very widespread in Antiquity. Modest funerals are fairly recent in

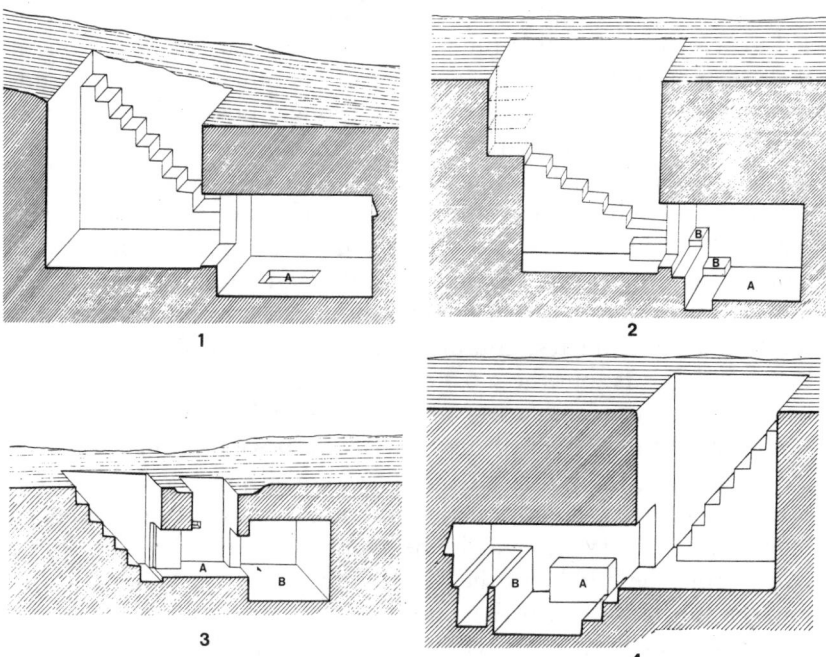

FIGURE 169   *Cross-sections of Punic hypogea from the cemeteries of the Sahel: 1 a tomb at Thapsus with a pit (A) dug in the floor of the funeral chamber; 2 a tomb at Thapsus with a low bench (A) and tiers (B); 3 a tomb at Mahdia with an antechamber (A); 4 a tomb at Mahdia with a bench (A) and a sarcophagus trough (B) (after* Dossiers Histoire et Archéologie, *no. 69).*

origin and in our societies are linked closely with the transmission of inheritances. The Smirat peasants had hardly anything to transmit.

The young generation of archaeologists trained at the Tunis National Institute of Archaeology and Art are actively interested in these cemeteries of the Sahel. Recent work undertaken in the sector of Mahdia has allowed early reports to be rectified, such as those of Dominique Anziani (1912, pp. 245–303) (figure 169). The architecture of these underground tombs, thus clarified in detail, reveals refinements which had sometimes escaped the first explorers, for example, the cushion-pillows or headrests set on the bench-beds in the funeral chambers (Ben Younès, 1985, pp. 23–61). Attention must be drawn especially to the importance of the excavation under way at present inland at the place known as El-Hkayma about fifteen kilometres south-west of Mahdia (Ben Younès, 1986 and 1988). Not far from this funerary deposit are the ruins, visible in their Roman state, of an ancient site of unknown identity, extending over about fifteen hectares. It was thought possible to recognize it as Tegea, a town not far from Aggar that features in the account of the battles waged by Caesar in 46 against Pompey and his supporters (Gsell, 1928, p. 111; Foucher, 1960, p. 13). At all events the tombs of El-Hkayma may be linked with this site, whatever its name. The results of two excavation campaigns at this cemetery not only confirm the principal contributions (on the structure of the tombs and funeral rites, notably) made by previous work on neighbouring deposits, but the most outstanding additional information has come from examination of the pottery. This reveals the skill acquired by the potters of the Sahel, who were no longer content with repeating the old repertoire of moulded pottery, but created original products, chiefly in the vast range of local imitations of black-glazed pottery, which developed greatly in the Punic world from the middle of the third century BC (Ben Younès, 1988, pp. 78–80). It is known that, following the example of Utica, the chief towns of Byzacium – Hadrumetum, Leptis, Thapsus, Acholla – abandoned Carthage in 146, when it was facing its final ordeal. In the case of Utica, this would be an expression of the jealousies built up in the course of a long-standing rivalry (Appian, *Libyca*, 75). We do not know the motives of the towns of the Sahel. Perhaps, having by then attained a fine agricultural and artisanal prosperity, they wanted to keep out of the torment to come.

8

Between East and West:
An Ambiguous Cultural Identity

At the very end of the ninth century BC, the Phoenicians from Tyre who had come to Africa settled in a 'barbarous' land, in the Greek sense of the word, that is to say, among or rather on the fringes of people who did not speak the same language as themselves and were not on the same cultural level. A little under two centuries later, the Dorians would get a foothold in Cyrene and, on the rim of the Barce plateau bordering the desert and a world that had remained in the Neolithic age, would establish a lastingly flourishing Hellenism free of any taint, whose finest jewels would be a marvellous poet, Pindar, and some of the most remarkable works of ancient sculpture. But there is no real comparison between the two situations. The Hellenism in Cyrenaica was never anything but a flourishing bridgehead, Greece's most unusual extraterritoriality, whereas Carthage, before becoming an African power, had since the beginning rubbed shoulders with the realities of the western Mediterranean that it sought to dominate. There was the risk – obviously very noticeable for us – of rapidly altering the oriental and Semitic culture of which it was the custodian, which had already started to become tinged with local influences in those places where the Phoenicians, earlier or simultaneously, had carried it into regions where the indigenous cultural personality was strong, as in southern Spain.

That risk of penetration and ultimate loss of identity was all the greater because the original Phoenician culture was already characterized by its absorbency. In Phoenicia itself, influences from Egypt had left a deep imprint, on which Mycenaean and then Greek contributions were superimposed. Arriving in Africa with Dido's followers, the civilization that had come from Tyre, by way of Cyprus, was already heterogeneous or, to express it in a more positive fashion, rich in its various components. This transplanted composite culture remained open and welcoming when it encountered local cultures in the West: indigenous and Greek in Sicily and Sardinia, Iberian in Ibiza. But, as I said at length earlier, until at least the beginning of the sixth century Carthage was largely *outside* Carthage. It therefore follows that its cultural identity in the archaic era must not be assessed on the basis of its specifically Carthaginian aspects alone, but must also take account of that tentacular dimension.

ARCHITECTURE

In the realm of the major arts, the Phoenico-Carthaginians may well look like poor relations, in comparison with Egypt and the Greek lands. One must admit the absence of great monumental art at Carthage and, more generally, among the Phoenicians in the West. But it must be conceded that this lack of monuments is due, at least in part, to the haphazardness of findings and the difficulty of

FIGURE 170 *Carthage: a cippus from the tophet (fifth century* BC*)
(Gallimard, 'Univers des Formes').*

making any significant ones, especially at the archaic levels of sites that have been seriously obstructed or even obliterated by the overlay of centuries.

To obtain some idea of Punic architecture in those very early times, one can nevertheless refer to its veritable simulation provided by the votive stelae, at Carthage itself and in the domain controlled by Carthage, chiefly in Sardinia and at Motya in Sicily. It will come as no surprise that the architectural type of these 'cippi-naiskoi' is frankly Egyptianate. Whether the image featuring in the framework of the doorway is a 'baetyl' (or a row of 'baetyls'), surmounted or not by the solar disc and the lunar crescent (figure 170), or a feminine representation with a disc (figure 171), or again a 'bottle-idol' (figure 172), the façade of these small-scale models of temples always presents an entablature whose architrave, acting as a lintel, is decorated with the winged solar disc, often stylized in the extreme, surmounted by a cornice with a frieze of *uraei* (figures 171 and 172), or an Egyptian moulding (figure 170). The constancy of this oriental reference is such that it is still to be found, in the third century, on a stele from the tophet at Sousse, on which this entablature motif, in a fairly degenerate form, coexists with fluted pilasters with capitals in the Corinthian style (figure 173). As for the cornice with the Egyptian moulding (its shape noticeably evolving

FIGURE 171 *Sulcis: a cippus from the tophet (sixth to fifth century BC) (after S. Moscati, Carthage, Milan, 1982).*

FIGURE 172   *A cippus from Nora (after S. Moscati, Carthage, Milan, 1982).*

as it travelled from east to west and down through the ages), it
would remain a major element of monumental art in the Cartha-

FIGURE 173   *Sousse: a cippus from the tophet (third century* BC; *Cintas's
excavations)*

FIGURE 174 *The Medracen in the region of Constantine, Algeria. On the right the Egyptian-style cornice can be seen in profile (after* Die Numider, Bonn, 1979)

ginian area right up to the end of Punic times: it is present in the third century in the great tomb of the Medracen, in the heart of Numidia, crowning its Doric entablature (figures 174 and 175); a little later it would also figure, projecting from the two storeys of the mausoleum at Dougga.

We must linger a while over this tomb at Dougga, the only great monument of Punic architecture still standing on Tunisian soil (Poinssot, 1958, p. 59). That is due to the restoration patiently carried out at the beginning of this century under the direction of Louis Poinssot, repairing the act of vandalism committed in the middle of the nineteenth century by the British consul in Tunis, who almost completely demolished the mausoleum in order to lay hands on the bilingual Libyan and Punic inscription, for which it had been famous for a long time. This text, now in the British Museum, is among those that permitted a first deciphering of the script of the

FIGURE 175 *The Medracen: detail of the Doric capitals, the architrave and the cornice with the Egyptian moulding (M. Bouchenaki).*

ancient Numidians. It informs us that the mausoleum was built for a native chief, Atban, probably a little before the reign of Massinissa (end of the third/beginning of the second century). But the inscription also gives the name of the architect, a Carthaginian, heading a team of Numidian workmen.

By itself, the storeyed mausoleum of Dougga sums up the Egypto-Greek syncretism which often characterizes what is left to us of Carthage's monumental art, from the Classical to the Hellenistic periods (figure 176). The bottom storey, which rests on a podium of five steps, is decorated on the corners by pilasters with Aeolic capitals ornamented with lotus flowers. The second storey, seated on three steps, presents a decoration of engaged fluted Ionic columns, supporting an architrave itself surmounted by a cornice with Egyptian moulding. The third storey is flanked at the four corners by pedestals that used to carry horsemen; the corner pilasters have lotus-flower capitals and, as on the second storey, support an entablature surmounted by a cornice with Egyptian moulding. On each face, in the large stone first course, is a bas-relief representing

FIGURE 176 *The Libyco-Punic mausoleum at Dougga (C. Poinssot).*

a four-horse chariot. The whole is topped by a pyramid flanked at the corners by the mutilated statues of sea-nymphs. The predominant impression left is of this juxtaposition of motifs of archaic Greek art (the horsemen, the quadrigae, the sirens), attached to an architectural structure (the tower mausoleum) whose origin is oriental and which had a good succession in Roman Africa. But the period of the Numidian kingdoms (third to second century BC) was the finest for this composite art, with very different forms of expression at Dougga and the Medracen, the fruit (as was recently written) of the meeting on African soil of an oriental-type despotic power and Greek art (Coarelli and Thébert, 1988, pp. 761–818).

These remains of funerary architecture in the Punic world owe their preservation to the fact that they are situated away from the great urban sites. It is probable that others will be discovered, but razed and reduced to the plan of their foundations, like the recently re-excavated mausoleum of Henchir-Bourgou, at Djerba, which is remarkable for its hexagonal outline, with alternately flat and

concave faces (Akkari-Weriemmi, 1985, pp. 189–96). In Tripolitania, at Sabratha, in present-day Libya, the finding of a sufficient
number of architectonic fragments has allowed the reconstruction
of a commemorative rather than funerary monument, the plan of
which is close to that of both the mausoleum of Siga (Beni Rhenane)
in the region of Oran, and of Henchir-Bourgou. But the resemblance to the Djerba monument is rather overshadowed by a more
pronounced development here of the concave faces, which gives the
monument more elegance and a grandeur further accentuated by its
position on a podium of six steps (figure 177). This 'Mausoleum B'
at Sabratha, which has been dated to the beginning of the second
century BC, carries the architectural reflection of the influence of
Hellenistic Alexandria in the region of the Syrtes (Di Vita, 1976,
pp. 273–86). Punic taste, however, is well and truly present in the
rich sculpted decoration, which borrows its motifs from both the
Orient and Greek archaism, with a slightly heavy and baroque

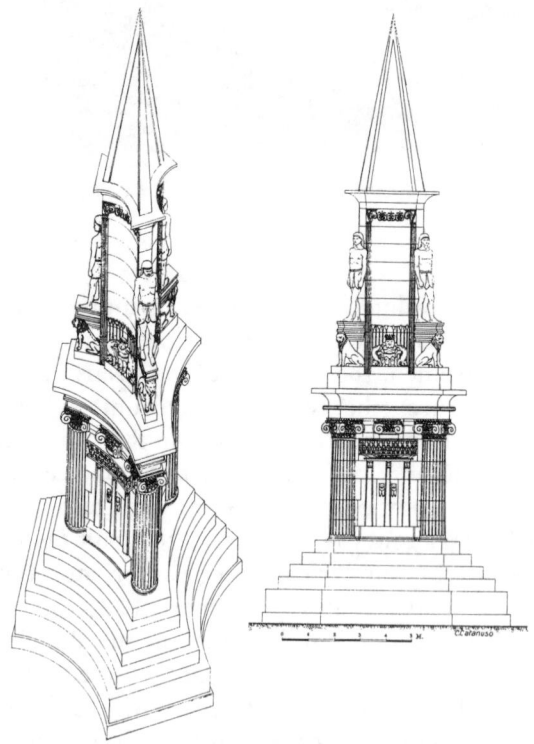

FIGURE 177 *Mausoleum B at Sabratha in Libya (drawings by C. Catanuso).*

profusion that is relieved by the elegance of the ensemble and the slenderness of the monument.

In Carthage itself and its closest hinterland, the Hellenistic period also provides us with the most numerous examples of architecture. Although no edifices have been found in their entirety, fragments throw light on the choices made for architectural decoration. The Carthaginians were very eclectic in the selection and execution of the architectural orders. They had a particular predilection for the Aeolic-type capital, which they seem to have adopted for their own by way of its Cypriot version, beginning from the fourth century BC. These scrolled capitals often feature in the decoration on stelae and are also very frequently used in the series of orders on mausolea, for example, at Dougga and Sabratha. Nearer to Carthage, from Medjez el-Bab comes a part of a limestone doorjamb decorated with a grooved pilaster surmounted by a capital of this type, probably part of a mausoleum datable to the end of the third century (figure 178). The Ionic column similarly plays a great role in architectural decoration in Carthage, starting from the fourth century at least, and perhaps also copied at first from Cypriot models. The use of this order has even been attributed to a sacred purpose, in that it has been found on architectural cippi sometimes collected from sanctuaries (Lézine, 1960, p. 43). Indeed, in the tophet of Salammbô, pillar-cippi noticeably square in section and crowned by Ionic capitals have been unearthed; one of them, in hard grey limestone, includes an abacus ornamented with eggs and darts above the volutes of the capital (figure 179). A stele from the same tophet, bearing as the chief subject of the lower section under

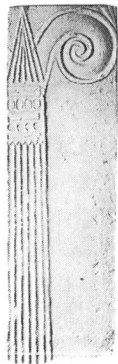

FIGURE 178   *A door-jamb with a pilaster surmounted by an Aeolic capital (Musée national du Bardo, Tunis).*

FIGURE 179   *A pillar cippus with an Ionic capital from the tophet of Salammbô (drawing by A. Lézine).*

FIGURE 180   *A stele from the tophet at Carthage (Musée national du Bardo, Tunis).*

the dedicatory inscription, a column with a highly stylized Ionic capital, supporting a sphinx, reflects the vogue in the third century (the date that can be given to this stele) for this architectural ornament, doubtless for reasons of 'taste' as much as for religious motives (figure 180). We know from Appian (*Libyca*, 96) that on the fronts of the shipsheds on the island and on the outer edge of the military harbour there were Ionic columns that gave the whole harbour the aspect of vast circular porticoes where this order prevailed.

A charming little monument carved out of a limestone block, which may well have been a small-scale model of a temple dedicated to Demeter and was doubtless deposited as an ex-voto, encapsulates both the architectural type of the late Punic temple derived from the Egyptianate *naos* (cf. above, p. 214) and the dominant taste relating to decoration, at a date that can be placed slightly before the fall of Carthage. This is the *naiskos* of Thuburbo Maius (Henchir Kasbat, not far from Carthage), which reproduces a building

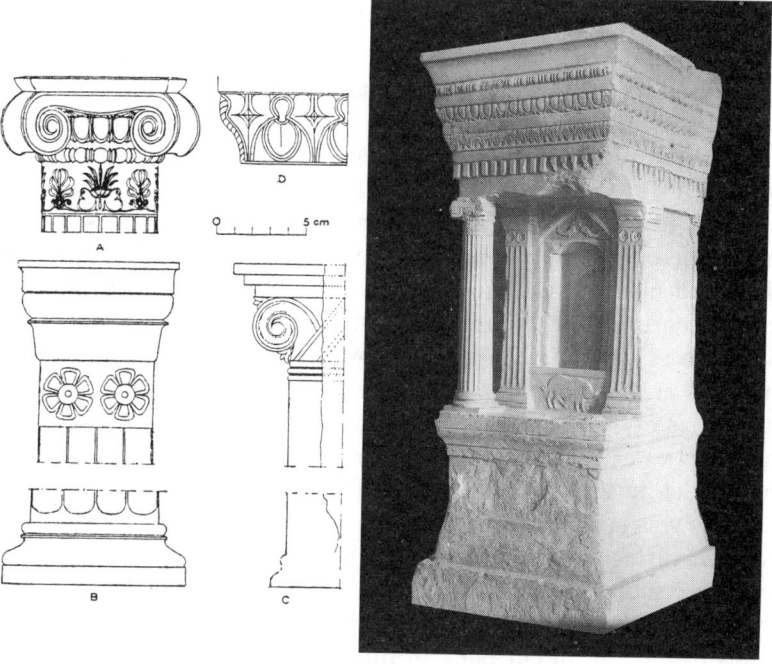

FIGURE 181 *The naiskos from Thuburbo Maius, photographed (right) before the restoration of a small column; left, details of the ornamentation (drawings by A. Lézine).*

composed of a *cella* preceded by a two-columned porch, the whole resting on a plinth (figure 181). The rather heavy entablature comprises, from top to bottom, a cyma recta, in which the Egyptian moulding is recognizable, then a line of beads and reels, a row of eggs and darts, an ogee moulding, and finally a row of denticles. Worthy of note is the quality of the capitals of the porch's small Ionic columns, which support this entablature, and especially the treatment of the neckings, decorated with seven-leaved palm fronds and separated from the capitals properly speaking by a chaplet of beads and reels. Behind the porch appears the façade of the *cella* hollowed in a recess flanked by two pilasters and surmounted by a pediment, on which two dolphins are face to face below a flower; a bas-relief representing a boar adorns the niche's base. The pilasters flanking it have capitals which are noteworthy for their neckings ornamented with six-petalled rosettes, while at the outer edges of the lateral façades the Aeolic order returns in the capitals of the pilasters (figure 181).

The monuments or fragments just mentioned are not made of marble, but carved out of sandstone or limestone. This is not surprising. Even in Rome itself, nothing was built in marble before the second half of the second century BC, by which time Carthage had ceased to exist. In any case, if marble had, exceptionally, been used in the construction of a public or religious edifice, how would it have been preserved in a city where everything that had not been pillaged at the time of its downfall was subsequently re-used or perished in the lime kilns? We shall see later that any surviving marble belongs to sarcophagi deeply buried in the soil and thereby preserved until the activities of excavators at the end of the nineteenth century. For monumental building (defences, temples and even houses) the Carthaginians resorted mainly to the sandstone of the cliffs at the tip of Cap Bon, which they worked at El-Haouaria at least as early as the seventh century. The relative distance from the quarries at the sea edge was compensated by easy transport of the blocks by sea along the coast. The material furnished by these quarries was easy to cut and saw, but rough and liable to split if its exposed surface was not coated. Perhaps that is why the Carthaginians were such able stucco-workers. As an example of their skill in ornamentation one could cite a projecting corner pillar which seems to have been cut back in thickness to be used as a funerary cippus, and which was one of the first finds in the excavations of the Salammbô tophet in 1922. Of course the stucco ornamentation applied to the core of El-Haouaria sandstone had suffered, but

FIGURE 182 *A projecting corner pilaster found in the excavations of the Carthage tophet (Musée national du Bardo, Tunis, with a drawing by A. Lézine).*

careful observation by Alexandre Lézine allowed him to reconstruct a very fine decoration, whose baroque exuberance suggests the influence of Hellenistic Sicily on this fragment, which is datable without doubt to the beginning of the third century BC (figure 182). Above the shaft, with its Ionic fluting, the necking is decorated with a frieze of palm fronds linked at their base by volutes; a few years ago one could make out, here and there, traces of a red 'paint' which might have been the 'seating' for the application of gold leaf. Whereas for the necking the stuccoist worked only on a sandstone surface left smooth, for the capital the decoration had first been sketched in the stone and then picked out more precisely by the application of stucco; it consists of a palm frond emerging from a bouquet of acanthus whose composition spreads across the width of the capital. This pilaster may have belonged to a prostyle temple in the Ionic order where it may have projected at the end of one of the *cella* walls (Lézine, 1960, pp. 79–84).

Rather curiously, the Carthaginians made scant and belated use of the Doric order, which they must, however, have known for a long time in Sicily, where it had been dominant since the end of the sixth

FIGURE 183   *The Souma of the Kroub, from a survey made by Ravoisié in the nineteenth century. Is it perhaps lacking a terminal pyramid?*

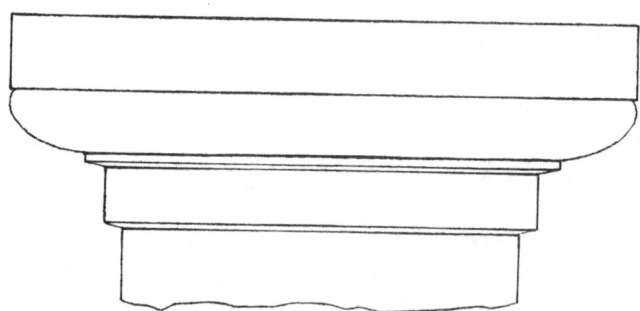

FIGURE 184   *One of the capitals of the Souma's second storey (Ravoisié survey).*

century. We have seen that order used on the Medracen, where Doric capitals of engaged columns support architraves surmounted by cornices with an Egyptian moulding (figure 175). A little later, around the end of the second century, they crop up again, on

FIGURE 185   *A Doric capital from Bordj-Djedid (A. Lézine).*

smooth-shafted columns, in the monument called the Kroub Souma, near Constantine (figures 183 and 184). In Carthage itself the oldest Doric capital does not appear to go further back than the beginning of the third century. This is the date that can be attributed to the example which Saumagne uncovered in his excavations at Bordj-Djedid. It will be seen that the echinus, which is rather bulbous, is connected with the shaft by three annulets, a flourish that leaves us rather far from the purest Doric tradition (figure 185). Above all, the shaft itself has fluting that is in fact Ionic, with ridges that are not at all sharp but shallow, giving quite a wide fillet, in a mixture of genres which can be paralleled elsewhere in the Hellenistic period. Recent excavations at Carthage of the levels of that date have considerably increased evidence of the use of this order in the Punic metropolis itself. A capital of very similar shape to that of Bordj-Djedid was recently uncovered by Friedrich Rakob in an investigation under the levels of the Roman *cardo XIII* (Rakob, 1989, p. 168). In the late Punic quarter on the hill of Byrsa, observations of numerous fragments collected enlighten us as to the techniques employed, particularly for shaping the columns. The fluting first cut on the sandstone shaft left sharp ridges which the subsequent application of the stucco, in two

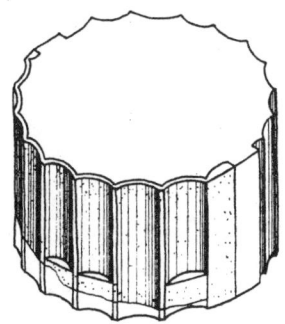

FIGURE 186   *A stuccoed column from Byrsa (P. Poncet, French archaeological mission).*

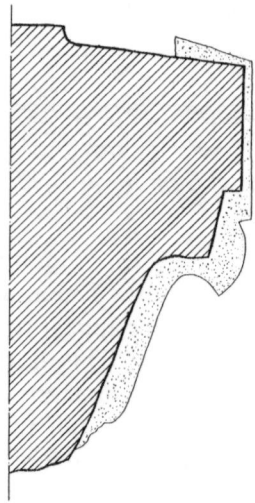

FIGURE 187   *A pilaster with a crow's beak capital from the Byrsa excavations (P. Poncet, French archaeological mission).*

layers, allowed to be reduced, producing a noticeably narrower fillet than on the shaft surmounted by Saumagne's capital (figure 186). In the Byrsa excavations, crow's beak cornices are associated with this Doric order, very few examples of which were found in the Carthaginian domain until just recently. There also we see the use of two techniques (figures 187 and 188), the first made by initially

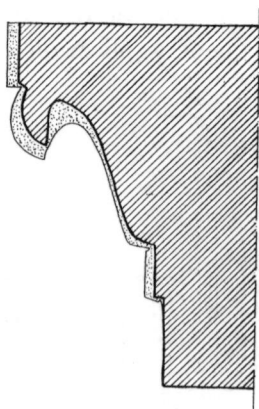

FIGURE 188   *A crow's beak cornice from the Byrsa excavations (P. Poncet, French archaeological mission).*

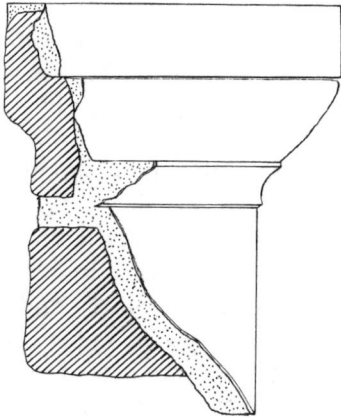

FIGURE 189 *A capital with a Doric column and a smooth shaft from the Byrsa excavations (P. Poncet, French archaeological mission).*

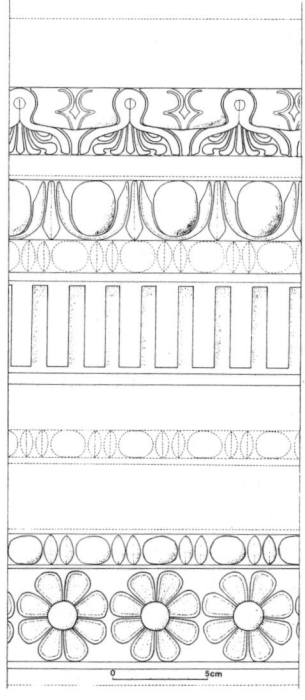

FIGURE 190 *Stuccoed and painted decoration from the interior of houses in Byrsa (collected by N. Ferchiou, drawn by G. Eriksson, French archaeological mission).*

carving out of the sandstone a pronounced and very sharp projection which the stuccoist then worked on, softening the curves; the second leaving to the stuccoist alone the task of shaping the crow's beak on a block of sandstone that is merely given an outline shape beforehand (Morel, 1982a, p. 184).

With more restricted modules, Punic architects also resorted to the Doric order for the interior decoration of Byrsa houses, as shown by a fragment of a smooth-shafted half-column, its core of El-Haouaria sandstone covered with a double coat of stucco (figure 189): first, a priming coat of between 15 and 20 mm in thickness, then a very fine and homogeneous 'skin' between 3 and 5 mm thick. Below the abacus, the echinus is connected to the shaft by a necking whose curve is emphasized by two reglets (Lancel, 1979, p. 195).

The expertise of Carthaginian stuccoists is also revealed in the architectural stuccoes moulded and fixed to decorate the upper parts of internal walls. There one finds the ornamental repertoire of the Hellenistic era (successive rows of leaves and darts, beads and reels, eggs and darts, denticles, rosettes), enhanced by multicolouring in which blues, yellows and pinks predominate (figure 190).

SCULPTURE

To anyone approaching it by sea, Carthage must have appeared a magnificent city, with the tall white walls of its wave-beaten ramparts, whose stucco gleamed in the sunshine, and its tiers of houses spreading upwards to the crest of the hills. Like all the opulent cities in the Mediterranean world, within its porticoes, temples and richest houses it concealed a wealth of works of art, especially sculpture. This is not pure hypothesis: after the capture of the town in the spring of 146 BC, Scipio brought back to Rome and exhibited in his 'triumph' a large number of statues and *objets d'art* which the Carthaginians, says Appian, had collected from all over the world during their long period of victories (*Libyca*, 135). In particular, the Roman general invited the Sicilians to come to identify and recover everything that the Carthaginians had formerly taken from them at Himera, Agrigentum, Gela and Segesta, notably statues, including the famous bronze bull made for Phalaris of Agrigentum (Cicero, *De signis*, 72–3). Thus we know that the Carthaginians had turned their city into a vast museum, which argues in favour of their taste if not of their own creativity. There is indeed a possibility of finding here, as in architecture, first an oscillation between East and West and then the same strong attraction exercised by the cultures of the classical world.

The large-scale sculpture of the Phoenicians from the Orient was mainly funerary. The large anthropoid sarcophagi of Sidon come to mind, which until the fifth century were rendered in a clearly Egyptianate style; the Nilotic style rivalled the timid Hellenization of the representations (Moscati, 1988, pp. 292–9). It is not surprising therefore to find these anthropoid sarcophagus covers at an early date (fifth century) in the provinces of the western Phoenicians, where the Semitic tradition had been more faithfully preserved: the sarcophagi of Cadiz (Gades), executed in alabaster, show recumbent figures with 'Greek' features, but with that remarkable fixity of the eastern monuments.

In western Sicily the situation was different. As we know, the Carthaginians had installed themselves there early, but in contact with another tradition which had been well established in the island in the seventh century, that of Greek statuary. It is therefore not surprising that the evidence from Sicily is particularly rich and, at the same time, that many specialists are reluctant to put it into a Punic perspective. However, several of the fragments of sculpture brought to light in the region and executed in the round have a direct connection with the figurative style exemplified by the productions of Phoenicia proper. Thus a stone torso found in the 'pool' of Marsala (and probably originating from Motya) recalls, except

FIGURE 191 *A torso from Marsala (Palermo Museum).*

in its nude breast, an eighth-century Egyptianate statue from Tyre in the Beirut Museum. The Marsala statue (in the Palermo Museum) wears an oriental-fashion loincloth like the Tyre model and bears witness to the fidelity in sixth-century Motya to canons of representation that are completely foreign to Greek art (figure 191). In the same way, the goddess seated on a throne between two sphinxes, unearthed at Pizzo Cannita and also in the Palermo Museum, makes clear reference to an oriental iconographic type, even if the treatment of the tunic suggests an Ionian influence (figure 192).

The most spectacular encounter between the oriental culture of the Carthaginians and Greek art is illustrated by a recent discovery, made at Motya in 1979, of an 'ephebe' which had scarcely emerged from the earth that miraculously preserved it before it provoked questions and comments. What could be more unusual and more beautiful at the same time? Larger than life (1.8 metres, without its missing feet) the statue is of a young man. The arms have disappeared, but it is easy to reconstruct at least the pose of the left arm, thanks to the spread fingers of the hand resting on the hip,

FIGURE 192 *A divinity seated on a throne between two sphinxes from Pizzo Cannita (Sicily) (Palermo Museum).*

thereby emphasizing the movement of that left hip which carries the weight of the body. The face with its frame of curly hair around the forehead – a characteristic of the archaic style – is treated in the 'severe' manner of Greek sculpture of the beginning of the fifth century, and that date may therefore be assumed for this marble, or at the very latest the middle of the fifth century. On the head, rivets indicate that it was probably encircled with a diadem or crown, doubtless in gilded bronze. But the distinctive character of this effigy and its enigmatic beauty is related to the garment the young man is wearing, in place of the customary 'heroic nudity' of classic Greek art: the very fine tunic, its long flowing pleats disclosing

FIGURE 193　*The 'ephebe of Motya' (Superintendent of Antiquities, Palermo).*

rather than concealing a body that is in fact very precisely revealed, whose freedom of movement is restrained only by that strange pectoral band, placed so high under the armpits, and closed in front by a metal buckle, which is missing now (figure 193). That last detail – the band or girdle – suggested that the person might be identified as an *auriga* or charioteer. But the celebrated charioteer of Delphi wears it less high up on a *chiton* that is very different, and in any case their respective attitudes rule out comparison. Nevertheless, if we are to believe one of the first and most knowledgeable commentators, we need to stay in the realm of circuses and horse races to understand this astonishing figure. If he is not the charioteer, perhaps the statue is the idealized image of the 'sponsor' of the games, a member of Motya's gilded youth, here represented after a triumph won in the arena, not by himself but by his driver (Tusa, 1986, pp. 143–52). The radiant youth of the subject in fact limits the range of hypotheses. Does it allow us to follow another line, which opens up as soon as we start to view that long tunic with its hundreds of pleats as a ritual garment, the white linen tunic girdled with a broad band, certainly purple in colour, worn by the priests of Herakles-Melqart at Gades, according to Silius Italicus (*Punica*, III, 24–8)? However, under the priestly garment we should not see a priest but the god himself, disguised to some extent and like a prototype of the 'disguised Hercules' (Falsone, 1987, pp. 420–7). This is an ingenious and attractive hypothesis to which, drawn by other paths and without prior knowledge of it, one of the best scholars of the eternal Mediterranean shortly afterwards gave his support (Fernandez, 1988, pp. 348–53). Must we, with Dominique Fernandez, attribute to its 'disturbing ambiguity' the fact that the Motya ephebe is still so little known to the public at large, compared with the fame so swiftly acquired by the bronze male warriors fished from the sea off Riace a few years ago? Possibly, provided it is borne in mind that the ambiguity is first and foremost cultural. The hand that sculpted the Motya marble with such quivering sensitivity was Greek: Pythagoras of Rhegium, who was active in Magna Graecia in the first half of the fifth century, has been suggested. But the garment, that long pleated robe of oriental origin, is Punic, and also Punic, in a city then controlled by Carthage, is the personage beneath the robe, man or god, or maybe someone royal. It was recently suggested that it might be Hamilcar, the loser at Himera (G. C. Picard, 1991, pp. 390–1). From that follows the loss of familiar points of reference, a cause of intellectual and aesthetic discomfort, which occurs frequently in these

FIGURE 194 *From the cemetery known as Sainte-Monique, the sarcophagus of 'the priestess' (G. van Raepenbusch, Musée national de Carthage).*

situations of cultural contact involving the western Phoenicians. In this respect the Motya ephebe has an emblematic value.

Is such a discovery imaginable in Carthage? Probably not, for the reasons given above. To Scipio's looting or 'recoveries' the course of centuries has added so much other pillage that to unearth a marble like that of Motya would be a sheer miracle. The funerary nature of Carthaginian sculpture is the result of that dual historical and archaeological situation. The tradition of sarcophagus covers with figures was maintained in the Punic capital until the Hellenistic era, and some were preserved in the depths of the underground tombs, in particular in the cemetery known as Sainte-Monique, on the present-day hill of Saïda, north of the town, where Père Delattre discovered notably two marble sarcophagi – now in the Carthage

Museum – which reveal the modifications that had been made to the oriental model. On a pitched roof with acroteria, of a Greek type, are figured in high relief not two 'gisants' (recumbent forms) but two 'statues' lying down, their feet resting on a pedestal.

One of them, in very deep relief, is a woman whose entire appearance shows a singular syncretism (figures 194 and 195). Her head is covered with a veil whose folds frame her face – rather like a *klaft* – and is topped by a falcon's head; the long pleated robe she is wearing, belted high and trimmed around the neck with a sort of aegis, has its lower part enveloped by two large wings, one folded over the other, which swathe the bottom of the body like a sheath; the right arm, extended along the body, holds a dove, while the left, bent up to waist height, holds a perfume phial. Egyptianate elements (the falcon, the crossed wings, peculiar to the iconography of Isis-Nephthys) are thus superimposed on a representation in which there is an underlying Hellenistic model, chiefly in the treatment of the face. The marble of this elegant figure (which people have wanted to recognize as a priestess, but it could be an image of Tanit) was painted, and the wings still bear clear traces of these coloured embellishments.

The personage who lies at her side in the Carthage Museum is a bearded man, clad in a long garment and represented according to a very frequently repeated iconographic type: the bent left arm holds a vessel in its hand, in a gesture similar to that of the

FIGURE 195 *The sarcophagus of 'the priestess': detail.*

FIGURE 196 *From the cemetery of Sainte-Monique: the sarcophagus of 'the priest' (G. van Raepenbusch, Musée national de Carthage).*

'priestess', and the right hand is raised, open palm foremost, not to 'bless', as is sometimes said, but in an attitude of prayer (figure 196). Was he a priest or a magistrate, as was believed by Père Delattre, who was impressed by the richness of this cemetery dated to the last years of the city and saw the tombs as those of notables (the 'cemetery of the Rabhs')? The 'Greek' construction of this sarcophagus lid is in contrast with the cover of a limestone ossuary that emerged from the same funerary setting (figure 197). The same beard, the same garment, the same gestures with both hands; but the personage whose head rests on what appear to be two large

FIGURE 197   *From the cemetery of Sainte-Monique: the sarcophagus of Baalshillek (Musée national de Carthage).*

cushions is pictured in flat relief, like the stelae, and in a fashion much closer to oriental tradition.

These differences in technique and material have sometimes inspired clear-cut opinions. In Gsell's view, for example – and later Carcopino's – the two large marble covers with their high-relief figures could have been cut and sculpted only by Greek hands. If they were not imported ready-made, then the most he would concede was that they were the work of Greeks settled in Carthage, working on marble from the Aegean to suit their clientele. Is there no known Punic sculptor? A statue base found at Ephesus bears in Greek the signature of 'Boethus, son of Apollodorus, Carthaginian', a label that was no doubt necessary in order to distinguish this Boethus from several homonyms, including the creator of the famous 'child playing with a goose', kept in the Capitoline Museum in Rome, and also Boethus of Chalcedon, the

FIGURE 198 *A funerary statue from Gammarth (Musée national de Carthage).*

slightly later sculptor who created the bronze group found in the underwater excavation of Mahdia, now preserved in the Bardo Museum. For Gsell there was no question that Boethus was a Greek, certainly born in Carthage but of a Greek father. We know, however, that outside Carthage the Carthaginians sometimes gave up their Semitic names for Greek ones, which sounded better in business dealings, a practice that reminds us, at least in spirit, of the

FIGURE 199 *A feminine funerary statue from Carthage (G. van Raepenbusch).*

FIGURE 200   A *funerary stele from Carthage (Louvre, Paris)*.

transcription into Greek characters of the name Mago on the amphora stamps.

What is true is that Carthage's funerary art mainly produced less
ambitious works, fashioned out of local limestone, which com-
municate an attitude towards death and the dead rather than seeking to meet aesthetic concerns. This is how we must regard the
funerary statues – appreciably smaller than life-size – which have
been unearthed in the Carthaginian cemeteries of the final period
(the third to the beginning of the second century). Whether masculine or feminine, their gestures all appear the same: stiff, even
hieratic, these figures placed on the tombs raise the right hand in an
attitude of prayer (or vow?), while the left holds either a dish or, in
the case of the female images, an object generally identified as a disc
(figures 198 and 199). These representations are even more schematic when they are executed in flat relief, in recesses scooped out of
pedimented stelae (figure 200).

CARVED STELAE AND BRONZES

Seventy odd years ago, in his absolute scorn for anything that did
not abide by the canons of classical art, Gsell disposed of the
Carthage stelae in a few irrevocable lines: 'It was obviously at
Carthage that the innumerable little stelae of local stone were
made, a common commodity with no artistic value' (Gsell, vol. IV,
1924, p. 210). This attitude can be explained if one takes into

account the tastes of the period. Greater attention to the 'peripheral' aspects of culture, greater sensitivity to cultural interaction have modified our perception of those 'innumerable little stelae'. Running over the course of centuries to thousands of examples in the sacrificial areas, they provide concrete evidence of pictorial representation which is not the same in all the provinces of the Punic world and which, in Carthage itself, went through a process of evolution.

The Carthaginian stelae of the archaic period (the end of the eighth century to the sixth) are 'aniconic', not to say abstract. Since, in addition, they are anepigraphic, their anonymous message is very bare; the geometric representation of a baetyl or sacred pillar, or of the 'bottle-idol', or a diamond shape (figure 201; cf. also figure 135, above). The human figure appears belatedly and still in a very stylized form, sometimes emphasized by an application of stucco on the panel of rough-hewn sandstone (figure 201).

In the same period, the craftsmen of Motya in western Sicily were developing a noticeably different iconography, of which it could be said that it was more faithful to its oriental origins, despite the proximity of the Greek cultural world, whose influence had not yet made itself felt (Moscati, 1988, p. 312). The human figure, at that time so rare in Carthage, was present everywhere, most frequently

FIGURE 201 *Archaic stelae from Carthage (Musée national du Bardo, Tunis, and Musée national de Carthage). Left, a stylized baetyl or sacred pillar with, exceptionally in the early period, a dedicatory inscription: 'This is the cippus MLK BᶜL dedicated by Mago, son of Hanno, to Baal Hammon' (Corpus Inscriptionum Semiticarum 5685). Centre: a diamond surmounted by a crescent moon pointing downwards; right: a schematic human outline, stuccoed.*

FIGURE 202   *Stelae from the Motya tophet (sixth century BC) (Istituto per la civiltà fenicia e punica, Rome).*

represented in front view, with fairly accentuated stylization, and sometimes in profile in an attitude of prayer (figure 202). The image is even frankly Egyptianate at times, as in the case of the double stele on which the two figures facing each other and wearing loincloths reproduce the gesture of adoration customarily addressed to the winged sun (figure 203). This is another illustration

FIGURE 203   *A stele from Motya (Istituto per la civiltà fenicia e punica, Rome).*

FIGURE 204 *A stele from Motya (Istituto per la civiltà fenicia e punica, Rome).*

of the subject of an ivory plaque recently brought to light in an archaic tomb of Byrsa, at Carthage (cf. above, figure 48a). Similarly very close to its Phoenician origins is the subject of the female figure, with a long robe and Egyptianate wig, crossing her arms over her bosom (figure 204).

In Carthage the stylistic evolution of the stelae was fairly slow. From the end of the sixth century the cippi, still cut from El-Haouaria sandstone, hardly changed form. They were, however, more elaborate and cippi-naiskoi began to appear, as I mentioned in connection with the indications they give on the earliest monumental architecture of the Punic city (above, figures 170–173). The 'sign of Tanit' also makes its first appearance on sandstone cippi around the end of the fifth century (cf. above, p. 201). But it was the transfer to another material, a grey, sometimes bluish limestone, very fine and dense, in a period that is difficult to fix exactly (about the end of the fourth century?), which mainly brought about a richer and far more varied iconography (C. Picard, 1976, pp. 67–137; 1982a, pp. 18–27). The shape of the stele becomes more Hellenized, with its triangular pediment often flanked by acroteria, in the fashion of funerary pillars of Greek type. In the finest examples a palm frond (but Greek, no longer Phoenician) occupies the area of the pediment, alternating with the raised forearm, the symbol of prayer (or a vow) and the 'sign of Tanit' (figures 205 to 210). The new shape allowed the sculptor a more exact and complex design, divided into sections separated by rows of motifs (eggs, beads)

FIGURE 205   *A stele from Constantine, Algeria (third to second century BC) (Louvre, Paris).*

FIGURE 206   *A stele from Carthage (third century BC) (P. Cintas).*

FIGURE 207 *A stele from Carthage (third century* BC*) (Musée national de Carthage).*

FIGURE 208 *A stele from Carthage (end of the third century* BC*) (Louvre, Paris).*

borrowed from Greek architectural decoration. In this layout the dedication is generally engraved in the middle position, the principal

FIGURE 209   *A stele from Carthage (P. Cintas).*

FIGURE 210   *Stelae from Carthage (from the third to the beginning of the second century* BC) *(Musée national de Carthage).*

ornamental motif taking its place in the lower register, often framed by the columns with Aeolic capitals which were so much in vogue, as I said, in the Punic city.

To ornament the lower part of the stele, the craftsman drew on a wide variety of decorative themes, animal (figures 205, 206 and 208), floral (figure 209) or those inspired by religious symbolism: caduceus, altar, cantharus (figures 207 and 210). Exceptionally, the usual shape of the stele is replaced by a little monument fashioned entirely in the form of a 'sign of Tanit' (figure 210). These developments end with stelae from which all relief is excluded, their decoration being simply incised on smooth surfaces. I have no hesitation in regarding them as the greatest successes of an art that is modest, yet often very elegant in its rendering, here of a stylized palm tree, flanked but not entwined by ivy between two Aeolic columns, or there of a floral composition inspired by acanthus but freely developed, in the same architectural frame (figure 211). Apart from these, on a stele of which luckily only the upper part is

FIGURE 211 *Stelae with incised decoration from Carthage (Musée national de Carthage).*

FIGURE 212　A hatchet-razor (Carthage, third century BC): on the left, an Egyptianate figure; on the right, a Hellenistic-style subject (after J. Vercoutter).

damaged, is the extremely sensitive engraving on stone of a young man's head and shoulders, his cloak fastened by a buckle. One needs to have some idea of the resistance of that hard limestone to the engraving tool in order to appreciate fully the spontaneity of this drawing, in which no reworking is apparent (figure 211).

It was also the engraving skills of the Carthaginian craftsmen, but on another material, bronze, that provided us with the rich range of hatchet-razors mentioned earlier in connection with the iconography of the god Melqart (above, p. 207). At that point I stressed the coexistence in the god's iconography, in the same period, of oriental features and representational schemas obviously borrowed from classical art. That coexistence is to be found more generally in the imagery developed by the incised motifs on these hatchet-razors. In the tombs of the Sainte-Monique cemetery from which most of them come, fairly varied subjects can be seen side by side: foliage, floral decorations, scenes of a Hellenistic kind. But the abundance of Egyptianate figures or Nilotic images is explained here in particular by the talismanic function of the hatchet-razors (C. Picard, 1967, p. 82; Acquaro, 1971, pp. 100–13). The group of razors in Hellenistic style forms an ensemble that is remarkable in particular for the quality of both design and execution (figure 212). In this case too, people have not failed to attribute such quality to Greek artists settled in Carthage (Vercoutter, 1945, pp. 306–7). In fact there is no serious reason for not crediting them with being able to engrave comparable decorations on stelae, as a specialist in this Hellenistic imagery so rightly states (C. Picard, 1979, p. 108).

TERRACOTTAS

Even more than the oriental Semites from whom they acquired their techniques, the Phoenicians of the West were brilliant exponents of the 'arts of the kiln', terracottas and pottery. We saw earlier (above, p. 61) that one of the greatest contributions of funerary archaeology at Carthage as far back as the end of the last century had been the discovery of masculine terracotta masks, and attempts were made to classify them by type, adding to the Carthaginian examples similar objects found later in Sardinia and Sicily: three types, according to Colette Picard (1967, pp. 10–19); four, according to Sabatino Moscati (1966, p. 206); five, according to Pierre Cintas (1946). About the end of the sixth century masks properly speaking appeared, 'protomes' or full masks with no opening at either eyes or mouth. The are characterized chiefly by a 'pastille' treatment of the hair and beard, created by little stamped circles or spirals. Some years ago it was still possible to make out touches of colour on the 'Saumagne mask' (above, figure 38); bright red on the cheeks, and the use of black and white for the eyes (C. Picard, 1967, p. 20). A masculine protome of a different type dating from the same era (the end of the sixth to the beginning of the fifth century) has a long tapering beard divided into two sections by a deep groove, and was found by Cintas in his excavations of the cemetery at Utica (figure 213a). This mask is the expression of an iconographic schema apparently also in vogue in Sardinia in the same period, as evidenced by a protome of very similar style and comparable size unearthed at Monte Sirai (figure 213b). There is the same 'pastille' work on the hair, the same treatment of the nose and cheek-bones underlined by a groove. However, some variations distinguish the moulds used to shape the two objects: at Utica the beard projects forward (but the craftsman's hand could have achieved this movement when the head came out of the mould); at Monte Sirai the eyes

FIGURE 213   *Masculine protomes with long beards: (a) from Utica
(P. Cintas) and (b) from Monte Sirai (Sardinia) (after S. Moscati,
I Fenici e Cartagine, Turin, 1972).*

have been retouched, and above all the ears are placed noticeably
higher in relation to the line of the eyebrows. A very fine specimen
kept in Cadiz Museum, and originating from this site, could almost
be superimposed on the Monte Sirai protome. Such similarities in
three distant places in the Phoenico-Punic world are easily explained if, as is thought (Moscati 1972a, p. 365; Ciasca, 1988,
p. 354), the long-bearded protome is the image of a divinity, necessarily produced following fixed rules; placing it in a tomb would
have been a votive gesture.

   Around the same period, a little after archaic times (the end of the
sixth century), a beautiful series of feminine protomes makes an
appearance in the Carthage tombs, and three types are distinguish-
able. The first is clearly Egyptianate: the figurine wears the *klaft*,
which leaves her well-defined ears prominent, in the oriental
fashion (figure 214); under the flat bandeau that holds her hair
back from her forehead and bears visible traces of yellow and black
paint, her eyebrows are shown in relief, at right angles to her nose.
The specimens discovered at Carthage in the tombs of Dermech and
Douimès (C. Picard, 1967, pp. 20–1) vary only minutely from one

FIGURE 214 *An Egyptian-style feminine protome from Tharros (Sardinia, sixth century BC) (Archaeological Museum, Cagliari).*

to another, due to retouching carried out on the object before firing. In themselves they fully resemble protomes of the same type brought to light at Tharros in Sardinia (figure 214) and Motya in Sicily, to such an extent that one might imagine they had all come from the same mould. It was as if the fixed image of the coffins of Egyptian mummies had been rigidly imposed and could not be contravened.

A second type, which could be called Graeco-Phoenician, shows how, a little later (the end of the sixth century), the influence of archaic Greek art modified the schemas of representation which still remained basically oriental. A good example is provided by a protome in the Bardo Museum, in Tunis, from one of the tombs excavated by Paul Gauckler at Dermech (C. Picard, 1967, pp. 22–3). A smooth bandeau across her forehead holds in place the hair which is drawn back to fall in two great tresses on either side of her face; in their treatment we rediscover the little stamped circles of the masculine long-bearded protomes (figure 215). A diadem composed of slim bars alternating with beads accentuates the height of her forehead. The oval of her face is elongated, with a triangular lower part and a pointed chin with a little dimple; her eyes are large and almond-shaped; her ears are still large and prominent, in oriental fashion, and her nostrils are pierced to accommodate a small ring, the *nezem*. More 'personalized' by retouching carried out after moulding, and by painted embellishments of which traces still survive on the example from Carthage, protomes of this type

FIGURE 215 A Graeco-Phoenician protome from Carthage (end of the
sixth century BC) (Musée national du Bardo, Tunis).

are less widespread outside the Punic capital, although an equivalent is known at Motya.

A third type often encountered in the tombs of Carthage from the
beginning of the fifth century consists of feminine protomes known
as 'Rhodian', because they are closely related to the representational schema of protomes made in Rhodes from the beginning
of the sixth century, probably under the influence of Phoenicia
proper, with which the island had strong connections; these
protomes were subsequently reproduced throughout the Greek
world and in particular at Delos. Beneath the veil that covers the
hair held under a smooth bandeau, and from which the 'pastille'
treatment has vanished, the oval face is smiling. Objects of this kind
have been found in large numbers in Sardinia, notably at Tharros,

as well as on Spanish sites and on Ibiza. They illustrate the growing obliteration of the major features of the oriental tradition in those sectors of the Punic world that were in contact with the Greek colonial world.

It is an absorbing task, but difficult and fraught with risk, to try to determine the factors that played a predominant role in establishing and popularizing an iconographic type. Thus the frequency of masks with a Silenus head – numerous at Carthage, but also in Sardinia, at Tharros and Sulcis in the fifth and sixth centuries, and based on archaic iconographic images – is attributed to the introduction of Dionysiac cults into the Punic domain (C. Picard, 1979, pp. 91–2). But one may wonder if that acclimatization of the iconography of Silenus and the Satyr did not benefit from the ubiquity, in the Punic cultural world, of the god Bes, whose powers and shape are so close to those of the satyrs and Silenus. To return to the Greek-style feminine images in the Punic area in the sixth and fifth centuries, it is clear that the Ionian kore established an image which gradually eclipsed the residual features of oriental typology. Nor is it surprising that this influence was particularly marked where contact with the culture of the Greek colonial world was closest, as witnessed by these feminine terracotta heads (but in the round: they are not protomes) from Motya, kept in the Whitaker Museum

FIGURE 216   *Hellenizing feminine figures from Motya (fifth century BC) (Whitaker Museum, Superintendent of Antiquities, Palermo).*

(figure 216). Like the famous marble ephebe, they belong in fact to Greek art.

In a geographical and cultural context less penetrated by Hellenism, the art of the Punic coroplasts presents a different physiognomy, sometimes heavily impregnated with local cultures. This is so in the Iberian world, and particularly Ibiza, where the Punic presence was long established (cf. above, p. 82) The cemetery of Puig des Molins has supplied plentiful statuettes datable to the fourth century, when local taste superimposed on Graeco-Punic models a naïve and baroque over-abundance of ornamentation (figure 217): immense and very elaborate diadems, heavy earrings, necklaces in the form of a many-tiered pectoral. These terracotta dolls (the size hardly exceeds about 30 centimetres) often wore a Semitic nose-ring, the *nezem*. Insularity played its part; this composite and original art developed in isolation, without any external circulation.

FIGURE 217   *Terracotta statuettes from the cemetery of Puig des Molins, Ibiza (fourth century* BC) *(Archaeological Museum, Ibiza).*

At Carthage, from the end of the fourth century, the world of terracottas clearly shows that the Punic capital had become a cultural melting-pot. To its initial vocation of acting as a relay point between East and West the town had added the function, which is specially affirmed in the Hellenistic period, of being a redistribution centre and an active place of exchange on a north-south axis. The exchange was of merchandise and consumer goods, and also of ideas, for instance, in the religious domain, where Carthage appears to have been more inclined to import than to export. Seen in the light of its influence on artistic and artisanal production, it is probably right to accord great importance to the official enthronement in the Punic city, in 396 BC, of the cult of the Greek goddesses from Sicily, Demeter and Kore. On a purely religious level, it is difficult to assess the true impact of the new cult. An attempt was made to do this by relating its introduction to the transformation, or rather the upheaval, thought to be discernible in the organization of the tophet of Salammbô in the first half of the fourth century (G. C. and C. Picard, 1970, pp. 148–50). According to this view, the triumph of Tanit in the tophet – where it was seen that at some

FIGURE 218 *Terracottas from the 'Carton chapel' at Carthage: left, a bearded divinity crowned with a plumed tiara; right, a type of Demeter kernophoros (Musée national du Bardo, Tunis).*

FIGURE 219   *A cult statue of a Punicized Demeter from Korba (Cap Bon) (Musée national du Bardo, Tunis).*

date, which is difficult to pinpoint precisely, she supplanted Baal Hammon – was linked both to the break with the 'monarchic regime' and the institution of an aristocratic regime after Himilco's defeat in Sicily, and also to the official enthronement in Carthage of the Sicilian goddesses, in reparation for the sacrilege committed by Himilco, who had permitted the looting of a temple to Demeter and Kore in Syracuse. It is an attractive and ingenious hypothesis, which we are prevented from verifying by the impossibility of reading so nice a chronology into the tophet's sequence of deposits.

On the other hand, it is quite certain that the iconographic type of the feminine votive terracottas was lastingly influenced by the representation of these goddesses. Excavations carried out in Carthage in the levels of the third and early second century have increased the findings of figurines of the Demeter *kernophoros* type, in which the goddess – or, more probably, her server – carries on her head not a basket (*kernos*), but more exactly a sort of incense-burning bowl. Particularly noteworthy are those from a group of votive terracottas found by Dr Carton in a 'chapel', mentioned earlier (cf. above, p. 213) in connection with temple architecture. In this group the *kernophoros* is in company with the representation of a bearded god, wearing a plumed tiara (like the *Sardus pater* of Sardinia), in which one can recognize an effigy of Baal Hammon (figure 218). The Sicilian goddess is also frequently represented in a divine posture, seated on a throne, with a treatment of detail conforming in every respect to that given her by Sicilian coroplasts (figure 219). At the same time, Punic craftsmen continued to make religious images whose appearance was still in the archaic-style Graeco-Punic tradition (figure 220). In the excava-

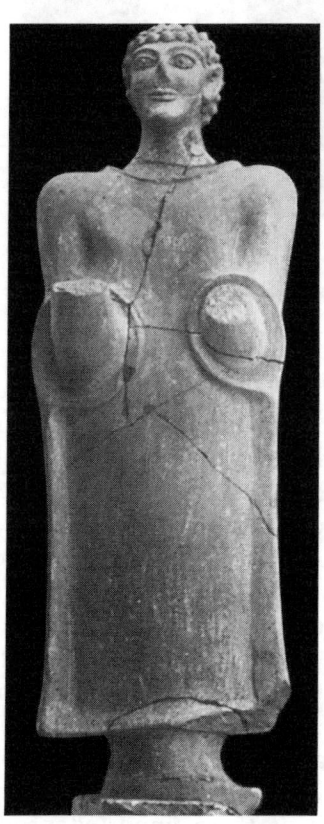

FIGURE 220   *A statue of a Punic worshipper in an attitude of prayer (third century* BC) *(Musée d'Utique).*

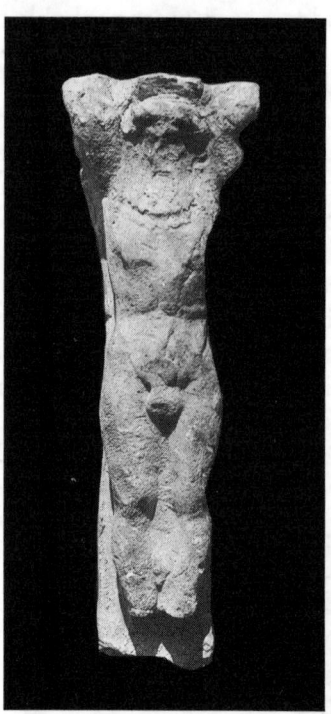

FIGURE 221 *An ornamental terracotta (French archaeological mission's excavations in Carthage) (S. Lancel).*

tions of the area of late Punic houses on Byrsa, some years ago the French archaeological mission discovered premises – no doubt a coroplast's shop – where figurines evidently fashioned on the eve of the destruction of 146 had been deposited. Alongside the usual Hellenistic knick-knacks (figures 221 and 222), two little statuettes of the god Bes, shown standing on a small cylindrical pedestal, awaited their purchaser, their colours still bright: brown for the face and the belt tied in front, light blue for the widely flowing beard (figure 223). But (was this a sign of the new times?) the traditionally shameless god was clothed and concealing his sex.

We shall discover a little later that, from about the middle of the third century, the Carthaginian housewife resorted with increasing frequency to imported tableware (chiefly from Italy) or to fairly successful imitations of these imported products. This must be ascribed to an economic war that was not the least aspect of what are called the 'Punic Wars'. Nevertheless, the Carthaginian potters

FIGURE 222 *Terracotta head of a female figurine (French archaeological mission's excavations in Carthage) (S. Lancel).*

FIGURE 223 *A painted terracotta statuette of the god Bes (French archaeological mission's excavations in Carthage) (S. Lancel).*

FIGURE 224   *Moulds (left) and prints on terracotta (right) from the
Carthage 'potter's workshop' (third century* BC) *(after P. Gauckler,*
Nécropoles puniques de Carthage, *Paris, 1915).*

persevered with their traditional output to the very end, maintaining a flow of 'typical' articles which, by their persistence, stood out
against a background of Hellenistic uniformity, for instance, the
little moulds which for want of a better name are known as 'cake
tins', and whose imprints in terracotta have sometimes been discovered in burials (were they in place of bread and cakes?) (Astruc,
1959, pp. 132–3). One of Gauckler's most interesting discoveries,
right at the end of the last century, in the middle of the archaic
cemetery of Dermech, was that of a group of potters' kilns, set up
there in the last years of the Punic city. It was plain to see that these
kilns had been in use up to the eve of the city's fall in spring 146.
There, amid the scraps and rejects from the kiln, the products of the
very last firings, was a whole set of these moulds, with their
imprints (figure 224); there were the ibis, the *oudja* eye, the Phoenician palm frond, eternal emblems of a Carthage which, in spite of
everything, had remained oriental.

'PHOINIKEIA GRAMMATA' AND 'LIBRI PUNICI'

No less than for its gods and its cults, Carthage is indebted to its Tyrian mother-country for its strongest mark of originality in the West and the essence of its cultural identity in a language, which is given material form for us in a script that for a while was unrivalled on those shores to which the Phoenicians spread from the end of the ninth century. Not for very long, if the truth is told: a mid-eighth-century dating is given to the earliest and one of the most famous examples of graffiti of the 'I belong to so-and-so' type, traced in Greek characters on the vessel known as 'Nestor's', a Euboean vase from the excavations of the cemetery at Pithecusae (Ischia) in the Bay of Naples (Hansen, 1983, No. 454). Moreover, it was the Chalcidians settled in southern Italy who brought into Etruria an alphabet which forms the basis of the first Etruscan written inscriptions, at the beginning of the seventh century (Briquel, 1991, pp. 615–16). More than a century would pass before the appearance of the earliest documents written in Latin, still with a Greek type of alphabet, transmitted by way of Etruscan. It is now suspected that the famous fibula of Praeneste, the oldest known evidence of a pre-literary archaic Latin, might be a forgery (Flobert, 1991, pp. 540–3). In the Iberian peninsula, where various writing systems were attested later, the earliest is 'Tartessian', in the southern part, and there is general agreement that it was modelled on the Phoenician alphabet (de Hoz, 1991, pp. 669–78). In the first written communications, Phoenician indisputably played a pioneering role in the West.

This role was direct but also indirect, since the Phoenician alphabet is at the origin of all those that developed from the starting-point of a 'proto-Greek' alphabet. The Greeks were in contact with Phoenician traders and had the opportunity (as early as the end of the second millennium, or rather around 800 BC? Discussion continues on the date and means of the borrowing: Amadasi-Guzzo, 1991, pp. 293–309) to appreciate the convenience, in commercial transactions, of this 'short' alphabet of twenty-two signs which they adopted deliberately – and gratefully – under the title of *Phoinikeia grammata* (Herodotus, V, 58–61; Diodorus, III, 67, 1). While they were borrowing their alphabet from the Phoenicians the Greeks were also borrowing part of the Semitic vocabulary relating to writing material – the papyrus leaf, *byblos*, a word destined for a long future, the writing tablet, *deltos* – or to the goods they had

PHOENICIAN (tenth century BC)			GREEK (eighth to seventh century BC)			Latin alphabet
Name	Alphabet	Transcription	Name	Alphabet	Transcription	
aleph	K K	ɔ	alpha	⇗A	Λ α	a
beth	Δ	b	bêta	8	B β	b
gimel	˥	g	gamma	˥	Γ γ	g
dalet	◁	d	delta	◁	Δ δ	d
hé	⫤	h	épsilon	⫤	E ε	é
waw	Y	w	digamma	⫟	F	
zayn	I	z	dzêta	I	Z ζ	z
heth	日 ⫤	ḥ	êta	目	H η	ê
ṭet	⊕	ṭ	thêta	⊗	Θ θ	th
yod	⁊	y	iota	I	I ι	i
kaph	↓	k	kappa	Ж	K ϰ	k
lamed	L	l	lambda	⋀	L λ	l
mem	⧊	m	mu	⋀	M μ	m
noun	⧕	n	nu	⋎	N ν	n
samek	⧧	s	xi	⧧	Ξ ξ	x
ʿayn	⊙	c	omicron	O	O o	o
pé	)	p	pi	˥˥	Π π	p
ṣadé	⍩	ṣ	san	⋀		
qoph	ⵁ	q	koppa	ⵁ		
resh	ⵗ	r	rhô	ⵗ	P ρ	r
šin	W	š	sigma	⅀ ⟨	Σ σ	s
taw	+	t	tau	T	T τ	t
			upsilon	Υ	Υ υ	u
			phi		Φ φ	ph
			khi		X χ	ch
			psi		Ψ ψ	ps
			ôméga		Ω ω	ô

FIGURE 225 *The Phoenician alphabet and its transmission into Greek (after* L'univers phénicien, *Paris, 1989).*

learned to know by way of the Phoenicians: gold (*chrysos*), linen (*byssos*), the tunic (*chitôn*) (Masson, 1967; Van Berchem, 1991, p. 144). It must be added, however, that the Greeks did not adopt this west Semitic alphabet without improving it. For the notation of their vowel range, which was far more extensive and precise than that of the Phoenicians, they employed several signs which in Semitic indicated laryngeal consonants for which they had no equivalent in their own phonology (figure 225).

That expresses both the strength and the weakness of this western Semitic alphabet, which was established at Byblos and Tyre at the beginning of the first millennium and imported in that form to the West. Its strength lay in its adaptability and ease of use, especially in account books and commercial documents, where what mattered was to record quantities and prices (letters had, in order, a numerical value which they maintained in Greek alphabets) and the identification of merchandise: there was hardly room for ambiguity in that. Its weakness, which would be revealed in more complex texts, lay in the fact that this alphabet was a consonantal skeleton. The Phoenicians, who had a scanty vowel system (only *a/i/u*) felt no need to indicate their vowels; writing the words was reduced to the consonantal root of two or more often three letters. The three letters of the word KTB (the root of the verb 'to write') were sufficient to put into script the various verbal moods and aspects of the act of writing, surely a source of uncertainty. But who read in that distant Antiquity? We must not forget that writing and even reading were activities involving technical know-how, that in those days there were infinitely more listeners than readers and that the latter were experienced professionals. Subsequently, in the course of their evolution, Semitic languages (Aramaic, Hebrew, Arabic) guarded against the risk of confusion by employing for the notation of at least the long vowels consonantal signs, which were used, as the specialists say, as *matres lectionis*, 'mothers' or 'generators of reading'. The Hebrew Bible and the Koran do not leave readers in a muddle that would be prejudicial to their understanding of the holy books. The Carthaginians had already begun to feel that need. In the epigraphic texts of Carthage's last years one sees the coexistence, in the writing of the same word, the one meaning 'tomb' (frequent in funerary inscriptions), of the bare consonantal skeleton QBR and, more rarely, the 'full form' QBᶜR, with the *ayn* used as *mater lectionis* in the second syllable (Bénichou-Safar, 1982, p. 195) (figure 226).

The first letter of this alphabet, *aleph* (Greek alpha, our *a*) is also used in late Punic to vocalize a syllable within a word. But it was

a

b

c

FIGURE 226   *Three examples of Punic writing of the Hellenistic period. Like all Semitic languages, they are read from right to left:* **a** *text on one line: 'Tomb (QPR) of the priestess Arisatbaal, wife of Melqarthilles' (Corpus Inscriptionum Semiticarum 5941);* **b** *'Tomb (QBᶜR) of the priestess Safonbaal, daughter of Hasdrubal, etc.' (CIS 5950);* **c** *votive stele: 'To the lady Tanit, face of Baal Hammon, and to the Lord Baal Hammon; vow made by Bodastart, son of Baal Hammon, grandson of Bodastart, because they have heard his voice' (CIS 185).*

above all in the field of foreign names, for which exactness in the rendering of the vowels was necessary, that the Carthaginians resorted to this sign, often used in the guise of a final vowel. It was thus in the Punic version of the Pyrgi sheets (above, p. 85), where *aleph* denotes the ending of the Etruscan chief's name *Thefarie*; and naturally afterwards for writing Latin names, thus for that of the great enemy *Roma*, which is transcribed as RMᵓ.

This method adopted by the Phoenico-Punic people for their alphabet is not the only cause of reading difficulty by epigraphists when they encounter an extended text that goes beyond the repetitive phrases of votive or funerary inscriptions. The actual writing of these words sometimes presents them with problems. Specialists in Latin epigraphy themselves find in their own field a development in the rendering of the capital letter, the *littera quadrata*, which became generalized throughout the Roman world in all kinds of categories of inscriptions on hard material. With all the more reason it was difficult to perpetuate a canonical form for characters that were not written according to almost geometric rules, like Latin capitals, but rather resembled what we call cursive script. In fact an evolution is noticeable, in both time and place, in the graphic rendering of this alphabet. People did not write in completely the same way, in the same period, in Sardinia and Carthage (figure 227). And in the Punic capital scripts varied. In the

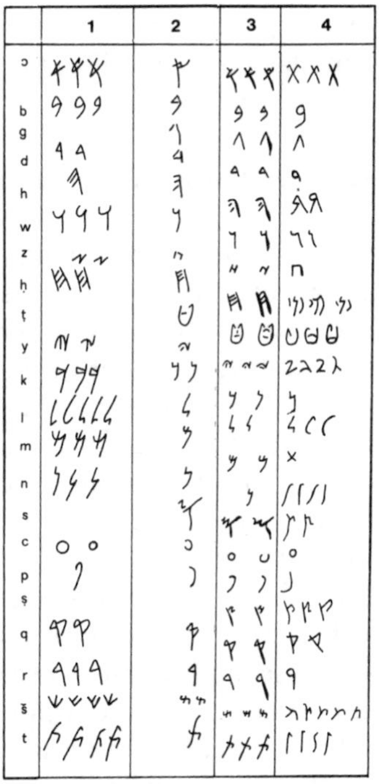

FIGURE 227 *Punic writing: 1 Pyrgi sheet (around 500 BC); 2 Sardinia (third century BC); 3 Carthage (third to second century BC); 4 Leptis Magna (first century BC to second century AD) (after M. G. Amadasi-Guzzo, 1990, pp. 12 and 29).*

'classical' period (the fifth to the third century), what distinguished Carthaginian writing from those observable elsewhere (Malta, Sicily, Sardinia) was, first of all, the very clear lengthening of the vertical strokes of signs such as the *aleph*, the *gimel*, the *qoph* and the *resh*; it was also their slant (to the right), as well as the frequently 'thick' line, which gave these letters their particular elegance due to the downstrokes and upstrokes (figure 226). Nevertheless, these variations are very slight and the relative uniformity must be credited to the schools for scribes (*sopherim*), who imposed standards on the stonecutters, from whom they must be distinguished (Bonnet, 1991, pp. 151–2). After the fall of Carthage, texts continued to be engraved on stone – these are neo-Punic; see below, p. 436 – which reveal a perceptibly altered, not to say debased, script with characters that become schematic and at times tend to merge. The cursive aspect of the letters is notably accentuated, which may be explained by the break in the scribal tradition of monumental texts: writing styles previously reserved for flexible materials – papyri, skin, parchment – were applied, with greater freedom, to stone (Amadasi-Guzzo, 1990, pp. 31–2).

PUNIC LANGUAGE AND LITERATURE

These days we measure the power of a language and its audience capacity by its 'imperialism', the extent of its use outside its own frontiers. History shows that the pre-eminence of a language is largely the result of the political weight of its nation or its land of origin in the international environment. At the time of Montesquieu or Voltaire there was no need for a Ministry of the French Language to ensure the cultural supremacy of French in Europe. But more recent history also shows that, in a context of intense international relations and an increased flow of communication, the need for a common language makes itself felt. And that language is the one that has been able to overtake the others, both by its simplicity, its ease of use, and because it seems to be linked with technical innovation and commercial development. In the Hellenistic era Greek played that role, before Latin took over from it and caused the retreat of 'Punicophony' in the whole of the western basin of the Mediterranean. A few centuries after the Greeks had welcomed the marvellous tool of the alphabet invented by the Phoenicians, the linguistic situation had turned in their favour. But the Punic language maintained its position in Africa, where it had long since eclipsed the indigenous tongue, Libyan, which never had official recognition, with the exception, under Massinissa and Micipsa, of a few texts found at Dougga, particularly the bilingual dedication of the famous mausoleum (above, p. 308). The official language of the Numidian and Moorish kingdoms was that of Carthage. The few administrative texts preserved there seem to be drawn up in Punic, like the boundary stone of Djebel Massouje which, as we have seen (above, p. 261) marked the limits of the *chora Thusca*, in the reign of Micipsa or some years after the fall of Carthage. The wording on coins of the Numidian kings is Punic, as well as on money struck by the Massaesylian kings of the West (Syphax, Vermina) and Massinissa's coinage in the east (Mazard, 1955, pp. 17–36) (figure 228). And since I have mentioned the Massylian king, Carthage's sworn enemy, I must not leave out as proof of his allegiance to the language of Carthage the little deed related by Cicero (*De signis*, IV, 103): one of his admirals having removed from the sanctuary of Juno in Malta – by which we can understand the temple of Tanit-Caelestis – some ivory tusks of enormous size in order to make a gift of them to his sovereign, Massinissa had them sent back with great pomp, by quinquereme, after having them engraved in Punic characters with words of apology and homage to the goddess.

As we shall see further on (below, p. 431), and as may be said in company with Gabriel Camps (1979, p. 48), beyond the apparent

FIGURE 228 *A coin of Massinissa; on the reverse, beneath the elephant, is an incomplete word in Punic characters: MSNSN, 'Massinissan' (Musée de Constantine, Algeria).*

paradox, 'Africa was never as Punic as after the sack of Carthage in 146.' This great specialist on Libyco-Berber Africa added: 'History, which enjoys symbols, shows us the sons of Massinissa receiving from the hands of Scipio Aemilianus manuscripts rescued from the fire, a material pledge of the spiritual heritage of Carthage.' That brings us to the delicate matter of the *libri Punici*; delicate and painful for, if the 'history' is not legend, and if they were really saved from the fire that devoured Carthage in the spring of 146, afterwards they did not escape the immense wreckage in which so many of Antiquity's literary works perished.

The Roman Senate seems to have had some presentiment of that disaster and to have come to terms with it when, according to Pliny the Elder (*NH*, XVIII, 22–3), it presented the African princes (*regulis Africae*) with Carthage's libraries after the city's fall, nevertheless deciding to ensure the survival of at least the twenty-eight books of the agronomist Mago by having them translated. As Pliny reminds us, Cato, the Latin specialist in rural economy, had died in 146, and we can speculate as to whether the favourable treatment reserved for Mago's works, in the context of the debates then agitating the Roman Senate between supporters and opponents of the Punic city's destruction (below, p. 410), might have been a sort of posthumous snub inflicted on Cato (Krings, 1991, p. 653). The translation might have been '*partly* the manifestation of an anti-Catonian reaction' (Heurgon, 1976, p. 447). The task of translating the treatise into Latin was entrusted to a person of noble origin, D. Silanus, an expert in the Punic tongue, and the book was subsequently also translated into Greek by Cassius Dionysius of Utica. The translations as well as the Punic original are lost, but we saw earlier that numerous extracts preserved among the Latin agronomists bear witness to the technical worth and cultural importance of Mago's work (Martin, 1971, pp. 37–52).

There remains that evocative word *bibliothecae* used by Pliny, which by itself suggests masses of books; or in actual fact, in that period, when we are talking of definitive, carefully edited copies, masses of papyrus scrolls or *volumina*. It is very tempting to take the word literally, to recall by way of comparison the libraries of Alexandria, even to suggest that those of Carthage could have been appreciably older than the famous Egyptian book collection, formed only at the time of the Punic Wars; the Carthaginians, it was said, could very well have imitated the example set in the seventh century by the Assyrian king Assurbanipal (Sznycer, 1968, p. 142). And one can also imagine the contents of those book cupboards:

archives and chronicles, of course, but also a whole religious literature, as a rather sombre story recounted by Plutarch (*De facie*, 26–30) tends to make us believe, when he speaks of sacred parchments saved at the time of the town's destruction and hidden for a while underground (Krings, 1991, p. 655). There is hardly any doubt that Carthage had a literature devoted to history, but in the Hellenistic era, at least, a good proportion of the chroniclers wrote in Greek. This is recognized as certain in the case of Silenos and Sosylos, Hannibal's historiographers – the second one named taught him Greek (Cornelius Nepos, *Hannibal*, 13, 3) – who accompanied him to Italy and recounted his campaigns and life. And when, in 205, Hannibal had his *res gestae* engraved on the inscription of Hera's temple at Cape Lacinion, he did so in both Punic and Greek, to ensure that the text gained a wider audience (Livy, XXVIII, 46, 16).

In his *Jugurthine War*, Sallust devotes a justly celebrated exposition to the ancient population of North Africa, based, he says, on the translation made for him of 'Punic books': 'ex libris Punicis qui regis Hiempsalis dicebantur' (*Jugurtha* 17, 7). Forgive me for quoting Sallust in Latin: the fact is that the whole problem lies in this use of the genitive for King Hiempsal, whether he is the first of that name, the son of Micipsa, grandson of Massinissa or, as has recently been suggested, Hiempsal II, son of Gauda (Kontorini, 1975, pp. 89–99). Those few words could just as well mean that the 'Punic books' were the work of the Numidian king, and one would then suspect him of having written them in Greek, in spite of their title (Krings, 1990, pp. 115–17); or that these books belonged to him or were in his possession, by no means surprisingly, for Hiempsal – whether the son of Micipsa or Gauda – was the descendant of those 'African kinglets' to whose lot had fallen the libraries of Carthage, according to Pliny. Sallust had had the honour, after Caesar's victory at Thapsus in 46, of being the first governor of the new province of *Africa nova*. The death of his protector two years later obliged him to leave Africa, but he had had time to gather a sound documentation on Numidia, which is the backdrop to his book and very much a presence in it. Whether he had in his hands, at that time, historical and ethnographic texts actually drawn up in Punic may be considered as a serious hypothesis. What became of those *libri Punici* afterwards? That would be a good starting-point for a historical novel.

Anyone attempting it could avail himself of an unexpected boost in the form of a few lines in a letter written at the very end of the fourth century AD by Saint Augustine to a grammarian in a nearby town, Madaura, the hometown of Apuleius, where he himself had been raised in his youth. To this Maximus, who wanted to be more Roman than the Romans of Rome, and made fun of indigenous names, Augustine (*Epistulae*, 17, 2) extolled the *libri Punici*, thanks to which so much knowledge and wisdom figured in mankind's heritage. But he added: 'as the most learned scholars relate', which means that he had not read them himself.

9

Carthage or Rome?

Not long ago this question in the form of an alternative was the title
of a book devoted to the Punic Wars (Brisson, 1973). It was
intended to signify that there was a moment, at the end of the third
century BC, when the Fates (to speak like the Ancients) appeared to
hesitate. The time was still far off when a barbarian, Alaric, would
pillage Rome at the head of his Gothic hordes. In the classical era
the only pressing danger the Eternal City had known had come
from the north, with the Gauls who had audaciously trodden on the
lower slopes of the Capitol. But those Celtic invaders were merely
ill-organized bands and Rome, at the beginning of the fourth century, was not yet that budding empire with everything to lose in a
major clash.

One and a half centuries later it was another matter entirely. The
Hellenistic Orient was rich, but lacked a guiding power. Alexander
was dead and Pyrrhus too. For the first time in the history of the
Mediterranean world the West would see a decisive confrontation
between two equally prosperous nations, one, Rome, in an almost
central position to the north of the other, Carthage, which was
more marginal geographically but had the advantage of occupying
a key position in the south, at the pivot of the two parts of the
Mediterranean basin. Can one speak of a north-south confrontation? Yes, provided the phrase is stripped of its economic significance, which means divesting it of almost all the geopolitical
substance it has for us. I think I have shown in the preceding pages
that Carthage, at the beginning of the third century, was a State
whose technical know-how, fleet and trading settlements along the
whole western Mediterranean perimeter placed it in the very fore-
front. However, it had at least two weak points: a professional
army, but for the most part made up of mercenaries, scarcely

homogeneous and of uncertain loyalty; a weak geographical cohesion and an insufficent territorial base, despite its enlargement in Africa. In contrast, Rome finally forced Etruria into submission before the middle of the third century. At the same time its victories over Pyrrhus assured its seizure of the whole of southern Italy and gave it the power to control Sicily, which the Greeks had defended against the Carthaginians for over three centuries and which the defeat of Pyrrhus left without a protector. What would Carthage do if western Sicily and then, the links in the chain becoming weak, Sardinia and Corsica were taken away from it? For centuries those islands had been the pivot of its maritime activity and the buttress of its trading enterprises towards the West.

THE 'FIRST PUNIC WAR' AND THE LOSS OF SICILY

Angebant ingentis spiritus virum Sicilia Sardiniaque amissae: not so long ago all budding humanists were familiar with this sentence of Livy's at the beginning of his account of the second Punic War (XXI, 1). The immensely proud man tormented by the loss of Sicily and Sardinia was Hamilcar Barca, father of Hannibal. He had all the more reason for being prey to such torment because, between 246 and 242, he had come within an ace of causing the Romans to lose their hold in Sicily. Thirty years later, his son would carry on to Italian soil the war of revenge in the spirit of which he had been brought up.

The loss of Sicily was the last unhappy act in a battle perpetually waged by Carthage to hold on at least to the invaluable strategic positions in the western part of the island (figure 229). I mentioned earlier the major phases of those ancient confrontations between Greeks and Carthaginians (above, pp. 88–91). At the very end of the fourth century, a treaty concluded in 306 between Rome and Carthage had fixed their positions, or more exactly fixed the respective limits on their intervention, by excluding Rome from Sicily and Carthage from Italy. It was a third-century Sicilian, Philinos, who passed on to us the clauses of that agreement, on which there is no reason to cast any doubt, in spite of those expressed about it by Polybius (III, 26, 3). The Greek historian, who was part of Scipio Aemilianus' circle in the middle of the following century, probably allowed himself to be persuaded by the Roman aristocrats of the futility of that treaty, rather than having to admit that Rome flouted it several decades later.

FIGURE 229 *Southern Italy and Sicily, with the area of Punic influence in the middle of the third century* BC *stippled.*

For in fact Rome did not respect the treaty. It so happened that bands of Campanian mercenaries – they had taken the name Mamertines, 'men of Mars', from the Oscan name, Mamers, the god of war – who, having come from the Bruttium across the straits, had for a long time been roaming Sicily, entering the service first of one side and then another, had seized Messina by force and had set up a kind of State there, in 288 BC. They lived peacefully for several years, while Pyrrhus, who had not sought to pick any quarrel with them, brought his brilliant Sicilian cavalry feats to an end after short-lived victories and finally left Sicily in 276, to go back and wage war for a few more months in southern Italy. On his departure he had weighed up the situation very clearly: 'What a battlefield,' he said, 'we are leaving to the Carthaginians and the Romans!' (Plutarch, *Pyrrhus*, 23). He was soon to be proved right, even if battle was engaged in a way he could not have foreseen.

The retreat of Pyrrhus had once again left the field open to the Carthaginians, except in the principality of Syracuse, where a new 'king', Hieron, consolidated his power in 270. The Mamertines of Messina swiftly entered into conflict with Hieron, on whose territory they were encroaching in the course of their plundering. In a difficult situation, they asked for Carthage's protection: a Punic admiral in command of a fleet moored in the neighbourhood (perhaps stationed at Lipari) dispatched a garrison to Messina's citadel. Shortly afterwards, and for reasons that remain obscure, those same Mamertines decided to make an appeal to Rome against their Carthaginian protectors. This took place in 264. It was a risky venture. Some years previously, after at first supporting them, the Romans had handled with scant ceremony the same turbulent ruffians who had helped themselves to the town of Rhegium on the other side of the straits, an attitude, as one of the shrewdest historians of republican Italy observed, 'which well illustrates the mixture of connivance and repudiation, premeditation and *laissez-faire* so characteristic of Roman imperialism in that period, endlessly carried onward by the mechanism of its conquests' (Heurgon, 1969, p. 338).

In fact, the Senate in Rome took no decision. But through the *Comitia centuriata*, convoked by the consuls, the people accepted the Mamertines' request, which in the eyes of the Latins was the equivalent of a *deditio*, a submission. For Carthage, the despatch of a Roman expeditionary corps to Sicily was a *casus belli*. Disembarking with a detachment not far from Messina, the consul Appius Claudius Caudex was *de facto* declaring war.

THE CAUSES OF THE CONFLICT AND ITS FIRST PHASES

Many questions have been raised, and will continue to be, about the real causes of the conflict. Polybius (I, 11) emphasizes that, faced with the waverings of the Roman Senate, the consuls could count on the feelings of the people, who had been 'put to the test by the

preceding wars', and whose hope of booty decided them in favour
of war. We shall see later what was actually the outcome of the
ruinous battles that lasted more than twenty years. At another level,
there is no doubt that the setting up of a Punic garrison in Messina,
only a few miles from Italian shores, jeopardized that 'Monroe
doctrine' which the treaty of 306 had put in concrete form. It has
recently been stressed that, in the years immediately preceding the
Romano-Punic war in Sicily, families of Campanian origin had
become predominant in Rome and they were more alive to the
danger represented by this proximity, aggravated as it was by that
of the Punic naval bases in the Aeolian islands (Heurgon, 1969,
p. 344). In fact the Atilii, who were Campanian, held the consulate
seven times between 267 and 245. This first Punic War would be
their war, as the wars against the Etruscans had been the business
of the Fabii. Going even further, emphasis has been laid on the
growing economic importance of Campania in those years, with its
agricultural wealth asserting itself, its wines increasingly exported
and its pottery output recently eclipsing that of Apulia and Tarentum (G. C. and C. Picard, 1970, pp. 183–4). The war in Sicily
would thus appear to have been decided upon under the influence
of a veritable commercial lobby, in order to defend its interests. Let
us note that all these motives were pushing in the same direction
and that the annexation of Sicily, in the middle of the third century,
could not be other than the best objective – certainly the most
obvious, for us – of Rome's new Mediterranean policy, which was
still feeling its way. We may recall the bragging of Petronius'
Trimalchio, the great landowner, three centuries later in the Tarentum region, who said he wanted to add Sicily to his property so as
not to have to leave home when the fancy took him to visit Africa
(Petronius, 48, 3). The joke is significant: Trimalchio the parvenu
landowner is daydreaming as the big Campanian landowners must
have done, their aspirations merging with those of the Roman
republic. 'Always more' is the motto of any imperialism.

I will not go into great detail here about a history of events rich
in ups and downs and reverses of fortune on both sides, and
recounted many times since the works of the German historian
J. Beloch and the French Stéphane Gsell (G. C. and C. Picard, 1970,
pp. 186–99; Brisson, 1973, pp. 27–98; Decret, 1977, pp. 154–69;
Nicolet, 1978, pp. 606–12; Huss, 1985, pp. 222–49). I will merely
keep to the main events and the principal developments. Hieron of
Syracuse, theoretically allied to the Carthaginians, saw which way
the wind was blowing and hastily gave his allegiance to the Romans

(263), guaranteeing to provide them with supplies throughout the duration of the war. The first important engagement took place shortly afterwards at Agrigentum, where the Carthaginians had concentrated contingents of mercenaries recruited in Spain, Gaul and Liguria, under the command of a general named Hannibal (262). At the end of a seven-month siege waged by an army under the command of two Roman consuls, the town was forced to surrender, but the Carthaginian general managed to escape with the greater part of his troops.

This setback, which caused many Sicilian towns, including Segesta, to rally to Rome, convinced the Carthaginians that they would not win against the legions in a pitched battle. They consequently modified their tactics, with troops contained in several well-fortified places, where the skill in siege-craft (in this instance the defence of strongholds) that they had learned from the Greeks – only recently had Pyrrhus proved himself to be the undisputed master of this military art – allowed them to keep the Romans in check. At the same time, light troops harassed the enemy supply convoys, and the mastery of the seas that the Carthaginians still enjoyed gave their swift vessels full scope to ravage the Italian coasts and land soldiers in the towns of the Sicilian littoral. For several years these tactics succeeded, all the better because, over terrain that they had known for a long time, the Carthaginians benefited from the continuity of command of experienced generals against consuls who were replaced each year.

This phase of the war marked a turning-point in Rome's military history. Conscious that it would stand no chance of gaining the upper hand without equipping itself with a navy, around 260 the Senate undertook to construct a fleet of 100 quinqueremes and 20 triremes. This occasion will bring to mind the fine story recounted by Polybius (I, 20), according to whom the Romans copied a Carthaginian ship that a manoeuvring error had let fall into their hands. In fact they called on the services of southern Italy's shipbuilding yards, in particular Tarentum, and it may be suspected that Greeks provided the pilots for this improvised fleet. After an unlucky initial attempt, it fell to the lot of a consul named Duilius to give Rome its first victory at sea after a combat in which the famous 'crow' worked wonders (above, p. 133). Thanks to this device, which allowed the enemy boat to be harpooned and held fast alongside, the Romans were able to avoid the tactic of ramming, favoured by Carthaginian sailors, and enforce that of boarding, where their naval troops could regain the conditions of battle that were

familiar to them. Thus at Mylae (Milazzo), between the Aeolian
Isles and the north coast of Sicily, the Carthaginians lost fifty vessels
and their admiral, the same Hannibal who shortly before had
escaped from the siege of Agrigentum, was crucified by his own
soldiers in Sardinia.

REGULUS' EXPEDITION IN AFRICA

Meanwhile, as the struggle dragged on and became bogged down in
Sicily, Rome resolved to strike at Carthage in Africa itself, as had
Agathocles half a century before. This expedition was entrusted to
the two consuls of the year 256, L. Manlius Vulso and M. Atilius
Regulus. According to Polybius (I, 25), a Carthaginian fleet tried
unsuccessfully to intercept the armada of 330 vessels that had set
off from Sicily. Landing was made on the south-east point of Cap
Bon at Clypaea (Kelibia), and the consuls installed themselves and
their troops in this strategic spot, which would assure their communications with Sicily and which, as we have seen, had been
fortified by the Carthaginians in earlier days (above, p. 265). Those
fortifications were unable to hold out for long, and the Roman
troops ravaged the rich country areas that had with great difficulty
recovered from the passage of Agathocles. It was very probably at
this time that the little city of Kerkouane, between Kelibia and Ras
ed-Drek, was captured and destroyed (above, p. 268). Shortly afterwards, on the orders of the Senate, Manlius Vulso brought the
larger part of the fleet back to Italy, while Regulus remained where
he was with forty ships, 15,000 foot-soldiers and 500 horsemen.

In the spring of 255 Regulus relaunched the campaign and won
an initial success at Adyn, probably Uthina (Oudna), not far from
Tunis (Fantar, 1989, pp. 82–3). Still following in Agathocles' footsteps, the Roman consul seized Tunis and set up his camp there (cf.
figure 230). The peace negotiations that the Carthaginians, their
backs to the wall, then conducted with him through the intermediary of a delegation came to an abrupt end, because of the
excessive demands of Regulus, who sought to impose nothing less
on his foe than the handing over of Sicily and Sardinia, not to
mention many other one-sided conditions, notably the buying back
of prisoners and payment of an annual tribute. Thereupon the
Carthaginians' courage revived, with the arrival, amid a troop of
mercenaries raised in Greece, of a Lacedaemonian officer named
Xanthippus, who was engaged as a technical adviser. Xanthippus

FIGURE 230   *Principal theatres of operations in the mercenaries' war (after S. Gsell).*

highlighted the errors committed by the Punic commanders during the last encounter: the legion must not be confronted on uneven terrain where its flexibility gave it the advantage over the Carthaginian phalanx, which was heavier and less manoeuvrable. On level ground, moreover, the cavalry and the elephants – those panzers of Antiquity – could play their part to the full.

So the Carthaginian army went off to camp not far from Tunis, and Regulus made the mistake of agreeing to fight on the terrain chosen by the enemy, where Xanthippus drew up the Punic battle line: the elephants covering the front in a single line, the phalanx behind, part of the mercenaries on the right wing, the more mobile among them as well as the horsemen in front of both wings (Polybius, I, 33). Regulus thought he would be able to withstand the impact of the elephants by ranging his maniples in deep order, giving a narrower front. This indeed was what happened, but his cavalry, fewer in number, turned tail, leaving his flanks unprotected. His left wing alone, which had eluded the elephants, penetrated the Punic right wing and gained some ground, avoided disaster and was able to rejoin its base at Clypea. But Regulus was taken prisoner, together with several hundred of his men.

Here a myth must be disposed of, painful though it may be to do so, for it is a part of our culture. Polybius does not breathe a word about Regulus after his capture on the battlefield, and it is likely that he died in obscurity in some Carthaginian gaol. But a number of later Latin writers (and not merely the minor ones, but Cicero, Livy, Florus, Valerius Maximus and Aulus Gellius) substantiated the lovely story we know: after years of captivity, the Carthaginians in 251–250 sent the former consul to Rome, his mission being to obtain the exchange of captives and, if possible, the cessation of hostilities. Regulus vowed an oath to return to Carthage if the negotiations failed, and they did fail because he advised the Senate to continue the war. Faithful to his vow, he went back to Africa, to die a terrible death by torture. In his treatise on *Duties*, Cicero did not fail to highlight this unparalleled *exemplum*, using all the resources of his eloquence, if not of his inmost conviction. What could be finer, on the plane of personal ethics, than the sacrifice of this man of duty? What better illustration could there be of the *fides Romana*, compared with the *fides Punica*, for which read Punic perfidy? In our collective consciousness, and in the *Petit Larousse* which, in France, is one of its guardians, the statue of Regulus, the hero of untouched honour, has remained intact.

The Romans had to wait more than half a century before setting foot in Africa again after this serious setback, which was further aggravated the next year, 254, by a veritable naval disaster. They had been able to build up a war fleet quite rapidly; but they still had to acquire experience of the sea and mastery of the maritime routes. While a fleet of 350 ships, according to Polybius (I, 36, 10), sent by Rome to repatriate the remainder of Regulus' expeditionary force, had swept aside a Punic naval force of 200 vessels which had come to encounter them, that brilliant success was cancelled out on the homeward journey by an error on the part of the two Roman consuls who, against the advice of their pilots, wanted to go along the southern coasts of Sicily and their dangerous waters. When they were off Camarina, a storm sent nearly all their ships to the bottom; only eighty escaped shipwreck. Again the following year, 253, the consuls C. Servilius Caepio and C. Sempronius Blaesus, very poor admirals, were no luckier. With a new, hastily prepared fleet, they sailed along the eastern shores of Tunisia and, having reached the island of Djerba (Meninx), let themselves be caught by the tide and ran aground in the shallows of the Syrtis Minor; they managed to get off only by jettisoning the whole of their ships' cargo. Returning to Palermo, they wanted to reach Italy by the most direct sea route: when they were right out to sea, a storm caused the loss of over 150 vessels. Following this new catastrophe, Rome gave up such distant maritime operations. The Carthaginians saw the removal of the danger that had threatened them so heavily on African soil and took new hope (Polybius, I, 39). It was during these years, in 247 precisely, that they widened their African lands by seizing distant Thevesta (present-day Tebessa, in Algeria), to the south-west of Carthage.

THE NAVAL BATTLE OF THE AEGATES AND THE END
OF THE SICILIAN WAR

In Sicily itself, the war continued with varying fortunes on both sides. There were setbacks at first for the Carthaginians. After the capture of their largest urban possession, Palermo, in 254, they found themselves reduced to their fortresses in the far west of Sicily, Lilybaeum (Marsala), where they had entrenched themselves after the destruction of Motya in 397, and *Drepanum* (Trapani), which was their naval base. The Romans spared no effort to gain possession of that base, and during the siege they put into operation procedures that, with hindsight, seem to be a rehearsal for what would succeed a century later in Carthage. The entry to the port was blocked by ships that were sunk there and then by a sort of improvised dike, which the sea's action, however, broke down, freeing the access. And the 20,000 soldiers that Rome had mobilized to besiege the town were unable to wear down the resistance of the 10,000 defenders under the orders of Himilco, the governor of the place. In 249 the consul Appius Claudius Pulcher believed he could make an end of it by catching the Carthaginian fleet by surprise in the harbour, with the aid of 120 vessels; that attempt ended in a serious setback and the loss, on the Roman side, of 93 ships (Polybius, I, 51). Several other daring feats of assistance by the Punic admirals along the Sicilian coasts discouraged their foe for a while from confronting them at sea.

A little later, to relieve Himilco, the valiant defender of Lilybaeum, Carthage dispatched to Sicily a young general destined for a great future, Hamilcar Barca. The latter, from his Sicilian *finistère*, stepped up maritime raids on the Italian coasts between 247

and 241. The better to defend the strongholds of Lilybaeum and
Drepanum, he installed himself on the acropolis of Mount Eryx
(Erice), not far from the temple formerly consecrated to Astarte (the
Erycine Venus of the Latins), an eagle's eyrie from which he
harassed the enemy, stationing his troops not far from his own
camp, in the direction of Palermo.

This war lasted more than twenty years, during which Rome in
particular had sunk enormous sums of money beneath the sea in the
form of hundreds of lost ships: 700, according to Polybius, against
400 for the Carthaginians. As the war effort could no longer be
subsidized from public funds, the Senate resorted to the private
means of those who had most to gain from victory and thus the
conquest of Sicily. Men of the ruling class, says Polybius (I, 59), that
is, those Campanian aristocrats we have already seen at the origins
of the conflict, either individually or grouped in consortia, provided
at their own expense fully-equipped vessels, on the sole condition
of being reimbursed for the amounts expended should victory
result. That is how a fleet of 200 ships, under the command of the
consul C. Lutatius Catulus, came to cut off Drepanum and Lilybaeum from all communication by sea. For its part, Carthage had
sent a squadron bringing reinforcements and supplies to Hamilcar.
The decisive naval encounter took place in the spring of 241 in the
vicinity of the Goat Islands (Aegates), offshore from the hideout
held by the Carthaginians. They were defeated. Hamilcar Barca,
who henceforth lost all hope of obtaining assistance by sea, received full powers from Carthage to engage in negotiations with the
Roman consul. From him he obtained the honours of war for his
soldiers and those of Gisco, the governor of Lilybaeum, in return
for the payment of a modest ransome. For Carthage, which now
occupied only the tiniest plot of Sicilian soil, the final peace treaty
might seem advantageous: it abandoned all claim to Sicily and the
Aeolian Isles. The financial clauses, light at first in the initial draft
of the agreement between the consul and Carthaginian negotiators,
were made more severe by the demands of the Roman people, says
Polybius (I, 63, 1). Carthage had to pay immediately 1000 Euboean
talents and 2200 more in ten yearly payments. If it is difficult for us
to evaluate with any precision how much that sum represented, at
all events it is clear that it fell far short of the total cost of the war
for the Romans.

Carthage lost much more from the affair than a little corner of
Sicily. It was the first stitch giving way in a fabric that was starting
to unravel. The two large islands to the north, Sardinia and Corsica,

now became vulnerable. Their defection would be the consequence – even if not immediately – of the financial difficulties that assailed the Punic state.

After the conclusion of the Peace of Lutatius, 20,000 men of the Punic armies remained in western Sicily, the vast majority of whom were mercenaries – the others were Libyans, Carthage's subjects – whom the clauses of the treaty banned from being demobilized on the spot. The task of repatriating them to Africa fell to Gisco, the governor of Lilybaeum. He did so very astutely, sending them in small groups, staggering the departures, to leave Carthage's government time to pay them off as they arrived and then to send the dismissed mercenaries back to their country of origin. But the Carthaginian Senate reacted like shopkeepers: they allowed the mercenaries back from Sicily to assemble in the city, hoping that by means of an overall negotiation they would be able to persuade them to agree to relinquish part of their pay (Polybius, I, II, 66). Then, as they were becoming a nuisance in Carthage itself, it was decided to regroup them in Sicca (Le Kef). There the military governor of Carthage's African territory, the same Hanno who several years earlier had enlarged its Libyan marches by seizing Theveste (Tebessa), concluded an address in which he stressed the desperate financial straits of the Republic, with the proposal to pay them off at a lower rate than the one previously agreed. The camp at Sicca contained a mix of Iberians, Gauls, Ligurians, Balearics, Greeks and Africans: speakers of many different languages, because of which, with the assistance of certain malicious officers, Hanno's speech became incomprehensible or unacceptable. All the more so since these men had nothing but mistrust for a leader under whom they had not served. The mercenaries rebelled and came in crowds to camp near Tunis. There, seeing that the threat they represented was alarming the Punic government, they raised the stakes: having obtained satisfaction as regards their dues, they then demanded reimbursement for their kit, their horses . . . The Senate in Carthage appointed Gisco as arbitrator.

The famous pages of Flaubert's novel, which are historically exact in broad outline since step by step they follow our sole source, Polybius, popularized the heroes of this rebellion. Like Polybius, Flaubert made a star of one of those 'half-Greeks', as the historian called them, often former slaves of Hellenic culture who had escpaed from the gaols of Sicily or southern Italy: Spendios, a Campanian who had turned renegade against the Romans and had everything to lose from a negotiated solution of this crisis with the Carthaginians. Besides his physical strength and courage, stressed by Polybius, he had something that the barbarians surrounding him often lacked: tactical intelligence and the gift of the gab. He had little difficulty in persuading the leader of the Libyans, Matho, to make common cause with him. During the preceding episodes Matho had shown himself to be an active agitator and, as an African, he lacked the resources to be able to flee far from Carthage's resentment. It was easy for him to make his compatriots believe that Carthage would take revenge on them, once the rest had gone back to their own countries. Through fear, the two men managed to eliminate all opposition in the mercenaries' camp and make them present a united front to Gisco. The latter, who had begun by settling with the mercenaries from foreign lands, told the Libyans demanding their due from him to address themselves to their general, Matho. This reply unleashed their fury; they hurled themselves on Carthage's coffers to loot them and, with Matho and Spendios stoking their anger to make them commit the irreparable act, they seized Gisco and his followers and put them in chains.

It was the start of an 'inexpiable war' (Polybius, I, 65, 6), that is to say, implacable, savage. The atrocious nature of the mercenaries' war, also called the 'African war' by Polybius, as opposed to the one waged chiefly in Sicily, has most to do with its aspects of civil war (the Libyans of the African territory were subjects of Carthage) and almost of revolution. The most recent historians (G. C. and C. Picard, 1970, pp. 199–203; Brisson, 1973, pp. 109–20; Decret, 1977, pp. 171–3; Huss, 1985, pp. 252–9) have laid emphasis on these aspects, which are not fully brought out in the Greek historian's account.

Matho and his allies hastened to send emissaries to the principal towns in Africa, urging them to seize the chance of liberty as regards Carthage and asking for their assistance. Those appeals received a broad response: nearly all the African populations, says Polybius (I, 70, 9), sided with the rebels and provided them with supplies and reinforcements. The majority of Libyans from the territories controlled by Carthage made common cause with the mercenaries; the women surrendered their jewellery. Matho and Spendios were thus able to amass large enough sums to give the mercenaries their back-pay and finance the uprising. Such solidarity is easy to explain: Carthage had put pressure on the Africans during the long war in Sicily, demanding for its armies half the crops and the payment of double tributes. Very soon, according to Polybius (I, 73, 3), 70,000 Libyans joined the mercenaries. These forces were divided into three groups. Two armies set off to besiege Utica on one hand and Bizerta (Hippo Dhiarrytus), which had remained loyal to Carthage, on the other. Another army corps, stationed near Tunis, cut off the isthmus and isolated the Punic capital from the mainland (figure 230). To free Utica the Council of the Elders appealed to Hanno, the conqueror of Theveste, who in fact at first scattered the besiegers, but spoiled that success by his negligence and spinelessness. Flaubert amused himself in his novel by portraying a caricature of an obese 'suffete' warming his ulcers in boiling hot steam-rooms, piggishly gorging himself with exotic or exquisite delicacies.

Here we see the reappearance of Hamilcar Barca, whom Polybius, echoing the Roman viewpoint in his assessment of the war in Sicily, considered to be the best war leader of the time (I, 64). Carthage entrusted him with command of the war against the insurgents, with newly recruited mercenaries, a few renegades from the enemy camp, and infantry and cavalry forces raised among the citizens, about 10,000 men in total. A bold manoeuvre – a surprise march along the sandy strip going from Gammarth to Ras el-Mekki, which at that time was in the process of closing the Gulf of Utica – enabled him to lift the siege of Utica and massacre several thousand mercenaries. Then the alliance he obtained with Naravas and his Numidian horsemen helped him to win a fresh victory. At the same time Hamilcar exercised a little cajolery: from among the prisoners he took into his forces those who rallied to him and let the others go, contenting himself with their promise not to fight Carthage in the future.

Then came the episode to which above all this war owes its title of inexpiable. The chief leaders of the rebels, Matho and Spendios to the fore, quickly weighed up the danger of divisions within their side that Hamilcar's clever tactic was provoking. To prevent it, a brutal response that would compromise everyone and leave no hope of turning back was proposed in assembly by a Gaulish chief, Autharitus, whose knowledge of the Punic language, of which many had rudiments, allowed him to make himself understood by almost all the mercenaries. Gisco, the former governor of Lilybaeum, who had conducted the first negotiations with them at Sicca, was still in their hands. Together with several hundred of his companions who had been held prisoner, he was put to death by the most atrocious tortures. Feelings ran high in Carthage, where the generals Hamilcar and Hanno were urged to unite their efforts to put an end to matters with the mercenaries. But their disagreement was the origin of an innovation in the appointment of the military leaders that might be termed 'democratic': the Council of the Elders agreed to relinquish their responsibility for choice in favour of the army itself. The army chose Hamilcar.

The year was 238. The war with the mercenaries had been going on for three years. Now events speeded up. Hamilcar managed to lure the greater part of the rebels, nearly 40,000 men, into a cirque or gorge which, says Polybius (I. 85, 7), 'was known as the Saw, because of its resemblance to that tool'. It has not been possible to identify this place exactly, called by Flaubert 'the gorge of the Axe'; it might be in the vicinity of Zaghouan or of Djebel Ressas (figure 230). There the mercenaries, already exhausted by famine, were massacred by Hamilcar's elephants. Spendios and the other chiefs were taken prisoner and crucified before the walls of Carthage, in the sight of Matho who was still besieging the town. He returned the Carthaginians' compliment by capturing and crucifying Hamilcar's second-in-command, named Hannibal – not to be confused with Hamilcar's son, who was at that time still a child. But it was the end of the story for the Libyan chief, who was soon taken prisoner in his turn, and his downfall brought in its wake the general submission of the Africans. Even Utica and Bizerta could not hold out for long. As for Matho, a mere native subject who nevertheless had succeeded in making Carthage tremble, he expiated that crime by undergoing through the streets of the town the cruel ordeal of a 'way of the cross', which inspired Flaubert in the last pages of his novel to a picture worthy of inclusion in an anthology of the horrors of the torture chamber.

Carthage had been within an inch of its downfall. But externally too, this war with the mercenaries worked out disastrously. During those three years of difficulties for the Carthaginians, the dominant group in the Roman Senate, who had imposed moderate peace terms in 241 on the outcome of the war in Sicily, had at first eschewed any initiative likely to worsen the situation of the vanquished. Of course, Italian traders had provided the rebels with supplies, and Carthaginian coastguards had caught several hundred of them. But Rome had subsequently recognized those wrongs, exchanged for the captured *negotiatores* the last Carthaginian prisoners still in captivity since the end of the Sicilian war, and authorized its merchants to export to Carthage's benefit while maintaining the blockade as far as the mercenaries were concerned. To the inhabitants of Utica, who had offered to hand over their town, Rome had replied with a refusal. Lastly, they had not followed up the proposals of the mercenaries of Sardinia, who had also revolted and invited the Romans to come and take possession of the island (Polybius, I, 83). Such moderation is astounding. Our sources explain it by Rome's concern to conform to treaty obligations, in particular that of 241, signed by C. Lutatius Catulus. One suspects also that another concern – for promoting economic imperialism beside a political and military imperialism that was still nascent – may account for such apparent leniency.

But Rome was keeping an ear turned to Carthage's internal politics. The dwindling influence of the Elders (among whom there existed a moderating element, such as Hanno, who were more interested in African development than in overseas ventures) in favour of a more direct democracy that benefited a leader feared by the Romans, like Hamilcar Barca, could not do other than worry Rome. That could explain the surprising volte-face in its attitude regarding Sardinia, in 238/237, at the end of the mercenaries' war. Some of those who had been based there, driven out by the hostility of the Sardinian tribes, had taken refuge in Italy. When they proposed to the Senate that the island, left so to speak in escheat, should be seized, this time their appeal was heard. Rome's interference was a real violation of the treaty of 241, which left Sardinia separate from the peace conditions. Carthage prepared to react by making ready an expedition that must have gathered together the army which Hamilcar would soon lead into Spain. The Roman Senate at once 'voted for war', which authorized its ambassadors to declare it if the Carthaginians did not yield. But Carthage, worn out by years of struggle, gave in. It had to renounce its claim to Sardinia and agree, moreover, to pay the Romans an additional indemnity of 1200 talents. Appointed to take possession of Sardinia in Rome's name, the consul T. Sempronius Gracchus also seized Corsica.

THE BARCIDS IN SPAIN

In a quarter of a century the positions of both sides on the chessboard of the western Mediterranean had altered profoundly. Henceforth in essence reduced to its African territory, which it had fortunately expanded, Carthage emerged from those decades of war in a marginalized state. In order to safeguard its role as a commer-

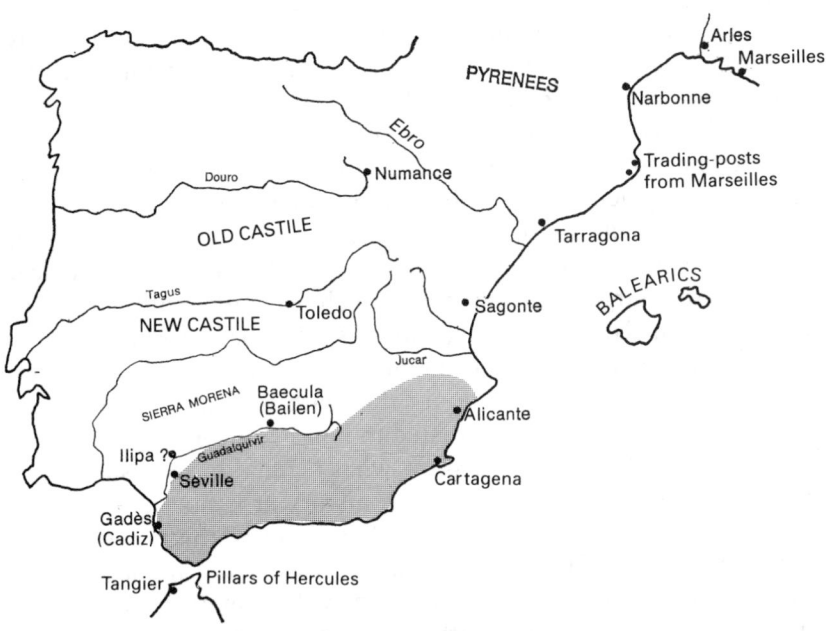

FIGURE 231   *The Iberian peninsula in the Punic era, with the probable extent of the 'Barcid kingdom' stippled.*

cial power, which needed operational bases outside Africa, it would look towards the west, to southern Spain where an old Phoenician settlement made it easier to establish itself (figure 231). This was the work of Hamilcar Barca, and modern historiographers have got into the habit, rather by linguistic exaggeration, of using the name 'Barcid kingdom' for this Iberian principality that sometimes seems like a family enterprise.

The young Hannibal, his son, was nine years old when Hamilcar, who was on the point of taking his army into Spain, made him solemnly swear on the altar of Zeus (read Baal Shamin), where he was making a sacrifice, never to be a friend of the Romans (Livy, XXI, 1, 4). Fifty years later, when he had taken refuge with Antiochus of Syria, himself hostile to the Romans but suspicious of Hannibal's loyalty, he revealed that oath, which had determined the course of his life and continued to dictate his actions (Polybius, III, 11). This detail goes far beyond mere anecdote, and there is no serious reason to look upon it, as has sometimes been done (Brisson, 1973, p. 132), as a later invention of Roman annalists anxious to justify morally Rome's aggressive policy towards Carthage. It confirms that state of mind in which Hamilcar approached his Spanish undertaking. It was not merely a matter of wiping out the undeserved defeat he had suffered in Sicily. Nor, even though it was one of the main objectives of this policy, was it only a question of basing a new prosperity for Carthage on the direct control of Andalusia's mining riches. Hamilcar took the longer view. He wanted to set up in the south of Spain a political and military administration comparable to the one the Carthaginians had established in Africa, and turn that large territorial base, which was sufficiently distant to be safe from Roman attacks, into a springboard from which to 'resume the venture that had momentarily been checked' (Decret, 1977, p. 179). There is no doubt that with such an aim Hamilcar went beyond the mission entrusted to him by his principals.

Efforts have been made to show what made the 'Spanish hour' a very original moment in Carthage's history. It is not an easy task, for the temptation must be resisted to identify the power established in Spain by Hamilcar and his successors as a monarchy of a Hellenistic type, based on the person of a charismatic leader and on a dynastic religion whose pantheon was believed to be recognizable in the triads of divinities who figure in the famous oath of Hannibal (above, p. 208). Did the Barcids, as has been written, create in Spain 'a State that was independent in fact if not in law' (G. C. and C. Picard, 1970, p. 213)? That assertion was based in particular on the effigies shown on coins from the south of Spain, which can be attributed to Barcid mints of the end of the third century (figure 232). They have been seen as portraits of Hamilcar Barca and his son-in-law Hasdrubal, represented as Hellenistic monarchs, crowned with laurel wreaths and wearing the royal diadem. The club visible on one of the coins – which is recognized as depicting Hamilcar – was in addition the sign of a desire to assimilate him to Herakles-Melqart, the great divinity of Cadiz. However, the identification of these heads as portraits of the Barcid chiefs is controversial. One must also consider with some suspicion an annalistic tradition going back to a Roman historian who was very hostile to Carthage, Fabius Pictor, according to which Hamilcar went to Spain on his own initiative, without the authority of the Carthaginian government and, following the death of his son-in-law and successor, Hasdrubal, attempted to overturn Carthage's constitution in order to institute royalty. The truth is that in Spain Hamilcar Barca benefited from a proconsulate of an assured duration – something that had often been so cruelly lacking for the Punic

FIGURE 232 *Hamilcar Barca (left) and his son-in-law Hasdrubal (right) on Punic coins from Spain. The person on the left, with the club, is represented following the Herakles-Melqart type (after L. Villaronga, 1973).*

generals in the Sicilian wars – backed by an army strongly united around their leader, who was endowed with fairly broad autonomy and who displayed certain dynastic aspects. When Hamilcar met his death in 229, drowning in the Jucar during a retreat from the Oretan Celtiberians, as his sons Hannibal and Hasdrubal the Younger were not of an age to succeed him, the army chose Hasdrubal the Elder, their brother-in-law, and Carthage was satisfied to ratify that choice.

I will not go into details here about the Iberian 'geste' of the Barcids, which perhaps belongs more to the ancient history of Spain than of Carthage. All the more so, since the very active archaeological work currently being carried out in the south of the country will no doubt chiefly result, as far as this period is concerned, in clarifying the realities of Punic settlement in the hinterland of Tartessus. The first act of Hamilcar, who was installed initially in Gades (Cadiz), was to reopen to Punic trade the gold and silver mines that should allow Carthage to pay off its debts. Anxious to extend the Carthaginian sphere of influence on the eastern coast as far north as possible, in 231 he set up his headquarters in a place known under the Greek name *Akra Leuke* (Cape Blanc), today Alicante. Hasdrubal consolidated his achievement and did not hesitate to found, on the same coast south of Alicante, a 'new Carthage' (in Latin *Carthago Nova*, Cartagena), considered by its contemporaries, whom Polybius echoes (III, 15), to be a capital city. The same historian (X, 10) has left us a description of the site of this town,

which he knew well, in which pride of place is given to the sumptuous palace built by Hasdrubal, who had taken as his second wife the
daughter of an Iberian king and whose proconsulate accentuated
the monarchic tendencies of the government of Carthaginian Spain.

Hasdrubal succumbed in 221 to the dagger of a Celtiberian
'patriot', but in Carthage's name he had signed an agreement in 226
with a Roman embassy, by the terms of which the Carthaginians
had been forbidden to 'make an armed crossing of the river Iber'
(Polybius, II, 13, 7; III, 27, 9). This was the Ebro, which empties
into the Mediterranean a little south of Tarragona and a fair way
north of Saguntum. It is likely that the Roman Senate were thinking
less of containing Carthaginian expansion than of ensuring Punic
neutrality in the dangerous situation created by the turbulence of
the Celtic tribes. But a difficulty in interpretation arises from a
passage in Polybius (III, 30, 2–3) where the Greek historian seems
to view Hannibal's attack on Saguntum as an infringement of the
agreement signed by Hasdrubal. To resolve this difficulty it must be
said that either Polybius was mistaken in thinking that Saguntum
was north of the Ebro (the expected identification of the 'river
Iber') or that the Iber mentioned in the treaty was not the Ebro, but
another river, namely the Jucar: the latter was the opinion sometimes held, in the wake of J. Carcopino (for example by G. C. and
C. Picard, 1970, p. 218). However, one only has to re-read Polybius
elsewhere (III, 6) to find the answer that he gives explicitly when,
recording the opinion of his contemporaries on the immediate
causes of the war, he says precisely, 'as first cause, the siege of
Saguntum by the Carthaginians and, as second cause, the crossing
by those same Carthaginians of the river that the people of the area
call Iber'. The treaty signed by Hasdrubal was dated 226. It is clear
that in 219, the year when hostilities broke out, Saguntum, south of
the Ebro, had become the ally of the Roman people and was in that
capacity immediately protected against Carthaginian encroachment
by the long-established clauses of Lutatius' treaty. The capture of
Saguntum thus became a *casus belli*, to which Hannibal would add
a second by crossing the *Iber*, Ebro, shortly afterwards. That he
was fully conscious of his actions emerges from the speech he made
to his soldiers, at the end of 218, on the eve of the battle of the
Ticinus (Ticino), mocking those Romans who would condemn you
to complete immobility if you listened to them: 'They do not keep
to the limits they set. "Don't pass the Ebro! Have nothing to do
with the Saguntines!" – "Is Saguntum on the Ebro then?" – "Don't
make the slightest move!" ' (Livy, XXI, 44, 5–6).

THE HANNIBALIC WAR OR THE 'SECOND PUNIC WAR'

In history and legend the figure of Hannibal is so large that it needs at least a book to contain it, even without taking account of the

FIGURE 233 *The bronze head from Volubilis (Morocco): to G. C. Picard a portrait of Hannibal; more commonly seen as Juba II (after Picard in Karthago, XII, 1968).*

second life he led in exile, to which he was forced after 195, by the hostility of the Romans and the ingratitude of his own people. At the very heart of that exceptional destiny, the few years' duration of the campaign that took him from Spain to the south of Italy are an almost inexhaustible topic for historians. On the crossing of the Alps alone a small library could be assembled!

We will therefore follow Hannibal without dwelling on every step of that gigantic adventure or trying to pinpoint all the facets of a rich and varied personality, who exerts a fascination that extends even into research about his physical appearance (G. C. Picard, 1967, pp. 104–8) (figure 233). At the time of the capture of Saguntum, in 219, he was just over twenty-five years old. Livy (XXI, 4, 2) closely followed the reflection of his image in the eyes of Hamilcar's veterans: 'It was,' thought the old soldiers, 'the young Hamilcar restored to them; they saw in him the same vigour in his features, the same energy in his look, the same manner, the same characteristics.' And the historian immediately adds that the young officer quickly came to be held in such regard that what he had inherited from his father was the least of his claims to popularity with the soldiers. Coloured by an obvious partiality when it touches upon the moral and religious aspects of the person, this justly famous portrayal highlights the fact that the war leader, despite limited experience, but possessing exceptional personal qualities, fully measured up to his prodigious challenge.

FROM CARTAGENA TO THE PO VALLEY

One last word, to assess the magnitude of the enterprise, before we let the Punic columns set off along the Spanish roads. A good century after the death of Alexander, no strategist could have devised an expedition that, by the length of its land journeys, the diversity of the territories and nations traversed, the natural difficulties overcome, surpassed the expeditions of the Macedonian in the East. Of course, the choice of a land itinerary was forced upon Hannibal: the condition of maritime inferiority and financial difficulties in which Carthage had found itself since the peace of 241 prevented it from building a fleet which might send an armada to the Italian shores, the more so since the island relay posts had been lost. The risk of making their way by mountains and valleys was thus necessary (figure 234). So that it should not be mere mad temerity, it had to be accompanied by a thorough preparation of the

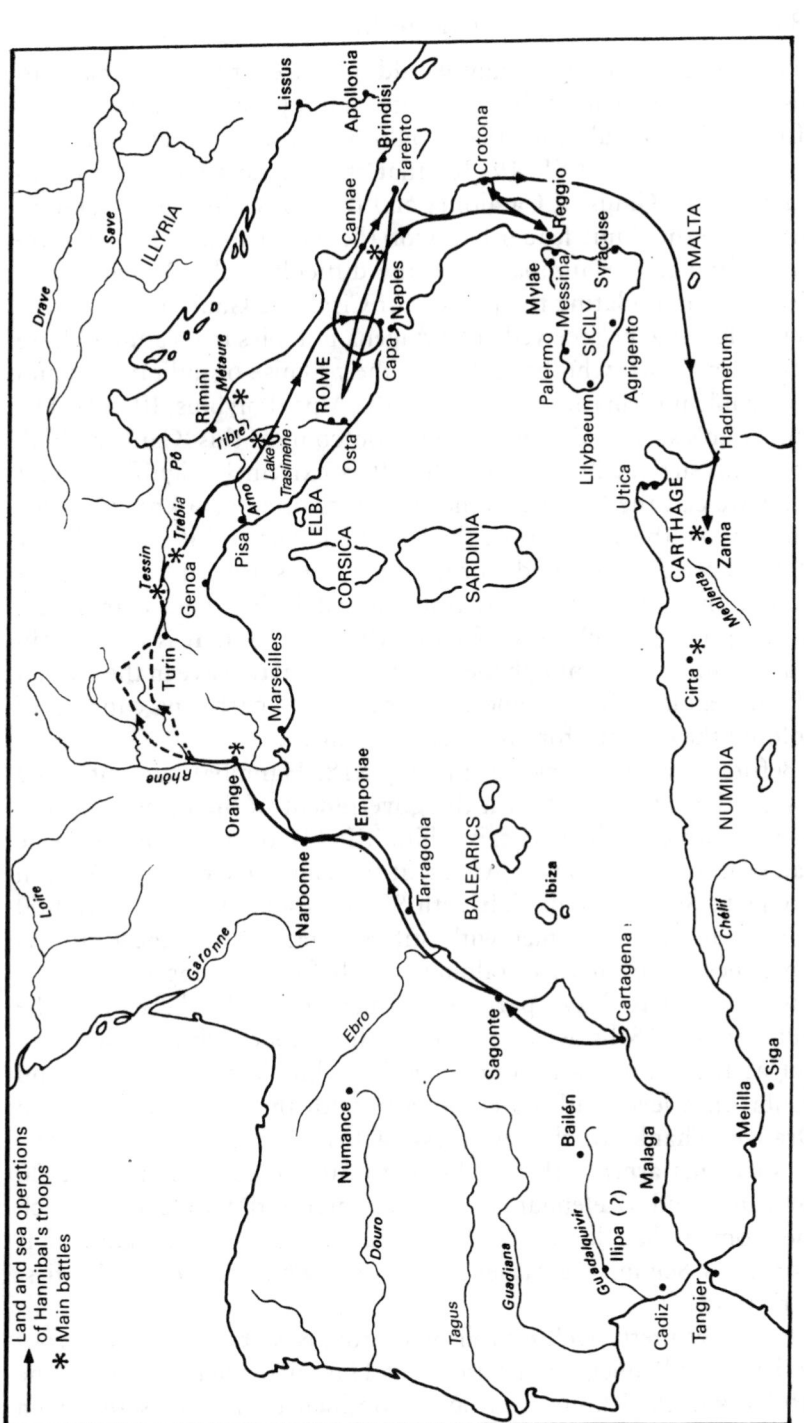

FIGURE 234 *From Cartagena to Zama (218–202 BC) (after F. Decret,* Carthage ou l'empire de la mer, *Paris, 1977).*

ground over which the army would advance. It was necessary to ensure at the very least the neutrality, and if possible the assistance, of the Celtic populations that would be encountered *en route*. We know from Livy (XXI, 19–20) that the Romans tried in vain to persuade the Gauls of Catalonia and the Roussillon to bar Hannibal's way; the Punic leader had won them over to his cause beforehand. Similarly, Hannibal knew the difficulties the Romans were having in assimilating the peoples of Cisalpine Gaul, in Italy itself. Before leaving, he received at Cartagena notables from among those Cisalpine Gauls, who brought him the promise of military aid and invaluable information on crossing the Alps (Polybius, III, 34). The campaign's success depended on the outcome of this 'Gaulish plan', up to his arrival in the Po valley. It is extremely significant that what we call the 'second Punic War' was often also known to the Romans as 'the war against the Carthaginians and the Gauls'. For all that, are there grounds for thinking that southern Gaul and the Roussillon in particular were transformed during those years into a 'Punic protectorate' (G. C. Picard, 1967, p. 165)? It is not certain that Hannibal had enough men at his disposal to leave in the *oppida* of the region – for instance, at Ensérune – garrisons capable of holding the country for any length of time.

Before leaving Cartagena, in May 218, Hannibal had entrusted his brother Hasdrubal with the government of Spain; with a wisdom for which Polybius praises him (III, 33), to ensure his safety he had sent Iberian troops to Africa, at the same time bringing African troops to Spain. Having left with 90,000 foot-soldiers and 12,000 horsemen, Hannibal met with stiff resistance from the Celtiberian tribes of southern Catalonia and, before crossing the Perthus pass, he had to leave part of his men there. At the end of the summer of 218 he was in sight of the Rhône, which he crossed not at Beaucaire, as is sometimes said, but farther upstream, no doubt on a level with its confluence with the Cèze, not far from Orange. Thanks to the swiftness of his march, he had managed to spare his army – then reduced to 50,000 foot-soldiers, 9,000 horsemen and 37 elephants – an encounter with two legions which the Romans had landed at Marseilles, under the command of P. Cornelius Scipio, the father of the one who was to be the first Africanus.

It is now pretty well established, though without decisive proof and thus still open to debate, that Hannibal went up along the left bank of the Rhône as far as its confluence with the Isère, which he then followed, to cut obliquely into the Maurienne and cross the Alps either by the Clapier pass or by the old passage of the Petit-Mont-Cenis. It has sometimes been pointed out that the Punic leader chose this somewhat long and not the most frequented route for political reasons: the Allobroges were divided, it is said, and Hannibal, always well-informed, might hope to gain something from that division by winning the favour of the victors whom he had supported (G. C. and C. Picard, 1970, p. 248; Brisson, 1973, p. 167). But could he have done anything else? His immediate objective in the summer of 218 was to reach the Po valley as quickly as possible to swell his army with the Celtic contingents he knew he could find there. Simply looking at the map, one would be tempted to say that the shortest route open to him was along the Ligurian coast. To commit himself to that, however, would have been sheer madness, for he would first have had to overcome the resistance of Marseilles, Rome's faithful ally, and then because, in those narrow routes along the littoral, he would have been the target for the ambushes of Ligurian brigands, and also vulnerable to any contributions from the Roman navy. The best route was what Antiquity knew as the 'Herculean way' – because it was supposed to have been opened first by Hercules, the eponymous hero of all the great routes in the ancient world – which went up the Durance and crossed the Alps at the Mont-Genèvre pass. A variation still much in use in the Middle Ages and up to the beginning of modern times turned right through the Guil valley and across the Queyras to reach the Traversette pass, near Monte Viso. But the landing of Scipio's legions at Marseilles had cut that route off from Hannibal, who could not have reached it without putting his army in grave danger in the vicinity of the Lubéron.

Hannibal's strategy had allowed for this eventuality and prepared an alternative itinerary, described above, which presupposed crossing the Rhône well upstream from Beaucaire. With that in mind, even before leaving Spain, he had secured in advance the services of native guides. He knew that the farther he went from the sea the less risk there was of encountering the Romans (Livy, XXI, 31, 2). In fact, as soon as Scipio had learnt of the arrangements made by his adversary, instead of dashing off in pursuit he entrusted his two legions to his brother Cnaeus for him to lead them into Spain, and he himself returned to Italy to wait resolutely, with another army, for the arrival of the invader on the Cisalpine plains.

The crossing of the great Alpine passes, undertaken at the end of the year, the beginning of winter, must surely have been a terrible ordeal, and it is probably wrong to make the customary assertion that the ancient writers wildly exaggerated the difficulties. (Livy, XXI, 36 quotes Polybius, III, 55, but adds to the following chapter, 37, the story of the vinegar poured on the burnt rocks, which others, from Pliny the Elder to Appian, by way of Juvenal, took up after him and which has prompted amateur historians to make a few fruitless practical experiments.) The truth is that the price of his speed (crossing the Alps took only a fortnight) had been high in human losses. He arrived among the Insubres, in sight of Turin, with an army reduced to 12,000 Africans and 8000 Iberians for infantry, with an additional 6000 horsemen. Those, says Polybius (III, 56), are the figures that Hannibal himself had had engraved on the famous stele of Cape Lacinium commemorating his *res gestae*.

FROM VICTORY TO VICTORY

The pages devoted by ancient historians to the campaign waged in Italy by the Punic leader during the following two years are little more than communiqués on his victories. The year 218 was not yet over when Hannibal overwhelmed Scipio, himself severely wounded, in the area of the Ticino, near Vercelli, and the Gauls serving in the Roman ranks turned against them to enter the service of the Carthaginians. In the very last days of December the other consul, T. Sempronius Longus, fell into a trap laid for him by Hannibal on the banks of the Trebbia, losing 20,000 men (figure 235). The Carthaginian leader, anxious to preserve the elite of his troops, had mostly lost Gaulish auxiliaries; but the damp and bitter cold had also ravaged his own ranks. Many horses and mules, and nearly all his elephants, had fallen victim to it. Hannibal spent the winter near Bologna, to restore his forces, joined by thousands of Gauls who had hastened to place themselves under his command. The Carthaginian appreciated their assistance, but mistrusted them and their proverbial instability, all the more because he could hardly control them in the field. On this subject Polybius (III, 78) relates a 'totally Phoenician ruse' by the Punic leader: to avoid being too easily recognized in his own camp, he had several wigs made, each suitable to one of the ages of life, and he wore them in turn, choosing appropriate clothing each time; even those closest to him, it seems, were hard put to it to recognize him.

Spring 217 was rough and rainy in northern Italy. The troops suffered greatly in the swampy regions of the Arno. The general

FIGURE 235 *From the Ticino to Trasimene, 218–217 BC. The triangles mark the sites of the victories of the Ticino, Trebbia and Lake Trasimene.*

himself, assailed by ophthalmia, lost an eye for want of proper attention. The sole remaining elephant served him as a mount. Thus was born the image that has come down through the centuries of the 'one-eyed chief riding a Gaetulian elephant'.

Having survived this bad patch, Hannibal swiftly took the initiative again, continuing his route through Tuscany, pillaging the surrounding countryside to attract the nearest Roman army, under the command of the consul Flaminius, and provoke it into an engagement. That took place on the day of the summer solstice, 21 June 217. Hannibal placed his army in the narrow plain bordering Lake

Trasimene and went to camp at the exit from the passage, after disposing troops along the heights that close this sort of defile to the north-east. In the space of three hours, says Livy (XXII, 6, 1), the matter was settled. The Romans lost 15,000 men, including their leader Flaminius, against only 2500 from the Punic ranks. Sticking to his method of dividing the Italian forces, after the battle Hannibal sent Rome's allies home without demanding a ransom, proclaiming that he had come to liberate them and not make war on them. For his part, the leader of the Punic cavalry, Maharbal, went to attack the other consul, C. Servilius, who had come to the rescue with 4000 horsemen, and they too were wiped out.

The Carthaginian leader did not, however, make the mistake of marching on Rome, which he was not strong enough to bring down. His sense of tactics, which was his principal strength since he was low in numbers, and his rapidity of manoeuvre, thanks in particular to his cavalry, would have been no help at all to him in a war of positions. Moreover, a siege would call for the use of machines that took a long time to make ready and put into operation. Hannibal chose rather to go from Etruria first to Picenum on the Adriatic coast, where he took advantage of the agricultural richness of the region to let his animals and men regain their health at leisure, and also to re-equip his African infantry with arms seized from the enemy at Trasimene.

In Rome, in the middle of 217, the political situation was unprecedented. Of the two consuls, one was dead while the other, Servilius, had kept his forces intact but was blocked at Rimini and cut off from all communication. Q. Fabius Maximus was appointed, with the prestige of two consulates and the censorship, to exercise the exceptional magistrature of 'dictator'. Hannibal was not slow to realize that the tactical choices ahead of him had altered. Vainly he tried to force into battle the man who would soon receive the surname Cunctator, 'the Delayer'. In Campania, where the prospect of the defection of Capua and its rich surrounding area had attracted the Punic leader, Fabius harassed the enemy and put him in danger of being encircled. Hannibal finally broke off this contact that was leading nowhere and went off to spend the winter of 217–216 and the following spring in Apulia. While he was overwintering in Geronium, not far from the Gargano, Rome gathered fresh hope and confidence after a few successes obtained by its soldiers. Furthermore, in Spain, where C. Cornelius Scipio had gained a foothold in the autumn of 218, events were turning to the Romans' advantage: Hanno, whose task had been to defend access to the 'Barcid kingdom' in Catalonia, had been defeated and taken prisoner. The next year, with the help of troop transports from Marseilles, the Romans gained further ground towards the south and established themselves firmly in the vicinity of Saguntum. Not only had they cut Hannibal off from the rear, but henceforth they would prevent him from drawing from the reserves on which he counted most. At the end of 217, the *comitia* in Rome appointed as consuls for the year Aemilius Paulus and a plebeian, Terentius Varro. Exceptional mobilization measures soon followed: eight legions were formed, and the head of the cavalry, Minucius, whose hotheadedness had brought him close to a disaster from which Fabius had saved him, received an important command. It was clear that Rome was making ready for a confrontation that it hoped would be decisive.

CANNAE (SUMMER 216)

That was just what Hannibal was waiting for. At the start of the summer he had left his camp to resupply his troops from the crops at harvest time. To precipitate events, he seized the citadel of Cannae, on the banks of the Aufidus (now the Ofanto in Puglia, a little south of the Gargano). There, on 2 August 216, the Romans came to offer him the combat he had so long desired. The paradox of that battle, without doubt the most celebrated in all Antiquity, certainly the most studied by modern strategists, is that there is still uncertainty about its exact location; on the right rather than on the left bank of the Aufidus (Brizzi, 1984, p. 42). A first-time reader will perhaps be surprised: of the tens of thousands of dead, and as many weapons left on the ground, is it possible that no traces survive? But arms and equipment were too precious to be left on the field of battle, and Livy (XXII, 51, 5) makes the precise point, if it were necessary, that immediately after the combat the Carthaginians gathered up the spoils. That left the bodies; those of the Punic soldiers were buried by their companions (Livy, XXII, 52, 6). Our sources are silent about what became of the dead from the Roman ranks, who were far more numerous. The discovery of a cemetery, not so long ago, on the right bank of the Aufidus, was taken to be that of those who had fallen in the battle. Since then a more careful examination has identified it as a burial ground of a much later date.

As regards the battles themselves, our sources (Polybius and Livy, but also Cornelius Nepos, Valerius Maximus, Frontinus) are sufficiently in agreement and precise to allow us to follow their development and even to plot the phases on a map, to the great satisfaction of lovers of war games. Facing the eight Roman legions, whose numbers were double his own (the consuls, with auxiliaries, could line up 90,000 foot-soldiers and 6000 horsemen), and to compensate at least in appearance for his numerical inferiority, Hannibal extended his army along a single line, with a front as wide as that of the Romans but much less in depth (figure 236). Above all, he made a tactical choice that would be studied in military schools right up to the nineteenth century. As usual, he placed his cavalry on the wings: Iberians and Celts on the left, Numidians on the right. In the centre he placed his Gaulish and Spanish foot-

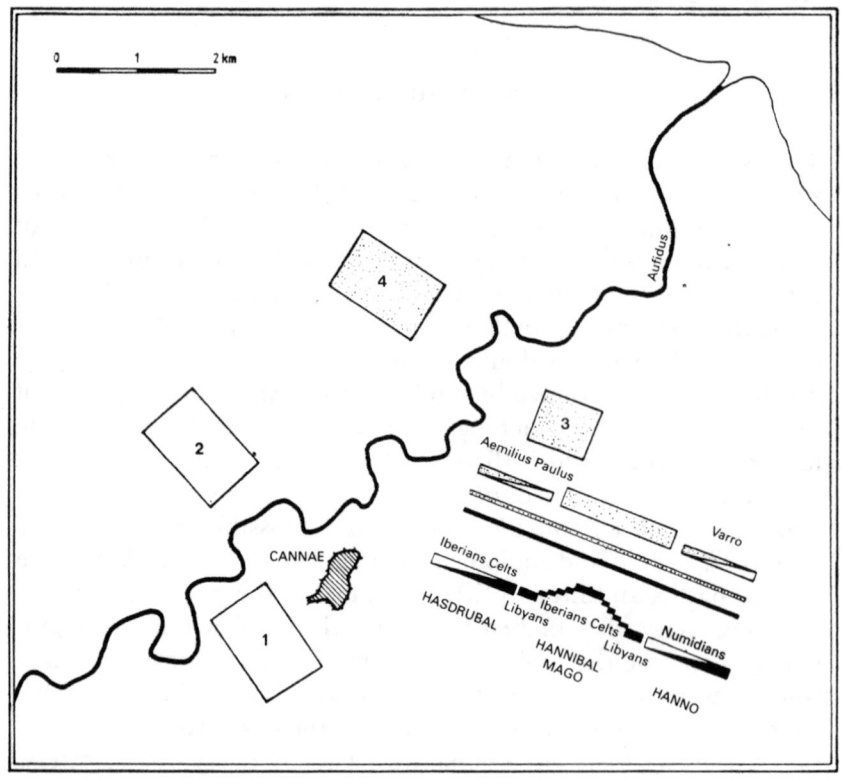

FIGURE 236 *The two armies in battle order before the engagement at Cannae in the summer of 216 BC: 1 Hannibal's first camp; 2 the second Punic camp; 3 the small Roman camp; 4 the large Roman camp (after W. Huss, Geschichte der Karthager, Munich, 1985).*

soldiers, in the form of the *umbo* of a shield, or a crescent with its convex side turned towards the enemy. Between the tips of the crescent and the cavalry wings, the Libyan foot-soldiers were disposed on either side in equal numbers. Hannibal was banking on the enemy assault falling mainly on the centre projection; he had foreseen, if not predetermined, that the Iberians and Gauls forming the projection on that front would yield under the thrust, and that the Roman infantry in their pursuit would then find themselves in line with the Africans who had only to wheel, one group to the right, the others to the left, in order to attack the flanks of the enemy thus engaged. Simultaneously, the Iberian and Celtic horsemen on the left wing, commanded by Hasdrubal, overwhelmed the Romans' right wing and, turning behind their lines, then attacked the left wing, which had resisted the Numidians, but which scattered when it was thus caught in a pincer movement. It only remained for the Punic cavalry to take from the rear the Roman infantry already caught in the net which, from the start of the engagement, had been fashioned by Hannibal's tactic of eliminating the centre. The Punic leader lost 4000 Gauls, 1500 Iberians and Africans and about 200 horsemen. On the Roman side it was sheer disaster: close on 70,000 men lay on the battlefield, including the consul Aemilius Paulus and the two consuls from the preceding year, Atilius and Servilius. Only Terentius Varro was able to get to Venosa, with a few dozen horsemen (Polybius, III, 116 and 117).

Was Rome immediately within reach of the victor? Maharbal, the leader of the Punic cavalry, believed so. He said as much to his master, whom he could well visualize dining three days later at the Capitol. Hannibal replied that he would have to think about it, and drew upon himself the rather piqued response from Maharbal, which Livy rendered in a phrase celebrated for its conciseness and as an example of asyndeton: 'Vincere scis, Hannibal, victoria uti nescis!' (Livy, XXII, 51, 2). In fact, the objections that could be raised against a forced march on Rome after Cannae had not changed since Trasimene, however much of a bloodbath had been inflicted on the Romans. Moreover, Hannibal had other war aims and another plan. Once the prisoners had been sorted out and those of the Italian allies sent back to their homes, he addressed the captive Roman soldiers, whose ransom he had fixed, and his words must be taken seriously: he was not, he told them, waging a war of extermination; he was fighting to maintain the rank (*dignitas*) of his nation and to achieve hegemony (*imperium*) (Livy, XXII, 58, 3). Hannibal therefore expected Rome to sue for peace; what he wanted was a victory recognized by a treaty that would overturn, in Carthage's favour, the humiliating situation born of the treaties of 241 (the loss of Sicily and the obligation to pay a heavy indemnity) and 236 (the loss of Sardinia) (Nicolet, 1978, p. 620). To attain that end, after Cannae Hannibal carried on intense diplomatic activity in the south of Italy, taking advantage of the destabilizing effect of his victory, which had alienated some of the Apulians, many Samnites, Lucanians and Bruttii from the Romans. In Carthage's name, the Punic leader made agreements with Italian states guaranteeing their autonomy, the maintenance of their laws and institutions, and that they would not see the imposition of tributes or a Carthaginian garrison. It was with Capua that Hannibal was at his most persuasive. Received by that city's Senate after concluding a pact of friendship, he promised its citizens that their town would soon be the capital of all Italy (Livy, XXIII, 10, 2). His plan was quite clear: to contain Rome in the north of Campania, while establishing a *de facto* protectorate over southern Italy (and Sicily), in short, as we might be tempted to put it today, to run the film backwards.

REVERSES IN SICILY AND SPAIN

At the same time, or more precisely in the following year, 215, Hannibal concluded a pact of alliance with King Philip V of Macedon, stipulating that the Macedonians, whose troops still counted among the best in that period, would support the Carthaginians, the two nations committing themselves not to sign a separate peace with their common enemy and to come to each other's mutual aid. In the text of that treaty, passed on by Polybius (VII, 9), the Punic divinities mentioned earlier appear (cf. above, p. 208), named in triads to reinforce a sworn oath, and seen sometimes as the pantheon not of Carthage but the Barcids (G. C. and C. Picard, 1970, p. 212). Philip V of Macedon was seeking possession of the eastern coast of the Adriatic in its entirety; in exchange he was prepared to look kindly on Carthage's plan of organizing an Italian confederation presided over by Capua, which would be its loyal supporter. The situation was developing along similar lines in Sicily, where the tyrant of Syracuse, Hieron, had died after a very long reign, leaving the succession under a regency to an adolescent, Hieronymos. Hannibal sent two of his officers to negotiate with the young prince's guardians: at the end of 215 a pact promised Syracuse domination over the eastern half of Sicily. The Syracusans immediately entered into war against Rome, which found itself deprived of the island's corn. The battles round about Syracuse that ensued and lasted three years clearly revealed the growing difficulties of the Carthaginians and their allies in exhausting Roman forces. The town was at first successfully defended, thanks to its powerful walls still reinforced by Archimedes' famous machines (Livy, XXIV, 34). But the land and sea forces sent by Carthage proved powerless to break the blockade imposed by the consul M. Claudius Marcellus. Syracuse fell in 212 and its brilliant defender met his end as an absent-minded old professor: amid all the noise and fury of the sacking of the town, still totally absorbed by the figures he was tracing in the sand, he let himself be killed, quite unrecognized, by a soldier (Livy, XXV, 31, 9).

Two years later, in 210, Agrigentum fell in its turn and the Carthaginians lost Sicily, this time without any hope of a return. In Italy itself Hannibal obtained a few successes in the extreme south, at Tarentum in particular, where the surrender of the town at last made a good port available to him, but they were short-lived. Rome had been able to rebuild a very strong army of a great number of men – twenty-five legions, in all nearly 200,000 men with the allied contingents – and it set out to wear down the Punic leader's forces and erode his positions. One by one the Romans retook the places that had been conquered or won by diplomacy in central and southern Italy. Capua, which Hannibal had hoped to turn into the pivot and model of his Italian policy, was attacked by six legions, appealed in vain to the Carthaginians and had to surrender in 211. Tarentum was lost in 209, and with it the hope of giving Carthage back the mastery of the region's coastal waters. Hannibal, who had believed he reigned over southern Italy, was in fact a virtual prisoner in Calabria.

In Rome, where there was no shortage of able strategists, it had been understood from the very start of the war that, if Hannibal could not easily be vanquished on Italian soil, it would be necessary to dry up the support for his expedition far to his rear, in other words, in Spain, where the fate of the battle was long undecided. In 215 Hasdrubal Barca had been routed by the Scipios' army south of the Ebro. But Carthage had reacted by assembling 12,000 foot-soldiers, 1500 horsemen and 60 vessels of war which were at first intended for the Italian theatre of operations but were directed to Spain under the command of Mago, the third son of Hamilcar Barca. At the end of 212 the two armies of Publius and Cnaeus

Scipio were slaughtered with their leaders. Two years later Publius Cornelius Scipio came to Spain, where his father and uncle had fallen. The future Africanus was then twenty-five years old, but since assuming his *toga virilis* eight years earlier, he had participated in most of the great encounters with Hannibal's troops: the Ticino, the Trebbia, Cannae. He had familiarized himself in the field with the Punic leader's tactics and manoeuvres, and would quickly reveal an equal genius for strategy. Despite his youth, he was moreover astonishingly careful about his image. He would undertake nothing, either in public or in private, without repairing to the Capitol to meditate, and this habit, which possibly reminded the Romans of the thaumaturgic king, Numa, had given rise to the belief that he was of divine origin. Some people even said that he was the offspring of a monstrous serpent that had sometimes been glimpsed in his mother's bed (Livy, XXVI, 19, 5–7). Scipio let them talk and kept up the mystery. Immediately on his arrival in Spain he seized Cartagena and the riches, machines and equipment held in the Barcid capital, together with the ships moored in the port.

In the spring of the following year, 208, Scipio penetrated into the interior of the country, in the direction of the high valley of the Guadalquivir, to lay his hands on the gold and silver mines that had long constituted Carthage's wealth. East of Cordoba he encountered the army of Hasdrubal Barca. The latter, finding himself in difficulties, broke off the engagement and managed to escape northwards. Crossing the Tagus, he made for the Pyrenees, which he crossed at their western extremity in order to avoid the Roman block in Catalonia (Livy, XXVII, 19, 1). By a feat comparable with that of his brother Hannibal, he was in sight of the Alps at the end of winter 208–207. Rome was alarmed by the possible renewal of the experience it had already suffered ten years before, aggravated this time if the two brothers succeeded in joining their forces in central Italy. But in the first place Hasdrubal lost time in besieging Piacenza, and the message setting a rendezvous with his older brother in Umbria was intercepted. The consul C. Claudius Nero, charged with the task of keeping Hannibal in Bruttium, was thus able to send a detachment of his troops to his colleague M. Livius, who was to bar Hasdrubal's way. The latter, overwhelmed by the combination of the two consular armies, was crushed and killed in combat on the Metaurus, not far from Rimini. The situation was becoming difficult for Hannibal. Four years earlier, in 211, the Punic leader, who must have been nursing the desire since Trasimene, had advanced, thanks to an incursion into the north of

Campania and Latium, as far as the vicinity of the Anio, a few kilometres east of Rome. He had camped there and had even advanced with 2000 horsemen as far as the Colline gate, reaching the foot of the walls with his troops (Livy, XXVI, 11, 1–3). The target he had fleetingly touched then must have seemed very distant to him in 207.

THE END OF THE AFFAIR

The alliance with Philip V came to an abrupt end. The King of Macedon had to face up to things elsewhere, in Greece itself; he also had to confront the King of Pergamum and the barbarians who were setting about his frontiers on the north. In 206, despite the mutual aid agreement made with the Carthaginians in 215, he ended by negotiating with Rome. One last attempt to come to Hannibal's assistance was made by Carthage in the spring of 205. Leaving Menorca with thirty ships and 15,000 men, Mago, his younger brother, landed in Liguria and seized Genoa and Savona. He found some support among the Ligurian and Gaulish populations of the Cisalpine region, where he managed to hold out for two years. Carthage obviously had it in mind that, by keeping up the threat in Italy itself, both north and south, the Roman armies would be held and prevented from carrying the war into Africa. But that calculation had already been frustrated: in 204, setting off from his Sicilian bases, Scipio had landed an army in Carthage's African territory. After failing at Utica and spending the winter not far away at the *Castra Cornelia*, in the spring of 203 he was victorious at the *Campi Magni*, in the basin of the middle Medjerda, over Carthaginian troops and their Numidian allies, whose chief, Syphax, he took prisoner. Carthage drew its own conclusions and recalled Hannibal and Mago from Italy soon afterwards. The latter, who was wounded, died during the return crossing.

10

The Final Ordeal

Rome's decision to carry the war into Africa had been a long time maturing, and the operation was most carefully planned. Such preparation had necessarily included negotiations with the indigenous princes. At the end of the third century BC, setting aside the western Maghreb, or present-day Morocco, where a Moorish kingdom lay, two kingdoms shared central North Africa between them, from the Moulouya in the west to the marches of Carthage's African territory in the east (figure 237). The larger of the two, in those years immediately before the end of Hannibal's war, was the western kingdom of the Massaesylian Numidians, whose king, Syphax, had his capital at Siga (Takembrit) near Oran. On a height dominating the town, Syphax – or his successor Vermina – had built a mausoleum, excavated and published recently (Rakob, 1979,

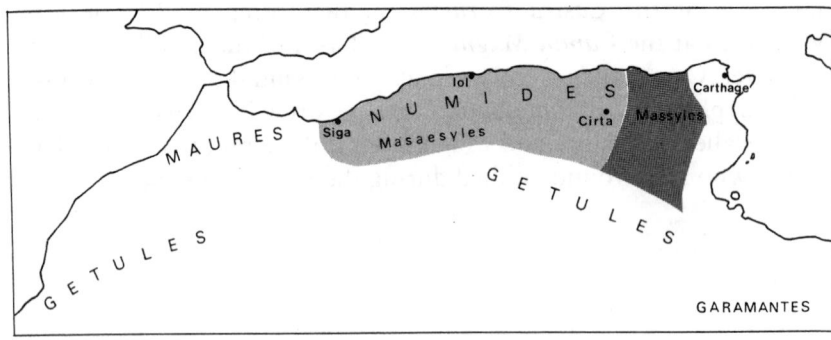

FIGURE 237 *The Massaesylian Numidian kingdom of Syphax (light grey) and the Massylian kingdom (dark grey), which Massinissa inherited at the end of the third century (drawn by S. Lancel after a map by G. Camps).*

FIGURE 238   *The Numidian mausoleum at Siga (a model of a reconstruction and a sketch) (after F. Rakob, in* Die Numider, Bonn, 1979*).*

pp. 149–57), which was very close in its design and elevation, though more sober, to the 'mausoleum B' at Sabratha (above, p. 310) (figure 238). At the eastern extremity of his kingdom Syphax had a second capital, Cirta (Constantine), though it appears that the Massaesylian possessions on the edge of Punic territory were then fairly recent acquisitions (Desanges, 1978a, p. 646). The other Numidian kingdom belonged to the Massylians, and was much smaller, probably with a very narrow sea frontage, between the Collo peninsula, in Algeria, and Khroumiria, in the north-west littoral zone of present-day Tunisia. The Medracen, north-east of Batna, whose architectural decoration I mentioned earlier (above, p. 307) has sometimes been identified as the mausoleum of the Massylian dynasty (Camps, 1973, p. 516). At the time of which we are speaking, 206, Massinissa had just succeeded his father Gaia at the head of this Massylian kingdom for a reign that would last more than half a century.

UNDER THE EYE OF THE NUMIDIAN PRINCES

As may well be imagined, these native princes had not remained passive onlookers in the struggle between Rome and Carthage. They had sided with one or the other, with successive loyalties. The Massylian king, Gaia, had provided Carthage with troops that had been taken to Spain, under the command of his son Massinissa, who had fought there alongside the Carthaginians between 212 and 206. Massinissa had thus been present in Spain at the downfall of Carthaginian power. Scenting a change in the wind, following the heavy defeat suffered by the Punic army at Ilipa, north of Seville, he sought an audience with Scipio, which took place at Gades. He offered his help to the Roman general if Rome should bring the war to Africa. Scipio, who had been able to assess the value of the Massylian cavalry, accepted the offer. As for Massinissa, his father had died in the meantime and he had to hasten back to his kingdom to defend his right to the succession. He triumphed over his rivals but, attacked by Syphax, had to go for some time into exile.

Syphax, for his part, after inclining for several years towards the Romans, with the idea that they would help him free himself from Punic supervision, had in the end allowed himself to be won over to an alliance with the Carthaginians. During the summer of 206 Scipio, accompanied by Laelius, had made the crossing from Cartagena to Siga, with two quinqueremes, to go to see the Massaesylian king. Having arrived in sight of the port of Siga, at the mouth of the Tafna, he had happened upon the triremes of Hasdrubal, son of Gisco, who after the defeat at Ilipa had embarked at Gades to return to Carthage and had made a landfall at Siga. Syphax invited the foes to share his hospitality. Hasdrubal emerged from that unexpected meeting even more impressed by Scipio than Syphax had been. With such a man, he said, 'the Carthaginians should not so much question why they had lost Spain as wonder how to keep Africa!' (Livy, XXVIII, 18, 9). As for Scipio, he went back to Cartagena thinking that he had won the Numidian king's alliance. Syphax had been flattered to exercise his good offices, but he did not care to have Carthage turn against him, since its untouched power in Africa was still to be feared, and he had become its immediate neighbour when, taking advantage of Massinissa's difficulties, he had annexed the Massylian kingdom. For the Carthaginians, with the imminent likelihood of war on their own ground, it was important to preserve the Numidian king's friendship. That was sealed by the marriage which, around the end of 205, united the Massaesylian king, who was growing old and was already the father of adult offspring, and Hasdrubal's daughter, Sophonisba – actually, Sophoniba, as one reads in Livy's best manuscripts, transcribing the Punic Çafonbaal, 'she whom Baal has protected'. Young, beautiful, educated, a musician, gifted with wit as well as charm, Sophonisba had everything it takes to attract a man and keep him. She enslaved Syphax, just as a little later she would captivate Massinissa when, in 203, he seized the palace of Cirta and immediately became her conquest, 'amore captivae victor captus', as Livy prettily puts it (XXX, 13, 18), to such an extent that he put her to death by poison rather than lose her by handing her over to Scipio – with the consent of this oriental woman, who preferred to die rather than live as a captive in the camp of her country's mortal enemies. Celebrated by painters of the European classical age, Sophonisba is indebted to Livy for her place in the gallery of outstanding women who mark the ancient history of North Africa, from Dido to Kahena.

Recalled by Carthage's Senate after the disaster suffered on the 'Great Plains', at the beginning of autumn 203 Hannibal rediscovered an Africa he had left as a child, which had mostly become quite foreign to him. He also mistrusted the Carthaginian senators, too often dominated by the political faction led by his family's old enemy, Hanno, whom he regarded, because of his cowardice, jealousy

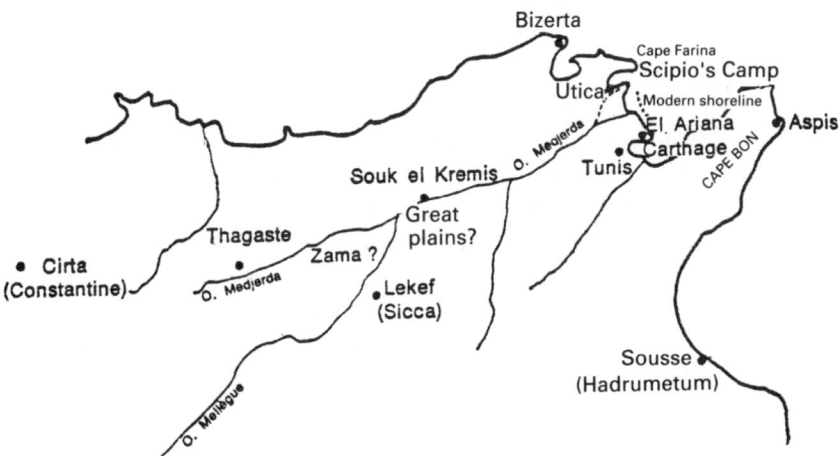

FIGURE 239 *The African theatre of operations at the end of the second Punic War.*

and campaigns of defamation against him, as the one truly responsible for the final failure in Italy. In fact, the Senate in Carthage had not waited for Hannibal to return before entering into negotiations with Scipio by means of plenipotentiaries dispatched to the Roman general's camp in Tunis. Hannibal disembarked at Leptis Minor (Lemta) and stayed in Byzacena to make his winter quarters, near Hadrumetum (Sousse) (figure 239). He thus kept his distance from the government in Carthage, while keeping enough between his forces and Scipio's army to maintain freedom to manoeuvre for the time being. Moreover, the Punic leader was on familiar ground on that coastal area of Byzacium: his family, as we have seen, had properties there, and his personal safety was assured.

THE CONFRONTATION BETWEEN HANNIBAL AND
SCIPIO AFRICANUS

In the spring of 202, a Carthaginian blow against Roman supply ships that had been driven on to the west coast of Cap Bon following a storm, and then the attack by Punic warships on the vessel carrying Scipio's negotiators, put an abrupt end – as was clearly desired by the belligerent part of Carthage's Senate – to the peace talks that had been going on for several months. Hannibal left his winter quarters and moved westward, to establish his camp about five days' march away, near Zama (Polybius, XV, 5, 3; Livy, XXX, 29, 2). This was undoubtedly – for there were two fairly close places with the same name in the region – the city that in the Roman period would be called Zama Regia, now Jama, thirty kilometres north of Makthar (G. C. Picard, 1967, pp. 204–5). Hannibal informed Scipio that he wanted to talk to him. The Roman general waited until he was joined by Massinissa and his 10,000 Numidian horsemen so that he could agree from a position of strength. There is no cause to doubt the historicity of that meeting, even if full credence cannot be given to the reconstruction – as was traditional in ancient historical accounts – of the subjects discussed by the two greatest war leaders of their time on the eve of their confrontation (Polybius, XV, 6–8; Livy, XXX, 30–1). It will at least be recalled that Hannibal was prepared to give up all Carthage's territorial possessions outside Africa, and any attempt to regain them, in order to save his country's fleet. Scipio refused, making war inevitable.

The time was the end of the summer or the beginning of the autumn of 202. The clash took place in the plain of Siliana, and for the account of its different phases one may trust Polybius (relayed subsequently in Latin by Livy), as he was a personal acquaintance of C. Laelius, Scipio's lieutenant, who was at Zama in charge of a cavalry wing. Hannibal had a slightly higher number of infantry than that of his adversary: 50,000 men, according to Appian (*Libyca*, 40), though he is not the surest guide; but his cavalry was inferior to that of Massinissa, Scipio's ally. Scipio, fearing the charge of the elephants – Hannibal had found eighty in Africa – had planned to pierce the three lines in which his infantry were arranged with corridors at right angles to the front, in such a way as to channel the charge and provide escape routes for his soldiers. Laelius and the Italian cavalry had been placed on the left wing, Massinissa and his Numidians on the right. Scipio's tactic succeeded beyond all expectations. The elephants mostly plunged into the corridors and crossed the whole of the battlefield without doing much harm to the Roman lines. Furthermore, the infantry battle did not proceed as Hannibal had foreseen: he had hoped to disorganize and break the Roman forces by the thrusts of his powerful front line, made up of mercenaries, then of the second line, with combined Carthaginians and Libyans, before finishing them off with his veterans, whom he had at first kept in reserve (Polybius, XV, 12, 7). But Scipio managed to reorganize his front by ordering his *principes* and his *triarii*, still unscathed, to take up a position in line with the front-line soldiers, the *hastati*. Above all, the Roman cavalry, who were vastly superior in number, with the back-up of the Numidians, had in the first place driven the Punic horsemen from the field and pursued them into the distance to prevent them from returning to the fray, and then fell on Hannibal's flanks and rear. It was a massacre and a rout. The Punic leader, with a tiny escort of horsemen, did not pause in his flight until he reached Hadrumetum.

THE CONSEQUENCES OF ZAMA: THE SUFFETATE AND HANNIBAL'S EXILE

Scipio no more had it in mind to destroy Carthage than Hannibal, fifteen years earlier, had really intended to try to seize Rome, although according to tradition debate on the matter had already begun in Rome. What the Roman Senate wanted was to prevent a future repetition of the venture that had started out in 218 from the Barcid kingdom in Spain. It was a matter of containing Carthage by confining it to Africa and keeping it in check, even on its own ground, in the west by means of the Numidian kingdom. The peace following the Zama defeat was thus concluded in 201 on terms that were far worse by comparison with what had been envisaged in the talks of 203. Carthage remained an independent State and kept its African territory as far as the *fossae punicae*, but had to restore Massinissa's kingdom to him, together with all the lands controlled by his Massylian ancestors. The Punic state had its hands tied militarily: it undertook not to make war in Africa or elsewhere without the agreement of the Roman people; it had to give up its elephants and not acquire others; abandon all its long ships (i.e. warships) except for ten (in place of twenty in the earlier talks). Lastly, it had to pay an indemnity which was at first fixed at 5000 talents in 203, but then increased to 10,000, payable in fifty yearly payments. On Scipio's orders the Carthaginian fleet was taken out to sea and burnt in sight of all. But it was the payment of the first annual tribute a little later that hit the hardest, among the Council of Elders. The lamentations of those whom he looked upon as shopkeepers drew a bitter laugh from Hannibal. It was, he told them, time for weeping when their arms were confiscated, their ships burnt and the State placed under political supervision. It was to be feared, he added, that the senators would shortly realize that in bewailing the loss of the money they had shed tears over the least of their misfortunes (Livy, XXX, 44, 4–11).

What followed, as we shall see, was to prove Hannibal right. As for him, he did not retire after the peace of 201. If we are to believe Cornelius Nepos (*Hannibal*, VII, 1–4), it seems that he remained at the head of the army which Carthage was allowed by the treaty to maintain for the defence of its territory, and we have seen that he appears to have used his veterans, transformed into farmers, to develop olive groves in Byzacium (above, p. 277). In Carthage the defeat had given rise to a political turmoil manifested more particularly by popular irritation against an oligarchy accused of negligence and prevarication in the conduct of public affairs. Hannibal was elected suffete for the year 196, in company with a colleague whose name history has not recorded.

The first thing he did was to summon a magistrate whom Livy (XXXIII, 46, 3) refers to as *quaestor*, that is, a person in charge of administering finances. This man, who belonged to the faction opposed to Hannibal and theoretically was accountable only to the

Council of Elders, refused to obey the suffete's order. Bearing in mind the separation of powers, he reckoned that he was in a strong position, all the more so because at the expiry of his term of office he would enter the order of judges – the Council of the Hundred or Hundred and Four – of which he would become one of the irremovable and powerful members. Hannibal had him arrested and brought before the Assembly of the People, who dismissed him and, at Hannibal's instigation, passed a law stating that in future judges would be elected for one year only and would not be eligible again immediately (Livy, XXXIII, 46, 6–7). By doing this the suffete had by-passed the Senate, which would normally have had to pronounce on this reform before the people, and had struck a hard blow at a veritable caste. This political attack was matched by another, this time financial. Hannibal had a detailed account of the state of public finances submitted: income, i.e. the product of taxation and taxes on goods, and expenditure, to which that income should be allocated. This budgetary inquiry having revealed the losses suffered by the Carthaginian State because of the misappropriation and plundering of the oligarchs, the suffete declared before the People's Assembly that the Republic did not need to tax its citizens in order to fulfil the obligations to the Roman Senate incurred by the defeat: all that was needed was to have the embezzled funds put back into the public coffers (Livy, XXXIII, 47, 1–2). In other words, make the prevaricators cough up.

The hatred that these enforced restitutions earned Hannibal may be imagined. Emissaries sent from Carthage to Rome accused the suffete of carrying on secret intrigues with King Antiochus of Syria, who was at that time hostile to Rome. Despite the reluctance of Scipio Africanus, who thought it unworthy of his country to become involved in the squabbles of Carthaginian internal politics, the Roman Senate sent three of its members to Carthage to indict Hannibal before his own Council of Elders. It was the summer of 195: the former suffete had finished his year's term of office and was thus vulnerable. He was not fooled by the rumours put about to explain the arrival of the three Roman senators, according to which they had come to settle arguments between Massinissa and the Carthaginians (Livy, XXXIII, 47). He had foreseen this possibility and discreetly left the town, with only two servants. The next day he was safely in one of his estates on the Byzacium coast, between Thapsus and Acholla. There a boat awaited him and took him to Cercina (Kerkenna island) and thither to Tyre: it was but the first stage in a long wandering, but almost symbolically Carthage's greatest man found his first refuge in the Phoenician mother-country from which Dido had departed over six centuries before.

CARTHAGE'S REVIVED PROSPERITY

Hannibal's possessions were confiscated and his house razed. However, the images offered by archaeology of the Punic city in the first few years of the second century BC are not those of destruction, but rather of construction; not images of stagnation, but rather of prosperity. Except for a brief reminder, I will not return here to the surprising vitality of urban development evidenced by the constructions of that date, in particular the zone on the south and south-west slopes of the hill of Byrsa. The chronological evidence was emphasized earlier; we have noted the standardized character of the dwellings built on land that was still vacant at this late date for residential occupation, and I suggested that the 'promoter' of these 'standard' homes might well be none other than the suffete of year 196 (above, p. 157). It is a simple hypothesis, to be sure. Much more worrying is the discovery made by British archaeologists working on the vestiges of the war harbour in the 'admiral's islet' of the circular lagoon. We saw (above, p. 176) that the chronology they claim for the monumental construction matching Appian's famous description (*Libyca*, 96) rests – in a fairly fragile fashion, I must repeat, but there is no cause to challenge it – on a few potsherds which date the complex of dry docks, or at least their last rearrangement, to several years before Carthage's destruction in 146. It was as if, some decades after the peace of 201, Rome no longer controlled or enforced respect for the ban imposed on the Punic state against arming more than ten long ships. Certainly, in our sources, there appears the urge of the Carthaginians, betrayed to the Senate in Rome around 170 by Gulussa, one of Massinissa's sons, to equip a large fleet, on the pretext of offering it to the Romans, theoretically their allies at the time, with the ulterior motive of turning it against them eventually; but Livy (XLIII, 3) reports the matter without giving it too much credence. This apparent distortion between the evidence of the texts and that of archaeology opens up one of those yawning gulfs that frequently give historians of Antiquity a touch of vertigo.

Whatever the truth about the irritating problem of the ports, it is certain that Carthage lost no time in regaining a real prosperity, to the extent that, at the end of ten years, it was able to propose to

Rome (which refused) the advance settlement of its war indemnities which were to have been staggered over fifty years (Livy, XXXVI, 4, 7). Recalling those years at the beginning of the second century, Appian (*Libyca*, 67) lays stress on Carthage's economic progress and population increase during the ensuing period, when its enforced pacifism allowed it to benefit to the full from its various products, notably in agriculture. The two countries had emerged exhausted from the long 'Hannibal's war'; but whereas Rome continued to wage war on Philip of Macedon, Antiochus of Syria and Perseus, Carthage was able to invest in lucrative activities the money formerly expended on arming war fleets, recruiting mercenaries and maintaining armies. Such is the customary revenge of the vanquished.

The size of grain supplies agreed by Carthage for Rome, at its request and in return for payment, as well as for the subsistence of Roman armies in the field, bears witness to Punic agriculture's capacity for setting aside large exportable surpluses during that period. In the year 200, 200,000 bushels of corn were dispatched to Rome, and as much to Macedonia, to supply the Roman expeditionary corps (Livy, XXXI, 19, 2). Ten years later, in 191, far larger quantities (including 500,000 bushels of barley destined for the Roman army) were requested by envoys of the Senate and supplied by Carthage, which boasted that it was willing to offer it without charge, but the Roman Senate refused (Livy, XXXVI, 4, 9). In 171 some Carthaginian delegates went to Rome to announce that a similar quota of barley and, in addition, a million bushels of corn were ready to be dispatched: on Rome's orders, they would be delivered to Macedonia (Livy, XLIII, 6).

On the level of ordinary commercial dealings, a literary text datable to the beginning of the second century confirms, if it were necessary, that business was continuing and that Carthaginian private trading was still present in Italy. The *Poenulus* ('The Carthaginian') is a *fabula palliata*, borrowing its theme from the Greek repertory, but the dialogue in this comedy, which was certainly performed around 190 BC, shows that the Romans of the period had a direct and familiar acquaintance with Punic traders. The one Plautus puts on the stage, under the passe-partout name of Hanno, is sketched without any fundamental hostility, but simply with the bantering language that foreign bazaar merchants have always provoked, especially on the part of those who secretly envy their *savoir-faire*. Hanno is a *gugga* (certainly a pejorative generic nickname), who wears rings in his ears and, like his slaves, is clad in a beltless tunic (the word *tunica*, let it be said in passing, was certainly borrowed from the Punic). As a good Carthaginian he knows all languages while pretending not to (*Poenulus*, v. 112), and thus expresses himself at first deliberately in Punic, which affords us about thirty lines of a jargon in which has been recognized – sometimes with difficulty – the language then spoken in Carthage as it was perceived by Latin ears (Sznycer, 1967). Punic was certainly known in Rome in that era, if for no other reason than contact with the numerous Carthaginian slaves procured in the war – the comic author of the next generation, Terence, was probably one of them – even if the vagueness of Milphio, in his attempts at dialogue with the old *gugga*, gives only a poor idea of that knowledge in practice. In fact, all that Milphio can say is 'Avo' ('Hail'), in which he barely strays from the Latin 'Ave', which means the same and also comes from the Punic (*Poenulus*, v. 977 ff.)

'Business as usual,' Hanno might have said, in Greek, the commercial language of the time. It would be nice to know what he had been selling overseas. 'Spoons, pipes and walnuts,' jokes Milphio (*Poenulus*, v. 1014), whom we must not believe, because we know that instead of translating the words uttered by Hanno, which he scarcely understands, to put people off the scent he is happy to substitute Latin words that resemble them phonetically (Sznycer, 1967, p. 134). Wild animals for the games held in Rome, hides, wool, metals (chiefly tin and silver), salted meats, farm produce (wax and honey, fruit and vegetables) are the most likely merchandise. Let us pause over one of them, about which the texts say little, but which archaeology attests in abundance, because of all these products it is the only one that is indestructible – pottery.

LATE PUNIC POTTERY

We saw earlier that Punic pottery, which was always in great demand in the domain of large containers (oil and wine amphorae), was inadequate for certain other needs. In the earliest era, in particular, products imported from Greece at first, notably Corinth, and then from Etruria were rivalling local pottery for use as drinking vessels and also for keeping perfumed oils (above, p. 58). Then, starting in the fifth century, Attic pottery with red figures, and more frequently black-glazed without designs, impressed Carthaginian housewives by its quality in a range of bowls, goblets and plates. In use, this thin-walled light pottery, resistant and ringing, with a glaze that was difficult to crack or damage, proved superior to common local pottery, which was heavier and more porous. The Attic pottery which came to Carthage until the middle of the fourth century was necessarily a pretty costly product; not that it was very luxurious in itself, but because it reached its destination at the end of a fairly roundabout route, probably punctuated by commercial middlemen. Beginning in the third century, imports from less far afield took over. Very careful re-examination of the pottery found at Carthage and in African Punic sites, dating from this period, has dashed the long-held idea that Magna Graecia (Sicily and South Italy) had become Carthage's principal supplier in this field in the Hellenistic period (Morel, 1980, pp. 29–75). Pottery originating from this area was to a great extent rivalled by more westerly imports, such as the grey pottery from the Iberian coasts, chiefly Ampurias, in Catalonia, which the Carthaginians were well placed to obtain at advantageous prices. At the same time they were developing for themselves the manufacture of crockery in hard and well-baked clay, brick-coloured when broken open but often greyish on the surface, and well represented in the form of little pots and casseroles with lids, which are present everywhere in the Hellenistic period on Mediterranean sites, where they seem to be a standardized product.

In the field of pottery, one must picture the western basin of the Mediterranean as a common market, wide open even in the context of situations of conflict, where the interaction of craftsmen was a common occurrence. The industrial and commercial presence of the Carthaginians played an important part. Recent excavations in Carthage and, in parallel, the great activity in archaeological investigations on the sites of the west coast of Spain, have resulted in a very noticeable re-evaluation of that presence, thanks to the identification as products of Carthage's African territory or the 'area of Punic influence' in the broad sense of the term (the Balearics, the western Iberian littoral, Sardinia, western Sicily: Lilybaeum, Segestum) of numerous types of black-glazed pottery (figure 240). In particular, over a fairly wide period between the end of the fourth century and the middle of the second, a quantity of examples of what are called 'plastic vessels' must be considered to be products of Carthage or the areas over which it had cultural influence. These are items of pottery in the shape of animals (for instance, dolphins, horses and pigs) or human beings: worth a special mention are the representations of negroes (a subject already in vogue in Greek pottery of the Classical period) and receptacles in the form of sandalled feet (Morel, 1990). Fragments of vessels of this type have

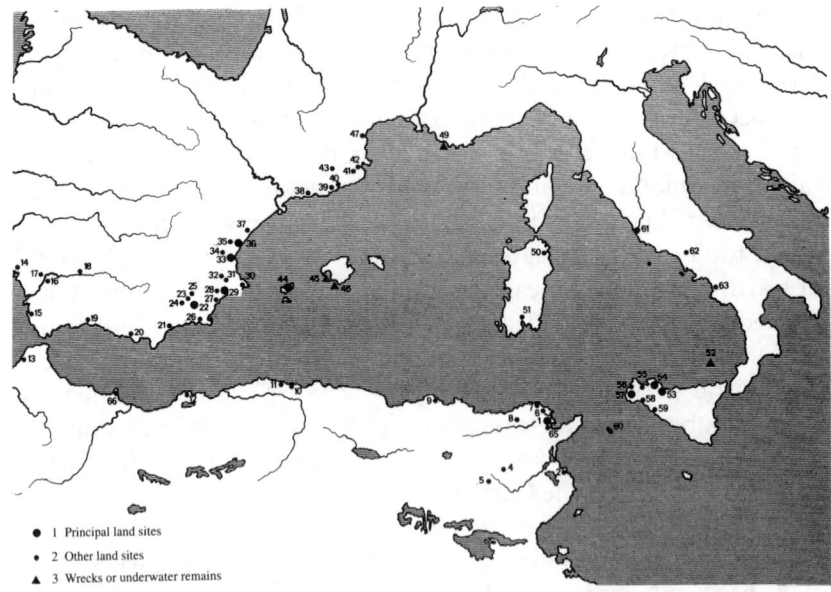

● 1 Principal land sites

• 2 Other land sites

▲ 3 Wrecks or underwater remains

FIGURE 240   *Sites in the western Mediterranean where black-glazed Punic or Punic-influenced pottery has been found (after J.-P. Morel). The abundance of this pottery will be noted without surprise on the Spanish coasts, but also in Sicily and Rome (no. 61).*

been found on sites in Italy, chiefly in Rome, where they had arrived in the crates of Carthaginian *guggas*. Carthage also produced, certainly from the middle of the third century (the era of the first Punic War), pottery in a light ochre clay, dense and very homogeneous, with slender walls – mainly in the form of plates with a broad rim and little cylindrical boxes or *pyxidia* – covered in a beautiful matt black glaze as solid and thick as the Attic black glaze that this pottery obviously aimed to supersede (it is the 'Byrsa 661 class' of Morel, 1982, pp. 53–4) (figure 241).

In the opposite direction, starting in the early years of the second century, from Italy or, more precisely, the Naples region, a flood of imports poured into Carthage of good quality pottery, known under the name of 'Campanian A pottery'. This term designates crockery – above all dishes, plates and bowls – which its clay, of dark ochre, and its glaze, black but often slightly bluish with metallic glints, allows to be easily distinguished from both the Attic pottery of the preceding period and the Punic black-glazed product just mentioned. Recent French excavations on the Byrsa hill allow the peak of these imports of Campanian pottery to be dated to the second quarter of the second century. They reached such a level

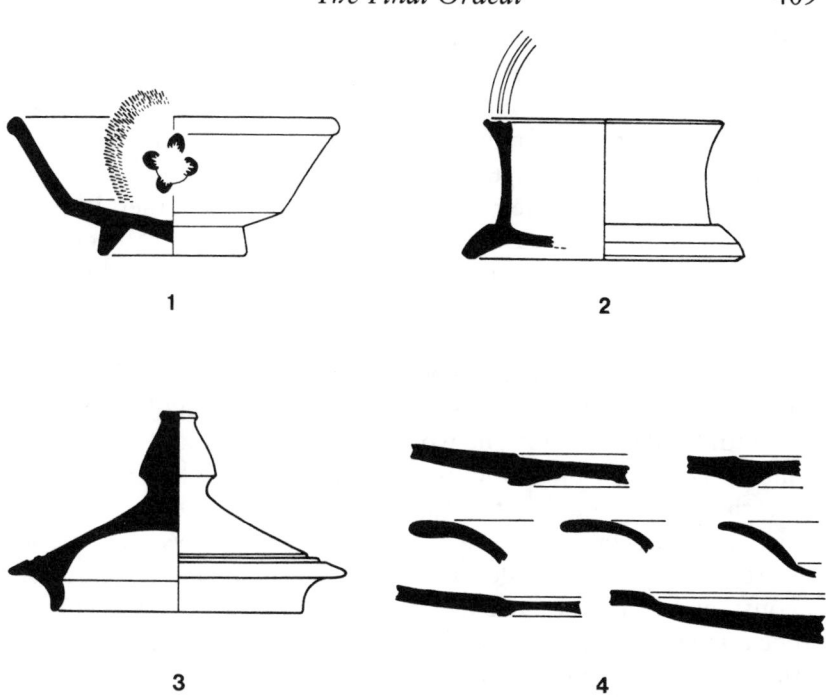

FIGURE 241   *Late Punic black-glazed pottery: 1 a little bowl of the Byrsa 401 type; 2 a pyxis of the Byrsa 661 type; 3 a lid of the Byrsa 661 type; 4 fragments of paterae and plates of the Byrsa 661 type (after J.-P. Morel).*

shortly before the fall of Carthage that the streets in this district were literally strewn with the debris of the crockery, thrown out unceremoniously when it was broken and useless. That massive presence, which incidentally does not exclude the local products mentioned above, must not be interpreted as a decline in Carthage's economic prosperity at the time. In the flow of trade, then very active between North Africa and central and southern Italy, via Sicily, Italian importers were certainly not making gifts to the Punic capital, which made up for importing manufactured goods by exporting its own products and its farming surpluses.

'DELENDA EST CARTHAGO!'

At some date between 153 and 152 there came to Carthage one of those Roman embassies that arrived from time to time to take stock of things or to arbitrate on conflicts between the Carthaginians and their Numidian neighbours. Among them was Cato the Elder, then aged eighty-one years, but still the active leader in the Roman Senate of the faction in favour of a preventive war against the Punic capital. Appian (*Libyca*, 69) and Plutarch (*Cato the Elder*, 26) recount that, during their mission, Cato and the other Roman ambassadors were struck by the air of prosperity in Carthage and the neighbouring countryside. In addition, according to Plutarch, Cato found the Punic city full of all kinds of weapons and buzzing with preparations for war; even the materials for building a fleet are said to have been collected (Livy, *Epitome of Book XLVII*). It was on his return from this embassy that, at every session of the Senate and until his death in 150, he would take up like an old refrain the sentence with which he punctuated each of his speeches, no matter what the point being debated: 'In any case I am of the opinion that Carthage must be destroyed.' And everyone knows the legend according to which, in order to give substance to what he felt to be a constant menace, he once brought to the Curia what he claimed to be a fresh fig picked in Carthage only three days before, adding: 'Ah yes, we have an enemy this close to our walls!'

There is scarcely any doubt that finding the old African enemy in such an insolent state of well-being worried and probably irritated Italian traders and business circles. It is not certain, however, that those worries and jealousies were directly at the root of the intervention decided upon shortly after Cato's death in 150. In fact there was a moderate party in the Roman Senate that was opposed to war, and it was headed by Scipio Africanus' own son-in-law, P. Cornelius Scipio Nasica. This great personage, who had held the highest offices, has been credited with a political philosophy of a very lofty view, according to which a great nation must accept coexistence with a fairly powerful external enemy, which by its very existence will exert sufficient pressure to maintain its own cohesion and save it from the risk of internal disintegration and the possibility of revolution. But it may well be that these ideas, whose inspiration came from certain curents of Greek political thinking and are seen to be circulating still in Cicero's *De Republica*, were attributed to Nasica after the event, perhaps in the time when the Gracchi, as we shall see, were interested in a first attempt to give the destroyed city rebirth (Nicolet, 1978, p. 626). In his *City of God* (I, 30), at the beginning of the fifth century AD, Saint Augustine, who was very aware of Carthage's pre-Roman past, was still crediting Scipio Nasica with having predicted the evils – foremost of which were the civil wars that would prove fatal to him – that too great an external safety brought to the Roman Republic. As reported by our sources from Diodorus to Plutarch, what these debates prove is at least that the Roman Senate was split over the attitude to be assumed *vis-à-vis* Carthage, and also that in the heart of the Senate the problem was seen in the framework of the whole of Rome's foreign policy (Dubuisson, 1989, pp. 283–5).

Nevertheless, fears of a possible reawakening of the enemy brought down by Scipio Africanus finally carried the day. In 151 the last of the fifty annual payments of the indemnity due under the terms of the treaty signed in 201 was paid by Carthage, which thus rid itself of the last burden still weighing – increasingly lightly – on its economic expansion. Nothing remained for those in favour of war but to find a pretext, which in fact presented itself when, in the following year, 150, the Carthaginians, exasperated by a new encroachment on their African territory by the Numidians, decided to counter-attack.

It may be remembered that one of the clauses of the 201 treaty forbade Carthage to make war – even a purely defensive one – without the agreement of the Roman people. Bound by that clause, Carthage's Senate had on several occasions during the preceding decades been forced to ask for Rome's arbitration in the differences that brought it into opposition with Massinissa. In particular, a text from Polybius (XXXI, 21) – preferable to Livy (XXXIV, 62) which places these events in 193, that is to say, at much too early a date – tells us that between 165 and 162 Massinissa ravaged the region of the *Emporia*, those village ports on the Syrtis Minor, between the Gulf of Gabès and Leptis Magna, which the Carthaginians had for centuries regarded, if not as territory under their direct administration, at least in their zone of influence. Rome was alerted but remained deaf to Carthage's complaints and allowed the Numidian king to have his way. Some ten years or so later, pushing his advantage, Massinissa set about the region of the Great Plains and the Carthaginian territory known as Thusca, a vast and rich area between the middle course of the Medjerda and the wadi Siliana. Once again, the Carthaginians implored the Roman Senate, who in the end dispatched to Africa the embassy including Cato the Elder, as we have seen, but that withdrew without settling the matter. Its patience exhausted, in 151–150 the Punic State put in power representatives of the popular party, who were more inclined than the oligarchy to offer some resistance. A Punic army, commanded by Hasdrubal the Boetharch ('commander of the auxiliary troops'), came to confront the Numidians in the defence of a town called Oroscopa, the location of which remains unknown (Appian, *Libyca*, 70). After an initial engagement with no decisive outcome, Hasdrubal's troops, surrounded and brought down by starvation, had to yield and were treacherously massacred. Massinissa thus stayed as master of his new conquests, which brought him to the very gates of Carthage's land.

But worst of all, Rome decided to use the opportunity of that desperate attempt to put an end to matters with its old enemy. Did the latest of Massinissa's successes arouse Rome's fear that he was on the point of achieving his ultimate aim, patiently furthered step by step since Syphax's eviction, of creating on Carthage's ruins a native kingdom the size of almost the entire present-day Maghreb, which would make him a force to be reckoned with? There are some historians who see the cause of the third Punic War in that concern. But it has also been pointed out that in 150 the Numidian prince, then aged eighty-eight years and on the point of disappearing, could hardly count on his heirs – in a succession that promised to be as difficult as the one which had brought him to power himself over half a century before – to realize such a grandiose enterprise (G. C. and C. Picard, 1970, p. 285). In fact, it is probably necessary to broaden the field of vision to the scale of the Mediterranean world to try to understand why, after controlling Carthage for half a century, Rome should seize the first legal pretext to hand in order to put a brutal end to their coexistence. In 168 a major event had occurred, the defeat at Pydna of Perseus, king of Macedon, which at last freed the Romans from their obsessive fear of a possible alliance between Carthage and the Antigonid dynasty. The end of the last great Hellenistic kingdom thus marked a real turning-point in the history of this period in the ancient world, springing the last bolt that still held back Roman imperialism. In the years that followed, and up till 152, Rome's forces had been sufficiently occupied by the hard campaigns that kept them mobilized in Spain against the Celtiberians. Two years later, the Senate's hands were free.

THE 'FINAL SOLUTION'

Rome opted for war, but did not declare it and concealed its intentions. However, at Carthage it was known that mobilization was taking place in Italy. Fear triumphed over the pride that had inspired resistance to the Numidian prince. Utica, scenting a change in the wind, defected and placed itself under the protection of Rome. Hasdrubal, condemned to death as the scapegoat, managed to escape, but the oligarchy, led by Hanno, returned to power and decided to trust in the 'good faith' of the Romans, sending an embassy to Rome which arrived there at the beginning of 149.

Meanwhile, on the Roman side, all arrangements had been made for war. The two consuls, Manilius and Censorinus, had already concentrated in Sicily the expeditionary corps and the fleet that would soon transport it to Africa. In Rome, the Punic embassy that had just made an act of submission before the Senate was given to understand that Carthage, as a pledge of its loyalty, must deliver 300 hostages within thirty days to the consuls at their headquarters in Sicily.

It was at Utica, where in the spring of 149 the consuls had just installed themselves and their troops, that the Punic delegation finally learned Rome's wishes: Carthage was to hand over all its weapons and war machines. Despite the protests of the people, the Carthaginian Senate complied. Appian (*Libyca*, 80) – following Polybius, XXXVI, 67, who gives the same figures – described the long train of carts carrying some 200,000 items of individual arms and 2000 throwing machines, ballistas and catapults, from Carthage to Utica. That done, it only remained to unveil to the disarmed Carthaginians the final phase of a plan that had been carefully kept secret. It was imparted at Utica to a deputation made up of thirty of the Punic state's principal men: the Carthaginians could remain free to live according to their laws, on condition that they abandoned their city, which Rome had determined to destroy, to go and settle wherever they pleased, provided it was at least eighty stadia (about fifteen kilometres) from the sea.

Such a diktat was the equivalent of a death sentence. There was no precedent in Antiquity for a state's surviving the eradication of what constituted it on the sacred plane: the destruction of its temples and cemeteries, the deportation of its cults, were a more surely mortal blow than displacing the population. But that displacement in itself, simply in material and non-religious terms, was the very negation of what for centuries had been the vocation and *raison d'être* of Carthage, a maritime State whose power and wealth relied on the feelers it sent out from its ports across the seas. Certainly, the wise use of its African territory, above all since the fourth century, had diversified its resources and increased its autonomy. But could the Carthaginians reasonably be expected to be won over by the consolatory words addressed to them, according to Appian (*Libyca*, 86–7), by the consul Censorinus: it would be greatly in their interest to give up the old passion for overseas expansion, which in the past had done them more harm than good? It is surely not accidental that, in Book II of his *Republic*, Cicero attributes to Scipio Aemilianus, the destroyer of Carthage, the development of the argument of which Censorinus' words, as reported by Appian, are merely the counterpoint (Heurgon, 1976, pp. 449–50). Romulus, says Scipio, had the wisdom not to choose a maritime location for Rome, as it would not have been at all suitable for a city founded with the hope of lasting and having empire over the world. If the Carthaginians really heard such speeches from the lips of Censorinus, they could only have felt them to be bitter derision. Stripped of its maritime outlets and withdrawn into its African territory alone, Carthage was condemned to be, at best, no more than an agricultural colony of Rome.

If the Roman consuls had hoped to spare themselves a war by persuading the Carthaginians to perform collective suicide, they were disappointed. When Rome's diktat was announced, popular fury swiftly followed despondency. As well as the representatives bringing the terrible tidings, senators accused of treason and Italian traders who happened to be in Carthage fell victim to it and were massacred. There was a rush to the city gates to close them, while the Carthaginian Senate decreed a state of war and freed slaves in order to enrol them. The 'boetharch' named Hasdrubal, who ran the campaign with about 20,000 men, was entreated to forget the death sentence against him and to direct military operations outside the town, while a general bearing the same name was charged with the defence of the town *intra-muros*. Energy born of despair performed prodigious feats: each day, improvised arsenals manufactured 100 shields, 300 swords, 500 javelins, 1000 projectiles for the catapults (Strabo, XVII, 3, 15; Appian, *Libyca*, 93). The women of Carthage offered their gold and, so it is said, gave their hair to be used as ropes for the machines.

The two Roman consuls without doubt underestimated that heroic determination. At all events, they were in no hurry to lay siege to a town that was still inadequately defended. Moreover, Massinissa's attitude did not encourage them to rush things. The old Numidian king, who was to die the following year, watched without enthusiasm as his Roman ally took the chestnuts from the fire in his place and did not hasten to lend a hand. It was not until the summer of 149 that the place was finally attacked, Manilius' mission being to break through its fortifications on the side of the isthmus, while Censorinus gave himself the task of attacking the theoretically weaker part of the great enclosing wall, the one which, to the south, linked the defences of the isthmus with the entry to the ports, running along the north shore of Lake Tunis.

THE SIEGE AND CARTHAGE'S DEFENCES

It did not take the Roman generals long to realize that seizing Carthage by sheer force, even when it had been disarmed by treachery, would be an arduous undertaking. In the manner of many large towns in the Hellenistic era, the town properly speaking, but also its *suburbia*, its residential quarters and surrounding semi-rural suburbs, were enclosed within a vast fortified envelope which protected the whole of the peninsula (figure 242). Indications that tally, provided by our sources, allow us to put its total length at about 22,000 or 23,000 Roman paces, or between 32 and 33 kilometres, a figure slightly above what is obtained by measuring on a map, taking account of the courses to be considered, which result, as we shall see, from the excavations carried out in the middle of this century. Unlike the single wall protecting the peninsula on its steep sides, to the north and the east, from present-day Gammarth and La Marsa as far as Sidi-bou-Saïd, the wall that cut across the isthmus over a width of about 5 kilometres was a triple one. According to Appian (*Libyca*, 95), each of its parts, about 30 feet (or a little less than 9 metres) in height, rose to 30 cubits (or about 15 metres), not including the crenellations or the towers that flanked the rampart at intervals of two *plethra* (a little less than 60 metres). Still according to Appian, each wall had two storeys; down below were stalls to house 300 elephants, and above, stabling for 4000 horses, stores for fodder and barley, and barracks for 20,000 foot-soldiers and 4000 horsemen. Such a description obviously calls for some corrections: Appian must be mistaken when he talks of three walls of the same height since, apart from the cost of the work, they would have presented more inconveniences than advantages for the defenders. By triple wall (*triplon teichos*) must be understood a triple line of defences of which only the principal wall could encompass in its thickness the sort of complex arrangements described by the Greek historian. It is the 'high wall' that a text of Orosius (*Historiarum adversus Paganos*, IV, 22, 5–6) presents as a freestone wall 30 feet wide (the measurement also

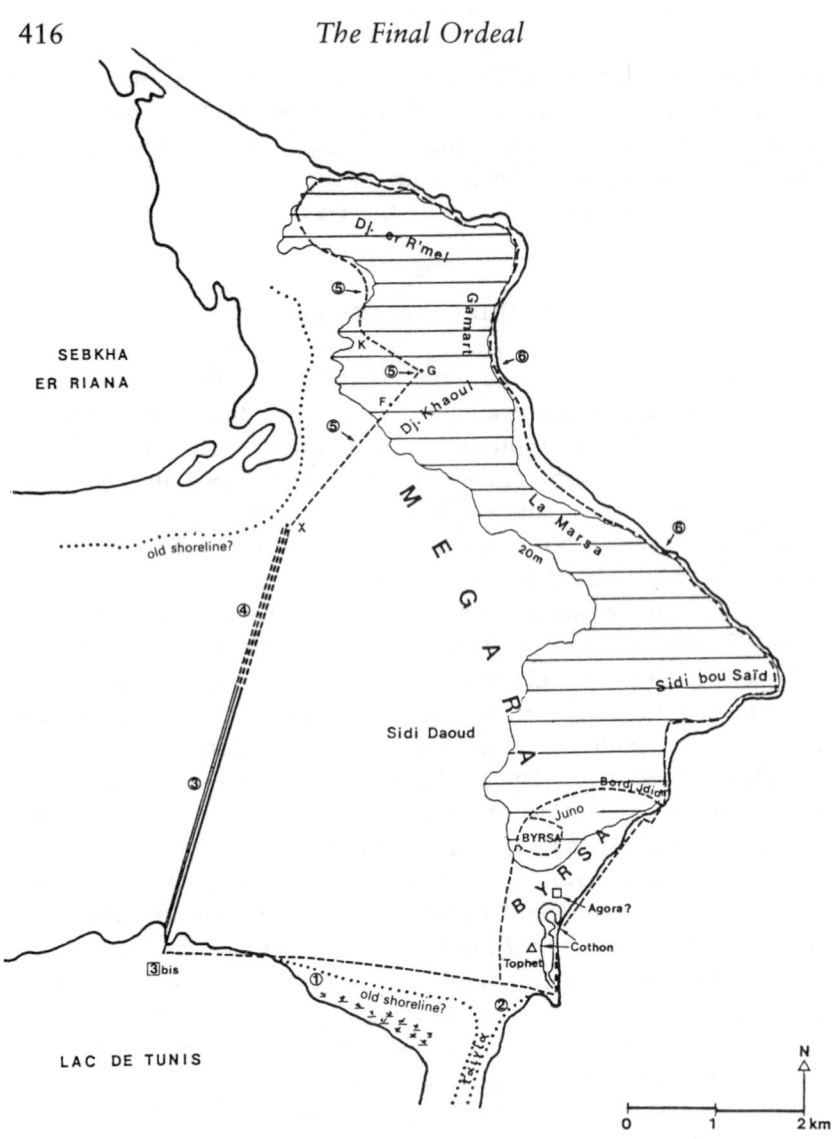

FIGURE 242 *Carthage's urban defences at the time of the third Punic War: realities and hypotheses (S. Lancel). 1 Hypothetical site of Censorinus' first camp (summer 149); 2 Censorinus' second camp on the* taenia *at the end of 149 (Appian,* Libyca, *99); 3 triple wall across the isthmus, the traces of which were found by General Duval; 3b the return of the triple wall in the form of a single wall towards the east, on the lake shore (discoveries of 1911 and 1950); 4 a hypothetical extension of the triple wall on the isthmus; 5 Scipio's attack in 147 on two points of the single wall in the north; 6 the hypothetical sites of Mancinus' failed attack, at the beginning of 147 (Appian,* Libyca, *113), by the coastal cliff.*

given by Appian) and 40 cubits high (about 20 metres instead of Appian's 15).

It was this triple defence that the consul Manilius attacked during the summer of 149. His first attempt was in vain (Appian, *Libyca*, 97). But the account of it that has come down to us throws some light on the nature of the fortification: Manilius had first to fill in the trench (*taphros*), then force the small wall (*brachu epiteichisma*), that is, the parapet surmounting it, before setting about the high walls (*upsèla teichè*). The Roman consul tried again shortly afterwards but, continues Appian (*Libyca*, 97, *in fine*), he finally had to give up attacking on that side, after a great amount of effort that resulted only in making a breach in the outer wall; and here the Greek historian uses the more appropriate term *proteichisma*. To be even more exact about the nature of these defences, let us slightly anticipate events to pick up a note from Polybius, one of the most valuable because it comes from an eyewitness who was present alongside Scipio Aemilianus in the aftermath of the siege and was himself an expert on siege-craft. In the autumn of 147 the Carthaginian general Hasdrubal tried to negotiate a truce, or at least to extricate himself personally, and to this end had an interview with Gulussa, the Numidian king and Rome's ally. The meeting took place on the isthmus: Hasdrubal crossed the high wall and stayed, says Polybius (XXXVIII, 7, 3), 'in the cover of the trench and the stockade'. These words of Polybius pinpoint Appian's terms: the outermost defence, towards the west, is the trench, bordered on the side of the high wall by a stockade, itself built on a small earth levee, and referred to by Appian sometimes as *epiteichisma* and sometimes, more correctly, as *proteichisma*.

The reader will perhaps be surprised that, if such monumental works were a reality, they have left hardly a trace on the ground. The archaeologist is less surprised, because he knows very well that at Carthage, where every stone that can be used for building is precious, all recoverable parts, even those from deep foundations, swiftly disappeared. However, following observations made from a plane and confirmed by aerial photography, military camps were positioned in 1949 by General Duval, Commander-in-Chief of the French forces in Tunisia, at various points marking out the track he had noticed, which cut across the isthmus from a north-north-east direction. This track, which might be supposed to reveal buried structures, was composed of three parallel bands. Excavation of the soil confirmed that tripartite division by revealing the existence, in several of the working areas opened up, of three principal elements:

FIGURE 243 *One of the banks pierced by post-holes found in General Duval's excavations on the isthmus of Carthage (J. Gintzburger).*

to the west, on the land side, a trench about 20 metres wide, followed by a 'bank' of about 4 metres, itself bordered on the east (thus on the town side) by a narrower trench about 5 metres wide. The most noticeable element in the graphic and photographic records remaining from this excavation (Lancel, 1989) is made up of these banks, which frequently present protuberances that may be seen as bastions. The bank and its bastions are often pierced by holes of between 30 and 40 centimetres in diameter, the bottoms frequently furnished with bases of amphorae, and it is reasonable to interpret them as post-holes (figure 243). There is general agreement (e.g. G. C. and C. Picard, 1982, p. 35) in recognizing traces of the Punic fortifications of the isthmus in the vestiges unearthed by those excavations, and more precisely the outer walls mentioned in the texts, as well as the trench and the stockaded bank. If General Duval had ordered investigations a few metres, or rather, a few dozen metres to the east of those structures, on the town side, he would have had the possibility of finding also the track of the principal wall, at least in the form of one of those 'negatives' which archaeologists working at Carthage now know well, but which were not so easy to perceive in his time.

At its southern extremity this triple fortification made an angle, from which was born the single wall going alongside Lake Tunis to join the harbour area, south of the town. During the summer of 149 it was the lot of Censorinus, the second consul, in command of the fleet, to attack this wall, concentrating, as Appian says (*Libyca*, 97), on its 'single corner', with the help of ladders set up on the lake shore, or from vessels moored on the lake near to its bank. This attempt having failed twice, Censorinus set up his camp at the foot of the rampart, on the lake shore. A little later, continues Appian (*Libyca*, 98), the consul partially filled in the lake to give himself more room to manoeuvre his siege machines, in particular his two battering-rams, one of which, manned by 6000 soldiers, succeeded in breaking down part of the wall, thus allowing the Romans to penetrate through the breach but without managing to maintain their hold there. From various details in Appian's text the approximate site of Censorinus' first camp may be inferred, and also, no doubt a short distance away, his attack platform, on a shoreline of the lake situated slightly to the north of the line on modern maps (figure 242). At the beginning of this century, exceptionally low waters allowed Dr Carton to observe, not far away from the shoreline of that time, wall structures certainly belonging to that south wall, at a point near to its join with the triple defence of the isthmus. And shortly after General Duval's excavations, examinations undertaken at the same point confirmed their presence (Lancel, 1989, pp. 273–6). To return to Censorinus, as the scorching midsummer heat had arrived – thus at the height of summer 149 – he could not stay long at the foot of that wall whose height prevented him from taking advantage of the off-sea breeze, those refreshing winds which, during Carthage's summer, come from the north-north-east quarter (Appian, *Libyca*, 99). It was for this reason that the consul then moved his camp seawards, setting it up on the sandy strip (the *taenia* or *glôssa* of our texts) near the mouth of the harbours that would become the bridgehead from which the final assault would be launched in 147.

Meanwhile 149 came to an end without the Romans being able to take advantage of the difficult position of Carthage, which was abandoned by the great Phoenician cities of the Sahel, Hadrumetum, Leptis, Thapsus and Acholla, following Utica's example (Appian, *Libyca*, 94). Trying to dislodge Hasdrubal, who, with his troops, held the Djebel Zaghouan region and intercepted communications with Byzacena, the consul Manilius let himself be taken by surprise in the bed of a wadi near Nepheris and escaped unscathed thanks only to the cool head and tactical sense of one of his tribunes, Scipio Aemilianus, son of Aemilius Paulus and adopted grandson of Scipio Africanus. Shortly before his death, with words borrowed from Homer (*Odyssey*, X, 495) crowning him, so to speak, with immortality, Cato the Elder had said of this young man, 'He alone is wise; the rest flit about like shadows.'

SCIPIO AEMILIANUS

At the beginning of 148, sensing that his end was nigh, Massinissa sent for Scipio Aemilianus to come to his capital, to help him settle the succession of the Numidian kingdom he had received from Africanus. But by the time Scipio Aemilianus arrived at Cirta (Constantine) the old king had died. Having the authority to arbitrate, the Roman officer arranged the succession judiciously, setting aside the sons born of concubines, and dividing the royal power among the three legitimate sons: Micipsa, who received the capital and the kingdom's administration, Mastanabal, the jurisdiction, and Gulussa, the command of the armies. Scipio returned with Gulussa, whose troops reinforced the Roman contingents. Shortly afterwards, he obtained another success with the surrender of Hasdrubal's chief lieutenant, Phamaias, who went over to the Roman camp with more than 2000 of his men. The rest of 148 passed with the position unaltered in Carthage. The two consuls leaving office were succeeded by L. Calpurnius Piso, who chose as legate L. Hostilius Mancinus, entrusted with the fleet. The two new leaders opted to carry on the war against those cities which had remained loyal to the Punic capital, to bring them down and thus deprive the Carthaginians of resources of food and manpower. In Cap Bon the strong defences of Clypea (Kelibia) resisted, but Neapolis (Nabeul) yielded to Piso and was sacked.

In the spring of 147 Mancinus, cruising with the fleet off the coast of Carthage, noticed that in the north sector of the town, on the Megara side, the rampart was poorly defended where the rocky coast made access difficult, either in the vicinity of Gammarth, or more probably where the heights of Sidi-bou-Saïd plunge into the sea by way of cliffs or steep slopes. A detachment of a few dozen men was sent to scale those slopes and prepare to get over the wall. The Carthaginians, seeing them raising their ladders, came out through a postern but were put to flight by the men in the commando group, who were then joined by Mancinus and the main body of the troop and gained a foothold inside the wall. But that improvised attack, carried out by men who were inadequately armed and without victuals, was in danger of turning into a disaster (Appian, *Libyca*, 113–14). The next day Mancinus and his men, numbering several hundred, had been driven back against the wall by the Carthaginians and were about to be crushed when they were saved by the unexpected intervention of Scipio Aemilianus.

Although he was not yet of the required age to fill this office, the *comitia* for the year 147 had in fact elected the adoptive grandson of Africanus. And the people made sure that he was appointed by name to command the army in Africa, instead of lots being drawn between the two consuls of the year. Scipio Aemilianus made up the necessary numbers by enlistment and landed at Utica, taking with him as lieutenant his most faithful friend, C. Laelius, and accompanied by two of the foremost Greeks, the philosopher Panaetius of Rhodes and the historian Polybius. His arrival at Utica happened to coincide with Mancinus' improvised expedition, and he at once went to his rescue. There are differing versions of what followed. According to Appian (*Libyca*, 114), Scipio took on board his vessels the Romans who were in difficulties, hastily sent Mancinus back to Rome and went to set up camp a short distance from Carthage. According to the Byzantine abridger of Dio Cassius, Zonaras, Mancinus was able to stay on with Scipio's help for a time in Megara, which allowed him in the following year, after Scipio had captured the town, to boast in Rome that he had been the first to penetrate it. He is said to have displayed in the forum a picture showing a map of Carthage, with representations of the different Roman attacks, standing by it and supplying details and explanations to anyone who wanted to hear them. It is not hard to believe that the operations in Africa excited imaginations in Rome; war games enthusiasts did not avoid the ridiculous or the odious. Plutarch relates that, at the time of the siege, a Roman knight at a feast had an enormous cake in the shape of the town served to his guests, who were invited to cut it into pieces. This anecdote is no doubt apocryphal.

Carthage's city wall remained the real hero of this long siege. After re-establishing order and discipline in his army, Scipio tried out the defences of the enemy system on several occasions during 147. He also made an attempt on the large suburban area of Megara, not however as Mancinus had done, coming from the open sea, but doubtless starting from the isthmus and going along the northern edge of the lower shore of the *sinus Uticensis* (the present-day

Sebkha er-Riana). At two points his men attacked what seems to have been a single wall, like the southern section bordering Lake Tunis. Here we come across a rather disturbing episode, likely to cast some suspicion on the credibility of our source (Appian, *Libyca*, 117); for Scipio's soldiers rather miraculously happened upon a tower (*purgos*) belonging to a private owner, certainly situated outside the rampart but so close that from the tower the Romans were able to throw an improvised bridge across to the top of the wall, gain a foothold on the curtain wall and open a gate to the main body of the troop, allowing 4000 men to get into Megara. Can anyone believe that the Carthaginians were so ill-advised as to leave standing in such proximity to their rampart a building ready-made to serve the plans of a possible attacker? But the doubt inspired by this event as reported by Appian does not reflect on the overall account of the undertaking, which is confirmed by another source. The attempt was merely a reconnaissance, for Scipio judged it imprudent to venture farther into this suburban zone, made up of gardens separated from one another by low walls and hedges, crisscrossed by a multitude of irrigation channels, in short, suitable for all kinds of ambush. He withdrew his troops, but the incursion at least had the result that Hasdrubal, fearing for the safety of the heart of the town following this strike, abandoned the camp he still held outside the wall, from which he could harass the enemy, to take refuge in Byrsa. And one of our sources specifies that the Punic general reinforced the town centre's own enclosing wall – the one, says Zonaras, IX, 29, that 'rose in front of the houses' – with trenches and stockades, in the manner of the external defences of the triple wall on the isthmus. The account of this phase is invaluable for us in that it adds to several other texts which suggest quite clearly that the name Byrsa applied not only to the citadel in the strict sense of the term, where we shall soon see the last survivors from the siege take refuge up on the hill, but also, in a broader sense, to the town of Carthage in its truly urban definition, as opposed to Megara (Lancel, 1988, pp. 69–70).

In this war of positions, shutting all Carthage's defenders within its walls was a turning-point that proved decisive. Scipio finished sealing them in by cutting off the isthmus, parallel with the Punic fortification, with an entrenched camp of a rectangular layout provided with towers, the middle one of which, topped by a high watchtower, allowed observation of everything that was happening in the Punic camp. Shortly afterwards, to complete the blockade and render any reprovisioning by sea virtually impossible, the

FIGURE 244 *In the foreground, cornice blocks from Carthage's sea wall in the Hellenistic period (third to second century BC); in the background, a modern drainage canal from the rectangular basin of the Punic commercial harbour; during the cutting of this channel the blocks were brought to light (F. Rakob).*

Roman general decided to close access to the ports by constructing a mole in the direction of their pierhead; its exact line is still disputed, as no trace of it has been discovered. It was obviously in Scipio's interest to keep this work as short as possible, while maintaining a sufficient distance from the south wall of the enclosure (the one ending at the ports) to ensure that those who had to labour on it were out of reach of shots. It is therefore probable that the mole went crosswise over the present-day small bay of Le Kram, starting from a point situated on the lagoon strip (the *taenia* or *glôssa* of our texts), between today's areas of Kherredine and Le Kram (figure 242).

A bitter struggle then began in this sector of the harbours. The Carthaginians had not waited until work on the mole was completed before finding an answer. Secretly, working mainly at night to avoid being seen, they prepared a new access to their harbours on the east side, probably starting from the circular basin of the military harbour, and at the same time contrived to fit out a small combat fleet with used materials and old patched-up boats. When both the ships and the new channel were ready, they made a breach in the wall of the town's sea front (figure 244); through that exit went several dozen triremes and quinqueremes, and a quantity of other smaller boats. The effect was one of total surprise, and the only mistake the Carthaginians made, says Appian (*Libyca*, 121), was not to take more advantage of it.

A mole is a dam, but it is also a bridge thrown from one point to another, and Scipio intended to use it in this way, to gain a foothold on the shelf of the outer harbour, the *choma* of the ancient authors, Falbe's quadrilateral for the archaeologists (above, p. 180). Anyone who knows the peaceful fishing port that the small cove of Le Kram is today will find it difficult to imagine the noise and fury that filled those parts in the days of autumn 147. On this quay the besieged had constructed an additional rampart, the better to defend it. Scipio had his siege machines moved along the roadway of the mole, and the Carthaginians burned them the first time in a desperate sortie. However, the attacker had the last word, establishing himself firmly on the landing stage and, in his turn, building a fortification to counter the low Punic rampart, from which the defenders were finally driven. At the beginning of the winter of 147–146, 4000 men were posted there by Scipio to hold this highly strategic point (Appian, *Libyca*, 125).

The dénouement was approaching. During the winter, with the help of Laelius and the Numidian king Gulussa, the consul managed to eliminate the pockets of resistance that still survived in the territories near Carthage, and in particular at the base of Cap Bon, around the city of Nepheris, which was captured after a long siege. In the following spring Scipio, who had kept his command although at the end of his consulate, decided that the time had come to finish matters with this crippled town, many of whose inhabitants had already succumbed to privation or their wounds.

THE FINAL ASSAULT AND DESTRUCTION OF CARTHAGE (SPRING 146)

One day in March or April 146 the final assault was ordered. It started from the quay of the outer harbour that had been held and fortified for several months by Scipio's men. Hasdrubal, believing that the attack would first target the rectangular basin of the merchant harbour, which in fact lay next to the quay, set fire to the neighbouring buildings, no doubt wooden warehouses. But Laelius, commanding the manoeuvre at that moment, made for the circular port and got his soldiers across its double enclosure by means of improvised bridges. The besieged were at the end of their strength and offered little resistance. Near the war harbour – and thus slightly north of this basin – stretched the esplanade of the great public square, the *agora*, of Greek texts. Scipio took possession of it and, as night had fallen, advanced no farther and camped there with his men (Appian, *Libyca*, 127). Next morning, the soldiers rewarded themselves for their trouble by invading the temple of Apollo, which apparently gave on to the square, and detaching with their sword-points the gold plates adorning the tabernacle of the god's chapel, in order to share them out.

The defences of the lower town having yielded, the final objective was the citadel of Byrsa, the last bastion of resistance, where tens of thousands of men, women and children had taken refuge. The consul called on 4000 men who had not yet been in the fight and made them converge on the citadel, in particular, making them advance along three streets which ascended to it from the square. These streets, says Appian (*Libyca*, 128), were bordered by six-storeyed houses, from the tops of which the Roman soldiers were attacked with all kinds of projectiles. These houses of six storeys – even if such precision must not be taken literally – were obviously multiple dwellings; it is all the easier to recognize in them the *insulae* or blocks recently unearthed by the French archaeological mission on the south-east slope of Byrsa, because the principal street on either side of which they stood lies on an axis that joins this slope of the hill in a straight line to the quarter adjacent to the edge of the war harbour (above, p. 168). It must therefore be one of the three streets along which the Roman legionaries advanced. That advance was difficult. They had to gain mastery over each of these houses in turn, and on reaching their roofs pass from one to the other, getting over the street space by means of beams used as makeshift bridges; the width of the cross streets in the quarter unearthed on Byrsa – averaging five metres – does not rule out the possibility of such a feat.

Meanwhile fighting was raging in the streets, where bodies hurled down from the upper floors added to the victims of the mêlée at ground level. Appian (*Libyca*, 129) has described these nightmare scenes with a precision of horrific detail unprecedented in an ancient account of this kind. A notable example is when the area had been delivered to the flames block by block and the walls knocked down, and the street cleaners came in the wake of the soldiers, with the task of clearing space for the passage of further attacking waves. Of course, apocalyptic descriptions of the capture of towns are one of the clichés of Hellenistic historical writing (Krings, 1989, pp. 334–5). But let us not be too hasty in suspecting Appian of having amplified the account of facts passed on by Polybius and gratuitously taking a morbid delight in portraying army servants using hooks to drag both dead and living to be flung pell-mell, with the debris of the houses, into pits from which still-moving heads and limbs could sometimes be seen emerging, only to be crushed by the galloping horses. Those atrocious scenes were the savage harvest of so much hatred sown on both sides. When Hasdrubal, the previous year, in his fury at the Romans' incursion into Megara, had had his prisoners mutilated and burnt in full view of their comrades on the ramparts of Byrsa, he could not have been unaware of what he would reap later. Archaeological excavation has also borne witness to these atrocities. Scipio's *lithologoi*, as Appian calls them, had not been able to clear the roads of every trace of these terrible combats and, under the blocks of stone that still obstructed them, in particular at the level of the crossroads of streets II and III, the discovery of human bones testified to the reality of the scenes described by the Greek historian. But the hundreds of men and women who perished at that time were buried in mass graves hastily created not far from there: these are the 'communal graves' discovered by Père Delattre in the neighbourhood west of the quarter (Lancel, 1988, pp. 85–6).

Six days and nights passed in this way. On the seventh, some of the besieged emerged from the citadel and came to implore Scipio to spare the lives of at least those who surrendered. And out came some 50,000 survivors to whom Scipio granted their lives, and who ended their days in slavery. There remained nearly a thousand renegades, who could expect no mercy; they sought a last refuge in the temple of Eschmoun, where they were joined by Hasdrubal and his family. At the last moment the Punic general weakened; holding a suppliant's branch, he came to prostrate himself before Scipio, begging for pity. The cowardice of a man was redeemed by a woman: dressed as if for a festival, Hasdrubal's wife stood on the high wall of the temple, facing the Roman general and her husband, whom she reproached for his betrayal. Then she cast herself and her children into the flames of the temple, which the renegades had set ablaze, and there they perished. On the city's last day this holocaust linked up in legend with that of Dido, the founding queen.

Throughout its history Carthage had always glowed red with the light of pyres. The one that consumed the city – and archaeologists find the carbonized layer everywhere, compacted by the centuries –

lasted another ten days. In 212 Marcellus had wept over the beauty of Syracuse, which his soldiers were making ready to take by storm and devastate. In front of the fire that destroyed Carthage Scipio, it is said, shed tears and spoke aloud these lines from Homer: 'A day will come when Ilium, that holy town, will perish, and Priam also will perish, and his people, so skilled in handling the spear' (*Iliad*, IV, 164–5). And in answer to Polybius, who asked him the reason for the quotation, he is said to have replied that he feared lest it might one day be used in regard to his own homeland. Nero, very much later, would carry this ham acting to the extent of declaiming the *Iliou Persis* before the blazing inferno in Rome which he himself had ignited. But on Scipio Aemilianus' part it was the desire and the means to exorcise fate. The cries ringing in his ears as Carthage burned were the cries of the town martyred above all others, the cries that ceaselessly obsessed Antiquity, of this protomartyr Troy; cries whose echo has not completely faded, those of the 'cruel night which for an entire people was an eternal night', as Racine would say.

Carthage entered its own night, and silence fell on the ruins of what had been one of the most beautiful towns in the ancient world.

11

The Double Survival

Besides its institutions and laws, three orders of reality on very different planes have always constituted a State, especially in Antiquity: its walls and the material expression of its urban existence; its temples and cults; its language and the written traces of its history and past. Walls may fall, temples disappear, books be carried away or destroyed; but that immaterial content formed by its language and its religion can escape and survive destruction or be reborn.

First of all, the walls. Certainly, Carthage was well and truly burnt and destroyed by Scipio in the spring of 146 BC. But using Appian's text as a point of departure (*Libyca*, 134), in which he reports that a ten-member commission dispatched by the Roman Senate ordered what was left of the town to be razed, a strange and gradual amplification developed in modern historiography. It is to Niebuhr, a pioneer in ancient history at the beginning of the nineteenth century, that we owe the picture of Scipio having a plough driven over the ruins of Carthage. The episode of the salt scattered on the soil first saw light through the pen of B. L. Hallward at the beginning of this century in the *Cambridge Ancient History*, and seems to have had its origin in the Bible, where we see in the Book of Judges (9:45) Abimelech sowing salt on the town of Sichem that he had destroyed. Such powerful images were destined for success, and it is not surprising to find them reproduced until fairly close to our own times. Recent excavations have enabled them to be reduced to a reality that is more modest in terms of the imaginary but nevertheless more reassuring for the archaeologist (figure 245). In the seventies, on the slopes of Byrsa, when we dug out walls that still sometimes reached two metres in height – but they were those of the 'six-storeyed houses' mentioned by Appian – journalists were able to write jokingly that the French archaeological mission was in

FIGURE 245 *Byrsa's Punic quarter under the heavy foundations of Roman Carthage's monumental centre (S. Lancel).*

the act of proving that, in spite of the elderly Cato's *delenda est Carthago*, Carthage had not been destroyed. It was on those very real and still partly standing vestiges of a martyred town, which it was forbidden to inhabit but not to visit as a tourist, that Marius came to sit, according to Plutarch (*Marius*, 40, 9), slightly more than half a century later when he had gone into exile to flee Sulla's dictatorship, meditating in his turn on the frailty of human affairs. And following the town's destruction, that was how it was for over a century, during which time Rome, established at Utica where the governor of the new African province resided, contented itself with 'watching over the corpse', to use Mommsen's phrase. The latter is more jocular than perfectly accurate, from the historical viewpoint; but it is true that the attempt at colonization for which C. Gracchus had taken the initiative in 122 came to nothing at the end of a year, and even that had remained on the fringe of the accursed urban perimeter of Carthage.

We must wait for the establishment of a new order in Rome before the ban affecting the ground of the destroyed city was lifted. We must attribute the decision to create a colony in Carthage to

Caesar, taken *in extremis* shortly before his death on the Ides of March 44. It would be given a real existence a little later by Octavian Augustus under the name *colonia Iulia Concordia Karthago*, subsequently to be strengthened in 29 by a *deductio* of colonists (Le Glay, 1985, pp. 235–47). Recent excavations have revealed that the new capital of the Roman province of Proconsular Africa took shape only gradually, and also that, in its material reality, at least on the fringes of the framework planned in theory, it never completely filled the street grid of *cardines* and *decumani* mapped out by the Emperor Augustus' surveyors (Hurst, 1985, pp. 149–55). This 'survey' had taken its origin from a central point situated on the summit of the hill of Byrsa, probably at the very place where the dramatic epilogue to six centuries of Punic Carthage's history had occurred. We saw earlier (above, p. 151) how, at the very end of the first century BC, an enormous rectangular platform was formed on the site of the original hilltop, intended to become the monumental centre of Roman Carthage (Gros, 1990, pp. 548–51). For the Roman town planners, a large level and orthogonal surface lent itself better to the construction of edifices of great size: a forum, a judicial basilica, temples bordered by porticoes. But above all, perhaps, on the political plane, by completely overturning the former aspect of the place, these huge earthworks offered the advantage of erasing a symbol, that of the focal point of the Punic city's power and its relentless resistance. When the excavation reached its close, what it revealed more obviously here than anywhere else in Carthage was the strong image of the remains of the Punic houses taken by storm in the spring of 146 on Byrsa's slopes, trampled down by the heavy and massive foundations of Roman Carthage's proud buildings (figure 245). After the death of the city came the burial of its last traces.

INSTITUTIONAL AND RELIGIOUS SURVIVAL

In great contrast to the town's second death was the astounding survival shown in the same period by its religion, language and, to a lesser extent, institutions.

Let us start with the latter. The most striking example of their vitality will take us to the strongly Punicized Numidian kingdom which formed the *pagus Thuscae* in the time of Carthage's independence (above, p. 261). At Makthar, the centre of that former Punic administrative district, which had remained an indigenous *civitas*, the municipal magistrates were suffetes, as in Hannibal's Carthage. But the epigraphic text that makes them known to us, and is datable to the second half of the first century AD, numbers three of them, instead of two in the former Punic capital, and in company with G. C. Picard (1957, pp. 39–40 and 61) it may be thought that the triumvirate – this college also sometimes appears under the Latin name in the Makthar texts – was due to the influence of Numidian customary law. Sometimes right up to the time of Trajan – in other words the apogee of the Empire – when Africa was already largely Romanized, a few other cities and not minor ones (Althiburos and Thugga in the same region, Leptis Magna in Tripolitania, Calama and Cirta in Numidia) preserved those magistracies inherited from Punic tradition (G. C. Picard, 1974, pp. 125–33). Near Makthar, in a little town named Magraoua (without doubt the ancient Macota) inscriptions have been found instancing the *baalim* ('notables') of Makthar at the time of the *rabs* ('chiefs', 'lords') Iasuchtan (a Libyan name) and Bodeschmoun (a Punic name). Similarly in the second half of the first century AD, and in cities of more modest size, the survival has been noted at municipal level of another form of official title of Carthaginian origin, borne by personages whose names are mentioned in the Semitic way, giving their forebears over one or two generations. Outside the colonies or *municipia* where the influx of population from Italy accelerated it within frameworks directly based on the Roman model, Romanization was in fact a slow process.

Of all those things that last, loyalty to the ancient gods and their cults is the most immaterial and thus that which has the greatest likelihood of withstanding change. For a long time yet – a century and a half, sometimes more – those divinities were invoked under their Semitic names. A few kilometres south-west of Makthar, at *Mididi* (Hr Medded), a recently discovered inscription (Ferjaoui, 1990, pp. 113–19), written in 'neo-Punic', lets it be known that the citizens of this town had dedicated a sanctuary to Astart, the Astarte whose *interpretatio* would soon be triumphant under the name of Venus but would never completely efface her original oriental character. But even more certainly and in a more lasting fashion, Tanit survived under the title of Juno Caelestis and Baal Hammon under that of Saturn. The great popularity and long persistence of the latter illustrate the perfect adaptation of Carthage's mighty god to an African religious mentality which his cult, maintained for centuries in a specifically Punic context, had largely contributed to fashioning.

FROM BAAL HAMMON TO AFRICAN SATURN

Of course, a modification is noticeable between Carthage's tutelary divinity and the great African god of the Roman era, and princip- ally a broadening of the religious field covered by the divine personality, to the point where the leading scholar on the subject has said that Saturn was Baal Hammon's disloyal heir (Le Glay, 1966, p. 68). Some have recently gone further, seeing in the trans- ition from Baal Hammon to Saturn – by likening him to Kronos, as he is shown on the stelae of El Hofra, near Constantine (Berthier, 1955, pp. 167–78) – the passage from a divinity of a transcendent nature, who does not mingle with men and acts through interces- sors (Tanit or Astarte), to a god who is certainly endowed with manifold and mighty powers, but is more familiarly ensconced in the bosom of the pantheon of divinities of Indo-European origin (G. C. Picard, 1990, p. 97). In fact, analysis of the imposing collec- tion of stelae relating to this divinity reveals an evolution at the end of which, in the third century AD, when the whole region was Romanized in depth, Saturn appears perfectly anthropomorphized, flanked by his attentive escorts, the Dioscuri, but without having lost any of the dreaded power of a demanding and almost unique god. In an initial phase, during the first century AD, the 'Lord Baal Hammon' was invoked by name in Punic in texts, usually inserted in very sober decoration, often reduced to a reproduction of the 'sign of Tanit', the lunar crescent, sometimes the caduceus, palms and bunches of grapes. These last designs, symbols of fertility, came to dominate in a series of stelae that are chronologically later, those known as the stelae of Ghorfa, a rich collection gleaned from different sites in central Tunisia, now dispersed between London, Paris, Vienna, the Bardo National Museum and Dougga. Recent research has enabled the origin of the majority of these stelae to be attributed to a small locality, Magraoua, near Makthar (M'Charek, 1988, pp. 731–60). On the monuments of this series dated to the second century, which bear a flat relief or one that stands out very slightly, the god is no longer named in a text that is in any case reduced to the Latin dedicatory formula or even nonexistent (figure 246). On some of these stelae with an especially exuberant decora- tion, this is divided into sections one above the other, one being occupied by a representation of Saturn brandishing a thunderbolt in his right hand, which likens him to Jupiter, and in his left holding a pine cone on a staff, which makes him a Liber Pater. Then in the

FIGURE 246   *Neo-Punic stelae: on the left, a stele from the Ghorfa series; on the right, a stele consecrated to Saturn on 8 November 323 (Musée national du Bardo, Tunis).*

third century came the fine collection of 'stelae to Saturn' – they usually bear, just below the triangular pediment, a band with the invocation in Latin: *Saturno Aug(usto) sacrum* – which are carved almost in the round, and where the power and glory of the god are truly manifested. One of the finest examples is a stele discovered quite a while ago at Siliana (figure 247): under the eagle on the pediment, which the god has in common with Jupiter, Saturn is enthroned in majesty, leaning on a sacrificial victim and holding in his right hand his symbolic attribute, the *harpe* or billhook, flanked by the Dioscuri, his attendants. The Victories framing the scene

FIGURE 247   *A stele to Saturn from Siliana, known as the 'Boglio stele'*
(third or beginning of the fourth century AD) (Musée national du Bardo,
Tunis; Gallimard 'Univers des Formes').

emphasize his triumphal nature: like the sun, which he also per-
sonifies, Saturn is invincible (*invictus*). Below, three ornamental
sections, pleasantly full of action, emphasize that Saturn reigns as
'lord and master' – he often bears the title *Dominus*, a translation
of the Punic *Adon* – not only over Cuttinus, the dedicant, who has
'acquitted himself of his vow, together with his family' (*votum
solvit cum suis*), but over an entire peasant society whose prosperity
he ensures. The scene of sacrifice, in which the lord of the estate is
seen placing granules of incense on the altar flanked by a ram and
a bull-calf, in the presence of women bearing fruit-filled baskets,
consecrates a happy abundance due to the work in the fields represented lower down and accomplished under the divinity's benevolent
patronage. 'There is no mystical uneasiness in this work,' it has
been said (G. C. Picard, 1954, p. 121). No apparent uneasiness
indeed. But can we look beyond appearances when observing these

images which obey rules of representation that are themselves changing?

Saturn as Baal Hammon's successor was not only the champion of African paganism; he continued to be an essential part of popular religion at a time when Christianity was increasingly gaining ground. A stele from the vicinity of *Vaga* (Beja), precisely dated 8 November 323 by a mention of the consuls for that year, shows him enthroned above a scene of sacrifice, accompanied by a sort of double in the form of a sun spirit and represented with that stiffness and fixity peculiar to the art of late Antiquity, in which it is often difficult to say how much is attributable to clumsiness and how much concern for hieratic imagery (figure 246). The text says that the ex-voto is the act of a priest, named M. Gargilius Zabo, who has celebrated his sacrifice under the presidency of the 'superior' (*magister*) of the priestly college (Beschaouch, 1968, pp. 253–68). This inscription joins others which allow us to glimpse the stages of allegiance to the god within the framework of a real clergy. Even before his birth the believer was first consecrated to Saturn by his parents' vow, then initiated at adolescence; thereafter he could remain an ordinary believer or pledge himself to divine service, that is, become a *sacerdos*. If that were the case, at the age of sixty-five he would celebrate a sort of jubilee by 'submitting to the yoke' of the god, to whom he then subjected himself completely (this is the rite of *intratio sub jugum*, where the Latin words used echo the ritual phrases of biblical texts) (Le Glay, 1988, pp. 232–4). Such texts show quite plainly the strength of the African Saturn's hold over souls and what his demands were. Let us not forget that nearly everywhere in Africa, from Sabratha in Tripolitania – where a recently discovered and still unpublished sacrificial area functioned at least until the time of Domitian – to the sites of deepest Numidia, at *Cirta*-Constantine and elsewhere, as far as Tipasa, on the coasts of Mauretania (above, p. 99), tophets continued to be in use. Certainly, a rite of substitution was generally practised, of *molchomor*, with lambs and kids for victims: *vita pro vita, sanguine pro sanguine, anima pro anima*, as it is written on the stelae of N'gaous. But human sacrifice remained under the surface, and this sacrificial tradition has recently been suggested as an explanation for the strange outbreaks of almost ritual suicides, notably in Numidia in the middle of the fourth century, that affected certain groups of Christians who were opposed to the established order, the *circumcelliones* (Lepelley, 1980, pp. 261–71). It will be remembered that, according to Tertullian, child sacrifice was still perpetrated in secret. There is a disturbing picture to be added to this record, dating from the same period. It comes to us from the account of the sufferings of Saints Perpetua and Felicitas, who were martyred at Carthage in 203. The text says that those condemned to death and exposed to the wild beasts in the amphitheatre were clad in ritual garments; for the men, that meant the attire of the priests of Saturn. As G. C. Picard rightly observed (1954, p. 134), it was a legal way of carrying on the old tradition of human sacrifice.

As for the name of the god, for us it is misleading and reductive. Under the name Saturn the Africans actually worshipped a cosmic god, lord of the sky and the earth, and of the infernal regions. Saturn is also Pluto, and like him *frugifer*, protector of harvests, and in fact he can be seen, in the Thinissut terracotta which belongs to the Roman period, wearing a *modius* (bushel) on his head, just like Pluto (above, figure 104). In popular religiosity he became confused with Jupiter, and an inscription from Constantine goes as far as making that confusion explicit in the introductory invocation: *Iovi Saturno Augusto*. Even if it did not reach the point of permitting its beneficiary to eclipse the other divinities of classical paganism completely, such syncretism turned the African god into a crude competitor for the unique god of the Bible. 'It was a step on the path towards monotheism,' wrote Gsell; yes, but along a parallel, not a convergent route. On his own, Saturn typified the deep current of Semitization that flowed through North Africa up till the end of Roman domination.

SURVIVALS OF THE PUNIC LANGUAGE

Carthage's ultimate revenge on its executioners was the extraordinary persistence of its language. Of course, the fall of Carthage brutally interrupted the practice of the official writing of Punic. But we saw with regard to the stelae that a cursive 'neo-Punic', which was increasingly altered and thus increasingly difficult to decipher, continued to be used until nearly the end of the first century AD, that is, two and a half centuries after the destruction of Carthage and its political death. In the end the skill of writing it disappeared, but orally the language stayed alive. People still spoke Punic, even if they no longer wrote it, or rather, it went on being written but in Latin characters or, more rarely, in Greek letters. In the middle of the third century AD, soldiers posted at Bu Ngem, a small fort of the Tripolitanian *limes* about a hundred kilometres south of the shores of the Syrtis Major, spoke a sort of pidgin made up of Punic mixed with Latin, which they sometimes transcribed on *ostraka* or scratched on the walls of their barrack-rooms (Marichal, 1979, pp. 436–7). Again in Tripolitania (the western regions of present-day Libya) there were findings in different sites – Leptis Magna, Zliten, Bir ed-Dreder, chiefly – of dozens of texts that long remained enigmatic, datable for the most part to the fourth century; they were first regarded as 'Latino-Libyan' inscriptions. We are indebted to the great Italian Semitic scholar G. Levi Della Vida for having actually recognized as 'Latino-Punic' some small texts – most frequently funerary inscriptions or dedications on monuments – in which, as in the Latin version of the Punic passages in Plautus' *Poenulus*, the Semitic words are transcribed in Latin (Levi Della Vida, 1963, pp. 65–91).

The 'Latino-Punics' of Tripolitania (conveniently gathered by F. Vattioni (1976, pp. 536–55) and M. G. Amadasi-Guzzo (1990a, pp. 107–8)) do not permit the slightest doubt about what should be understood by *Punica lingua* when, at the beginning of the fifth century, Saint Augustine presented it, on the same level as Latin, as the language of the Christians in Africa (*Tractatus in epistulam Iohannis*, 2, 3). The Bishop of Hippo even stated precisely: *Punica, id est Afra*, 'Punic, that is to say, African,' for in his view the very debased Punic that was spoken almost everywhere around him was, in contrast to the universality of Latin, the cultural mark that was specifically *African*. The language was all around him, and first of all at Hippo, his episcopal town. The sermons he delivered there contain many allusions to Punic; before his faithful flock, when he refers to a Punic proverb he always quotes it in Latin because, he says, not all his listeners could speak Punic, which means that a good many understood it (*Sermones*, 167, 4). He himself had a fairly limited knowledge of Punic, as may be seen, among other texts, in a moving passage from a dialogue with his son Adeodatus, still an adolescent, on the meaning of a Punic word (*De magistro*, 13, 44). To tell the truth, it was chiefly in rural circles that Punic was indispensable to communication and also pastoral activities (Lancel, 1982b, pp. 270–3). Knowing Punic was a necessary if not a sufficient condition to be a cleric or bishop in Numidia's country areas and little townships (the present-day Algerian east and the frontier zone with Tunisia). To quote but one instance, it was that competence alone which decided Augustine to elevate to the episcopacy, in an area bordering on his vast diocese of Hippo, a young cleric of the name of Antoninus, whose conduct would soon cause him bitterly to regret that decision.

When Saint Augustine died within the walls of Hippo that had been laid low by the Vandal hordes in 430, people had been speaking Punic in Africa for over a thousand years. If a culture's capacity to take hold is measured by the length of life and survival of its language, that figure deserves consideration. And Dido's language – but was it really the same, so many centuries later? – certainly outlived the arrival of the Vandals. It was very probably still being spoken when Belisarius regained control of Africa for the Byzantines in the sixth century. The end of the ancient world, in North Africa, favoured the constitution of cultural cells. We can bet that Punic-speaking pockets were still surviving when, 150 years later, other Semites from Arabia implanted a brand-new Islam in what was called the Maghreb. And there is no shortage of sympathizers who think that this Islam and its cultural environment found a ready-made breeding ground there (Fantar, 1990a, p. 66). But that is another story.

CARTHAGE'S ARCHAEOLOGICAL RENAISSANCE

Carthage's second survival is due to the men of our own time, to those – scholars or the simply curious – who, although generally humanists who had read their authors, refused to let themselves be locked into the 'closed corpus' – as E. Leroy Ladurie said somewhere – of classical sources. Polybius and Diodorus, Livy and Appian are essential reading, as is proved by the frequency of references to them in the preceding pages. They supply the plot and the essence of this history that runs over several centuries. But their gaze is one that falls on a vanquished state, above all viewed in its involvement in a chain of circumstances leading to its downfall. And if one kept to the texts, Carthage would be no more than the ultimately unfortunate and always slightly abstract partner of Magna Graecia, then of Rome. It was archaeology that restored its personality, an ambiguous personality I have frequently stressed, as might be expected of a culture mediating between East and West.

Archaeological recognition of Carthage and Punic civilization is recent: it goes back slightly more than a century. Who could be surprised? In the Middle Ages and the dawn of modern times, in that Ifriqiya so prodigiously rich in traces of the past, what leapt to the eyes of travellers were the often remarkable heights of still-standing monuments from the Roman era. Rarely was their attention held by a pre-Roman building preserved in the middle of a clearly later monumental context. Nevertheless, that was the case at the beginning of the seventeenth century when a member of the Aix parliament, Nicolas Fabri de Peiresc, dissuaded a former prisoner of the Barbary pirates who had been freed and then converted to Islam, Thomas d'Arcos, from despoiling the Dougga mausoleum of its Punico-Libyan inscription (Février, 1989, pp. 26–8). We have seen (above, p. 307) that others did not have the same restraint. In the eighteenth century, several European travellers left accounts of their expeditions in 'Barbary' (Brahimi, 1976), but the ruins they described were Roman. It was an exception when they were able, like Thomas Shaw, an English chaplain in residence in Algiers for a dozen years or so around 1730, to notice a monument from a preceding era, in this instance the 'Kbour er-Roumia' or 'Tomb of the Christian Woman', near Tipasa.

It happened that certain of those travellers, sometimes famous ones, were disappointed. Such was the case with Chateaubriand who, returning from his trip to Greece and the Holy Land, came to Tunis in 1807 and naturally made the excursion to Carthage; unfortunately the site at that time was bare and desolate, no longer bristling with still identifiable monuments as El Bekri had seen it in the eleventh century and El Idrissi in the twelfth. Meanwhile, Carthage had been used as a quarry, not only for the building of Tunis nearby, but also of Kairouan and, overseas, of Genoa and Pisa, when Andrea Doria, Charles V's admiral, had seized La Goulette in 1535. Chateaubriand made a note of the impression he retained of his route between the cisterns of La Malga and Byrsa: 'To proceed from the public cisterns to the hill of Byrsa one goes along a rough road . . . The summit of the Acropolis has even ground, dotted with tiny pieces of marble, and is visibly the site of a palace or temple. If one opts for a palace, it would be Dido's; if a temple is preferred, one should recognize that of Aesculapius' (*Itinéraire de Paris à Jérusalem*, Pléiade edition, p. 1202). The great writer, who knew his classics, thus amusingly indicated the tracks to follow. We shall see that his advice was not wasted.

In Carthage itself it was a Dane, C. T. Falbe, his country's consul-general in Tunis, who carried out real pioneering work a quarter of a century later. He spent several years compiling an archaeological map of Carthage, which he published in Paris in 1833 with his *Recherches sur l'emplacement de Carthage*. On this outstanding document, on which more than a hundred points of special interest were recorded and itemized, Falbe had also noted very exactly the line of tracks that cut across one another at right angles on the

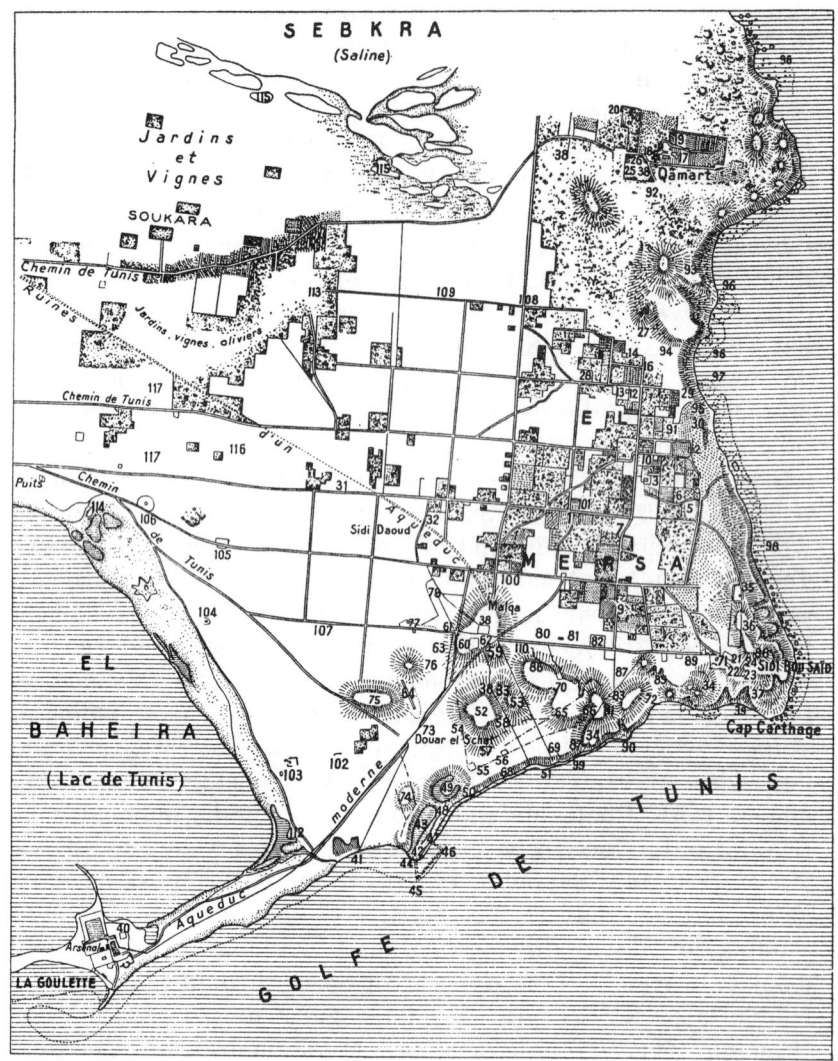

FIGURE 248　*The archaeological map of Carthage drawn up by C. T. Falbe.*

isthmus as far as La Malga between the village of La Soukra and Sidi-bou-Saïd, forming squares with sides of 2400 feet, which we have since learnt gave material indications of the rural planning decided by the Gracchi in 122 BC (figure 248). The site of Carthage entered the age of archaeological research with this map on which the plateau at the summit of Byrsa – Falbe's point 52 – still appeared as that bare, rectangular level space seen by Chateaubriand twenty-five years earlier. Reference is still made today to this document, which invaluably froze the condition of places that have sometimes been profoundly altered since then, notably in the area of the ports and regarding the coastline in general. In 1974, when the Danish mission started work under the auspices of the international campaign sponsored by UNESCO, they chose to set up their operational site at point 90, determined a century and a half earlier by their illustrious compatriot.

In the middle of the nineteenth century initiatives increased. Dido's city was perceived as an advanced bastion in the West of the East that was then so fashionable. As the discovery of ancient Egypt had marked the beginning of the century, the rediscovery of Carthage, and soon of the whole of ancient North Africa, was the concern of those years of waning romanticism. In 1837 the Society for the Exploration of Carthage was created, naturally including Falbe among its members, under the presidency of Dureau de la Malle, who in 1835 published his *Recherches sur la topographie de Carthage*. Of course, in keeping with the spirit of the times, its rules included certain clauses that are regrettable today, like the one which, in order to finance research, envisages the sale of excavated articles either to private individuals or to museums. That was how the Englishman, Nathan Davis, who explored the entire littoral zone, in the vicinity of Falbe's points 34 and 87, enriched the British Museum with a fine series of Roman mosaics with floral decoration (G. C. Picard, 1984, p. 13). In 1861 he published the results of his excavations under the title: *Carthage and her Remains*.

FLAUBERT IN CARTHAGE

One morning at the end of April 1858 Gustave Flaubert landed at Tunis, arriving by sea from Philippeville. We know the reasons for this voyage, which lasted only a month. The writer was sweating blood and tears over the novel that he then called *Carthage*. As he himself said, with a spirit that matched his despondency in his correspondence of that period, to glean information he had swallowed volume upon volume – ninety-eight, he wrote to one of his correspondents! – learned memoir upon learned memoir. In a letter addressed to Ernest Feydeau during the summer of 1857, he seemed to resign himself to the fact that in this book, whose chief character would ultimately be Carthage 'archaeology is only a probability'

(*Correspondance*, Pléiade edition, p. 749). And then, dissatisfied with himself, with the 'colour' that he decidedly could not see, he resolved upon this expedition. He wasted no time, going as far as Utica and Bizerta, spending whole days on horseback at the site of Carthage, where he met Nathan Davis. At the beginning of May he was able to write to his friend Louis Bouilhet: 'I know Carthage *in depth* and at all hours of the day and night' (*Correspondance*, p. 810). And the precision of the observations that he made on many aspects of the site in his *Notes de voyage* (vol. II, ed. Conard, 1910, pp. 310–19) bears witness that it was not mere boastfulness on his part. He returned to Croisset at the end of June 1858, convinced that his book, as he wrote to Ernest Feydeau at the time, had to be 'completely redone, or rather, done' (*Correspondance*, p. 817), but with his eyes filled and his ears still ringing with what he had sought in vain in books. With that momentum he would work almost three years longer before publishing *Salammbô* in 1862.

Though it may not have done much for Flaubert's more lasting renown, the book – which created a considerable stir in its day – was in its own way of great service to the cause of Carthaginian archaeology. The writer, fairly consciously, had been borne along by the powerful wave of interest in orientalism, widespread in those days. If it is added that his journey to Turkey and Greece in 1850, with his friend Maxime du Camp, had aroused his enthusiasm, and that since college he had been an assiduous reader of Michelet, it is understandable that he was tempted by the adventure of a historical novel that was both African and oriental. Much read, many times republished, the novel had the effect of adding its imaginary dimension to the movement of ideas it had excited, including minor matters, which are by no means the least durable. Carthage's modern toponymy still bears signs of the book: the area of the ancient ports, Salammbô, owes its name to the heroine, and Hamilcar's ravine, which cuts a gash in the southern flank of the promontory of Sidi-bou-Saïd, prolongs the echo of the famous introductory sentence that Flaubert was pleased to declaim aloud, testing its sonority: 'It was in Megara, a suburb of Carthage, in the gardens of Hamilcar.'

While Nathan Davis was completing his excavations in the lower town, Charles-Ernest Beulé arrived at Byrsa to undertake his own. The year was 1859 and this archaeologist, better known for having 'discovered' the Propylaeum of the Acropolis at Athens, was unable to meet Flaubert. But the memory of the writer still hung in the air of Carthage and, moreover, Beulé had read the *Itinéraire de Paris à Jérusalem*. It is therefore not surprising to see him include the 'supposed ruins of Dido's palace' on the map that he published at the end of his exploration of the plateau of Byrsa (figure 249). Like

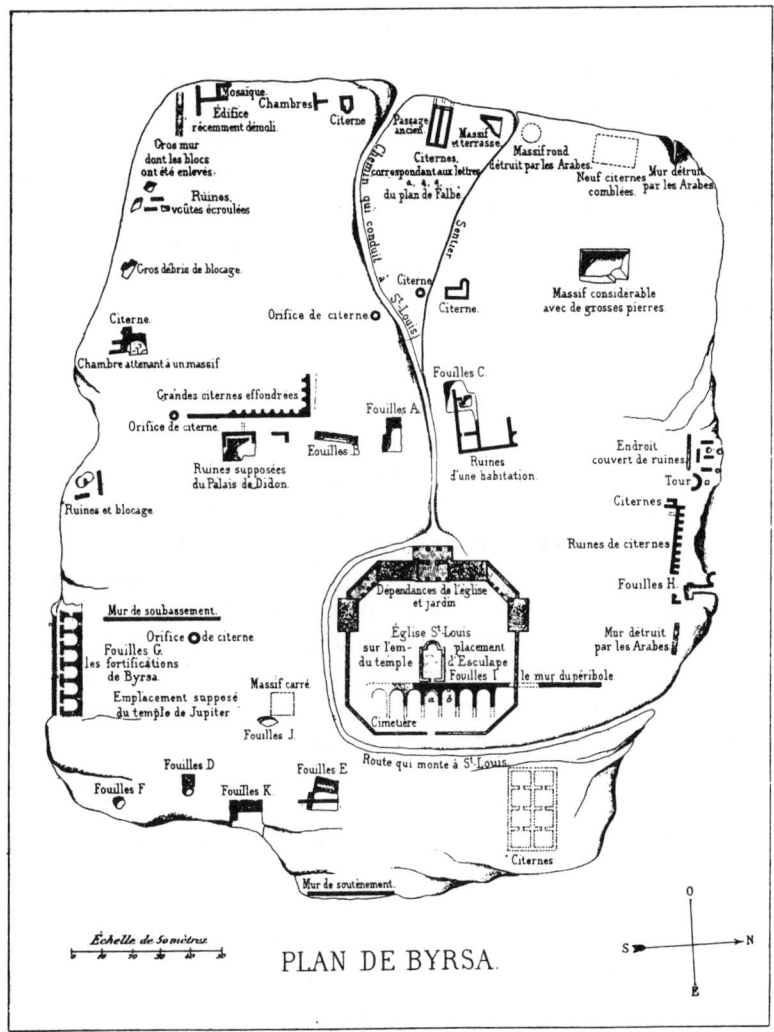

FIGURE 249 *Plan of the site of Beulé's excavations at Byrsa. Note, centre left, the indication of the 'assumed ruins of Dido's palace' and, below centre, of the 'temple of Aesculapius' under the Gothic chapel dedicated to Saint-Louis, recently built at the time the plan was drawn up (after* Fouilles à Carthage, *Paris, 1861, plate I).*

most of those probing the ground of Carthage at that time, Beulé was guided by a preoccupation with finding traces of the earliest city. Unaware of the nature of the level space on which he found himself (above, p. 430), and very keen to lay his hands on the enclosure of the citadel taken by storm in the spring of 146, he let himself be deceived by the Roman retaining walls corseting the largely artificial plateau, which he took to be the enclosing wall. However, in the last metres of a very deep excavation, he had come across real Punic vestiges: not those of 'the interior of Byrsa's walls', as he believed, but those of the houses destroyed and burnt by Scipio's soldiers in their advance towards the citadel. He was thus the first to come into contact with the layer of the burnt town and to be astonished by it, to the point where he considerably exaggerated its importance: 'The rock was covered, in several rooms, by a layer of ash a metre and a half thick' (Beulé, 1861, p. 55).

Punic Carthage began to come back to light, even if there was still some hesitation between reality and fiction. The fiction was the fanciful reconstructions suggested for both Utica and Carthage by Daux, an engineer sent by Napoleon III between 1865 and 1867. But very real were some 2000 Punic stelae unearthed by E. de Sainte-Marie, who had been sent out by the Académie des Inscriptions et Belles-Lettres, at various points of the site where these votive monuments, which certainly originated from the tophet, had been scattered in the Roman era. The ship on which a great number of them had been loaded, to be taken to the Louvre, was wrecked on its arrival, which is why for over a century several hundred of these stelae have been lying on the bottom of Toulon harbour.

THE BEGINNINGS OF SCIENTIFIC INVESTIGATION

The last quarter of the nineteenth century proved decisive for the rediscovery of Carthage, in particular of Punic Carthage. Already the collection of votive stelae gathered at La Manouba in the garden of Sidi Mustapha Kaznadar, the Bey of Tunis's minister – it was this which had attracted the attention of E. de Sainte-Marie to these monuments – had shown that in the Regency itself there was interest in such an ancient past. This interest could do no other than facilitate great projects to recover that past, even if they were foreign. In 1875 two White Fathers were sent to Algiers by the future Cardinal Lavigerie, then an archbishop, to keep an eye on the upkeep of the chapel erected in 1841, on the orders of Louis-Philippe, to the memory of Saint Louis, which had been built facing the sea on the Byrsa plateau, at the supposed site of the temple of Eschmoun. They were soon afterwards joined by a young missionary returning from America, who was to be the first chaplain of Saint Louis: the reverend Père Delattre (Gandolphe, 1950, p. 287). Cardinal Lavigerie's aims were twofold: first of all to work in Carthage *ad maiorem Dei gloriam* under the French flag; but also, under the same flag, to succeed in another, scientific enterprise, whose aims he set out in a letter addressed to the Académie des Inscriptions et Belles-Lettres in April 1881. One month later, the Bardo Treaty placed Tunisia under French protection and, the following year, a decree by the Bey set up a Department of Antiquities and regulated methods of archaeological research.

Père Delattre did not wait to start work. For nearly half a century, this strong figure of a red-haired and bearded colossus was to be seen going tirelessly from one excavation to another, spending his time equally between uncovering palaeo-Christian monuments and excavating in the Punic cemeteries. I mentioned earlier (above, p. 25) how much the archaeology of the earliest Carthage owes to his activities. By the start of the twentieth century, thanks to his efforts and also the talent of Paul Gauckler, the second director of the young Tunisian Department of Antiquities, the subterranean world of the dead had delivered up the essentials of the information that might have been hoped from it. It remained to carry on in the domain of the living, wherever there was ground still accessible, investigations that were delicate in another way, requiring of the archaeologist a skill in approach, a refinement in instrumentation, a sensitivity in perception, a personal effacement before the object of his research, which are the requirements of our own time. That was the task of the following generations. I will not repeat here those to whom, after the pioneers of the nineteenth century, we are indebted for our knowledge of the town of Dido and Hannibal. Without them, French or Tunisian, German, American or British, writing a book such as this, in which their names recur so often, would have been an impossible undertaking.

A few years after Père Delattre had been installed at Byrsa, the little museum that he had built in the shadow of the cathedral and the White Fathers' seminary already contained thousands of items. These collections are now housed in the vast buildings of the novitiate, which have become the National Museum of Carthage. It is here that I will leave my readers. Before visiting the Punic quarter on the south side of the hill, their understanding of which will be made easier by the information and the model exhibited on the ground floor, they will admire the marble recumbent statues brought to light by Père Delattre in the cemetery then known as Sainte-Monique. Then they will go up to the museum's first floor, where the objects they see will in their own fashion tell them about six centuries and more of the Punic city. Above all, they will go to one of the high windows in the façade, from which the view extends from the heights of Sidi-bou-Saïd, on the left, and to La Goulette, on the right. There history broadens out together with the landscape. In front of them, in the foreground, down below, beyond the cenotaph where Saint Louis maintains a more discreet presence, their gaze falls on what remains of one of the most enormous basilicas in Roman Africa, where at the very end of the fourth century AD Augustine's best friend, Alypius, was nearly the victim of a judicial error (*Confessions*, VI, ix, 14). Then, beyond the rim of the plateau, the view drops to the lower town. Still farther, the outlines of Cap Bon close the Gulf of Carthage and bar the horizon. In clear weather they may be able to sense, rather than see, closing the vista towards the open sea, the cone of the Isle of Zembra, which they had noticed on the port side as they arrived by boat. Perhaps that was where Elissa-Dido took some respite before accomplishing at Byrsa the founding act of this entire history.

Chronological Overview

Around 1200

Invasion of Phoenicia by populations from Anatolia and the Aegean Sea to whom the Egyptians give the generic title 'Peoples of the Sea'. Ras Shamra-Ugarit (which did not recover), Sidon and Tyre are sacked. Shortly afterwards, Rameses III checks a new wave of 'Peoples of the Sea' in a naval battle recounted in pictures on the walls of his funerary temple of Medinet Habou. Meanwhile, the Philistines settle on territory – eventually to be Palestine – situated between Phoenicia and Egypt.

Between 1100 and 1000

Recovery of the Phoenician towns (Byblos, Sidon, Tyre). Beginnings of Phoenician expansion in the eastern, then western Mediterranean. **1110**: legendary date of the founding of Gades (Cadiz); **1101**: legendary date of the founding of Utica. First Phoenician landings in Sicily.

Around 1000

The golden age of the coastal cities of Phoenicia. **969–935**: reign of king Hiram I in Tyre; alliance with king Solomon (972–932), David's successor on the throne of Israel in Jerusalem.

Between 900 and 800

The Nora inscription. First Phoenician landings in Sardinia and on the coasts of southern Spain. **814**: traditional date of the founding of Carthage.

Between 800 and 700

753: traditional date of the founding of Rome. Greek colonization in southern Italy and Sicily, in the second half of the eighth century. First archaeological evidence at Carthage: tophet of Salammbô, earliest dated tombs, Euboean pottery from the deepest investigations in the archaic settlement. Phoenician foundations in Andalusia (Almuñecar, Trayamar, Toscanos), Malta, Sardinia (Tharros, Sulcis, Bithia) and Sicily (Motya).

Between 700 and 600

Phoenician cities battling with the Assyrian power (siege of Tyre by Asarhadon in 671). Great development of the archaic cemeteries at Carthage in the first half of the seventh century (cemeteries of Dermech, Douimès, Juno, Byrsa). First extension of the earliest settlement. 654: founding of Ibiza in the Balearics (by Carthage?). Around 650: founding (by the Phoenicians of Gades?) of Mogador, on the Atlantic coast of Morocco. Founding of Cyrene by the Greeks and Leptis Magna by the Phoenicians.

Between 600 and 500

Around 600: foundation of Massalia (Marseilles) by the Greeks of Phocaea. Development of Phoenico-Punic colonization in Sardinia (Monte Sirai) and western Sicily (Palermo, Soluntum). First Punic staging-posts on the north coast of the Maghreb (Mersa Madakh, Tipasa). 535: victory at Alalia (Aleria, Corsica) of the Carthaginians and Etruscans over the Phocaeans. 509: first treaty between Rome and Carthage. Around 500: the Etrusco-Punic gold sheets from Pyrgi.

Between 500 and 400

480: battle of Himera, in Sicily, and defeat of Hamilcar by Gelon of Syracuse. Middle of the fifth century: beginning of Carthage's establishment of an African territory. 409: destruction of Selinunte and recapture of Himera by the Carthaginians. 405: treaty signed by Dionysius the Elder, acknowledging the Carthaginians' possession of western Sicily.

Between 400 and 300

397: destruction of Motya by Dionysius the Elder; Himilco founds Lilybaeum (Marsala) next to Motya, but fails at Syracuse. Introduction of the cult of the Sicilian goddesses (Demeter and Kore) to Carthage. 348: second treaty between Carthage and Rome. 310–307: Agathocles, tyrant of Syracuse, comes to Africa, ravages Cap Bon but fails at Carthage; failure of Bomilcar's *coup d'état*. 306: third treaty between Rome and Carthage.

Between 300 and 200

Around 275: when Pyrrhus of Epirus returns to Italy after failing at Lilybaeum, the Carthaginians reoccupy western Sicily and extend their control over a large part of the island. 264: the Romans intervene at Messina against a garrison set up by the Carthaginians. 264–241: First Punic War or Sicilian War. 260: Roman naval victory at Mylae (Milazzo); 256: Regulus in Africa. 241: victory of the Roman fleet at the Aegates islands; Carthage asks for peace and loses Sicily. **241–238:** Mercenaries' War or African War. Rome annexes Sardinia and Corsica. **237–229:** founding by Hamilcar Barca of a Punic 'kingdom' in southern Spain. **221:** Hasdrubal, Hamilcar Barca's son-in-law, founds Cartagena. **219:** siege and capture of Saguntum by Hannibal, son of Hamilcar Barca. **218–202:** Second Punic War or 'Hannibal's war'. Crossing of the Alps (winter **218**); Hannibal's victories at the Ticino, the Trebbia (**218**) and Lake Trasimene (**217**). Battle of Cannae and defection of Capua (**216**). Alliance between Carthage and Philip V of Macedon (**215**); Hannibal, in control of southern Italy, makes an incursion as far as Rome (**211**). Victories of P. Cornelius Scipio (Africanus) in Spain and end of Punic domination in the Iberian peninsula. Scipio lands in Africa (**204**), wins a victory at the *Campi Magni* and takes Syphax (**203**). Back from Italy, Hannibal is defeated by Scipio at Zama (**202**). The peace treaty concluded in **201** confines Carthage to its African territory, takes away its fleet, places it under Rome's political supervision and imposes the payment of a heavy war indemnity.

Between 200 and 146

Hannibal elected suffete (**196**), but has to go into exile soon afterwards. Prosperity of Carthage in the first half of the second century, attested especially by the results of recent archaeological excavations (Byrsa area and war harbour). **150:** Rome considers the decision taken by Carthage to respond with military action to Massinissa's latest encroachments on its territory as a *casus belli*: the beginning of the Third Punic War. Disarmed by treachery, the Carthaginians refuse to submit to Rome's diktat (**149**). After a siege lasting three years, the town is taken by storm and destroyed in the spring of **146**.

Bibliography

Acquaro, Enrico. 1971: *I rasoi punici*. Rome: CNR.
—— 1988: Scarabs and amulets. In *The Phoenicians*, Milan: Bompiani.
—— 1988a: Bronzes. In *The Phoenicians*, Milan: Bompiani.
Akkari-Weriemmi, Jenina. 1985: Un témoignage spectaculaire sur la présence libyco-punique dans l'île de Djerba: le mausolée d'Henchir Bourgou. *Reppal*, I (Tunis, Institut National d'Archéologie et d'Art), 189–96.
Amadasi-Guzzo, Maria Giulia. 1967: Le iscrizioni fenicie e puniche delle colonie in occidente. *Studi Semitici*, 28.
—— 1990: *Iscrizioni fenicie e puniche in Italia*. Rome.
—— 1990a: Stato degli studi iscrizioni latino-puniche della Tripolitania. *Africa Romana*, VII, 101–8.
—— 1991: 'The Shadow Line'. Réflexions sur l'introduction de l'alphabet en Grèce. In *Phoinikeia Grammata*, Actes du Colloque de Liège, 15–18 décembre 1989, Namur, 293–309.
Anziani, Dominique. 1912: Nécropoles puniques du Sahel tunisien. *Mélanges de l'École française de Rome*, 32, 245–303.
Astruc, Myriam. 1951: *La Nécropolis de Villaricos*. Madrid.
—— 1959: Empreintes et reliefs carthaginois de terre cuite. *Mélanges de l'École française de Rome*, 71, 107–34.
Aubet, Maria Eugenia. 1974: *See* Ferron, Jean and Aubet, M. E.
—— 1980: Marfiles fenicios del Bajo Guadalquivir II. *Studia Archaeologica* (Valladolid), 63.
Aubet-Semmler, Maria Eugenia. 1982: Zur Problematik der orientalierenden Horizontes auf der Iberischen Halbinsel. In H. G. Niemeyer (ed.), *Phönizier im Western* (Madrider Beiträge, 8), Mainz: Philipp von Zabern, 309–35.
Baradez, Jean. 1959: Nouvelles recherches sur les ports antiques de Carthage. *Karthago*, IX, 47–78.
Barreca, Ferrucio. 1983: Le fortificazioni puniche sul Capo Bon. II. Ras ed-Drek. In *Prospezione archeologica al Capo Bon*, II, Rome: CNR, 17–28.
—— 1984: Gli eserciti annibalici. *Rivista di Storia dell'Antichità*, XIII–XIV, 43–68.

Bartoloni, Piero. 1976: *Le stele archaiche di Cartagine*. Rome: CNR.

—— 1988: Ships and navigation. In *The Phoenicians*, Milan: Bompiani, 72–7.

Basch, Lucien. 1987: *Le Musée imaginaire de la marine antique*. Athens.

Ben Abed, Aïcha. 1990: *See* Soren, David, Ben Abed, Aïcha, and Slim, Hédi.

Benigni, Giulio. 1975: Il 'segno di Tanit' in Oriente. *Rivista di Studi Fenici*, 3, 17–18.

Bénichou-Safar, Hélène. 1981: A propos des ossements humains du tophet de Carthage. *Rivista di Studi Fenici*, 9, 5–9.

—— 1982: *Les Tombes puniques de Carthage. Topographie, structures, inscriptions et rites funéraires*. Paris: CNRS.

—— 1988: Sur l'incinération des enfants aux tophets de Carthage et de Sousse. *Revue de l'histoire des religions*, CCV, 1, 57–68.

Ben Younès, Habib. 1981: *La présence punique au Sahel*. Dissertation, Université de Tunis.

—— 1985: Rapport sur la campagne de fouilles effectuée dans la grande nécropole punique de la région de Mahdia. *Reppal*, I (Tunis: Institut National d'Archéologie et d'Art), 23–61.

—— 1986: La nécropole punique d'El Hkayma, mars 1984. *Reppal*, II, 31–67.

—— 1987: Le vase de Smirat et la victoire sur la mort. *Reppal*, III, 17–32.

—— 1988: La nécropole punique d'El Hkayma, septembre 1985. *Reppal*, IV, 49–159.

Bérard, Victor. 1930: *La Résurrection d'Homère*. Paris.

Berthier, André and Charlier, René. 1955: *Le sanctuaire punique d'El Hofra*. Paris.

Beschaouch, Azzedine. 1968: Une stèle consacrée à Saturne le 8 novembre 323. *Bulletin archéologique du Comité*, 253–68.

Beulé, Charles-Étienne. 1861: *Fouilles à Carthage*. Paris.

Bisi, Anna Maria. 1966: Le influenze puniche sulla religione libica. La gorfa di Kef el-Blida. *Studi e materiali di storia delle religioni*, 37, 85–112.

—— 1967: *Le stele puniche* (Studi Semitici, 27). Rome.

—— 1968: I pettini d'avorio di Cartagine. *Africa*, III, 11–51.

—— 1970: *La ceramica punica. Aspetti e problemi*. Naples.

—— 1979: Les sources syro-palestiniennes et chypriotes de l'art punique. *Antiquités africaines*, 14, 17–35.

—— 1980: La diffusion du 'smiting god' syro-palestinien dans le milieu phénicien d'Occident. *Karthago*, 19, 5–15.

—— 1982: Simboli animati nella religione fenicio- punica. *Religioni e Civiltà* (Bari), ns 3.

—— 1983: Importazioni e imitazioni greco-geometriche nella piu antica ceramica fenicia d'occidente. In *Atti I Congresso Internazionale di Studi Fenici e Punici*, Rome, 693–715.

Blazquez, José Maria. 1975: *Tartessos y los origenes de la colonización fenicia en occidente*. 2nd edn. Salamanca.

Bondi, Sandro Filippo. 1988: City planning and architecture. In *The Phoenicians*, Milan: Bompiani, 248–81.

Bonnet, Corinne. 1986: Le culte de Melqart à Carthage: un cas de conservatisme religieux. In *Studia Phoenicia*, IV: *Religio Phoenicia*, Namur, 209–22.

—— 1988: *Melqart. Cultes et mythes de l'Héraklès tyrien en Méditerranée* (Studia Phoenicia, VIII). Namur-Leuven.

—— 1991: Les scribes phénico-puniques. In *Phoinikeia Grammata*, Actes du Colloque de Liège, 15–18 novembre 1989, Namur, 147–72.

Bordreuil, Pierre. 1986: Attestations inédites de Melqart, Ba'al Hammon et Ba'al Saphon à Tyr. In *Studia Phoenicia*, IV: *Religio Phoenicia*, Namur, 71–86.

Boucher, Étienne. 1953: Céramique archaïque d'importation au musée Lavigerie de Carthage. *Cahiers de Byrsa*, III, 11–86.

Brahimi, Denise. 1976: *Voyageurs français au XVIIIe siècle en Barbarie.* Lille and Paris.

Briquel, Dominique. 1991: L'écriture étrusque d'après les inscriptions du VIIIe siècle avant J.-C. In *Phoinikeia Grammata*, Actes du Colloque de Liège, 15–18 novembre 1989, Namur-Leuven, 615–31.

Brisson, Jean-Pierre. 1973: *Carthage ou Rome.* Paris: Fayard.

Brizzi, Giovanni. 1984: *Annibale: strategia e immagine.* Spoleto.

Camps, Gabriel. 1961: *Aux origines de la Berbérie. Monuments et rites funéraires protohistoriques.* Paris: AMG.

—— 1973: Nouvelles observations sur l'architecture et l'âge du Médracen, le mausolée royal de Numidie. *CRAI*, 470–517.

—— 1979: Les Numides et la civilisation punique. *Antiquités africaines*, 14, 43–53.

—— 1986: L'araire berbère. In *Actes du IIIe Colloque international d'histoire et d'archéologie de l'Afrique du Nord, Montpellier, 1–5 avril 1985*, Paris: CTHS, 177–80.

Caquot, André. 1981: [Article on] Rephaïm. In *Dictionnaire du Bible, Supplément*, fasc. 55, Paris, col. 344–57.

Carter, T. H. 1965: Western Phoenicians at Lepcis Magna. *American Journal of Archeology*, LXIX, 2, 123–32.

Carton, Louis. 1911: Le port marchand et le mur de mer de la Carthage punique. *Revue archéologique*, 18, 229–55.

—— 1913: *Documents pour servir à l'étude des ports et de l'enceinte de la Carthage punique.* Paris: Leroux.

—— 1929: *Sanctuaire punique découvert à Carthage.* Paris: Geuthner.

Casson, Lionel. 1971: *Ships and Seamanship in the Ancient World.* Princeton, NJ: Princeton University Press.

Charlier, René. 1955: *See* Berthier, André, and Charlier, René.

Chelbi, Fethi. 1983: Quelques aspects de la civilisation carthaginoise à l'époque hellénistique. *Cahiers des Études anciennes* (Quebec), XVI, 79–87.

—— 1984: Découverte d'un habitat punique sur le flanc sud-est de la colline de Byrsa. In *Actes du Ier Colloque international d'histoire et d'archéologie de l'Afrique du Nord, Perpignan, 14–18 avril 1981*, published as *Bulletin archéologique du Comité*, ns 17B, 21–33.

Ciasca, Antonia. 1988: Masks and protomes. In *The Phoenicians*, Milan: Bompiani, 354–69.

Cintas, Pierre. 1946: *Les Amulettes puniques.* Tunis.

Cintas, Pierre, 1947: Le sanctuaire punique de Sousse. *Revue africaine*, nos 410–411, 1–80.

—— 1948: Un sanctuaire précarthaginois sur la grève de Salammbô. *Revue tunisienne*, 3rd series, no. 1, 1–31.

—— 1949: *Fouilles puniques à Tipasa*. Algiers: Direction des Antiquités de l'Algérie.

—— 1950: *Céramique punique*. Paris: Klincksieck.

—— 1954: *Contribution à l'étude de l'expansion carthaginoise au Maroc*. Paris: AMG.

—— 1968: Le signe de Tanit. *Archéologie vivante*, 1–2, 4–10.

—— 1970–6: *Manuel d'Archéologie punique*. 2 volumes. Paris: A. and J. Picard.

Cintas, Pierre, and Gobert, E.-G. 1941: Smirat. *Revue tunisienne*, nos 45–47, 83–121.

Clerc, Gisèle. 1986–7: *See* Leclant, Jean, and Clerc, Gisèle.

Coarelli, Filippo, and Thébert, Yvon. 1988: Architecture funéraire et pouvoir: réflexions sur l'hellénisme numide. *Mélanges de l'École française de Rome, Antiquité*, 100, 2, 761–818.

D'Agostino, Bruno. 1977: Tombe principesche dell'orientalizzante antico da Pontecagnano. *Monumenti Antichi dell'Accademia dei Linceo*, 49, Misc. II, 1.

Davis, Nathan. 1861: *Carthage and her Remains*. London.

Decret, François. 1977: *Carthage ou l'empire de la mer*. Paris: Seuil.

de Hoz, Javier. 1991: The Phoenician origin of the early Hispanic scripts. In *Phoinikeia Grammata*, Actes du Colloque de Liège, 15–18 novembre 1989, Namur, 669–78.

Delattre, Albert-Louis. 1921: Tombeaux puniques de la colline de Junon. *CRAI*, 96–9.

Demargne, Pierre. 1951: La céramique punique. *Revue archéologique*, 44–52.

Desanges, Jehan. 1967: Rex Muxitanorum Hiarbas (Justin, XVIII, 6, 1). *Philologus*, 111, 304–8.

—— 1978: *Recherches sur l'activité des Méditerranéens aux confins de l'Afrique*. (Collection École française de Rome, 38). Rome.

—— 1978a: L'Afrique romaine et libyco-berbère. In Claude Nicolet (ed.), *Rome et la conquête du monde méditerranéen. 2 – Genèse d'un empire* (Collection 'Nouvelle Clio'), Paris: Presses Universitaires de France, 627–56.

—— 1990: La localisation du 'Beau Promontoire' de Polybe. *Karthago*, XXII (1988–9), 19–31.

Desanges, Jehan, ed. 1980: Pline l'Ancien, *Histoire naturelle, livre V*, 1–46. Paris: Collection des Universités de France.

—— 1992: *Dictionnaire de la civilisation phénicienne et punique*. Paris: Brepols.

Di Vita, Antonino. 1969: Le date di fondazioni di Leptis e di Sabratha. In *Hommages à Marcel Renard*, III (Collection Latomus, 103), Brussels, 196–202.

—— 1976: Il mausoleo punico-ellenistico B di Sabratha. *MDAI, Römische Abteilung*, 83, 273–86.

Di Vita-Évrard, Ginette. 1986: La Fossa Regia et les diocèses d'Afrique Proconsulaire. *Africa Romana*, 3, 34–58.

Dubuisson, Michel. 1989: Delenda est Carthago. Remise en question d'un stéréotype. *Studia Phoenicia, X: Punic Wars*, 279–87.

Dupont-Sommer, André. Une nouvelle inscription punique de Carthage. *CRAI*, 116–33.

Eisfeldt, Otto. 1935: *Molk als Opferbegriff im Punischen und Hebräischen und das Ende des Gottes Moloch*. Halle.

Ellis, Simon. 1987: Excavations at Carthage, 1986. *CEDAC, Carthage, Bulletin*, 8, 12.

Falbe, C. T. 1833: *Recherches sur l'emplacement de Carthage*. Paris.

Falsone, Gioacchino. 1987: La statue de Motyè. Aurige ou prêtre de Melqart? In *Stemmata. Mélanges offerts à J. Labarbe*, Liège/Louvain-la-Neuve, 420–7.

Fantar, Mhamed Hassine. 1970: *Eschatologie phénicienne-punique*. Tunis: Institut National d'Archéologie et d'Art.

—— 1978: La cité punique de Thapsus. In *Actes du IIe Congrès international sur l'étude des cultures de la Méditerranée occidentale*, Algiers, 59–70.

—— 1984, 1986: *Kerkouane, cité punique du cap Bon (Tunisie)*. Volumes I and III. Tunis: Institut National d'Archéologie et d'Art.

—— 1985: A Gammarth avant la conquête romaine. In *Actes du IIe Colloque international sur l'histoire et l'archéologie de l'Afrique du Nord Grenoble, 5–9 avril 1983* (= *Bulletin archéologique du Comité*, ns 17B), 3–18.

—— 1989: Regulus en Afrique. *Studia Phoenicia, X: Punic Wars*, 75–84.

—— 1990: Ba'al Hammon. *Reppal*, V, 67–105.

—— 1990a: Survivances de la civilisation punique en Afrique du Nord. *Africa Romana*, VII, 53–70.

Fedele, F. and Foster, G. 1988: Tharros: ovicaprini sacrificiali e rituale del Tofet. *Rivista di Studi Fenici*, 16, 29–42.

Ferchiou, Naidé. 1987: Deux témoignages de l'architecture religieuse de la Carthage hellénistique. *Rivista di Studi Fenici*, 15, 15–35.

—— 1990: Habitats fortifiés pré-impériaux en Tunisie antique. *Antiquités africaines*, 26, 43–86.

Ferjaoui, Ahmed. 1990: Dédicace d'un sanctuaire à Astart. In *Hommages à Maurice Sznycer*, I (= *Semitica*, XXXVIII), 113–19.

Fernandez, Dominique. 1988: *Le Radeau de la Gorgone. Promenades en Sicile*. Paris: Grasset.

Ferron, Jean. 1958: Le médaillon de Carthage. *Cahiers de Byrsa*, VIII, 45–6.

—— 1968: Le mythe solaire de la résurrection des âmes. *Archéologia*, 20, 52–5.

—— 1969: Les statuettes au tympanon dans les hypogées puniques. *Antiquités africaines*, 3, 11–33.

Ferron, Jean, and Aubet, Maria Eugenia. 1974: *Les Orants de Carthage*. Paris.

Février, James Germain. 1960: Essai de reconstitution du sacrifice molek. *Journal asiatique*, 167–87.

Février, Paul-Albert. 1967: Origines de l'habitat urbain en Maurétanie Césarienne. *Journal des Savants*, 107–23.

—— 1980: Les rites funéraires de la nécropole orientale de Sétif. *Antiquités africaines*, 15, 91–124.

—— 1989: *Approches du Maghreb romain*. Volume I. Aix-en-Provence: Édisud.

Flobert, Pierre. 1991: L'apport des inscriptions archaïques à notre connaissance du latin pré-littéraire. *Latomus*, 50, 521–43.

Foster, G. 1988: *See* Fedele, F. and Foster, G.

Foucher, Louis. 1960: César en Afrique. Autour d'Aggar. *Cahiers de Tunisie*, no. 31, 11–17.

Frost, Honor. 1989: The prefabricated Punic war ship. *Studia Phoenicia*, X: *Punic Wars*, 127–35.

Gandolphe, Pierre. 1950: Saint-Louis de Carthage. *Cahiers de Byrsa*, 1, 269–306.

Garbini, Giovanni. 1981: Continuità ed innovazioni nella religione fenicia. In *Atti del colloquio in Roma: la religione fenicia* (= *Studi Semitici*, 53), Rome, 34–6.

Gauckler, Paul. 1915: *Nécropoles puniques de Carthage*. Part 2. Paris.

Gharbi, Maya. 1990: Les fortifications préromaines de Tunisie: le cas de Kelibia. *Africa Romana*, VII, 187–98.

Gobert, E.-G. 1941: *See* Cintas, Pierre, and Gobert, E.-G.

Gomez Bellard, Carlos. 1990: *La colonización fenicia de la isla de Ibiza*. Madrid: Ministry of Culture.

Gran Aymerich, José Maria Jean. 1979: Prospections archéologiques au Sahara atlantique (Rio de Oro et Seguiet el Hamra). *Antiquités africaines*, 13, 7–21.

Gras, Michel. 1985: *Trafics tyrrhéniens archaïques* (Bibliothèque de l'École française d'Athènes et de Rome, 258). Rome.

Gras, Michel, Rouillard, Pierre, and Teixidor, Javier. 1989: *L'Univers phénicien*. Paris: Arthaud.

Grimal, Pierre. 1969: *Les Jardins romains*. 2nd edn. Paris: Presses Universitaires de France.

Gros, Pierre. 1990: Le premier urbanisme de la colonia Julia Carthago. Mythes et réalités d'une fondation césaro-augustéenne. In *L'Afrique dans l'Occident romain (1ᵉʳ siècle avant J.-C.-IVᵉ siècle après J.-C.)*, (Collection de l'École française de Rome, 134), Rome, 547–73.

Gsell, Stéphane. 1921–8: *Histoire ancienne de l'Afrique du Nord* (abbreviated as *HAAN*). Volume I, 3rd edn, 1921; volumes II and III, 2nd edn, 1921; volume IV, 2nd edn, 1924; volume VIII, 1928. Paris: Hachette

Guerrero, Victor M. 1989: Las anforas Cintas 282/283 y el commercio de vino fenicio en occidente. *Saguntum*, 22, 147–64.

—— 1989a: L'épave de Binisafuller (Minorque). Un bateau de commerce punique du IIIᵉ siècle avant J.-C. *Studia Phoenicia*, X: *Punic Wars*, 115–24.

Halff, Gisèle. 1965: L'onomastique punique de Carthage: répertoire et commentaire. *Karthago*, XII, 61–145.

Hansen, P. H. 1983: *Carmina epigraphica graeca saeculorum VIII–V.A. Chr.* Berlin.

Harden, Donald. 1927: Punic urns from the Precinct of Tanit at Carthage. *American Journal of Archeology*, XXXI, 297–310.

—— 1937: The pottery from the Precinct of Tanit at Salammbô, Carthage. *Iraq*, IV, 59–89.

—— 1962: *The Phoenicians*. London. (See additional bibliography for later editions.)

Heurgon, Jacques. 1965: Les inscriptions de Pyrgi et l'alliance étrusco-punique autour de 500 avant J.-C. *CRAI*, 89–104.

—— 1969: *Rome et la Méditerranée occidentale jusqu'aux guerres puniques*. (Collection 'Nouvelle Clio', 7). Paris: Presses Universitaires de France.

—— 1976: L'agronome carthaginois Magon et ses traducteurs en grec et en latin. *CRAI*, 441–56.

Hurst, Henry. 1979: Excavations at Carthage, 1977–1978: fourth interim report. *Antiquaries' Journal*, LIX, 1, 19–49.

—— 1985: Fouilles britanniques au port circulaire et quelques idées sur le développement de la Carthage romaine. *Cahiers des Études anciennes* (Quebec), XVII, 143–56.

Hurst, Henry, and Stager, Lawrence. 1978: A metropolitan landscape: the Late Punic port of Carthage. *World Archaeology*, 9, 333–46.

Huss, Werner. 1985: *Geschichte der Karthager (Handbuch der Altertumswissenschaft*, III, 8). Munich.

—— 1986: Hannibal und die Religion. *Studia Phoenicia*, IV: *Religio Phoenicia*, 223–38.

Hvidberg-Hansen, F. O. 1979: *La déesse TNT. Une étude sur la religion cananéopunique*. Copenhagen.

Icard, François. 1923: Découverte de l'area du sanctuaire de Tanit. *Revue tunisienne*, 1–11.

—— 1923a: *See* Vassel, Eusèbe, and Icard, François.

Jodin, André. 1966: *Mogador, comptoir phénicien du Maroc atlantique*. Tangier.

—— 1967: *Les établissements du roi Juba II aux îles Purpuraires (Mogador)*. Tangier.

Karageorghis, Vassos. 1973: *Excavations in the Necropolis of Salamis, III*. Cyprus.

Kelsey, Francis. 1926: *A Preliminary Report on the Excavations at Carthage, 1925*. (Supplement to the *American Journal of Archeology*.) New York: Macmillan.

Koch, M. 1984: *Tarshish und Hispanien*. Berlin.

Kontorini, V. 1975: Le roi Hiempsal II de Numidie et Rhodes. *Antiquité classique*, 44, 89–99.

Krings, Véronique. 1990: Les libri Punici de Salluste. *Africa Romana*, VII, 109–17.

—— 1991: Les lettres grecques à Carthage. In *Phoinikeia Grammata*, Actes du Colloque de Liège, 15–18 novembre 1989, Namur, 649–68.

La Blanchère, R. de. 1888: Fouilles à Sousse. *Bulletin archéologique du Comité*, 149–54.

Lancel, Serge. 1968: Tipasitana III: la nécropole pré-romaine occidentale de Tipasa. *Bulletin d'archéologie algérienne*, III, 85–166.

Lancel, Serge, 1980: La céramique phénico-punique de la nécropole archaïque de Byrsa: quelques remarques préliminaires. In *Actes du Colloque sur la céramique antique*, Carthage, 23–24 juin 1980, CEDAC, Carthage, Dossier I, 1–7.

—— 1981: Fouilles françaises à Carthage. La colline de Byrsa et l'occupation punique. Bilan de sept années de fouilles. *CRAI*, 156–93.

—— 1982a: Tipasa de Maurétanie. Histoire et archéologie. I. État des questions des origines préromaines à la fin du IIIᵉ siècle. In *Aufstieg und Niedergang der römischen Welt*, II, 10, 2, Berlin and New York, 739–86.

—— 1982b: La fin et la survie de la latinité en Afrique du Nord. *Revue des Études latines*, 59 (1981), 269–97.

—— 1983: *La colline de Byrsa à l'époque punique*. Paris: Édition Recherches sur les Civilisations.

—— 1983a: Ivoires phénico-puniques de la nécropole archaïque de Byrsa, à Carthage. In *Atti I Congresso Internazionale di Studi Fenici e Punici*, Rome, 687–92.

—— 1984: Remarques sur la topographie urbaine de la Carthage punique. In *Actes du Iᵉʳ Colloque international sur l'histoire et l'archéologie de l'Afrique du Nord* (= *Bulletin archéologique du Comité*, ns 17B), 35–53.

—— 1985: La renaissance de la Carthage punique. Réflexions sur quelques enseignements de la campagne internationale patronnée par l'Unesco. *CRAI*, 727–51.

—— 1988: Les fouilles de la mission archéologique française à Carthage et le problème de Byrsa. *Studia Phoenicia*, VI: *Carthago*, 61–89.

—— 1989: L'enceinte périurbaine de Carthage lors de la troisième guerre punique: réalités et hypothèses. *Studia Phoenicia*, X: *Punic Wars*, 251–78.

—— 1990: Problèmes d'urbanisme de la Carthage punique à la lumière des fouilles anciennes et récentes. In *Carthage et son territoire dans l'Antiquité*, Actes du IVᵉ Colloque international, Strasbourg, 1988, Paris: CTHS, 9–30.

Lancel, Serge (ed.) 1979: *Byrsa I. Mission archéologique française à Carthage. Rapport préliminaire des fouilles, 1974–76*. (Collection de l'École française de Rome, 41). Rome.

—— 1982: *Byrsa II. Mission archéologique française à Carthage. Rapports préliminaires des fouilles 1977–1978 (niveaux et vestiges puniques)*. (Collection de l'École française de Rome, 41.) Rome.

Lantier, Raymond. 1923: *See* Poinssot, Louis, and Lantier, Raymond.

Lapeyre, G.-G. 1935: Fouilles récentes à Carthage. *CRAI*, 81–7.

—— 1939: Fouilles du musée Lavigerie à Carthage. *CRAI*, 294–300.

Leclant, Jean. 1968: Les talismans égyptiens dans les nécropoles. *Archéologie vivante*, 1, 2, 95–113.

—— 1980: A propos des étuis porte-amulettes égyptiens et puniques. In *Oriental Studies presented to B. S. J. Isserlin*, Leiden, 102–7.

Leclant, Jean, and Clerc, Gisèle. 1986–7: Nuntii. III. Découvertes d'objets égyptiens et égyptisants hors d'Égypte. *Orientalia*, 55, 3, 318–19 and 56, 3, 388–9.

Le Glay, Marcel. 1966: *Saturne africain, histoire*. Paris.

—— 1985: Les premiers temps de la Carthage romaine. In *Histoire et archéologie de l'Afrique du Nord*, IIe Colloque international, Grenoble, 5–9 avril, 1983, Paris: CTHS, 235–47.

—— 1988: Nouveaux documents, nouveaux points de vue sur Saturne africain. *Studia phoenicia*, VI: *Carthago*, 187–237.

Lemaire, André. 1984: La stèle araméenne de Barhadad. *Orientalia*, 53, 337–49.

Lepelley, Claude. 1980: Iuvenes et circoncellions: les derniers sacrifices humains de l'Afrique antique. *Antiquités africaines*, 15, 261–71.

Leveau, Philippe. 1984: *Caesarea de Maurétanie, une ville romaine et ses campagnes*. (Collection de l'École française de Rome, 70.) Rome.

Levi Della Vida, Giorgio. 1963: Sulle iscrizioni 'latino-libiche' della Tripolitania. *Oriens Antiquus*, II, 65–95.

—— 1971: Magistrature romane e indigene nelle iscrizioni puniche Tripolitane. In *Studi in onore di Edoardo Volterra*, VI, Milan, 457–69.

Lézine, Alexandre. 1959: Résistance à l'hellénisme de l'architecture religieuse de Carthage. *Cahiers de Tunisie*, 26–27, 247–61.

—— 1960: *Architecture punique. Recueil de documents*. Paris, Presses Universitaires de France.

—— 1968: *Carthage, Utique. Études d'architecture et d'urbanisme*. Paris.

Lipinski, Édouard. 1987: Les racines syro-phéniciennes de la religion carthaginoise. *CEDAC, Carthage, Bulletin* 8, 28–44.

Little, John. 1975: *See* Yorke, Robert A. and Little, John.

Longerstay, Monique. 1990: Les peintures rupestres des haouanet de Khroumirie: aspects techniques et répertoire iconographique. *Revue archéologique de Picardie*, 1–2, 119–31.

—— 1990a: Représentations de navires archaïques en Tunisie du Nord. Contribution à la chronologie des haouanet. *Karthago*, XXII, 33–44.

Lonis, Raoul. 1978: Les conditions de la navigation sur la côte atlantique de l'Afrique dans l'Antiquité: le problème du retour. In *Afrique noire et monde méditerranéen*, Dakar-Abidjan, 147–70.

Marichal, Robert. 1979: Les ostraka de Bu Njem. *CRAI*, 436–7.

Martin, René. 1971: *Recherches sur les agronomes latins et sur leurs conceptions économiques et sociales*. Paris.

Masson, Émilia. 1967: *Recherches sur les plus anciens emprunts sémitiques en grec*. Paris.

Mauny, René. 1960: *Les Navigations médiévales sur les côtes sahariennes antérieures à la découverte portugaise (1434)*. Lisbon.

Maurin, Louis. 1962: Himilcon le Magonide. Crises et mutations à Carthage au début du IVe siècle avant J.-C. *Semitica*, XII, 5–43.

Mazard, Jean. 1955: *Corpus nummorum Numidiae Mauretaniaeque*. Paris: AMG.

M'Charek, Ahmed. 1988: Maghrawa, lieu de provenance des stèles punico-numides dites de la Ghorfa. *Mélanges de l'École française de Rome, Antiquité*, 100, 2, 731–61.

Meijer, F. J. 1984: Cato's African figs. *Mnémosyne*, XXXVII, 117–24.

Merlin, Alfred. 1918: Tombeaux de la colline dite 'de Junon'. *Bulletin archéologique du Comité*, 288–312.

Monod, Théodore. 1973: Les monnaies nord-africaines anciennes de Corvo (Açores). *Bulletin de l'Institut de la fondation de l'Afrique noire*, série B, XXXV, 231–4.

Monod, Théodore, 1979: A propos de l'île Herné (baie de Dakhla, Sahara occidental). *Bulletin de l'Institut de la fondation de l'Afrique noire*, série B, XLI, 15–20.

Morel, Jean-Paul. 1969: Kerkouane, ville punique du cap Bon: remarques archéologiques et historiques. *Mélanges de l'École française de Rome*, LXXXI, 473–518.

—— 1975: L'expansion phocéenne en Occident. *Bulletin de Correspondance hellénique*, XCIX, 853–96.

—— 1980: Les vases à vernis noir et à figures rouges d'Afrique avant la deuxième guerre punique et le problème des importations de Grande-Grèce. *Antiquités africaines*, 15, 29–90.

—— 1982: La céramique à vernis noir de Carthage-Byrsa: nouvelles données et éléments de comparaison. In *Actes du Colloque sur la céramique antique*, CEDAC, Carthage, Dossier 1, 43–61.

—— 1982a: Le secteur B (1978). In Serge Lancel (ed.), *Byrsa II*, 181–213.

—— 1983: Les importations de céramiques grecques et italiennes dans le monde punique (V^e–Ier siècle). In *Atti I Congresso Internazionale di Studi Fenici e Punici*, III, Rome, 731–40.

—— 1990: A propos des vases plastiques à vernis noir de Carthage. *Bulletin archéologique du Comité*, ns 22–23.

Mosca, Paul. 1975: *Child Sacrifice in Canaanite and Israelite Religion: a Study in Mulk and MLK*. PhD thesis, Harvard University.

Moscati, Sabatino. 1966: *Il mondo dei Fenici*. Milan: Il Saggiatore.

—— 1972: L'origine del 'segno di Tanit'. *Rendiconti dell'Accademia dei Lincei*, 371–4.

—— 1981: Un bilancio per TNT. *Oriens Antiquus*, XX, 107–17.

—— 1987: Il sacrificio punico dei fanciulli: realtà o invenzione? *Rendiconti dell'Accademia dei Lincei*, 3–15.

—— 1988: Sarcofaghi et Stelae. In *The Phoenicians*, Milan: Bompiani.

Moscati, Sabatino, and others. 1972a: *I Fenici e Cartagine*. Turin: UTET.

Nicolet, Claude. 1978: Les guerres puniques. In Claude Nicolet (ed.), *Rome et la conquête du monde méditerranéen. 2 – Genèse d'un empire*, (Collection 'Nouvelle Clio'), Paris: Presses Universitaires de France, 594–626.

Niemeyer, Hans Georg. 1984: Die Phönizier und die Mittelmeerwelt im Zeitalter Homers. *Jahrbuch des römisch-germanischen Zentralmuseums*, 31, 3–94.

—— 1990: A la recherche de la Carthage archaïque: premiers résultats des fouilles de l'université de Hambourg en 1986 et 1987. In *Carthage et son territoire dans L'Antiquité*, IVe Colloque international, Strasbourg, 1988, Paris: CTHS, 45–52.

Niemeyer, Hans Georg (ed.) 1982: *Phönizier im Westen. Die Beiträge des internationalen Symposiums über 'Die phönizische Expansion im Westlichen Mittelmeerraum'*, Cologne, 24–27 April 1979, (Madrider Beiträge, 8). Mainz: Philipp von Zabern.

Pallary, Paul. 1922: Note sur les débris osseux trouvés dans le sanctuaire de Tanit à Salammbô, près Carthage. *Bulletin archéologique du Comité*, 223–6.

Paskoff, Roland, Hurst, Henry, and Rakob, Friedrich. 1985: Position du niveau de la mer et déplacement de la ligne du rivage à Carthage

(Tunisie) dans l'Antiquité. *Comptes rendus de l'Académie des Sciences de Paris*, série II, no. 13, 613–17.

Pellicer Catalan, Manuel. 1962: Excavaciones en la nécropolis punica 'Laurita' del Cerro de San Cristóbal (Almuñecar, Granada). *Excavaciones arqueologicas eñ España*, 17.

Picard, Colette. 1967: Sacra Punica. *Karthago*, 13, 3–115.

—— 1967a: Thèmes hellénistiques sur les stèles de Carthage. *Antiquités africaines*, 1, 9–30.

—— 1968: Genèse et évolution des signes de la bouteille et de Tanit à Carthage. *Studi Magrebini*, II, 77–87.

—— 1976: Les représentations du sacrifice molk sur les ex-voto de Carthage (suite et fin). *Karthago*, XVIII (1975–6), 5–116.

—— 1979: Les représentations du cycle dionysiaque à Carthage dans l'art punique. *Antiquités africaines*, 14, 83–113.

—— 1982: Les navigations de Carthage vers l'ouest. Carthage et le pays de Tharsis aux VIII\e-VI\e siècles. In H. G. Niemeyer (ed.), *Phönizier im Westen*, Mainz: Philipp von Zabern, 167–73.

—— 1982a: Les sacrifices d'enfants à Carthage. *Archéologia*, no. 69, 18–27.

—— 1990: Les sacrifices molk chez les Puniques: certitudes et hypothèses. In *Hommages à Maurice Sznycer*, II (= *Semitica*, XXXIX), 77–88.

Picard, Gilbert. 1945: Le sanctuaire dit de Tanit à Carthage. *CRAI*, 443–52.

Picard, Gilbert-Charles. 1954: *Les Religions de l'Afrique antique*. Paris.

—— 1957: *Civitas Mactaritana* (= *Karthago*, VIII).

—— 1966: L'administration territoriale de Carthage. In *Mélanges offerts à André Piganiol*, III, Paris, 1257–65.

—— 1967: *Hannibal*. Paris: Hachette.

—— 1974: Une survivance du droit punique en Afrique romaine: les cités suffétales. In *I diritti locali nelle provinze romane* (Accademia Nazionale dei Lincei, quaderno 194), Rome, 125–33.

—— 1983: Est-il possible d'écrire une histoire de Carthage? In *Atti I Congresso Internazionale di Studi Fenici e Punici*, Rome, 5–10 novembre, Rome: CNR, 279–83.

—— 1984: La recherche archéologique en Tunisie des origines à l'indépendance. *Cahiers des Études anciennes* (Quebec), XVI, 11–20.

—— 1990: Ba'al Hammon et Saturne dans l'Afrique romaine. In *Hommages à Maurice Sznycer*, II (= *Semitica*, XXXIX), 89–97.

—— 1991: Mythe et histoire aux débuts de Carthage. In *Atti II Congresso Internazionale di Studi Fenici e Punici*, I, Rome: CNR, 385–92.

Picard, Gilbert-Charles, and Picard, Colette. 1970: *Vie et mort de Carthage*. Paris: Hachette.

—— 1982: *La Vie quotidienne à Carthage au temps d'Hannibal (III\e siècle avant J.-C.)*. 2nd edn. Paris: Hachette.

Pisano, Giovanna. 1988: Jewellery. In *The Phoenicians*, Milan: Bompiani.

Poinssot, Claude. 1958: *Les Ruines de Dougga*. Tunis: Institut National d'Archéologie et d'Art.

Poinssot, Louis, and Lantier, Raymond. 1923: Un sanctuaire de Tanit à Carthage. *Revue de l'histoire des religions*, 31–68.

Ponsich, Michel. 1967: *Nécropoles phéniciennes de la région de Tanger* (Études et travaux d'archéologie marocaine, III.) Tangier.

—— 1982: Lixus: informations archéologiques. In *Aufstieg und Niedergang der römischen Welt*, II, 10, 2, Berlin and New York, 817–49.

—— 1982a: Territories utiles du Maroc punique. In H. G. Niemeyer (ed.), *Phönizier im Westen*, Mainz: Philipp von Zabern, 429–44.

Pritchard, James B. 1978: *Recovering Sarepta, a Phoenician City*. Princeton, NJ: Princeton University Press.

Quillard, Brigitte. 1971: Les étuis porte-amulettes carthaginois. *Karthago*, XVI, 5–32.

—— 1979: *Bijoux carthaginois. I – Les Colliers*. Louvain-la-Neuve.

Rakob, Friedrich. 1979: Numidische Königsarchitektur in Nordafrika. In *Die Numider*, Bonn, 119–71.

—— 1984: Deutsche Ausgrabungen in Karthago. Die punischen Befunde. *MDAI, Römische Abteilung*, 91, 1–22.

—— 1987: Zur Siedlungstopographie des punischen Karthagos. *MDAI, Römische Abteilung*, 94, 333–49.

—— 1989: Karthago. Die frühe Siedlung. *MDAI, Römische Abteilung*, 96, 156–208.

—— 1990: La Carthage archaïque. In *Carthage et son territoire dans l'Antiquité*, IVᵉ Colloque international, Strasbourg, 1988, Paris: CTHS, 31–43.

Ramon, Juan. 1981: *La producción anforica punico- ebusitana*. Ibiza.

Rebuffat, René. 1976: D'un portulan grec du XVIᵉ siècle au *Périple d'Hannon*. *Karthago*, XVII (1973–4), 139–51.

—— 1988: Les nomades de Lixus. *Bulletin archéologique du Comité*, ns 18B, 77–85.

—— 1988a: Voyage du Carthaginois Hannon de Lixos à Cerné. *Bulletin archéologique du Comité*, ns 18B (1982), 198–200.

Ribichini, Sergio. 1985: Temple et sacerdoce dans l'économie de Carthage. In *Histoire et archéologie de l'Afrique du Nord*, IIᵉ Colloque international, Grenoble, 5–9 avril 1983, Paris: CTHS.

—— 1987: *Il tofet e il sacrificio dei fanciulli* (Collection Sardo, 2). Sassari.

Richard, Jean. 1961: *Étude médico-légale des urnes sacrificielles puniques et de leur contenu*. MD thesis, Université de Lille.

Rougé, Jean. 1975: *La Marine dans l'Antiquité*. Paris.

Rouillard, Pierre. 1989: *See* Gras, Michel, and others.

Ruiz-Mata, D. 1985: La ceramicas fenicias del Castillo de Doña Blanca (Puerto de Santa Maria, Cadiz). *Aula Orientalis*, III, 241–63.

Saumagne, Charles. 1923: Notes sur les découvertes de Salammbô: 1: sur les sacrifices humains; 2: sur les monuments. *Revue tunisienne*, 3–23.

—— 1928: Vestiges de la colonie de C. Gracchus à Carthage. *Bulletin archéologique du Comité* (1928–9), 648–64.

—— 1931: Notes de topographie carthaginoise. II. Sondages aux abords des anciens ports. *Bulletin archéologique du Comité* (1930–1), 654–9.

—— 1960: Le 'lungomare' de la Carthage romaine. *Karthago*, X (1959–60), 157–70.

Scheid, John, and Svenbro, Jesper. 1985: Byrsa. La ruse d'Elissa et la fondation de Carthage. *Annales ESC*, 328–42.

Schubart, Hermanfrid. 1982: Phönizische Niederlassungen an der iberischen Südküste. In H. G. Niemeyer (ed.), *Phönizier im Westen*, Mainz: Philipp von Zabern, 205–34.

Seefried-Brouillet, Monique. 1982: *Les pendentifs en verre sur noyau des pays de la Méditerranée antique*. Rome.

Simonetti, A. 1983: Sacrifici umani e uccisioni rituali nel mondo feniciopunico. Il contributo delle fonti letterarie. *Rivista di Studi Fenici*, 11, 91–111.

Slim, Hédi. 1990: *See* Soren, David, and others.

Smet, Jean-Jacques de. 1913: Fouilles de sépultures puniques de Lemta (Leptis Minor). *Bulletin archéologique du Comité*, 327–42.

Soren, David, Ben Abed, Aïcha, and Slim, Hédi. 1990: *Carthage: Uncovering the Mysteries and Splendors of Ancient Tunisia*. New York: Simon and Schuster.

Speranza, F. 1974: *Scriptorum Romanorum de re rustica reliquiae. I. Ab antiquissimis temporibus ad aetatem Varronianam, accedunt Magonis de agri cultura fragmenta*. Messina.

Stager, Lawrence. 1978: The Punic project. In *Annual Report, The Oriental Institute, University of Chicago, 1977–78*, 19–37.

—— 1978a: *See* Hurst, Henry, and Stager, Lawrence.

—— 1979: Archaeological news. *CEDAC, Carthage, Bulletin* 2, 31–2.

—— 1980: The rite of child sacrifice at Carthage. In J. G. Pedley (ed.), *New Light on Ancient Carthage*, Ann Arbor: University of Michigan Press, 1–11.

Stager, Lawrence, and Wolff, Samuel. 1984: Child sacrifice at Carthage: religious rite or population control? *Biblical Archaeology Review*, January-February, 31–51.

Svenbro, Jesper. 1985: *See* Scheid, John, and Svenbro, Jesper.

Sznycer, Maurice. 1967: *Les Passages puniques en transcription latine dans le* Poenulus *de Plaute*. Paris: Klincksieck.

—— 1968: La littérature punique. *Archéologie vivante*, 1, 2, 141–8.

—— 1978: Carthage et la civilisation punique. In Claude Nicolet (ed.), *Rome et la conquête du monde méditerranéen. 2. Genèse d'un empire* (Collection 'Nouvelle Clio', 8bis), Paris: Presses Universitaires de France, 545–93.

—— 1986: Le problème de la 'Megara' de Carthage. In *Histoire et archéologie de l'Afrique du Nord*, IIIᵉ Colloque international, Montpellier, 1–5 avril 1985, Paris: CTHS, 123–35.

Teixidor, Javier. 1989: *See* Gras, Michel, and others.

Thébert, Yvon. 1988: *See* Coarelli, Filippo, and Thébert, Yvon.

Thuillier, Jean-Paul. 1982: Timbres amphoriques puniques écrits en lettres grecques. In *Colloque sur la céramique antique*, Carthage, 23–24 juin 1980, *CEDAC*, Carthage, Dossier 1, 15–20.

—— 1985: Nouvelles découvertes de bucchero à Carthage. In *Il commercio etrusco arcaico*, Atti del incontro di studio in Roma, 5–7 dicembre 1983, Rome, 55–63.

Tlatli, Salah Eddine. 1978: *La Carthage punique*. Paris: Maisonneuve and Tunis: Cérès Productions.

Tusa, Vincenzo. Lo scavo del 1970. In *Mozia-VII*, Rome: CNR, 7–81.

464 *Bibliography*

Tusa, Vincenzo, 1978: La necropoli arcaica e adiacenze. In *Mozia–IX*, Rome: CNR, 7–65.

—— 1986: Il giovane de Mozia. *Rivista di Studi Fenici*, 14, 143–52.

Vallet, Georges. 1958: *Rhegion et Zancle. Histoire, commerce et civilisation des cités chalcidiennes du détroit de Messine*. Paris.

Van Berchem, Denis. 1967: Sanctuaires d'Hercule-Melqart. Contribution à l'étude de l'expansion phénicienne en Méditerranée. *Syria*, 44, 73–109 and 307–38.

—— 1991: Commerce et écriture. L'exemple de Délos à l'époque hellénistique. *Museum Helveticum*, 48, 129–45.

Vassel, Eusèbe. 1923: Les enseignements du sanctuaire punique de Carthage. *Annales de l'Académie des sciences coloniales*, 3–51.

Vassel, Eusèbe, and Icard, François. 1923a: Les inscriptions votives du temple de Tanit à Carthage. *Revue tunisienne*, 3–20.

Vattioni, Francesco. 1976: Glosse puniche. *Augustinianum*, XVI, 3, 505–55.

Vegas, Mercedes. 1989: Archaische und mittelpunische Keramik aus Karthago, Grabungen 1987–1988. *MDAI, Römische Abteilung*, 96, 209–59.

Vercoutter, Jean. 1945: *Les objets égyptiens et égyptisants du mobilier funéraire carthaginois*. Paris: Geuthner.

Villard, François. 1959: Vases attiques du Ve siècle avant J.-C. à Gouraya. *Libyca*, VII, 1–12.

Villaronga, Leandro. 1973: *Las monedas hispano-cartaginesas*. Barcelona.

Vuillemot, G. 1965: *Reconnaissances aux échelles puniques d'Oranie*. Autun: Musée Rolin.

Warmington, B. H. 1961: *Histoire et civilisation de Carthage*. Paris: Payot.

Weil, Raymond. 1961: *Aristote et l'histoire*. Paris.

Wolff, Samuel. 1984: *See* Stager, Lawrence, and Wolff, Samuel.

Xella, Paolo. 1985: Quelques aspects du rapport économie-religion d'après les tarifs sacrificiels puniques. In *Histoire et archéologie de l'Afrique du Nord*, IIe Colloque international, Grenoble, 5–9 avril 1983, Paris: CTHS, 39–45.

—— 1991: *Ba'al Hammon. Recherches sur l'identité et l'histoire d'un dieu phénicopunique*. Rome: CNR.

Yorke, Robert A. and Little, John. 1975: Offshore survey at Carthage (Tunisia). *International Journal of Nautical Archaeology and Underwater Exploration*, 4, 1, 94–8.

Additional Bibliographical Notes for the English Edition

Henry Hurst
Museum of Classical Archaeology,
University of Cambridge

Lancel's bibliography covers publications in all languages up to 1991. One or two more recent ones are listed here, together with a few more specifically for English-speaking readers.

The Phoenicians (including Carthage)

Aubet, Maria Eugenia. 1993: *The Phoenicians and the West*. Translated by Mary Turton. Cambridge: Cambridge University Press.

Culican, W. 1991: Phoenicia and Phoenician colonization. In John Boardman et al. (eds), *Cambridge Ancient History*, 2nd edn, vol. III part 2, chapter 32.

Harden, Donald. 1980: *The Phoenicians*. 2nd edn, revised. London: Penguin.

Moscati, Sabatino. 1968: *The World of the Phoenicians*. Translated by A. Hamilton. London: Weidenfeld and Nicolson (paperback, Cardinal, 1973).

Carthage (general)

Briscoe, J. 1989: The Second Punic War. In A. E. Astin et al. (eds), *Cambridge Ancient History*, 2nd edn, vol. VIII, chapter 3.

Ennabli, A. (ed.) 1992: *Pour Sauver Carthage*. Tunis: UNESCO and Institut National d'Archéologie et d'Art.

Harris, W. V. 1989: Roman expansion in the West [especially part IV, Rome and Carthage]. In *Cambridge Ancient History*, 2nd edn, vol. VIII, chapter 5.

Hurst, Henry. 1987: Carthage: the Punic City. In Barry Cunliffe (ed.), *Origins: The Roots of European Civilisation*. London: BBC Books, chapter 10.

Pedley, J. G. (ed.) 1980: *New Light on Ancient Carthage*. Ann Arbor: University of Michigan Press.

Picard, Gilbert-Charles, and Picard, Colette. 1968: *The Life and Death of Carthage*. Translated by Dominique Collon. London: Sidgwick and Jackson.

Raven, S. 1993. *Rome in Africa*. 3rd edn. London, Routledge.

Scullard, H. H. 1989: Carthage and Rome [including the First Punic War]. In F. W. Walbank et al. (eds), *Cambridge Ancient History*, 2nd edn, vol. VII part 2, chapter 11.

—— 1989a: The Carthaginians in Spain. In A. E. Astin et al. (eds), *Cambridge Ancient History*, 2nd edn, vol. VIII, chapter 2.

Warmington, B. H. 1969: *Carthage*. 2nd edn. London: Robert Hale.

Carthage (the tophet and harbours, including recent American and British work)

Brown, S. 1991: *Late Carthaginian Child Sacrifice and Sacrificial Monuments in their Mediterranean Context* (JSOT/ASOR Monograph Series, no. 3). Sheffield: Sheffield Academic Press.

Hurst, Henry. 1994: *Excavations at Carthage. Volume II, 1. The Circular Harbour, North Side. The Site and Finds other than Pottery* (British Academy Monographs in Archaeology, no. 4). Oxford: Oxford University Press, chapter 3 (with S. Gibson), The Punic Shipsheds, and chapter 4, The Topography and Development of the Punic Harbour.

Hurst, Henry, and Stager, Lawrence. 1978: *See* main bibliography.

Stager, Lawrence. 1982: *See* main bibliography.

Index

The names of places are in **bold** type, the names of people and divinities in *italics*.